Here's What You Get on the CD:

The CD included with the second edition of the *MCSE: Internet Explorer 4 Administration Kit Study Guide* contains invaluable programs and information to help you prepare for your MCSE exams. You can access and install the files on the CD through a user-friendly graphical interface by running the CLICKME.EXE file located in the root directory.

System Requirements: 486/100MHz, 16MB RAM, 2×CD-ROM, SoundBlaster-compatible sound card, 640×480, 256-color display, Windows 95/98/NT 4 or later.

The Sybex CD interface is supported only by Windows 95, Windows 98, and Windows NT.

The Sybex MCSE Edge Tests for Internet Explorer 4 Administration Kit

Test your knowledge with *The Sybex MCSE Edge Test for Internet Explorer 4 Administration Kit*, a custom version of The Edge Tests, designed exclusively for Sybex by The Edge Group. All of the questions from your Sybex MCSE Study Guide are presented in an advanced testing engine, to further aid in your studies. We've included versions of the test for Windows 95, Windows 98, and NT 4 systems.

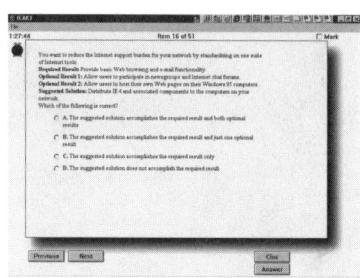

Network Press MCSE Study Guide Sampler

Preview chapters from the best-selling line of MCSE study guides from Sybex. We've also included a copy of the Adobe Acrobat Reader, which you'll need to view the various preview chapters. From the core requirements to the most popular electives, you'll see why Sybex MCSE Study Guides have become the self-study method of choice for tens of thousands seeking MCSE certification.

Microsoft Train_Cert Offline *Update and* Internet Explorer 4.0

Look to Microsoft's *Train_Cert Offline Update*, a quarterly snapshot of Microsoft's Education and Certification Web site, for all of the information you need to plot your course for MCSE certification. You'll need to run *Internet Explorer 4.0* to access all of the features of the *Train_Cert Offline* Web site, so we've included a free copy on the CD. To install *Internet Explorer 4.0*, run the IE4SETUP.EXE file located in the MICROSFT\IE4\CD folder. To install the *Train_Cert Offline* Web site to your system, run the SETUP file located in the MICROSFT\OFFLINE folder.

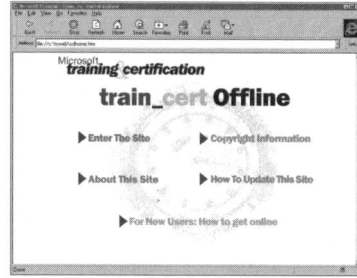

Please consult the README file located in the root directory for more detailed information on the CD contents.

MCSE: Internet Explorer 4
Administration Kit Study Guide

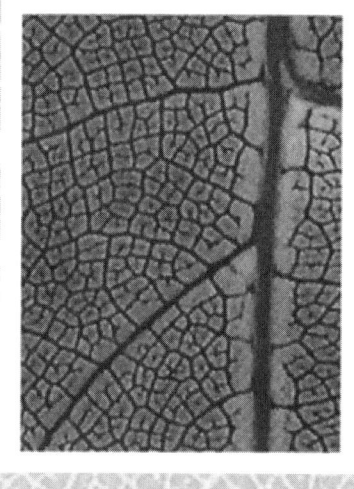

MCSE: Internet Explorer 4 Administration Kit Study Guide

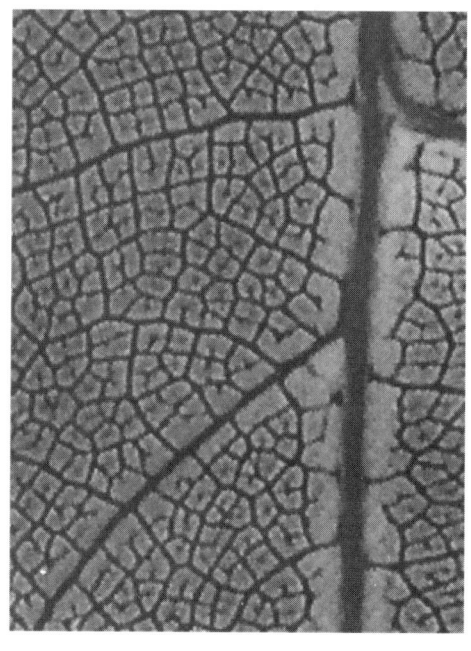

Charles Perkins
James Chellis

San Francisco • Paris • Düsseldorf • Soest

Associate Publisher: Guy Hart-Davis
Contracts and Licensing Manager: Kristine Plachy
Acquisitions & Developmental Editor: Neil Edde
Editor: Brianne Hope Agatep
Technical Editor: Jim Cooper
Book Designer: Bill Gibson
Graphic Illustrator: Tony Jonick
Electronic Publishing Specialist: Robin Kibby
Production Coordinators: Charles Mathews, Julie Sakaue
Indexer: Nancy Guenther
Companion CD: Ginger Warner
Cover Designer: Archer Design

Screen reproductions produced with Collage Complete.

Collage Complete is a trademark of Inner Media Inc.

SYBEX, Network Press, and the Network Press logo are registered trademarks of SYBEX Inc.

TRADEMARKS: SYBEX has attempted throughout this book to distinguish proprietary trademarks from descriptive terms by following the capitalization style used by the manufacturer.

Microsoft® Internet Explorer ©1998 Microsoft Corporation. All rights reserved. Microsoft, the Microsoft Internet Explorer logo, Windows, Windows NT, and the Windows logo are either registered trademarks or trademarks of Microsoft Corporation in the United States and/or other countries.

The CD Interface music is from GIRA Sound AURIA Music Library ©GIRA Sound 1998.

The author and publisher have made their best efforts to prepare this book, and the content is based upon final release software whenever possible. Portions of the manuscript may be based upon pre-release versions supplied by software manufacturer(s). The author and the publisher make no representation or warranties of any kind with regard to the completeness or accuracy of the contents herein and accept no liability of any kind including but not limited to performance, merchantability, fitness for any particular purpose, or any losses or damages of any kind caused or alleged to be caused directly or indirectly from this book.

Photographs and illustrations used in this book have been downloaded from publicly accessible file archives and are used in this book for news reportage purposes only to demonstrate the variety of graphics resources available via electronic access. Text and images available over the Internet may be subject to copyright and other rights owned by third parties. Online availability of text and images does not imply that they may be reused without the permission of rights holders, although the Copyright Act does permit certain unauthorized reuse as fair use under 17 U.S.C. Section 107.

SYBEX is an independent entity from Microsoft Corporation, and not affiliated with Microsoft Corporation in any manner. This publication may be used in assisting students to prepare for a Microsoft Certified Professional Exam. Neither Microsoft Corporation, its designated review company, nor SYBEX warrants that use of this publication will ensure passing the relevant exam. Microsoft is either a registered trademark or trademark of Microsoft Corporation in the United States and/or other countries.

Library of Congress Card Number: 98-86638
ISBN: 0-7821-2309-0

Manufactured in the United States of America

10 9 8 7 6 5 4 3 2

Microsoft®
CERTIFIED PROFESSIONAL
Approved Study Guide

November 1, 1997

Dear SYBEX Customer:

Microsoft is pleased to inform you that SYBEX is a participant in the Microsoft® Independent Courseware Vendor (ICV) program. Microsoft ICVs design, develop, and market self-paced courseware, books, and other products that support Microsoft software and the Microsoft Certified Professional (MCP) program.

To be accepted into the Microsoft ICV program, an ICV must meet set criteria. In addition, Microsoft reviews and approves each ICV training product before permission is granted to use the Microsoft Certified Professional Approved Study Guide logo on that product. This logo assures the consumer that the product has passed the following Microsoft standards:

- The course contains accurate product information.
- The course includes labs and activities during which the student can apply knowledge and skills learned from the course.
- The course teaches skills that help prepare the student to take corresponding MCP exams.

Microsoft ICVs continually develop and release new MCP Approved Study Guides. To prepare for a particular Microsoft certification exam, a student may choose one or more single, self-paced training courses or a series of training courses.

You will be pleased with the quality and effectiveness of the MCP Approved Study Guides available from SYBEX.

Sincerely,

Holly Heath
ICV Account Manager
Microsoft Training & Certification

MICROSOFT INDEPENDENT COURSEWARE VENDOR PROGRAM

To Joseph

Acknowledgments

Thanks, James, for thinking of me when you needed a writer. Thanks again, Mike, for asking that question—"What do you know about NT?" Also, thanks to the crew at Sybex—Brianne and Jim, especially for putting up with my long sentences and meandering style, but also Robin, Charles, and Julie, without whom this book would just be a bunch of text files somewhere, rather than this handsome volume taking up valuable bookshelf space around the world. Thanks to Tony for transforming my drawings into art, Ginger for her hard work on the CD, and Liz for keeping my editorial crew up and running. Guy, Neil, and Kristine, you must be nuts for letting me do this one more time...

—*Charles Perkins*

Contents at a Glance

Table of Contents

Table of Exercises

Introduction

The Microsoft Certified Systems Engineer (MCSE) certification is *the* hottest ticket to career advancement in the computer industry today. Hundreds of thousands of corporations and organizations worldwide are choosing to deploy Windows NT and complementary software products, such as Internet Explorer. The explosion of interest in Internet Explorer has created a tremendous need for qualified personnel and consultants to help implement and support this critical product on networks worldwide. The MCSE certification is your way to show corporations and organizations that you have the professional abilities they need.

This book has been developed in alliance with Microsoft Corporation to give you the knowledge and skills you need to prepare for a popular elective in the MCSE certification program. This elective is Exam 70-079: Implementing and Supporting Microsoft Internet Explorer 4.0 by Using the Microsoft Internet Explorer Administration Kit.

Whether you are just getting started or are ready to move ahead in the computer industry, the knowledge and skills you have are your most valuable assets. Microsoft, recognizing this asset, has developed its Microsoft Certified Professional (MCP) program to give you credentials that verify your ability to work with Microsoft products effectively and professionally. The MCP credential designed for professionals who work with Microsoft networks is the Microsoft Certified Systems Engineer (MCSE) certification.

Certified by Micrososft, this book covers a broad range of topics related to one of Microsoft's key products. You will acquire a solid understanding of the fundamentals of the Internet Explorer Administration Kit (IEAK). Here you will also find the information you need to acquire a solid foundation in the field of computer networks, prepare for the IEAK exam, and take a big step toward MCSE certification.

Is This Book for You?

If you want to learn the basics of how the IEAK works, this book is for you. You'll find clear explanations of the fundamental concepts you need to grasp. If you want to become certified as a Microsoft Certified Systems Engineer (MCSE), this book is also for you. *Microsoft Certified Professional Magazine* recently completed a survey that revealed the average MCSE is earning around $70,000 (US) per year, while the average MCSE consultant is earning more than $95,000 per year. If you want to acquire the solid background you need to pass Microsoft's most popular elective exam, take a step closer to your MCSE certification, and boost your career efforts, this book is for you.

You can read the entire *MCP Magazine* annual salary survey at http://www.mcpmag.com.

What Does This Book Cover?

Think of this book as your guide to the Internet Explorer Administrator's Kit, and to those Microsoft Internet products that it helps you customize. You will learn the basics of installing and using Microsoft's Internet tools, including:

- Internet Explorer 4

- Microsoft Outlook Express

- Microsoft NetMeeting

In addition, you will learn how to perform important tasks, including:

- Installing the IEAK

- Building your own custom version of IE 4

- Including your own custom components in your custom IE 4 package

- Centrally administering deployed browsers and other Internet software

- Establishing browser security and locking-down browser settings in a LAN environment

- Optimizing and troubleshooting IE 4 and the standard IE 4 components (Outlook Express, NetMeeting)

How Do You Become an MCSE?

Attaining Microsoft Certified Systems Engineer (MCSE) status is a serious challenge. The exams cover a wide range of topics and require dedicated study and expertise. Many people who have achieved other computer industry credentials have had troubles with the MCSE certification process. This challenge is, however, why the MCSE certificate is so valuable. If achieving MCSE status was easy, the market would be quickly flooded by MCSEs and the certification would quickly become meaningless. Microsoft, keenly aware of this fact, has taken steps to ensure that the certification means its holder is truly knowledgeable and skilled.

To become an MCSE, you must pass four core requirements and two electives. Most people select the following exam combination for the MCSE core requirements for the 4.0 track (the most current track):

Client Requirement

70-073: Implementing and Supporting Windows NT Workstation 4.0

Networking Requirement

70-058: Networking Essentials

Windows NT Server 4.0 Requirement

70-067: Implementing and Supporting Windows NT Server 4.0

Windows NT Server 4.0 in the Enterprise Requirement

70-068: Implementing and Supporting Windows NT Server 4.0 in the Enterprise

For the electives, you have about 10 choices. Two popular electives at present are:

70-059: Internetworking Microsoft TCP/IP on Microsoft Windows NT 4.0

70-079: Implementing and Supporting Microsoft Internet Explorer 4.0 by Using the Microsoft Internet Explorer Administration Kit

For a more detailed description of the MCSE program, go to
`http://www.cyberstateu.com/text/mcp.`

This book is a part of a series of Network Press MCSE study guides, published by Sybex, that covers four core requirements as well as the electives you need to complete your MCSE track.

Where Do You Take the Exams?

You may take the exams at any of more than 800 Authorized Prometric Testing Centers (APTCs) and VUE Testing Centers available around the world. For the location of a testing center near you, call 800-755-EXAM (755-3926) or call VUE at 888-837-8616. Outside the United States and Canada, contact your local Sylvan Prometric or VUE registration center.

To register for a Microsoft Certified Professional exam:

1. Determine the number of the exam you want to take.

2. Register with the Sylvan Prometric or VUE registration center that is nearest to you. At this point you will be asked for advance payment for the exam—as of September 1998 the exams are $100 each. Exams must be taken within one year of payment. You can schedule exams up to six weeks in advance or as late as one working day prior to the date of the exam. You can cancel or reschedule your exam if you contact the testing center at least two working days prior to the exam. Same-day registration is available in some locations, subject to space availability. Where same-day registration is available, you must register a minimum of two hours before test time.

3. You will receive a registration and payment confirmation letter from Sylvan Prometric.

You may also register for your exams online at http://www.sylvanprometric.com/ or http://www.vue.com/ms/.

When you schedule the exam, you'll be provided with instructions regarding appointment and cancellation procedures, ID requirements, and information about the testing center location.

Microsoft requires certification candidates to accept the terms of a Non-Disclosure Agreement before taking certification exams.

What the IEAK Exam Measures

The IEAK exam covers concepts and skills required for the customization, deployment, and support of Internet Explorer 4 and associated components (Outlook Express, Microsoft NetMeeting, Microsoft Chat, and so on) in Corporate, Internet Service Provider, and Internet Content Provider environments. It emphasizes the following areas of IEAK use:

- Standards and terminology
- Planning
- Implementation
- Troubleshooting

This exam can be quite specific regarding IEAK requirements and operational settings, and it can be particular about how administrative tasks are performed in the operating system. It also focuses on fundamental concepts relating to use of the IEAK and installation of the custom packages. Careful study of this book, along with hands-on experience with the operating system itself, will help you prepare for this exam.

Microsoft provides exam objectives to give you a very general overview of possible areas of coverage by the Microsoft exams. For your convenience we have added in-text objectives listings at the points in the text where specific Microsoft exam objectives are covered.

Exam objectives are subject to change at any time without prior notice and at Microsoft's sole discretion. Please visit Microsoft's Training & Certification Web site (www.microsoft.com/Train_Cert) for the most current exam objectives listing.

How Microsoft Develops the Exam Questions

Microsoft follows an exam development process consisting of eight mandatory phases. The process takes an average of seven months and contains more than 150 specific steps. The phases of Microsoft Certified Professional exam development are:

1. Job analysis

2. Objective domain definition

3. Blueprint survey

4. Item development

5. Alpha review and item revision

6. Beta exam

7. Item selection and cut-score setting

8. Exam live

Microsoft describes each phase as follows:

Phase 1: Job analysis   Phase 1 is an analysis of all the tasks that make up the specific job function, based on tasks performed by people who are currently performing the job function. This phase also identifies the knowledge, skills, and abilities that relate specifically to the performance area to be certified.

Phase 2: Objective domain definition   The results of the job analysis provide the framework used to develop objectives. The development of objectives involves translating the job function tasks into a comprehensive set of more specific and measurable knowledge, skills, and abilities. The resulting list of objectives, or the objective domain, is the basis for the development of both the certification exams and the training materials.

Phase 3: Blueprint survey   The final objective domain is transformed into a blueprint survey in which contributors—technology professionals who are performing the applicable job function—are asked to rate each objective. Contributors may be selected from lists of past Certified Professional candidates, from appropriately skilled exam-development volunteers, and from within Microsoft. Based on the contributors' input, the objectives are prioritized and weighted. The actual exam items are written according to the prioritized objectives. Contributors are queried about how they spend their time on the job, and if a contributor doesn't spend an adequate amount of time actually performing the specified job function, his or her data is eliminated from the analysis.

The blueprint survey phase helps determine which objectives to measure, as well as the appropriate number and types of items to include on the exam.

Phase 4: Item development   A pool of items is developed to measure the blueprinted objective domain. The number and types of items to be written are based on the results of the blueprint survey. During this phase, items are reviewed and revised to ensure that they are:

- Technically accurate

- Clear, unambiguous, and plausible

- Not biased for any population subgroup or culture

- Not misleading or tricky

- Testing at the correct level of Bloom's Taxonomy

- Testing for useful knowledge, not obscure or trivial facts

Items that meet these criteria are included in the initial item pool.

Phase 5: Alpha review and item revision   During this phase, a panel of technical and job function experts reviews each item for technical accuracy, then answers each item, reaching consensus on all technical issues. Once the items have been verified as technically accurate, they are edited to ensure that they are expressed in the clearest language possible.

Phase 6: Beta exam   The reviewed and edited items are collected into a beta exam pool. During the beta exam, each participant has the opportunity to respond to all the items in this beta exam pool. Based on the responses of all beta participants, Microsoft performs a statistical analysis to verify the validity of the exam items and to determine which items will be used in the certification exam. Once the analysis has been completed, the items are distributed into multiple parallel forms, or versions, of the final certification exam.

Phase 7: Item selection and cut-score setting   The results of the beta exam are analyzed to determine which items should be included in the certification exam based on many factors, including item difficulty and relevance. Generally, the desired items are those that were answered correctly by anywhere from 25 percent to 90 percent of the beta exam candidates. This helps ensure that the exam consists of a variety of difficulty levels, from somewhat easy to extremely difficult.

Also during this phase, a panel of job function experts determines the cut score (minimum passing score) for the exam. The cut score differs from exam to exam because it is based on an item-by-item determination of the percentage of candidates who answered the item correctly and who would be expected to answer the item correctly. The cut score is determined in a group session to increase the reliability among the experts.

Phase 8: Exam live   Microsoft Certified Professional exams are administered by Sylvan Prometric.

Tips for Taking the IEAK Exam

Here are some general tips for taking the exam successfully:

- Arrive early at the exam center so you can relax and take one last review of your study materials, particularly tables and lists of exam-related information.

- Read the questions carefully. Don't be tempted to jump to an early conclusion. Make sure you know *exactly* what the question is asking.

- Don't leave any unanswered questions. They count against you.

- Many examinees find that it is helpful to mark and then skip all multiple choice scenario questions until all other questions have been answered. Then you can gauge how much time is remaining and the number of scenario questions to be answered.

- Use a process of elimination to get rid of the obviously incorrect answers first on multiple-choice questions that you're not sure about. This method will improve your odds of selecting the correct answer if you need to make an educated guess.

- Save the hard questions for last because they will eat up the most time. You can move forward and back through the exam.

How to Use This Book

This book can provide a solid foundation for the serious effort of preparing for the IEAK exam. To best benefit from this book, you might want to use the following study method:

1. Study a chapter carefully, making sure you fully understand the information.

2. Complete all hands-on exercises in the chapter, referring to the chapter so that you understand each step you take.

3. Answer the exercise questions related to that chapter. (You will find the answers to these questions in Appendix A.)

4. Note which questions you did not understand and study the corresponding sections of the book again.

5. Study each chapter in the same manner.

6. Before taking the exam, try the Sybex MCSE Edge Test included on the CD that comes with this book in order to become familiar with the test-taking process. The Edge Tests include simulations of the actual Microsoft exam. It is an excellent way to make the best use of your SYBEX study guides and your limited study time. For more information about The Edge Tests visit www.edgetest.com.

If you prefer to use this book in conjunction with classroom or online training, you have many options. Both Microsoft-authorized training and independent training are widely available. CyberState University offers excellent online MCSE programs across the Internet, using the SYBEX materials. Their program also includes an online lab where you can aquire hands-on experience working with Microsoft products, as well as videos, exam preparation software, chat forums, and lectures, all centered around the SYBEX MCSE Study Guide series. You can reach CyberState at 1-888-GET-EDUCated (888-438-3382) or www.cyberstateu.com.

To learn all the material covered in this book, you will need to study regularly and with discipline. Try to set aside the same time every day to study and select a comfortable and quiet place in which to do it. If you work hard, you will be surprised at how quickly you learn this material. Good luck.

What's on the CD?

The CD contains several valuable tools to help you study for your MCSE exams:

- The Sybex MCSE Edge Test for IEAK
- Microsoft's Train_Cert Offline
- Microsoft's Internet Explorer 4.01

Contact Information

To find out more about Microsoft Education and Certification materials and programs, to register with Sylvan Prometric, or to get other useful information, check the following resources. (Outside the United States or Canada, contact your local Microsoft office or Sylvan Prometric testing center.)

Microsoft Certified Professional Program — (800) 636-7544   Call the MCPP number for the latest information about the Microsoft Certified Professional program and exams.

Sylvan Prometric Testing Centers — (800) 755-EXAM   To register to take a Microsoft Certified Professional exam at any of more than 800 Sylvan Prometric testing centers around the world, or to order this Exam Study Guide, call the Sylvan Prometric registration center.

VUE Testing Centers — (888) 837-8616   To register to take a Microsoft Certified Professional exam at a VUE testing center call the VUE registration center.

Microsoft Certification Development Team — http://www.microsoft .com/Train_Cert/mcp/examinfo/certsd.htm   Contact the Microsoft Certification Development Team through their Web site to volunteer for one or more exam development phases or to report a problem with an exam. Address written correspondence to: Certification Development Team; Microsoft Education and Certification; One Microsoft Way; Redmond, WA 98052.

Microsoft TechNet Technical Information Network — (800) 344-2121

Use this number to contact support professionals and system administrators. Outside the United States and Canada, call your local Microsoft subsidiary for information.

Microsoft Related Training Resources

- http://www.microsoft.com/train_cert/train/
- http://www.cyberstateu.com/text/catalog/nt.htm

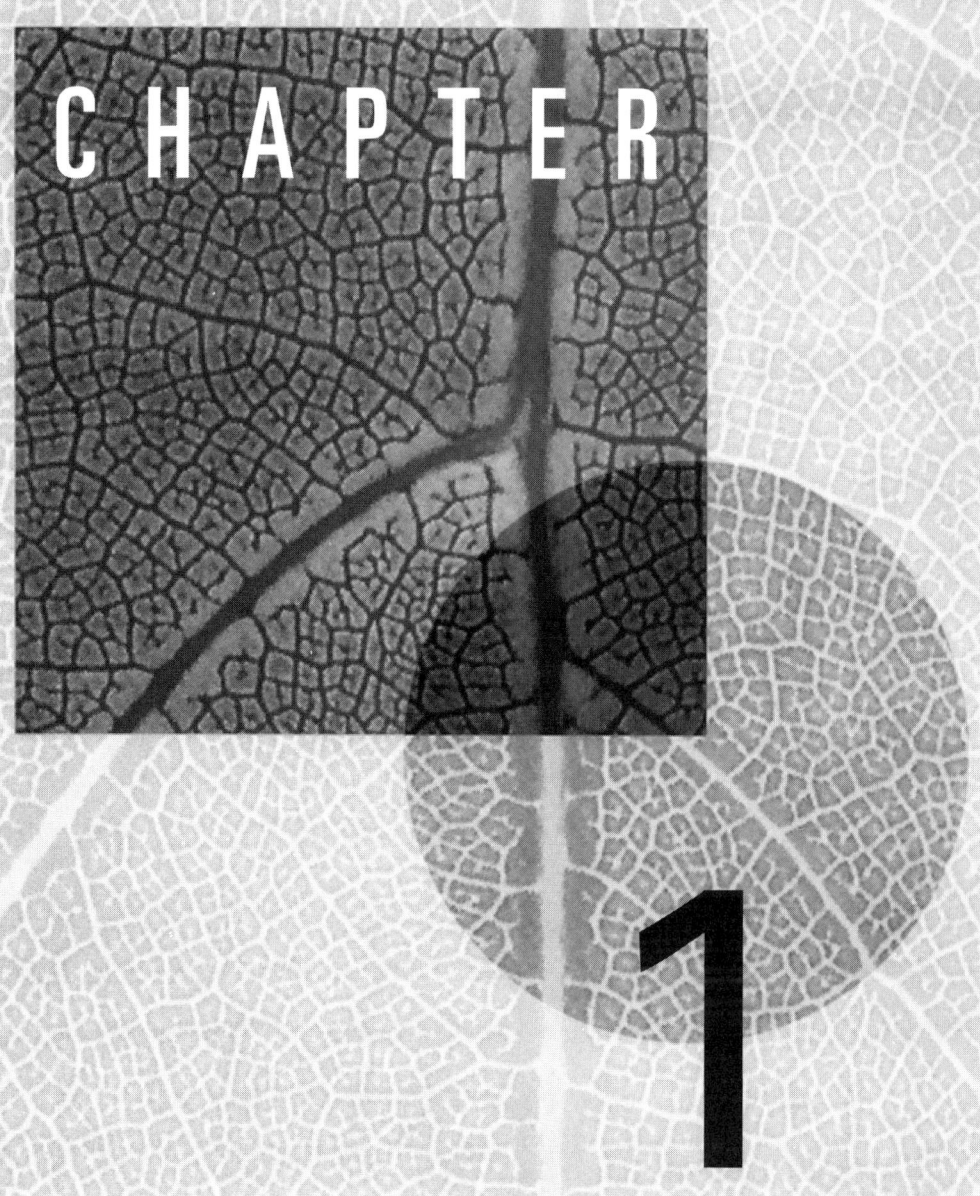

CHAPTER

1

Exploring Internet Explorer

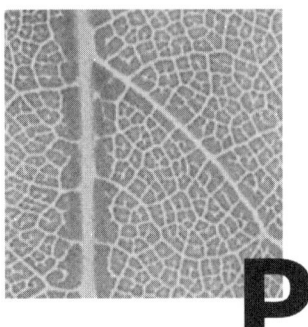

Proficiency with Internet Explorer requires a familiarity with the Internet itself, with the protocols and standards of the World Wide Web (HTTP and HTML, specifically), and with commonly used Internet tools and Web browser extensions. You also need to know the features and capabilities of Internet Explorer 4 and the other programs (Outlook Express, NetMeeting, NetShow, etc.) that are distributed with it. This chapter gives you an overview of the technology that will be discussed in greater detail in the rest of this book.

What Is This Web Thing Anyway?

How something works depends a lot on the environment in which it operates. Understanding a fish presumes that you know something about water (water is wet, buoyant, relatively easy to move through, sometimes clear, not quick to change temperature). Remove a fish from its environment and it doesn't behave very fish-like anymore (it flops around instead of swimming).

Similarly, in order to understand Internet Explorer you need to understand its environment, which is the World Wide Web. The Web is based on the technology that forms the Internet, so in order to understand the Web you have to know how the Internet works as well. This section briefly describes the following topics:

- The Internet

- The World Wide Web—what it is, what it's good for, and how it works

- The functions of a Web browser
- A bit about HTML

If you are familiar with how the Internet works, skip ahead to the section on the World Wide Web. If you are familiar with Web servers, HTML, and HTTP, skip ahead to "Beyond the Web," which introduces tools that move beyond hypertext use of the Web.

The Internet

People talk about the Internet as though it is one big thing, mythical, like Godzilla or Kansas. However, the Internet is not one big thing; it is how a group of things (computers, big and little) are tied together. It's not a monolithic organization with a single direction and a controlling group; it's a society of interconnected computers.

The Internet, like the economy, is a concept. You can't touch it. But you know it exists by participating in it. Start a business or just buy a loaf of bread, and you participate in the economy. Similarly, connect to your local area network or to an Internet service provider, and you are "connected to" the Internet.

Governments, companies, and other organizations link computers together to form networks. There are two types of networks: Computers linked together at a single location, such as a school or office building, form a *local area network* (LAN). LANs are usually connected with cables specifically designed to carry computer data. Computers linked together at different locations (such as across the town, across the state, or across the world) form a *wide area network* (WAN). WANs are usually linked together by telephone lines or other types of leased lines.

In 1969, the Advanced Research Projects Agency of the Department of Defense (ARPA) created a WAN to link researchers and Department of Defense research centers. In addition to the great deal of the research done at universities, they also conducted studies on the networking protocols used in the WAN. This research was further developed into the *Transmission Control Protocol / Internet Protocol* (or TCP/IP) *suite*, the protocols used over the Internet.

You can learn a great deal more about TCP/IP in the Sybex Network Press book *MCSE: TCP/IP Study Guide*. After you've absorbed its contents, you should take the MCP TCP/IP test (an elective towards your MCSE certification and a core requirement for the MCPS Internet Specialist certification).

During the 1970s most of the larger universities in the United States and many research centers throughout the world linked themselves together using the same TCP/IP protocols, extending the original network, called ARPANET, beyond its original scope of linking Department of Defense computers. The extended network became known as the *network of networks* (because many schools and organizations already had LANs linking their local computers), or the *Internet*.

As corporations joined with universities to develop technologies (especially computer technologies) and turn those technologies into commercial products, the corporations joined their networks to the Internet as well. University alumni and researchers who joined corporations often convinced their new employers that they needed Internet access, and so the Internet moved into the business world.

Although ARPA and its successor, the Defense Advanced Research Projects Agency (DARPA), created the nucleus of the Internet, these organizations did not control the Internet. For a while ARPA and DARPA guided the Internet's evolution. Because the government subsidized the Internet *backbone* (the main high-speed links connecting geographic areas), it controlled Internet access by limiting commercial traffic. Eventually, DARPA decreed the Internet "research program" a success and spun off support of the backbone to private industry (mostly to the long-distance telephone companies). Today, no single organization is "in charge" of the Internet.

The Internet, as well as being a network of networks, is a network of cooperating organizations and companies. Internet service providers allow personal computer users and small companies to connect to the Internet. Many Internet service providers may compete in a geographical area. The ISPs connect to a network access point, which is a central geographical place where the high-capacity Internet backbone links come together to exchange data. Several long-distance telephone companies compete to link the network access points (two major competitors are AT&T and Sprint). The various organizations compete with other companies at the same level for providing Internet service, but cooperate with the organizations "above" and "below" them in the service chain. See Figure 1.1 for a conceptual diagram of the Internet.

FIGURE 1.1

The Internet is a web of computers linked by telephone lines.

The Internet links computers around the world. What you do with the link is a matter of software. One of the earliest software programs written to use the Internet protocols is *Telnet*. Telnet allows you to connect to and use Unix computers with a command-line interface. Another program that has been around a long time is *FTP* (File Transfer Protocol), which is both a program and the protocol it uses. It allows you to store and retrieve files on any remote computer that supports FTP.

The Internet is the realm of protocols and operating systems. Its purpose is to transport data. What that data is and what you use the Internet for is another matter entirely. You can put information on your computer (connected to the Internet) and let other computers on the Internet access that data. This is the realm of Web servers and Web clients, respectively.

The Internet connects computers. World Wide Web servers make information available to computers connected to the Internet. World Wide Web browsers allow you to view information stored on a Web server. The World Wide Web requires the Internet to function.

The World Wide Web

Most early Internet programs were command-line programs (the 1969 genesis of the Internet was *long* before the Macintosh showed the world how nice graphics can be). The World Wide Web changed all that. Instead of requiring you to know arcane commands, the World Wide Web gives you a graphical view of the Internet. The Web is easy to use; it is also easy to create Web pages and to link them to other Web pages. You don't have to learn esoteric programming languages to create a simple Web site. You can create Web pages with a simple text editor. There are other tools—such as Microsoft FrontPage Express—that make creating Web pages even easier. The more complex Web pages do require some programming, however.

What Is the Web?

Although the World Wide Web uses the Internet, the Web is based on another concept entirely. That concept is *hypertext*, and it is referred to in the names of the standards and protocols that the World Wide Web uses: Hypertext Markup Language (HTML) and Hypertext Transport Protocol (HTTP).

Hypertext is based on the idea that electronic documents, unlike paper documents, are dynamic (i.e. changing and interactive). When you run across an interesting word or concept in a printed newspaper article, for instance, you must go to a dictionary, encyclopedia, or library to look up the reference yourself. At best, the article will cite references in footnotes. However, if a hypertext article is displayed for you on a computer screen, the computer can bring the references right to you. Instead of merely giving the reference name, the hypertext article contains pointers to a web of interrelated documents, each with links to more articles with similar subjects or examples or "digressionary" (but interesting) subjects. To access these documents, all you have to do is click the reference link.

Consider a computer support technician looking for help diagnosing and fixing a recalcitrant video adapter. The technician knows that the adapter is manufactured by Nifty Video, and that they have a Web site. The technician goes to the home page of Nifty Video (probably `www.niftyvideo.com`). Nifty Video's home page, a default hypertext document, contains hypertext links to information about Nifty Video products, including device drivers and frequently asked questions (FAQ) lists (a good first place to look for help when experiencing a problem). The technician clicks on the link to the frequently asked questions document. A hypertext document that lists the questions appears. The technician can then use the hypertext to select the corresponding question to find a solution to the video problem.

A hypertext document can contain links to just about anything. A document summarizing the rise and fall of the Roman Empire might have links to detailed biographies of each of the Roman leaders, and also contain other links to the political differences between republics and empires. A hypertext quarterly report for a company can include links in summary sections to detailed reports on the performance of company divisions as well as links to the company's products, detailed by geographic region. A personal home page can contain links to the interests and hobbies of the person who created the page.

The World Wide Web delivers what hypertext promises—and more. The Web goes beyond merely linking textual documents. Web features such as JavaScript and CGI allow the user to interact with individual Web pages. Web servers can create Web pages that are based on dynamic information such as the weather or the contents of a database. Some Web pages even display the moment-by-moment state of coffee machines and soda vending machines (so you can know whether your next drink will be fresh or even available if you happen to be near the Web-enabled device).

The World Wide Web markup language (HTML) and protocol (HTTP) allow any Internet site to provide (or *host*) Web pages. Any Web page can refer to another Web page, even without the other page's knowledge. You don't have to ask anyone's permission (outside of your own company or organization) to set up a Web site. This open method of linking documents makes it incredibly easy for people to set up their own Web pages and to make the information on them available to anyone on the Internet.

What Is the Web Good For?

In a few short years, the Web has become indispensable to the flow of information around the globe and within organizations. It is an integral part of how people communicate and how organizations manage their projects and business.

Even more recent than the explosion of popular interest in the World Wide Web has been a rapid migration toward the use of Internet technologies, including browsers, to form "mini-Internets" within organizations. These "mini-Internets" are known as *intranets*. Browsers, of course, form a core piece of this important recent development in intra-organizational communication.

There are two questions you should ask yourself when looking at Internet and Web technology: What can it do for me as an individual? What can it do for my company?

For Individuals: You can use the World Wide Web to search for product information, download changes to software and firmware, keep abreast of information published in electronic newsletters, research any subject from auto mechanics to zoology, and much more.

You can also publish your own information on the World Wide Web. If you have a constant connection to the Internet, the information can be stored on your workstation or on your LAN server. If you have a dial-up connection, your Internet service provider usually will provide space on its server for your World Wide Web information.

For Organizations: By empowering the individual to work more effectively, the Web also helps businesses do business. In addition to expediting individual-centric tasks, a business can directly benefit from the Web by providing a new arena for advertising, making it easier for customers to find information about products and services, giving users of products another feed-back channel to the product producers, and establishing another marketplace for buying and selling products (one with lower overhead than maintaining a presence in the traditional person-to-person marketplace of store fronts and office buildings).

A company Web page announces to the world that that company has products or services to sell. People searching the Web can evaluate if the products or services detailed in the Web page meet their needs. Companies that take an aggressive stance in Web-based advertising can purchase screen space (in the form of links with graphics) on commonly accessed Web pages maintained by other organizations such as search engines and Web page directories.

After a customer purchases a product, the company Web site can keep the user happy with the purchase by maintaining useful information about it, such as how to perform tasks with it, how to solve common technical problems, and what is the latest version.

Customer-support Web sites often provide an avenue for customers to give feedback about the product and ask questions about its use. Sometimes these Web pages even provide an area for customers to help other customers and establish a community of users. These types of Web pages are sometimes called *bulletin board systems* (BBS).

What most people think about when discussing Web-based commerce is buying and selling products over the Web. A company that sells products and can deliver them in mail-order fashion can accept orders (usually with a credit card) over the Web and have them delivered by Federal Express or

United Parcel Service. If the product the company makes is composed of information (such as software, timely news or statistics, or entertainment), the product itself can often be delivered over the Web as well.

How the Web Works

The Web is pretty simple considering how much you can do with it. When you view information on the Web, the information has to come from somewhere. That somewhere is a Web server. Something has to put that information up on your computer screen, and that something is a Web browser. When you understand how the Web browser and the Web server do their jobs (including how they communicate with each other) you know how the Web works.

Web Servers   A Web server is a program that runs on a computer on the Internet (it can be pretty much anywhere on the Internet, so long as other computers on the Internet can access it). The Web server just listens for requests for Web pages, and when it gets a request it sends out the requested page.

In order for the Web server to understand a request for a hypertext document, the request has to be formatted a specific way. The HTTP protocol embodies the rules for how requests are submitted to the Web server and how the resulting hypertext document is sent back.

Web servers can store and send more than just hypertext documents. They can also send pictures, sound files, animations, spreadsheets, programs, word processing documents, and any other kind of file that can be stored on a hard disk drive. It doesn't matter to the Web server what kind of file it is, because all the Web server has to do is identify the file and send it out.

Modern Web servers go one step beyond just sending the document. Sometimes the requested file doesn't actually exist. The Web servers can run programs to generate files on the fly—the current stock prices, a picture of the lobby of an office building, or a current weather map. Or if the user wants a list of all those documents with the words "IPO" and "Biomedical" in them, the Web server can find those files and generate a new document that lists them.

Some Web servers also give you control over who may access the hypertext and other files. These servers also often support other advanced security features such as Secure Socket Layer encryption of HTTP communication,

Digital Certificates to assure the authenticity of the server, and the ability to make one computer and Web server appear to be many computers and Web servers (useful for companies that are hosting Internet information for other companies).

There are many Web server programs available today. Some Web servers run on only one operating system, others are portable and have versions for almost any computer. Microsoft provides three Web servers, one for each of its operating systems:

- Personal Web Server—(For Windows 95) This Web server provides simple Web page hosting services and some support for dynamically generating Web pages (via CGI and scripting languages).

- Peer Web Services—(For Windows NT Workstation) This Web server gives Workstation users the ability to host Web pages that take advantage of Active Server Pages technology and Internet Server Application Interface (ISAPI) filters. Peer Web Services is limited in the number of simultaneous HTTP requests it can satisfy.

- Internet Information Server—(For Windows NT Server) This is the Web server Microsoft provides for businesses to place information on the Internet. This full-featured product does everything that Peer Web Services does and has, in addition, more security features (including authentication and encryption), virtual Web server support, bandwidth throttling, and additional administration and reporting tools.

Web Browsers and HTML   The Web browser displays what the Web server stores, produces, and sometimes generates. If the Web server sends a hypertext document, the Web browser displays it on the user's screen. If the server sends a sound file, the browser plays it through the computer's speakers. If the server sends a spreadsheet, the browser finds the appropriate spreadsheet application and launches it with the document.

The Web browser has to know how to display the hypertext data to the user. For this reason, hypertext documents on the Web have a standard format called Hypertext Markup Language (HTML). An HTML document is also commonly called a Web page.

The following is the source of an HTML document (the source is what is contained in the document before the Web browser interprets it and displays it to the user). See Figure 1.2 for a view of Internet Explorer displaying that same document.

```
<HTML><HEAD>
<TITLE>The Random Quotations Page</TITLE></HEAD>
<BODY background="images/grback5.gif">
<p align=center>

<IMG SRC="images/rq2.gif" ><BR>

<small>[<a href="index.html">Quotations Page</a> | <a href =
"qotd.html"> Daily </a> | <a href="qotw.html">Weekly</a> |
<a href="mqotd.html"> Motivational </a> | Random | <a
href="search.html">Search</a> | <a href="add.html">
Contribute </a> | <a href="links.html">Links</a> | <a
href="books.html"> Books </a>  | <a href="mail.html"> Email
</a>]</small></p><HR><UL>

<LI>The following quotations were chosen randomly when you
loaded this page. Reload the page for a new set of quotes,
or use the options and button below.</UL>

<form method="get" action="randquote.cgi"><input
type="submit" value="Reload">
  using: <select name=file>
<option value=20thcent>20th Century Quotations
<option value=altq>alt.quotations archives
<option value=barry>Dave Barry Quotations
<option value=bywomen>Quotations by Women
<option value=coles>Cole's Quotables
<option value=deep>Deep Thoughts - Jack Handey
<option value=devils>The Devil's Dictionary
<option value=mgm selected>Michael Moncur's collection
<option value=motivate>Laura Moncur's Motivational Quotes
<option value=usenet>The USENET fortune file
<option value=wright>Steven Wright quotations
</select> Number of quotes: <select name=number>
<option value=1>1<option value=2>2<option value=3
selected>3<option value=4>4<option value=5>5
<option value=6>6<option value=7>7<option value=8>8<option
value=9>9<option value=10>10
</select><BR><DL>
```

```
<DT><B> H. L. Mencken (1880-1956):</B><DD>"An idealist is
one who, on noticing that roses smell better than a cabbage,
concludes that it will also make better soup."

<DT><B> Anonymous:</B><DD>"Nobody knows the age of the human
race, but everybody agrees that it is old enough to know
better."

<DT><B> Ashleigh Brilliant:</B><DD>"I either want less
corruption, or more chance to participate in it." </DL>

<HR><p align=center>[<a href="index.html">Quotations Page</
a> |<a href="qotd.html">Daily</a> | <a
href="qotw.html">Weekly</a> |<a href="mqotd.html">
Motivational </a> | Random | <a href="search.html"> Search
</a> | <a href="add.html">Contribute</a> | <a
href="links.html"> Links </a> | <a href="books.html">Books</
a>  | <a href="mail.html"> Email </a> ] </p> </BODY> </HTML>
```

FIGURE 1.2

Michael Moncur's Random Quotations Page has formatted text, a form created with HTML tags, and links to other Web pages.

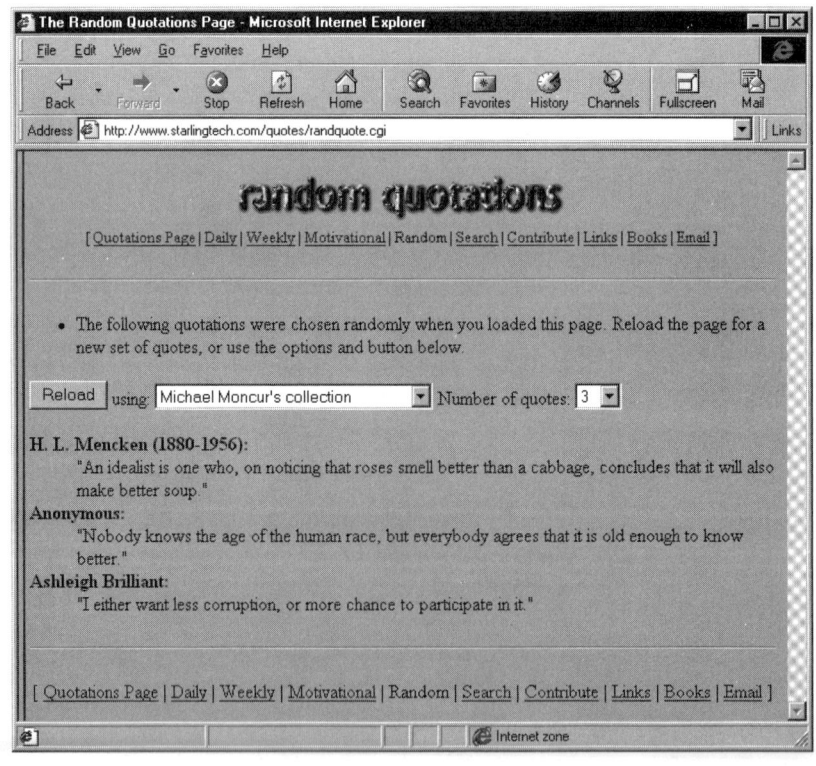

An HTML document is a text document that is made up of text, links, and tags. It is the links that make HTML hypertext, and it is the tags that make it extendable and visually rich. When the Web browser receives an HTML page to display, it formats the text in the document according to the tags. The Web browser will ignore any tasks it doesn't know how to handle. Web browser plug-ins teach the Web browser how to handle new tags. When you click a link (which is a special form of tag) it requests the document specified by that link.

Tags in HTML are identified by the angle brackets, < and >, that surround them. Although there are many different tags defined in the HTML standard, only a few are used in the previous example. You should not see the tags in the document when it is displayed by the Web browser (if you do see them, something has gone horribly wrong). The tags tell the Web browser how to display the text in the document or the tags tell the Web browser how the document is structured.

To view the HTML source code of a Web page, view that page in IE 4 and select Source from the View menu.

The <B> tag, for example, tells the Web browser to start displaying the text in a bold font. The </B> tag tells the Web browser it should stop displaying the text in bold (many HTML tags come in pairs like that). The <HR> command draws a horizontal line across the Web page and the <IMG SRC=*URL*> tag identifies an image to display. The <HTML>, <HEAD>, </HEAD>, <BODY>, </BODY>, and </HTML> tags, however, describe the structure of the document instead of specifying how to display it.

You may notice that some of the HTML tags in the previous example are in uppercase and some are in lowercase. HTML is not case sensitive, which means that <p> means the same thing as <P>, and <html> means the same as <HTML>, <Html>, or even <hTmL>.

Links to other Web documents use the <a href=*URL*> and </a> tags. Within the <a href=*URL* > tag is the URL to the linked document, and what the user clicks on to go to the page goes between the two tags. Web browsers usually underline, draw a box around, or otherwise signify that this is a link to another document. In Internet Explorer, the cursor turns from a pointer to a hand when you move it over a link.

A Word about URLs Every resource on the Internet, including Web pages and FTP files, has a unique reference name that you can use to access that specific document. This reference name is called a *Uniform Resource Locator* (URL). The part of an `<a href="`*URL*`">` tag between the quotes is the URL, as is the contents of the Address field in the Web browser. URLs consist of a number of elements:

- The service that provides the resource (followed by a colon—most browsers will default to `http` if you don't provide a service)

- The address of the server that contains the resource (preceded by two slashes, and either in the form of a domain name or an IP address)

- The path to the document on the server's file system (each directory is preceded by a Unix style forward slash no matter what operating system the server actually runs)

- The name of the resource (preceded by slash)

So for instance, the following URL requests the default HTML page in the VirtualNT directory from the HTTP service of the server `internetropolis.com`:

```
http://www.internetropolis.com/VirtualNT/default.html
```

All URLs follow this format regardless of the service being used or the document being retrieved.

Web Browsers and Plug-Ins With a Web browser you can access far more than just Web pages. Quite often a link on a Web page points to something other than an HTML file (such as a MIDI music file or a QuickTime animation file). Part of the great flexibility of the Web is that it is easy to configure your Web browser to handle more than just HTML data.

Plug-ins are code modules that extend the power of a Web browser without requiring changes to the browser itself. When a Web server sends data to a browser, it also tells the browser what kind of data the server thinks it is (it tells the browser the Multimedia Internet Mail Encoding, or MIME, type of the data). The browser calls plug-ins whenever a Web server sends it data that it doesn't have the built-in capability to handle.

If a needed plug-in is not installed on your computer, and the HTML tag tells the browser where on the Internet to get the plug-in, the browser will pop up a dialog box and ask you whether you want to go to the manufacturer's Web site and download it. If you answer yes, the browser often can attach to the manufacturer's site, download the plug-in, install it, link back to the source site, and then begin streaming the content to the plug-in for display.

Internet Explorer plug-ins must be written specifically for the Windows architecture and are developed in compiled languages such as C++. There are plug-ins available to display almost any kind of data, from sound and video to 3-D virtual worlds. Consider the following three plug-ins:

Virtual Reality Modeling Language (VRML) is a client/server 3-D rendering package that allows Web browsers to load a description of a 3-D space (for instance, the coordinate points that specify the corners of a cube), which is then rendered inside their Web browser. You can then move through the VRML space using your browser. Your browser transmits your current location to the server and receives the data required to render that location. VRML data is much smaller than it might seem; for instance, rendering a cube requires the transmission of only six numbers.

Shockwave is a plug-in that supports frame-based video streaming. The Shockwave plug-in receives video frames and displays them with your browser. Shockwave is based on Macromedia's Director product that evolved from HyperCard on the Mac/OS.

RealAudio provides support for real-time audio over the Internet. By installing the plug-in and then browsing to a RealAudio server, you'll hear whatever content is being Webcast at that moment. Many radio stations use RealAudio to simulcast over the Internet to reach a larger audience than their broadcast area. You can even use RealAudio to listen to radio stations from other countries.

Scripting and Extending Web Browsers Plug-ins are a great idea, but they don't really fulfill the need for applications that can be quickly developed and delivered over the Web without additional cost—especially for simple content such as advertising banners and animation. Most Web browsers now include interpreters for script languages that allow Webmasters to create all types of interactive content that would not be possible with simple Hypertext Markup Language documents. Four types of active content are now common on the Web:

JavaScript/JScript is a scripting language created for Netscape Navigator based on the syntax of Java. JavaScript has the broadest browser support of any easy-to-use language. JScript is Microsoft's version of JavaScript, which includes a few features that make more effective use of the Internet Explorer Web browser and the Windows operating system.

VBScript is a scripting language created for Internet Explorer and based on the syntax of Visual Basic. Internet Explorer is the only browser that supports VBScript, and it's not likely that any non-Microsoft browsers will ever support it.

ActiveX controls are compiled plug-ins that can be automatically downloaded and installed to provide application-like user-interface controls on a Web page. ActiveX is only supported by Microsoft browsers.

Java is a complete interpreted programming language based on the syntax of C++. Java is supported by more Web browsers than any other sort of dynamic content.

More about JavaScript and JScript   Netscape recognized the need for a client-based scripting language for its Web browsers to take care of many simple programmatic functions for the user, such as rotating graphic banners or scrolling messages across the screen. Java could do this, but as a complete programming language with a development environment, Java was too complex for anyone who wasn't a professional programmer.

JavaScript is a simple but powerful language that does not have to be compiled or linked into applets that are downloaded. The JavaScript codes are simply inserted into the body of the HTML document. When the page is read by the browser, the browser interprets any embedded JavaScript codes.

JavaScript does not allow access to your computer outside your Web browser. It is not possible to create viruses or Trojan horses with JavaScript, nor is it possible to extract information about you with JavaScript. Figure 1.3 shows you an example of what JavaScript can do.

JavaScript is best for Internet Web pages that need straightforward animation, scrolling text, or other simple programming requirements.

Exercise 1.1 shows you how to use a JavaScript-enabled Web page.

FIGURE 1.3

A game written
entirely in JavaScript

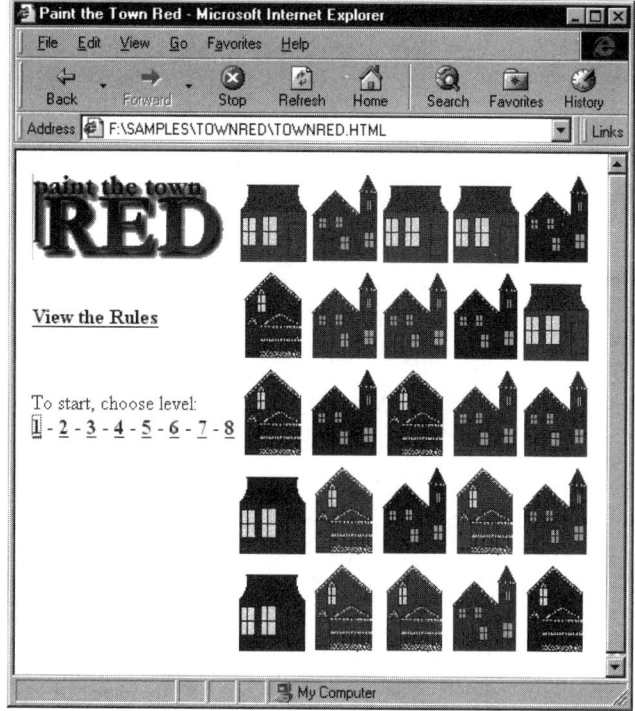

EXERCISE 1.1

Browsing a JavaScript Web Page

1. Launch Internet Explorer 4.

2. Type **//<CD-ROM>/townred/townred.htm** into the Address field of
your Web browser.

3. Click View the Rules for an overview of the rules.

4. Play to your heart's content.

More about VBScript Although JavaScript is a good interpreted object-
oriented language for general Web browsing, it doesn't support many of the
fundamental features of the Windows operating systems. This lack of support is intentional—JavaScript wasn't developed with just Windows in
mind. It works perfectly well on any platform.

Microsoft created VBScript, which is comparable to JavaScript, primarily to assist in the creation of Internet-based client/server database applications. Like Visual Basic before it, its primary purpose is the rapid development of front ends for SQL database servers. VBScript doesn't run on other Web browsers (e.g., Netscape Navigator) though.

Like JavaScript, VBScript does not allow access to your hard drive or other executing programs, so it cannot be used to propagate malicious software or to extract information from your computer.

VBScript is perfect for Intranet environments based on Microsoft operating systems and applications, as it interfaces well with Visual Basic for Applications and ActiveX controls. It's not well suited for Internet Web sites, because it only works with Internet Explorer.

More about ActiveX   ActiveX is Microsoft's technology for extending the user interface capability of HTML and scripting languages. ActiveX controls (such as buttons, pick lists, menus, and check boxes) allow you to embed controls in your HTML forms that make them look like Windows applications. ActiveX was developed specifically to make Web browser–based database clients resemble database clients that can be created with Visual C++ or Visual Basic.

ActiveX controls are more closely related in design and implementation to plug-ins than they are to Java applets or to scripts. ActiveX controls are compiled programs that are downloaded once and permanently installed into your browser.

ActiveX technology is most appropriate for Intranet or Internet servers where security isn't a major issue and similar software is in use.

More about Java   Java is a powerful new programming language for developing applets that run inside Web browsers or applications that run independently on your computer. Java is similar to many industrial programming languages (e.g., C or C++) except that it is not compiled to the native machine language of the target computer. Rather, Java is compiled to a "virtual machine," or a fictitious machine language. The resulting fictitious machine code is called Java byte code, which can be interpreted by a Java run-time interpreter or compiled to the native machine language of your computer by a just-in-time (JIT) compiler.

The important difference between Java and more traditional languages is that the distribution of byte code, rather than machine code, allows the same application to run on any computer that has a Java runtime interpreter or compiler. For instance, a word processor written in 100 percent pure Java (i.e., Java that doesn't make use of any machine-specific libraries) could run on a Macintosh, a PC, or a Unix workstation without any modification at all.

Because Java can run virtually on any machine, it's the perfect language for developing active content in your Web pages if your customers are using a variety of computers. Like HTML, Java is designed to work the same on any computer.

Java may be the most important new programming language development in the past few decades. Although the factors that make Java important were not invented or developed specifically for Java, it is the first language to embody so many different factors. Although a single organization (Java-Soft, a wholly owned subsidiary of Sun Microsystems) tightly controls the development of Java, it has gained wide acceptance among software and hardware developers. Here are Java's strong points:

- Truly object-oriented architecture.

- Syntactically similar to C and C++, so it's easy for programmers to learn.

- Interpreted virtual machine is completely cross-platform.

- Easily speed optimized at both compile time and runtime.

- Language-based object component model facilitates code reuse.

- Standard I/O libraries designed for Internet communication.

- Virtual machine can be embedded in applications like Web browsers to support the development of applets.

- Virtual machine byte code is dense, requires very little bandwidth, and can be just-in-time compiled for extra speed.

- Embedded virtual machines create safe environments that prevent security leaks in distributed applications.

EXERCISE 1.2

Exploring Java Sites on the Web

1. Launch Internet Explorer.

2. Type **http://langevin.usc.edu/Fred/** in the address line.

3. Click the View Fred's World hypertext link. Wait for the Java game to load. It may take a while, depending on the speed of your connection to the Internet. After it loads, you will see a 3-D maze.

4. Use your mouse or the arrow keys to walk through the 3-D maze. This 3-D full-motion game is written entirely in Java. It runs well on Macintoshes, PCs, and Unix machines.

5. Type **http://www.kona.lotus.com** in the address line of your Web browser.

6. Click eSuite Demos ➤ eSuite Intranet Demo.

7. Click Start Demo.

8. Complete the marketing form and click Submit.

9. Accept the software license agreement form.

10. Click Sales Forecast.

11. Change some of the numbers in one of the cells with a white background. Notice that all the related cells change. This fully functional spreadsheet is written entirely in Java.

12. Close the Web browser when you are finished.

Although Java applets running in Web browsers have no access to your computer (they can only access files on the originating server), Java applications that you run on your computer (independent of the Web browser) can access files on any Internet server that allows Internet access. You can easily implement server services entirely in Java, which means that you can provide some custom services that Internet Information Server does not support (e.g., a Telnet client or a chat server). Running the Java server application (or *servlet*) on your IIS server allows users who download a client applet in their

Web browser to connect to the Java server running on your Internet server. In this manner, you can create complete client/server applications written entirely in Java.

Beyond the Web

The World Wide Web is the big Internet service that everyone talks about (and usually confuses with the Internet itself), but there are other services and tools out there that are arguably as important and that have been around for much longer. The most common services are as follows:

- **Internet mail,** known to most as e-mail, is one of the oldest and still one of the most useful Internet services. Millions of messages are exchanged daily within and between companies and individuals worldwide via Internet mail.

- **FTP** is a command-line interface used to transfer files between archives on the Internet and your computer (you can also use your Web browser to access FTP sites).

- **Telnet** is a tool that gives Internet clients a command-line interface to Internet server computers. Telnet is often used by Network integrators and administrators to remotely configure and administer network devices. Telnet is the simplest of all Internet protocols, so many embedded devices use Telnet for configuration. Also, with Telnet, many hand-held computers can remotely control larger general purpose computers.

- **Internet news** gives individuals with common interests (from cooking to large system database administration) a new way to exchange information on almost any subject. Internet news works like a huge subject-based bulletin board system. You can subscribe to newsgroup topics that interest you, then follow the public discussions posted in that newsgroup.

Internet Mail

You can use Internet mail to send e-mail messages to other individuals anywhere in the world. If you have a dedicated Internet connection and your

LAN e-mail package is set up to route e-mail to the Internet, you do not have to do anything special to send Internet mail.

With Outlook Express (which comes with a full installation of Internet Explorer 4) you can either use Microsoft Exchange Server to route your e-mail to the Internet or use the SMTP and POP protocols to send and receive mail by contacting Internet mail hosts directly. E-mail packages (Outlook Express included) have many features that make exchanging electronic mail over the Internet easier, including:

- Address books

- Inboxes and outboxes

- Mailboxes for specific correspondence

- Delayed message sending and offline mail reading

- Multiple e-mail account access

- Automatic mail forwarding and mail access

- Mail filters and automated mail processing

- File attachment and flexible mail formats

See Figure 1.4 for a view of Outlook Express.

FIGURE 1.4

Microsoft's e-mail software, Outlook Express, can send messages over the Internet.

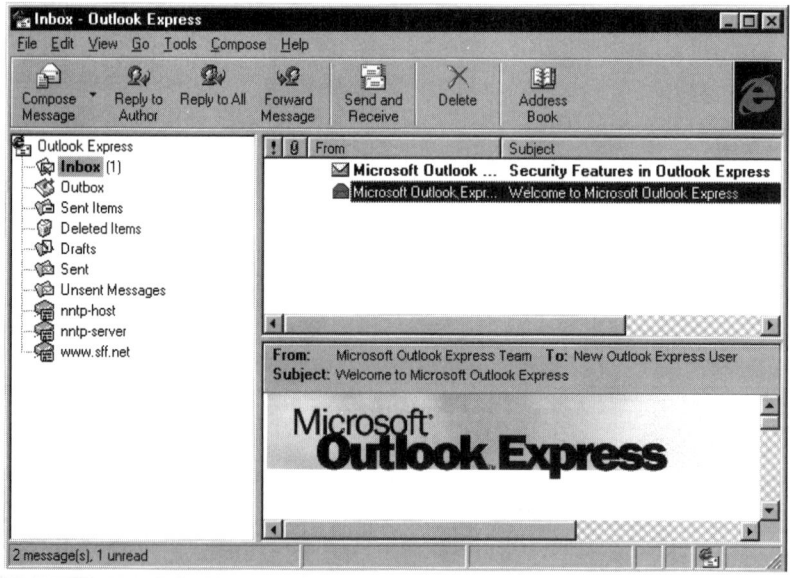

In Exercise 1.3 you will send an e-mail message over the Internet using Microsoft's Desktop e-mail software in Windows 95 or Windows NT.

EXERCISE 1.3

Sending an Internet E-Mail Message Using Microsoft Exchange

1. Launch Outlook Express (Double-click the Inbox or Outlook Express icon on the desktop).

If the e-mail package is not configured, you may have to configure it. The Installation Wizard will guide you through the process. If you have difficulty installing the software, consult the documentation that came with the software.

2. Select New Message from the Compose menu.

3. Type **mcseieaksg@aol.com** in the To box.

4. Type **Exercise 1.3** in the Subject box.

5. Type the following sentence in the text area of the window: **Exercise 1.2 completed. I will be a Microsoft Certified Systems Engineer soon.**

6. Select File ➤ Send.

7. *If you are working offline* (check your configuration and refer to step 1): Select Tools ➤ Deliver Now Using ➤ Internet Mail option in the Inbox of the Microsoft Exchange window.

8. Select File ➤ Exit.

FTP

File Transfer Protocol (FTP) is a protocol for transferring files over the Internet. Many FTP utilities are available for Windows NT and Windows 95. Microsoft ships an FTP utility with the Windows NT and Windows 95 operating systems; it is installed when you install the operating system.

The FTP utility is a *command-line utility*; that is, you type commands from within the utility to perform the file transfer operations. You can set up an icon that will start the FTP utility or you can invoke it from the command line.

Many graphical FTP utilities are available. Several are free to download from the Internet. These utilities provide a graphical interface and translate the actions you perform on graphical objects (such as selecting a file from a file list on a remote computer and then clicking Get) into the textual commands that the FTP protocol expects (e.g., get filename). See Figure 1.5 for an example of Microsoft's client FTP software being used.

You can use modern Web browsers as download-only FTP clients. If you want to upload a file, you'll have to use an FTP utility.

FIGURE 1.5

Microsoft's FTP command-line utility retrieves files over the Internet.

```
Command Prompt - ftp ftp.cdrom.com                              _ □ ✕
Microsoft(R) Windows NT(TM)
(C) Copyright 1985-1996 Microsoft Corp.

D:\>ftp ftp.cdrom.com
Connected to wcarchive.cdrom.com.
220 wcarchive.cdrom.com FTP server (Version wu-2.4(17) Sat Jun 22 21:37:48 PDT 1
996) ready.
User (wcarchive.cdrom.com:(none)): anonymous
331 Guest login ok, send your complete e-mail address as password.
Password:
230 Guest login ok, access restrictions apply.
ftp> bin
200 Type set to I.
ftp> hash
Hash mark printing On (2048 bytes/hash mark).
ftp> get index.txt_
```

Telnet

Telnet is a utility that gives you a text terminal interface to another computer over a TCP/IP network. Telnet is usually used to connect to a remote Unix computer.

If your Internet service provider provides you with a Unix shell account, Telnet is most likely how you will access that shell account. If you have a dial-up connection, your mail will probably be delivered to this account. Although accessing this e-mail account is easier if you use a TCP/IP e-mail package as described above, you can use Telnet and the Unix shell account command-line programs to send and receive e-mail. You may also have to use the Unix command line in order to manage World Wide Web files in this Unix account if you are using an Internet service provider to publish your Web pages to the Internet.

Windows NT and Windows 95 come with a Telnet utility that is installed when you install the operating system and the TCP/IP protocol. See Figure 1.6 for an example of Telnet being used.

FIGURE 1.6

Telnet enables you to access command-line accounts on other computers.

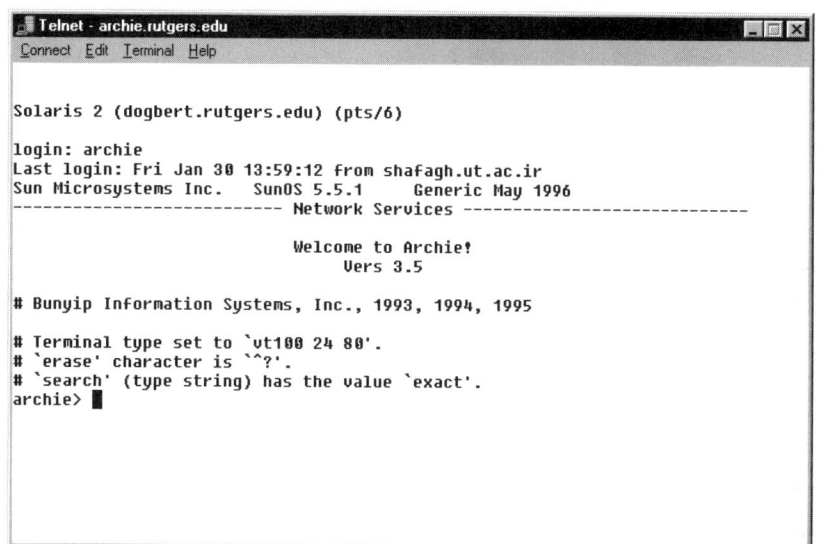

```
Telnet - archie.rutgers.edu                                    _ □ X
Connect  Edit  Terminal  Help

Solaris 2 (dogbert.rutgers.edu) (pts/6)

login: archie
Last login: Fri Jan 30 13:59:12 from shafagh.ut.ac.ir
Sun Microsystems Inc.   SunOS 5.5.1    Generic May 1996
------------------------- Network Services -------------------------

                        Welcome to Archie!
                           Vers 3.5

# Bunyip Information Systems, Inc., 1993, 1994, 1995

# Terminal type set to `vt100 24 80'.
# `erase' character is `^?'.
# `search' (type string) has the value `exact'.
archie> █
```

Internet News

Internet news is a worldwide replicated bulletin board network with tens of thousands of topics that individuals around the world discuss constantly. You will find that it is an unparalleled resource for solving technical problems, especially computer and computer networking problems. For any problem you face, you can be assured that someone has probably already faced that problem and found a solution. Many progressive companies use newsgroups to provide technical support.

Internet newsgroups are not limited to technical subjects. You will find newsgroups on topics ranging from boat building to politics. The subjects of newsgroups are only as limited as the interests and imaginations of the individuals on the Internet.

In order to access Internet news, you will need to install a newsreader program and have access to a Internet news server supplied on your network or by your Internet service provider (most Internet news servers are limited to subscriber access). Many newsreaders are available for most operating systems, and you may find other Internet tools that include a newsreader. Both Internet Explorer and Netscape contain a newsreader in addition to the Internet e-mail package. See Figure 1.7 for an example of Internet news being used.

FIGURE 1.7

With Outlook Express you can keep up with your current newsgroup as well as send and receive mail.

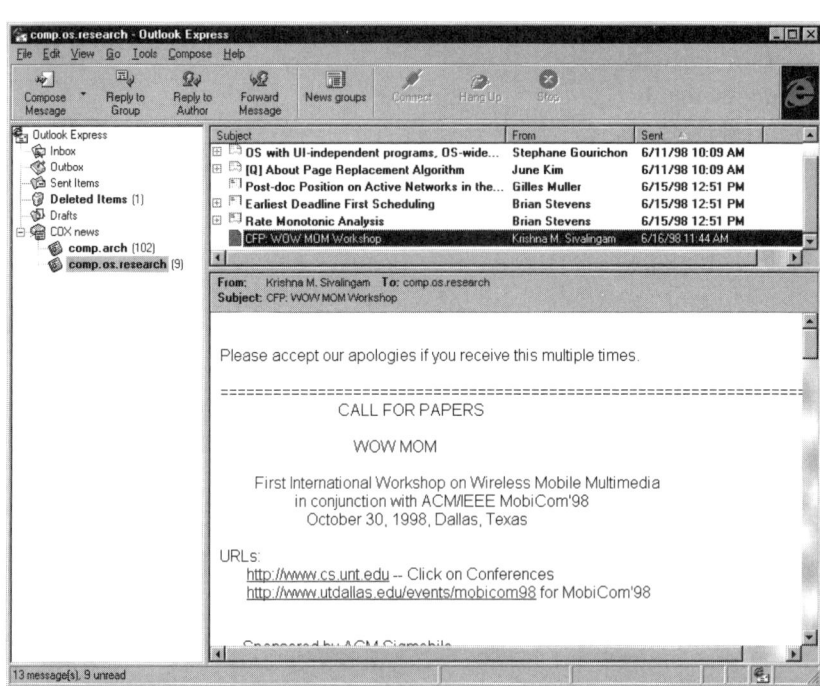

Internet Explorer and Friends

Now that you have a good understanding of what the Internet and the World Wide Web are about, you should take a look at exactly what comes with Internet Explorer 4. First, look at Internet Explorer itself, then check out the optional components that come with the full installation of IE 4 or can be downloaded from Microsoft, as follows:

- Internet Explorer 4
- Microsoft Chat
- Microsoft FrontPage Express
- Microsoft Web Publishing Wizard
- Microsoft NetShow Player
- Microsoft Wallet
- Microsoft Outlook Express
- Microsoft NetMeeting
- Microsoft Interactive Music Control (+With Synthesizer)
- Microsoft VRML 2 Viewer
- Microsoft Agent
- Macromedia Shockwave Director
- Macromedia Shockwave Flash
- Microsoft Script Debugger

Internet Explorer 4

Internet Explorer 4 provides the traditional features of an Internet Web browser and more. Much more. So much more, in fact, that many companies have accused Microsoft of trying to take over the World Wide Web entirely. You will explore the features of IE 4 in greater detail in Chapter 3, but a summary is appropriate here.

Supported Platforms

It is in Microsoft's best interest to see that Internet Explorer is used as widely as possible, so they have ported IE to many different platforms, including:

- Windows 95
- Windows NT

- Windows 3.*x*
- Various flavors of Unix (currently only the Solaris version is available)
- MacOS

New Features in IE 4

Internet Explorer 4 provides a number of features that are an improvement on Internet Explorer 3. They include (but are definitely not limited to) the following:

Accessibility Features   This set of features includes settings for blind and low-vision users, for hard of hearing individuals, for people with physical impairments, and for people with seizure disorders. Settings include font and image options, color restrictions, captioned system sounds, keyboard navigation and focus/selection changes, as well as suppressing video, animation (including blinking), and sounds.

Active Setup   IE 4 makes it easy to customize your Web browser by downloading the exact Web browser components you want from the Internet.

Automatic Configuration   You can get all the settings for your Web browser from a centrally managed location, rather than configuring it yourself.

Collaborative Features   The NetMeeting and Chat helper applications make it easy to communicate with others over the Web in real time.

Security Features   Security zones, certificates, and secure electronic transactions features help protect your communications with commercial and private Web servers over the Internet.

Web and Desktop Integration   Your favorites show up in the Start menu, the Taskbar has new icons for channels and frequently accessed sites, and Web content can appear directly on your desktop and in your screensaver.

Webcasting   With IE 4 you can subscribe to Web pages and to active channels (which are specially formatted Web sites). Your computer will automatically scan for new information and (if you configure it to do so) download that information to your hard drive.

Features of IE 4

Internet Explorer 4 is a feature-rich program and the following list is by no means exhaustive. Review the following to get an idea of what IE 4 provides:

Navigation History   IE 4 keeps track of the Web sites you have accessed most recently and will present you with a list of them to revisit.

Autocomplete   When you type a portion of an address you have already visited (and is still in the history bar), IE 4 will type out the rest of the address for you.

Explorer Bars   IE 4 allows you to configure sidebars with links to other Web-located information, making it easy to get to frequently accessed sites. IE 4 comes with four Explorer bars already configured for you—Search, Favorites, History, and Channels.

Caching and Offline Browsing   Every object IE 4 retrieves from the Internet is stored in a temporary Internet files folder. Whenever an HTML file refers to a Web resource, IE 4 checks to see if it is already in the temporary folder (the cache), and if it is (and the file has not expired) IE 4 displays that file instead of retrieving it from the Internet. This considerably speeds up frequently accessed Web sites. A side effect of this, which IE 4 capitalizes on, is that you can access Web sites you've already visited when not connected to the Internet by retrieving the Web pages from the cache.

Frames   This feature organizes data on Web pages in rectangular areas and allows Web pages to include other Web pages in a nested manner.

Style Sheets   Web page designers can encode the appearance of their Web pages (colors, fonts, etc.) in style sheets, and IE 4 will use those style sheets as well as allow you to specify your own or override specific settings of Web page–specified style sheets.

Tables   IE 4 can present information in tabular form.

Client-Side Image Maps   IE 4 can reduce the processor load on Web servers by selecting hypertext links within images itself rather than requiring the Web server to determine which part of the image the user clicked in.

Animated Images   IE 4 supports the animated GIF standard.

DirectX Multimedia Technologies   IE 4 can write directly to video memory, accelerating Web-based video.

Java Applets and Scripting   Web pages viewed with IE 4 can include Java programs.

ActiveX Controls and Visual Basic Scripting   Web pages viewed with IE 4 can include ActiveX controls and VBScript programs.

Start Menu and Taskbar Integration   You can place Web pages in the Start menu and Taskbar. The Taskbar includes new quick-access icons, and the Favorites menu shows up in the Start menu.

Desktop Explorer Integration   You can view folders on your hard drives as Web pages and customize how you view them by editing HTML template files.

Active Desktop Integration   You can place Web content, including automatically updated text and graphics, on the Windows Desktop background and in a Windows screensaver.

Active Channel and Web Page Subscription (Webcasting)   You can have IE 4 automatically check Web sites for updated Web pages. You can also subscribe to specially formatted Web pages with organized content called channels.

Accessibility Options   You can configure IE 4 to make Web browsing easier for the impaired by custom configuring fonts, colors, pointers, and sounds.

Internet Explorer 4 also includes some advanced security measures to help usher in that much-touted era in which we purchase everything, and run our entire lives, from the comfort of home. Other security features are designed to restrict access to certain Web sites. Among the security features are:

- A "Content Advisor"
- A "Profile Assistant"
- Encryption capabilities
- Microsoft Wallet
- Security Certificates
- Security Levels
- Security Zones

Chapter 8 of this book will focus heavily upon Internet Explorer 4 security.

Additional IE Components Distributed with IE 4

Internet Explorer 4 doesn't do everything (although it tries to). To provide a complete suite of Internet tools Microsoft has included a suite of Internet tools with the IE 4 package. You will learn how to configure these tools in Chapter 4. A full installation of IE 4 includes the following:

Microsoft Chat   This tool lets you interact with other Internet users in real time, providing virtual spaces, or "rooms," in which people can meet and converse. Microsoft chat supports the exchange of typed text as well as a cartoon-based visual interaction environment.

Microsoft FrontPage Express   Microsoft makes creating Web pages easier by bundling FrontPage Express with IE 4. This package automates Web page editing and management and assists transferring Web pages from a workstation, where they are being developed, to a Web server where they may be accessed. FrontPage Express lets you graphically manipulate Web pages and makes linking Web pages together easy.

Microsoft Web Publishing Wizard   The Web Publishing Wizard automates the process of connecting to an Internet service provider (or other Web server) and transferring Web site data to that server.

Microsoft NetShow Player   NetShow accepts and plays continuous streams of video and audio broadcast over the Internet.

Microsoft Wallet   Microsoft Wallet is a repository for Web payment information including contact information and credit card numbers. It stores the information in encrypted form and supports Internet commerce standards such as Secure Electronic Transactions and Secure Socket Layer communications.

Microsoft Outlook Express   Outlook Express is your Internet mail box. You can send and receive mail from Internet SMTP and POP mail servers as well as IMAP servers such as Microsoft Exchange. You can attach files to your mail, encrypt and decrypt information, send visually appealing mail using HTML tags, and set filters and rules for handling incoming messages.

Microsoft NetMeeting   With NetMeeting you can collaborate over the Internet in real time. NetMeeting supports the Internet and telecommunications videoconferencing standards, allowing you to set up video and audio links over Internet protocols. NetMeeting also supports whiteboard collaboration, text-based chat, file sharing, and application sharing.

Microsoft Interactive Music Control (also with Synthesizer)   An ActiveX control for interactive "music" creation and composition corresponding to user actions. The control with synthesizer supports the use of dedicated music hardware.

Microsoft Script Debugger   This tool helps you find problems with misbehaving VBScript and JScript programs.

Additional IE 4 Components Available for Download

There are some components extending IE 4 functionality that are not distributed with the Web browser but that you can download if you need them. Chapter 3 will show you how to connect to the Microsoft Web site and download these additional components for your Web browser. Some downloadable components are:

Microsoft VRML 2 Viewer   The VRML 2 Viewer displays to the user 3-dimensional objects in the Web browser, allowing the user to "walk through" the scene and view the VRML objects from many angles.

Microsoft Agent   This package makes it easy for Internet software to engage you in a help dialog, similar to the "paperclip" entity in Microsoft Office applications. With any luck it will never be used.

Macromedia Shockwave Director   With Shockwave Director you can create multimedia presentations for delivery over the Internet. The presentations can include text, animations, buttons, banners, maps, and logos.

Macromedia Shockwave Flash   The Shockwave Flash component decodes and displays Shockwave presentations created with Shockwave Director.

Supplemental Web Fonts   This package includes the following fonts for use with IE: Arial, Comic, Courier, Impact, and Times Roman.

Internet Explorer Sound Pack   This component provides auditory cues for when pages open or finish loading, sites are found, and so on.

Task Scheduler   This component gives you a graphical interface that you can use to configure your computer to perform scheduled Internet tasks.

Multi-Language Support   This component extends the Web browser to browse Web pages displaying text written in languages other than English.

Summary

Internet Explorer 4 is the tool Microsoft gives you to access the Internet. Since Microsoft wants you to use IE 4 on Microsoft operating systems, IE 4 contains almost any conceivable feature that makes the Web easier to use, and it integrates nicely with Windows 95 and Windows NT. IE 4 comes with Web browser extensions in order to display information other than HTML data. When you install a full version of IE 4 you get applications that let you use other Internet services such as e-mail, Web video broadcasting, Internet videoconferencing, and Internet chat rooms.

This chapter introduced you to the Internet and the World Wide Web, and showed you the software Microsoft would like you to use to access these new information services. A sophisticated user of Web browsers and other Internet tools will find the features of IE 4 powerful and friendly, but the very flexibility of IE 4 introduces a new problem—a network administrator or Internet service provider must be able to configure each IE 4 feature to work properly in newly installed and continuously maintained computers, especially when the computer users may not be very knowledgeable about computers. The next chapter introduces you to the Internet Explorer Administrator's Kit, which makes IE 4 and add-on tools much easier to deploy in a network or ISP environment.

Review Questions

1. You want to enable Internet traffic on your LAN. What protocol must the router that links your LAN to the Internet support?

   A. NetBEUI

   B. TCP/IP

   C. Ethernet

   D. IPX/SPX

2. What protocol does the Web browser and Web server use to exchange hypertext files?

   A. IPX/SPX

   B. HTML

   C. HTTP

   D. Java

3. You have performed a full installation of Internet Explorer 4, and you want to chat with other users on the Internet. What else do you need to add to your Windows 95 computer in order to use Microsoft Chat?

   A. The Microsoft Chat package from the Add/Remove Components section of Active Setup

   B. Windows 95 OSR2

   C. The Windows NT Option Pack

   D. Nothing, Microsoft Chat is included with a full install of IE 4

4. You want to use an electronic whiteboard to collaborate with coworkers over the Internet. What package should you use?

   A. Microsoft Chat

   B. Microsoft NetShow

   C. Microsoft NetMeeting

   D. Microsoft Outlook Express

5. Which of the following platforms does Internet Explorer not run on?

   A. Windows 95

   B. Windows 3.11

   C. MacOS

   D. OS/2

6. Which Web technology does not work in non-Microsoft Web browsers?

   A. JavaScript

   B. HTML

   C. Java

   D. ActiveX

7. Which of the following is a complete and correctly formed URL?

   A. `www.microsoft.com`

   B. `\\www.memetech.com\default.htm`

   C. `ftp://www.starlingtech.com/pub/archive.z`

   D. `http/www.niftyvideo.com/products.asp`

8. You have performed a full installation of Internet Explorer 4. You want to view and manipulate three-dimensional figures in your IE 4 Web browser. What else do you need to add to your Windows 95 computer in order to add this capability to IE 4?

   A. The VRML 2 Viewer package from the Add/Remove Components section of Active Setup

   B. Windows 95 OSR2

   C. The Windows NT Option Pack

   D. Nothing, the VRML 2 Viewer is installed with a full install of IE 4

9. You want to send and receive encrypted e-mail over the Internet. Which tool should you launch?

   A. Outlook Express

   B. NetMeeting

   C. Chat

   D. Macromedia Shockwave Flash

10. You want to run a Web server on your Windows 95 computer. What Microsoft Web server provides this capability?

   A. Peer Web Services

   B. Internet Information Server

   C. Personal Web Server

   D. Windows Web Server

11. You use a Windows NT Workstation computer with a standard installation of IE 4 to browse a Web page that has a JScript program embedded in it. The JScript program has an error but you are not given the option of running the Microsoft Script Debugger to determine what the problem is. Why is this?

   A. The Microsoft Script Debugger only runs under Windows 95, not Windows NT.

   B. The Full installation of IE 4 does not include the Microsoft Script Debugger.

   C. You must enable debugging in the User Manager or User Manager for Domains program.

   D. You must install the Microsoft J++ software development environment to debug JScript programs.

12. Which two browser extension technologies are only supported by Internet Explorer?

   A. JavaScript

   B. VBScript

   C. ActiveX

   D. Java

13. Which of the following tools are not distributed with IE 4?

   A. NetMeeting

   B. Outlook Express

   C. J++

   D. NetShow Live

14. You want to write a simple program that will run on the majority of Web browsers, including non-Microsoft Web browsers. Which technology should you choose?

   A. ActiveX

   B. JavaScript

   C. VBScript

   D. C++

15. Who controls the Internet?

   A. The International Standards Organization

   B. The National Security Agency

   C. The Department of Defense

   D. No single person or group

16. You want to reduce the Internet support burden for your network by standardizing on one suite of Internet tools.

Required Result: Provide basic Web browsing and e-mail functionality.

Optional Result 1: Allow users to participate in newsgroups and Internet chat forums.

Optional Result 2: Allow users to host their own Web pages on their Windows 95 computers.

Suggested Solution: Distribute IE 4 and associated components to the computers on your network.

Which of the following is correct?

A. The suggested solution accomplishes the required result and both optional results.

B. The suggested solution accomplishes the required result and just one optional result.

C. The suggested solution accomplishes the required result only.

D. The suggested solution does not accomplish the required result.

17. You manage a heterogeneous network containing Windows 95, Windows NT, MacOS, and Linux computers. You want to use the same Web browser on all the computers in your network. You would also like to use the same software on all of the computers for e-mail, videoconferencing, and newsgroup reading.

Required Result: Select a Web browser that will work on all computers in your network.

Optional Result 1: Select software packages for e-mail and news reading that will work on all the computers in your network.

Optional Result 2: Select software packages for videoconferencing that will work on all the computers in your network.

Suggested Solution: Choose Internet Explorer 4, Outlook Express, and Microsoft NetMeeting.

Which of the following is correct?

A. The suggested solution accomplishes the required result and both optional results.

B. The suggested solution accomplishes the required result and just one optional result.

C. The suggested solution accomplishes the required result only.

D. The suggested solution does not accomplish the required result.

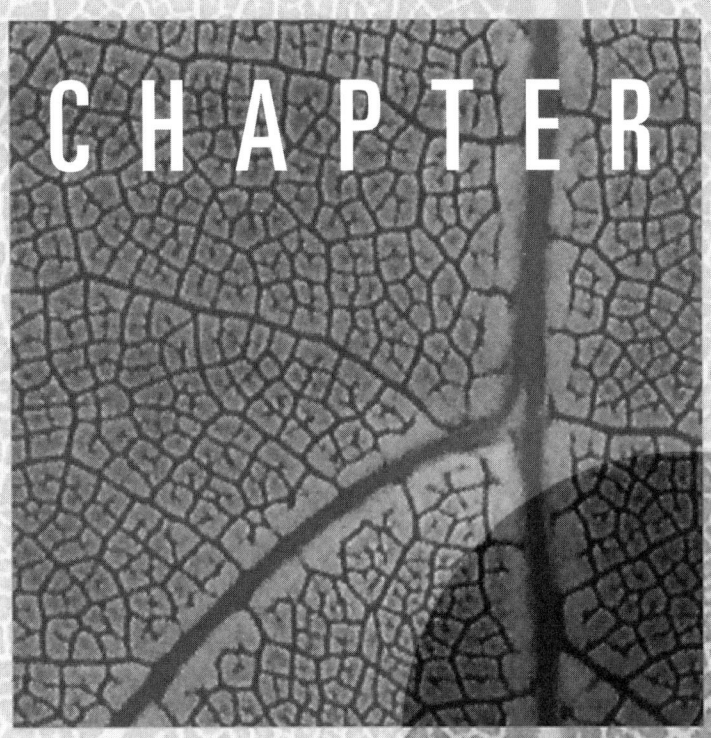

CHAPTER

2

Examining the Internet Explorer
Administration Kit

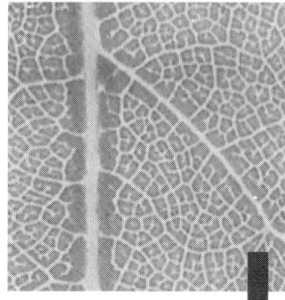

I t is a network administrator's job to keep the network running smoothly and to provide a consistent, useful view of the network for users. As time goes on, more of the user's network experience is through the Internet—using search engines to find facts, getting news updates from Web sites, exchanging data by e-mail, reading Internet news, and maintaining organizational information using Intranet applications that interface with Web-based databases. Keeping all of it working and consistent can be difficult.

In addition, Internet Explorer 4 shows Microsoft's intent to merge Microsoft Windows and the Internet. With Active Desktop Update, the users can have HTML on their desktop background in place of the background pattern or image, and hard drive folders that act like Web pages. Favorite URLs show up in the Start menu, and channels show up in the Taskbar. Users now expect these customizing features, but they also need a consistent view of resources. Inconsistent client configuration settings make it difficult for network administrators to help users. Network administrators' traditional management of the user's desktop must now include managing Internet tools, especially the browser.

Microsoft has provided a tool to help network administrators manage their local portion of the chaos that is the Internet. That tool is the Internet Explorer Administration Kit (IEAK). With the IEAK, administrators can create custom distributions of IE 4 and Windows Desktop Updates that are already configured to connect to local network services and that can be centrally managed more easily than a default or separate configuration of IE 4. The administrator can also configure all of the Web browsers and helper applications at once instead of configuring each separately when they are installed on the client computers.

Getting the IEAK

Microsoft distributes Internet Explorer at no charge. However, you are not free to do whatever you want with IE 4. Microsoft is very particular about people distributing it, and they are especially particular about people distributing a modified copy. The software is still proprietary to Microsoft; you just don't have to give them money to use it.

The process for getting and using the IEAK reflects Microsoft's desire to retain control of Internet Explorer 4. You can get the software a number of ways (including by downloading it from the Internet or by purchasing it on CD-ROM from Microsoft). However you get it, you will have to get (but not necessarily pay for) a license for the IEAK from Microsoft in order to use it.

Before you install the IEAK, however, you should make sure that the computer has sufficient memory, processing power, and hard disk space to run it.

IEAK Requirements

Since the IEAK customizes Internet Explorer 4, the IEAK needs some space for IE 4 files and more for IEAK specific files. The IEAK is not terribly processor intensive, nor does it require a great deal of RAM. The IEAK does require Internet Explorer 4 and either Windows 95 or Windows NT. Microsoft's requirements for IEAK are summarized in Table 2.1.

T A B L E 2.1 IEAK Requirements	**Component**	**Requirement**
	Processor	486/66
	Operating System	Windows 95 or Windows NT 4
	RAM	8MB Windows 95/16MB Windows NT
	Hard Drive Space	40 to 60 MB to install
	Hard Drive Space	40 to 100 MB per custom package

The space required for IEAK depends primarily on the kind of Internet Explorer 4 package you will be putting together. If you only need the files to put together a standard installation of IE 4, then you need about 43MB of free hard drive space to hold the files. For an enhanced installation, the files use approximately 50MB. A full installation uses approximately 59MB. This space is required to be located on the hard drive containing your `Program Files` directory (usually the C drive).

Note that you still need space for the custom package you will put together, and that can be up to twice as much as the space required for a general Internet Explorer 4 installation. This can be on a different drive than the `Program Files` directory, even on a network share. Table 2.2 shows you the space and component requirements of each type of distribution.

T A B L E 2.2 Required Space and Components for Standard, Enhanced, and Full Distributions	Type	Components	Space Required
	Standard	IE 4, Outlook Express, ActiveMovie	43MB
	Enhanced	IE 4, Outlook Express, ActiveMovie, FrontPad	50MB
	Full	IE 4, Outlook Express, NetMeeting, FrontPage Express, Microsoft Wallet, NetShow, ActiveMovie	59MB

Downloading from the Web

Getting the IEAK from the Internet is a little bit more complicated than downloading Internet Explorer 4. Microsoft wants to be sure you've seen and agreed to the license agreement before you use the IEAK. You have to go through a registration process and receive (through e-mail) a logon password for the secure site. Then you will receive an ID number that will allow you to use the IEAK once it has been downloaded. The IEAK will be downloaded and installed to your Program Files folder. Exercise 2.1 shows you how it's done.

Downloading and installing IEAK requires Internet Explorer 4.

EXERCISE 2.1

Downloading the IEAK from Microsoft's Web Site

1. Launch Internet Explorer 4.

2. In the Address field, enter **http://ieak.microsoft.com/gettheieak.asp**, and click OK.

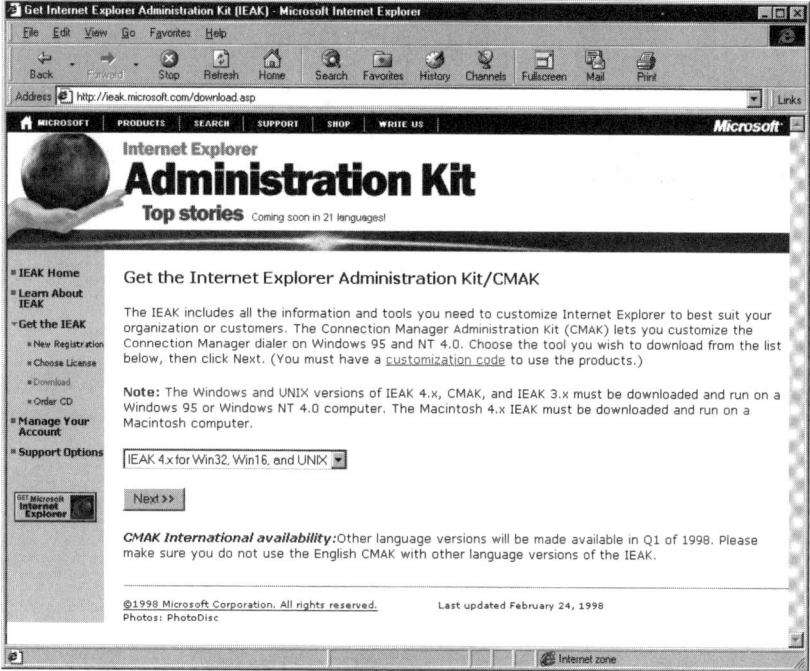

3. Click New Registration in the left column.

4. Enter your e-mail address, name, and company. Click Enter.

EXERCISE 2.1 (CONTINUED)

5. Go to your e-mail program and get the password from the e-mail message from Microsoft.

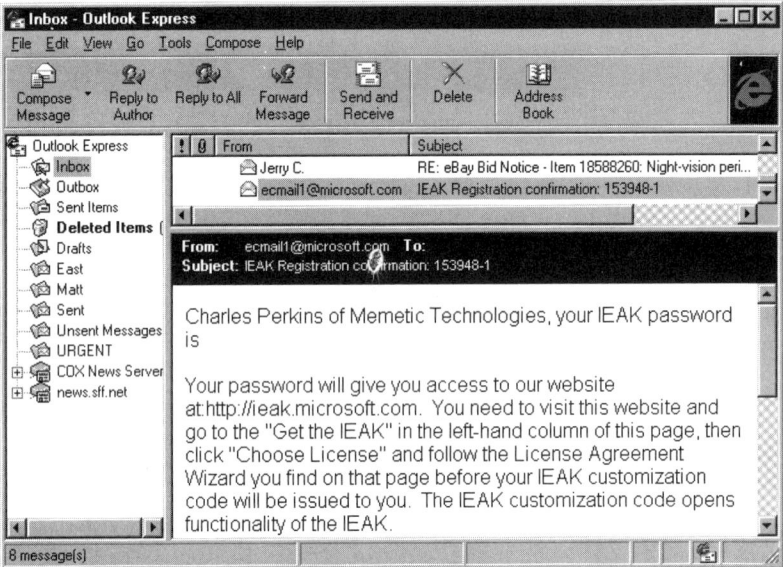

6. Go to Internet Explorer and click the login link at the bottom of the page.

7. Enter your password in the Password field, and then click OK.

8. Enter your job title, address, telephone and fax numbers, and corporate URL. Click Next.

9. Select Both ≻ 1-100 for IE, NetMeeting, and Outlook Express, and click Next.

10. Select Other, click Next, click Proceed, and then click the License Agreement Wizard link at the bottom of the page.

11. Select To Companies Within Your Organization, and click Next.

12. Select Yes. Click Next.

13. Read the license agreement, then click I Accept.

14. Click Get Internet Explorer Administration Kit.

15. Select Download the IEAK 4 link.

16. Select a site near you, and click Next.

17. Click Install Now, click OK, and then click Review Your Licenses.

18. Note the customization code for IEAK 4.

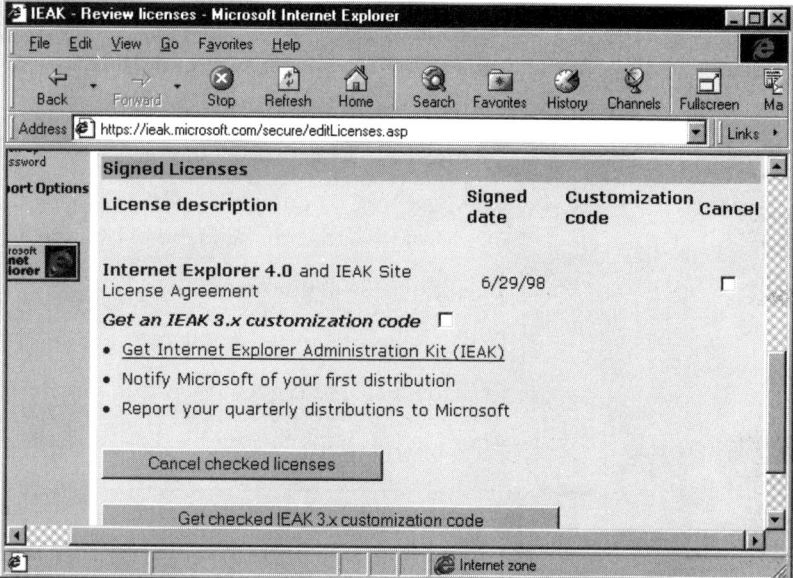

After you've downloaded the IEAK, it is installed in the IEAK folder of your `Program Files` directory. Three new items will show up in the Start menu, all under Microsoft IEAK:

- IEAK Help

- IEAK Profile Manager

- IEAK Wizard

Loading from CD-ROM

Loading the IEAK from CD-ROM is much quicker than downloading it from the Internet. You can get the CD-ROM a number of ways—one of which is to order it from Microsoft's Web site (http://ieak.microsoft.com/). You can also get the CD-ROM as a part of the *Microsoft Internet Explorer Resource Kit*, which is available at many bookstores that carry computer books, including online bookstores (such as http://www.amazon.com/). Exercise 2.2 guides you through installing the IEAK from CD-ROM.

EXERCISE 2.2

Installing the IEAK from CD-ROM

1. Insert the IEAK CD-ROM in the CD-ROM Drive.

2. Open the My Computer icon, and then open the icon representing the CD-ROM drive that contains the IEAK CD-ROM.

3. Open the i386 subdirectory.

4. Double-click the Setup.exe icon.

5. Click the Install Internet Explorer Administration Kit option.

6. After the files copy to your hard drive, click OK.

Installing from CD-ROM places the files in the IEAK folder of your Program Files directory. IEAK Help, IEAK Profile Manager, and IEAK Wizard appear in the Start menu.

IEAK Features

Now that you have the IEAK, what can you actually do with this mystical tool of Internet Explorer management? This section will explore the IEAK. An overview of what comprises the IEAK and how the IEAK can help Internet content providers, Internet service providers, and corporate network administrators.

IEAK Components

When you install the IEAK, a set of files and folders are created in the IEAK folder of the `Program Files` directory. Links in the Start menu are made to the IEAK Wizard, the Profile Manager, and the HTML Help files. The IEAK folder contains the following two executable programs, which comprise the main functionality of the IEAK:

Ieakwiz.exe   This is the IEAK Wizard, which guides you through the process of customizing Internet Explorer 4.

Profmgr.exe   This is the program that you use to create autoconfiguration files for Internet Explorer 4 and associated programs.

The following are folders in the IEAK folder:

Iebin   This folder will contain the files used to build the Internet Explorer 4 custom package. It is empty until you run the IEAK for the first time. The files will be retrieved from the Internet.

Help   The IEAK Help pages are stored in this folder.

Reskit   This folder contains useful tools, programs, and sample files for customizing Internet Explorer 4 components that will be collected into a custom software package using the IEAK.

Tools   This folder contains utility programs used by the IEAK to create custom distributions.

The following folders will be created the first time you run the IEAK:

Download   This folder stores the Internet Explorer CAB files used to create the Internet Explorer 4 distributions.

Policies   This folder stores the autoconfiguration files that can be used to configure installed versions of Internet Explorer 4.

The `Reskit` folder itself contains several folders, including:

Addons   This contains add-on components for Internet Explorer 4 and code signing tools for signing your custom components.

Corp   This folder contains files that help manage Internet Explorer 4 on a LAN.

Graphics Here you will find sample graphics and graphics manipulation programs.

ISP This folder contains tools that help users connect to your ISP site and tools that help manage an ISP service.

Functions of the IEAK

Now you have the IEAK, you see what has been installed, and you agree that centralized management can be a good thing. But what can you actually do with the IEAK?

The IEAK was designed to allow you to put together a version of Internet Explorer 4 that fits your organization's needs. The specific options you have in putting together your own distribution of IE 4 depends on how you will distribute the resulting package. You have different options if you are an Internet content provider, Internet service provider, or corporate administrator. The common and specific features of each option are described in this section.

New Features

The IEAK 4 Wizard has new features that will be appreciated by users of previous versions of the IEAK. The *INS Editor* (which is used to edit files with the INS extension) has been extended and renamed to be the IEAK Profile Manager. The IEAK 4 has added the following features since IEAK 3.02:

- You can customize the Active Setup Wizard bitmap and title bar.

- You can have up to 10 custom components that will be installed along with Internet Explorer 4.

- You can have up to 10 installation options (including Standard, Full, and Custom) which users of your custom version of Internet Explorer 4 can choose from.

- You can preconfigure Internet Explorer 4 with up to 10 download site options for the users to retrieve the CAB files for your custom version of IE 4.

- You can specify a custom browser welcome message.

- You can specify Active Desktop components that will be installed with Internet Explorer 4.

- You can append a custom User Agent string.

If you are an Internet service provider and you want to make a previously configured Internet Explorer 4 available to your users, you have the following new options available:

- You can include the Internet Connection Manager in the custom version of Internet Explorer 4.

- You can add a channel and/or delete channels that directly compete with your service.

- You can create a single-floppy distribution of Internet Explorer 4 (in other words, an IE 4 `Setup.exe` program that fits on a floppy disk and downloads the files it needs from your Web site).

- You can establish proxy settings for Internet Explorer 4 and add-on components.

If you are using the IEAK in corporate mode, you have the following new options available to you:

- You can specify the inclusion and customization of Active Desktop.

- You can completely customize the Channel bar.

- You can specify a *silent installation* (an installation that does not give feedback to the user while being installed).

- You can set the browser to autoconfigure at set times and on a regular basis.

- You can create system policies and restrictions.

- You can establish security zones.

- You can configure Authenticode settings.

- You can establish site certificates.

- You can configure how the My Computer and Control Panel folders appear in Web view.

IEAK Roles

With version 4 of the IEAK, there are three licensing roles, each with its own set of options and features for the IEAK. These roles reflect Microsoft's three target audiences: Internet content providers, Internet service providers, and corporate administrators. The license for IEAK that you receive from Microsoft will reflect which one of those three roles you chose on the Microsoft Web site. If you want to use the IEAK in multiple roles, you will need to get multiple licenses and report the number of Internet Explorer 4 packages you distribute under each license.

Internet Content provider   Many developers of Internet software distribute a Web browser with their software, and information services distribute Web browsers to provide access to their services. Organizations that make Internet software or provide information services over the Internet are called an Internet content provider (ICP). One of the three modes of the IEAK is specifically tailored to meet the needs of an ICP that wants to distribute a custom version of Internet Explorer 4 with their products.

Internet content provider users of the IEAK can use the Wizard to do the following:

- Modify how the setup program starts and appears (such as changing logos and title bars, as well as setting installation options)

- Provide Internet Explorer and add-on components as a complete package for download or on distribution media

- Specify a location for updated or additional add-on components other than the default Microsoft location

- Specify language versions for the Internet Explorer 4 custom build

- Configure automatic Internet software distribution

- Configure the default locations of the Start, Search, and Support HTML pages

- Pre-load the Favorites list

- Add a channel and/or delete competitor channels in the Channel bar

- Configure the custom distribution to use the referral server to establish an Internet service account for the user

When you distribute IE 4 with your software, you are required by the license agreement for the IEAK to display the Microsoft logo on your software packaging and promotional material, including your Web site. You can find various formats of the logo at `Reskit\Graphics\Samples\Cpyr_art`.

Internet Service Provider   If you provide Internet connections to your customers (over dial-up lines, cable modems, leased phone lines, or even radio), your customers may not have a Web browser yet. Microsoft makes it easy for you to provide your customers with a preconfigured version of Internet Explorer that will automatically go to your Web page first, and will correctly handle proxy and other settings. The ISP license mode of the IEAK is specifically designed for Internet service providers.

The following IEAK features are available to you in Internet service provider mode:

- Modify how the setup program starts and appears (such as changing logos and title bars, as well as setting installation options)

- Provide Internet Explorer and add-on components as a complete package for download or on distribution media

- Specify a location for updated or additional add-on components other than the default Microsoft location

- Specify language versions for the Internet Explorer 4 custom build

- Configure the default locations of the Start, Search, and Support HTML pages

- Pre-load the Favorites list

- Add a channel and/or delete competitor channels in the Channel bar

- Integrate service sign-up over the Web with an Internet Explorer 4 custom package and a Web-based sign-up server

As with an ICP, an ISP that provides Internet Explorer 4 for download or on distributed installation media (such as a CD-ROM) to customers is required by the license agreement for the IEAK to display the Microsoft logo in software packaging and promotional material, including Web sites. You can find various formats of the logo at Reskit\Graphics\Samples\Cpyr_art.

Corporate Administrator   The third target audience for the IEAK, corporate administrators, have a different set of available options, and the corporate administrator's options are greater than those of an ICP or ISP. The client computers on a company network are usually a more controlled environment than the home user's computer. The corporate administrator not only needs to distribute a standard set of features, but also needs to be able to change the settings remotely, without reinstalling the software.

The following IEAK features are available to corporate administrators:

- Modify how the setup program starts and appears (such as changing logos and title bars, as well as setting installation options)

- Provide Internet Explorer and add-on components as a complete package for download or on distribution media

- Specify a location for updated or additional add-on components other than the default Microsoft location

- Specify language versions for the Internet Explorer 4 custom build

- Configure the default locations of the Start, Search, and Support HTML pages

- Configure Windows Desktop Update, including Web view of window objects, Active Desktop items, and the Autoconfigure mechanism

- Configure software update channels

- Prevent users from changing desktop, browser, and add-on features (lock-down)

- Pre-load the Favorites list

- Add a channel and/or delete competitor channels in the Channel bar

- Pre-install certificates, and block users from downloading other certificates (see Chapter 7 for a discussion of certificates and other browser security issues)

- Pre-set ratings settings, which allow you to restrict the browser from viewing Web pages according to voluntary ratings of the page's violence, language, nudity, or sex

- Establish a corporate disclaimer for outgoing news postings and e-mail messages

- Configure security zones

- Specify proxy settings

- Manage Internet profiles

The IEAK and IE 4 Licenses

Microsoft allows you to use and distribute Internet Explorer 4 at no charge (in legal terms, royalty free), but that does not mean that you can, with no strings attached, modify it and give it out. Microsoft is very explicit about what you can and cannot do with IE 4 and the IEAK. The licenses you agree to, when you download the IEAK and when you install IE 4, spell out the terms of the agreements (see Figure 2.1 for a view of the license you agreed to in Exercise 2.1).

F I G U R E   2.1

The Microsoft IEAK license agreement limits what you can do with the IEAK.

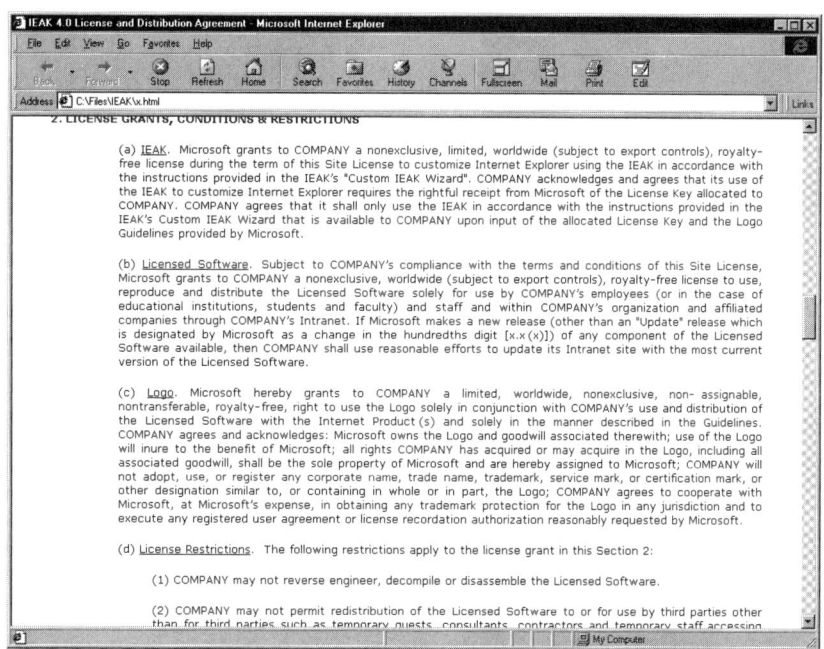

The big issues for most people who want to use the IEAK to customize Internet Explorer 4 are what modifications they can make to enhance their own company's image (branding), what they must do when Microsoft updates its software, and what distribution reports they must make to Microsoft.

Microsoft is sensitive about its logo. Don't mess with the gyrating "e", and make sure that your Web page and product packaging use the appropriate Microsoft artwork to reflect that Internet Explorer 4 is being distributed if that is what you are doing. You can, however, change the Active Setup bitmap, the Toolbar bitmap, the Autorun bitmap (if you are creating a CD-ROM distribution), the default Welcome page, and the Outlook Express Infopane.

If you are an Internet service provider or an Internet content provider, you may add a channel of your own and/or remove channels that compete with your service. You can't remove other channels, though, because Microsoft wants to maintain a consistent experience for users of its software. If you are preparing Internet Explorer 4 for a captive audience (such as the employees in your company), you can, as a corporate administrator, be more free with what you do with channels.

You can only include and distribute Internet Explorer 4 with 128-bit security if you reside in the United States or Canada. This is due to United States munitions-export regulations.

Microsoft periodically makes improvements to Internet Explorer 4 and add-on components. The IEAK license agreement states that if you want to distribute Microsoft software you must make an effort to stay current. When Microsoft makes an upgrade to software, other than an update release, you must make the upgraded software available. An update release can be identified by version number change in the hundredth digit (i.e. from 1.02 to 1.03); anything greater must be made available to your customers.

Microsoft requires that you report how many copies of Internet Explorer you distribute in your role as an ICP, ISP, or corporate administrator. You must immediately report the first distribution(s) you make. Thereafter, you must report additional distributions quarterly. If your organization distributes Internet Explorer 4 under more than one role (such as both a corporate administrator for your LAN and as an ICP for customers of the software you produce), you must separately report the number of copies distributed under each role.

Summary

The Internet Explorer Administration Kit helps you manage the distribution of Internet Explorer 4 by allowing you to pre-configure Internet Explorer 4 settings for your environment. The IEAK doesn't take up that much disk space (up to 60MB to download and up to an additional 100MB per distribution), and doesn't require much in the way of processing power (a 486/66 will do). The IEAK does require IE 4 for download and usage.

You can download the IEAK from Microsoft's Web site or you can purchase it on CD-ROM. You can order the CD-ROM from Microsoft's Web site, or you can get the IEAK along with other nifty tools by purchasing the *Microsoft Internet Explorer Resource Kit* at your local computer bookstore. No matter how you obtain the IEAK, you will still have to go to Microsoft's Web site and get an IEAK license number to actually use the software.

You have a choice of using the IEAK in one of three modes: ISP, ICP, and corporate administrator. An ISP and ICP are more limited in their options of modifying Internet Explorer 4 because Microsoft wants to maintain some consistency for users of their software. A corporate administrator has more freedom in making changes.

When you use the IEAK to customize software, you must abide by the IEAK license agreement which requires you to report back to Microsoft the number of copies of Internet Explorer 4 you distribute. You must report your first distribution immediately and update your distribution report each quarter thereafter.

In order to use the IEAK most effectively, you need to know what all the Internet Explorer 4 and add-on features are. The next chapter will guide you through the features and capabilities of IE 4 (including installing IE 4) so that you will know what you're modifying with the IEAK Wizard.

Review Questions

1. You want to change the versions of Internet Explorer 4 that you distribute with your Internet Stock Quote application so that they reflect your company's image. Which of the following items are you not allowed to change?

   A. The default Web page

   B. The Taskbar image

   C. The spinning "e"

   D. The Active Setup bitmap

2. You want to distribute Internet Explorer 4 on a CD-ROM with your Internet-based multiplayer video game. Which licensing role should you choose?

   A. Corporate administrator

   B. ISP

   C. ICP

   D. ICQ

3. You provide dial-up access to the Internet for people in your community. You want to make it easier for your customers, many of whom do not already have a Web browser, to get on the Web. You decide to include Internet Explorer 4 with your installation software. Which licensing role should you choose?

   A. Corporate administrator

   B. ISP

   C. ICP

   D. DNS

4. Your company network is comprised of four LANs with mixed Windows 95 and Windows NT Workstation computers. You have two RAS servers allowing remote connection to your network. You want to ease your Internet support burden by crafting a custom version of Internet Explorer 4 that is pre-configured for your network and that uses the Autoupdate feature of IE 4. Which licensing role should you choose?

A. Corporate administrator

B. ISP

C. ICP

D. DSP

5. You manage an ISP service, and you make a custom version of Internet Explorer 4 available for download on your Web site. You also distribute it on CD-ROM to new customers. How should you report to Microsoft your distributions?

A. Monthly, combined CD-ROM and downloaded totals

B. Yearly, CD-ROM and downloaded totals separately

C. Quarterly, combined CD-ROM and downloaded totals

D. Quarterly, CD-ROM and downloaded totals separately

6. You provide information to clients over the Internet. You have a free service and a for-fee service. You want to structure the services as channels. How many channels can you add to the Channel bar with your ICP license?

A. One

B. Two

C. Three

D. Zero

7. You chair the Committee for Moral Profundity. You provide information over the Internet on good sites for children to visit. You want to make a "safe" version of Internet Explorer available for download from your Web site, but you don't like some of the channels that Microsoft has established in the Channel bar. How many of these channels can you remove?

A. One

B. Two

C. Three

D. Zero

8. You want to include several custom components for encrypted financial data exchange over the Internet with your custom version of Internet Explorer 4. How many custom components can you include?

A. Zero

B. One

C. Three

D. 10

9. You want to make installing your version of Internet Explorer 4 as flexible as possible. How many installation options (standard, custom, full, and so on) can you configure in the IEAK?

A. Zero

B. Three

C. Five

D. 10

10. You want to build your own custom Internet Explorer 4 package containing all of the general IE 4 components. How much space do you need to download the components, run the IEAK, and contain the resulting custom IE 4 package?

A. 60MB

B. 80MB

C. 110MB

D. 160MB

11. What are your options for getting the IEAK? Choose all that apply.

A. Download it from Microsoft's Web site

B. Purchase it on CD-ROM from Microsoft's Web site

C. Purchase the Internet Explorer Resource Kit

D. Load it from the Windows 95 installation CD-ROM

12. You used the INS Editor with the previous version of the IEAK. You find that it is not included in the new IEAK. What has replaced it?

A. User Manager for Domains

B. System Profile Editor

C. Profile Editor

D. Syscon

13. You have included the Microsoft add-on package Fluff version 1.04 in your custom installation of Internet Explorer 4. Microsoft came out with Fluff version 1.05 a month later. What are your obligations according to the IEAK license?

A. You must make version 1.05 available to your customers.

B. You must upgrade all of your customers to version 1.05.

C. You don't have to do anything.

D. You must renew your IEAK license with Microsoft.

14. You have included the Microsoft add-on package Fluff version 1.04 in your custom installation of Internet Explorer 4. Microsoft came out with Fluff version 1.10 a month later. What are your obligations according to the IEAK license?

A. You must make version 1.10 available to your customers.

B. You must upgrade all of your customers to version 1.10.

C. You don't have to do anything.

D. You must renew your IEAK license with Microsoft.

15. You need to provide graphic images to the printing department for the promotional packaging of your product containing IE 4. Where can you get the images?

A. `http://www.microsoft.com/images/presskit`.

B. You must order the images from Microsoft; they will be delivered in 2-5 working days by Federal Express.

C. You can scan and use images from other Microsoft products such as Windows 95 or Windows NT.

D. Get them from `Reskit\Graphics\Samples\Cpyr_art` in the IEAK directory.

16. Your company provides for automatic futures trading over the Internet. Customers can trade using any Web browser, but you have developed a custom IE 4 ActiveX control that makes trading much more intuitive. The ActiveX control requires your Web site to be in the Trusted Sites zone of the IE 4 Web browser. You want to distribute a custom IE 4 package that increases your company's product visibility (through the branding options of the IEAK), and you want to precon-figure the security zones settings of IE 4, as well as comply with Microsoft's license restrictions.

Required Result: Comply with Microsoft's license restrictions.

Optional Result 1: Brand IE 4 to increase company product visibility.

Optional Result 2: Customize IE 4 settings to allow proper operation of the ActiveX control.

Suggested Solution: Use the IEAK to create a custom IE 4 package. Supply a custom toolbar bitmap, custom Active Setup bitmap, custom logo to replace the spinning 'e', and a custom Outlook Express info-pane. In the Policies section of the IEAK, preconfigure the security zones of the custom package with your site listed in the Trusted Sites zone.

Which of the following is correct?

A. The suggested solution accomplishes the required result and both optional results.

B. The suggested solution accomplishes the required result and just one optional result.

C. The suggested solution accomplishes the required result only.

D. The suggested solution does not accomplish the required result.

17. Your company provides for automatic futures trading over the Internet. Customers can trade using any Web browser, but you have developed a custom IE 4 ActiveX control that makes trading much more intuitive. The ActiveX control requires your Web site to be in the Trusted Sites zone of the IE 4 Web browser. You want to distribute a custom IE 4 package that increases your company's product visibility (through the branding options of the IEAK) and preconfigure the security zones settings of IE 4, as well as comply with Microsoft's license restrictions.

Required Result: Comply with Microsoft's license restrictions.

Optional Result 1: Brand IE 4 to increase company product visibility.

Optional Result 2: Customize IE 4 settings to allow proper operation of the ActiveX control.

Suggested Solution: Use the IEAK to create a custom IEAK package. Supply a custom toolbar bitmap, custom Active Setup bitmap, and a custom Outlook Express infopane.

Which of the following is correct?

A. The suggested solution accomplishes the required result and both optional results.

B. The suggested solution accomplishes the required result and just one optional result.

C. The suggested solution accomplishes the required result only.

D. The suggested solution does not accomplish the required result.

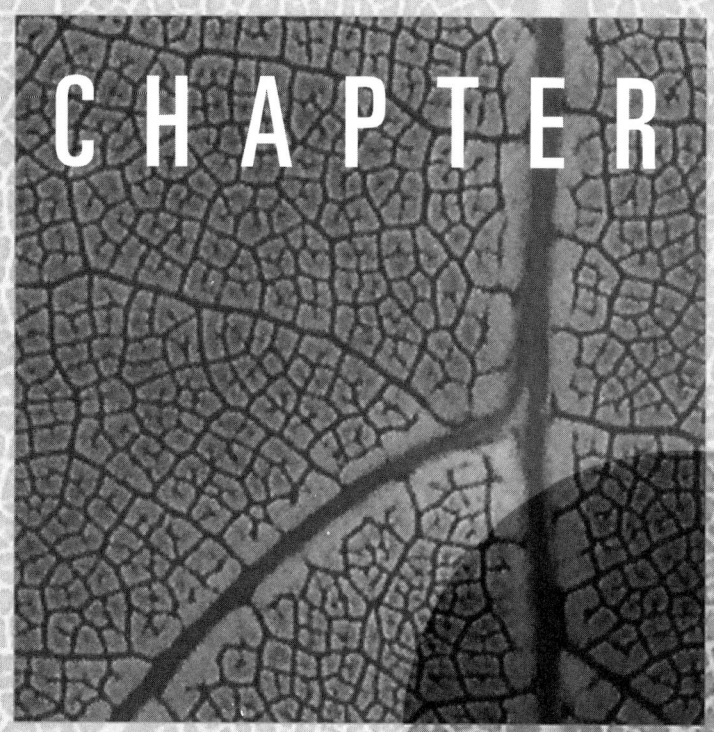

CHAPTER

3

Installing and Working
with Internet Explorer

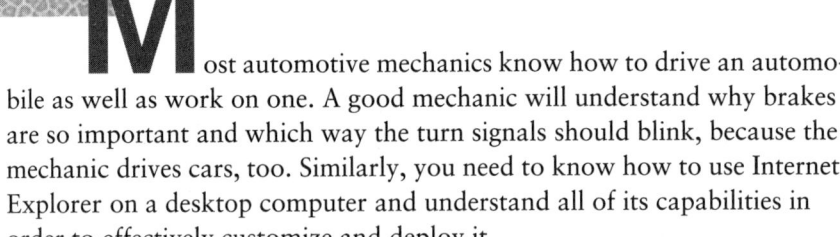

ost automotive mechanics know how to drive an automobile as well as work on one. A good mechanic will understand why brakes are so important and which way the turn signals should blink, because the mechanic drives cars, too. Similarly, you need to know how to use Internet Explorer on a desktop computer and understand all of its capabilities in order to effectively customize and deploy it.

This chapter covers the following aspects of using Internet Explorer on a desktop computer:

- Installing Internet Explorer

- Configuring Internet Explorer

- Using and customizing the Internet Explorer Web browser

- Adding and removing components

- Uninstalling Internet Explorer

This chapter will concentrate on core features of Internet Explorer 4, including navigation, subscription, Active Desktop, and channels. Also, it will describe companion software to IE4, including Outlook Express and NetMeeting.

Installing Internet Explorer

The Internet Explorer Administration Kit gives you the tools to customize an Internet Explorer 4 installation. In order to use the IEAK effectively, you need to understand how IE 4 is installed in its normal, uncustomized form. When distributing IE 4 to the client computers in your LAN or guiding ISP clients through the process of installing your version of IE 4, you will have to know all the installation options.

Microsoft ✔ *Exam* *Objective*

Install and configure Internet Explorer 4.0, with or without the Windows Desktop Update, on computers that run various operating systems. Operating systems include:

- Microsoft Windows NT Server 4.0
- Microsoft Windows NT Workstation 4.0
- Microsoft Windows 3.*x*
- Microsoft Windows 95
- Macintosh

How you install Internet Explorer 4 depends on the sources of the IE 4 files and the operating system. This section shows how to install (from CD-ROM or downloaded from the Internet) IE 4 on the following operating systems:

- Windows 98
- Windows 95 and Windows NT Workstation and Server
- Windows 3.*x* and MacOS

Windows 98

You don't have to install Internet Explorer 4 on Windows 98—Microsoft ships Windows 98 with IE 4 preinstalled. However, Microsoft is sure to come out with upgrades to its Web browser, and you need to know how to install those upgrades. The installation process will be substantially the same as for Windows 95 and Windows NT.

The same features of Internet Explorer 4 will be available to users of Windows 98, so you should familiarize yourself with the features of IE 4 and the process of creating your own version of IE 4. In addition, administering the security and centrally controlling the configuration of browsers in a network is the same, so don't throw out your IEAK just yet.

Windows 95 and Windows NT

Windows 95 is Microsoft's mass-market consumer operating system, and Windows NT is Microsoft's operating system of the future; so it isn't surprising that Microsoft has made it easy to install Internet Explorer 4 on these operating systems. With the Active Setup feature, all you need to install IE 4 on these computers is the IE4Setup.exe program (which can fit on a single floppy disk) and a connection to the Internet (or some other network service that contains the IE 4 setup files).

Both Windows 95 and Windows NT use the same installation process, with the Active Setup and ACME Setup programs. Internet Explorer 4 has similar requirements for the two operating systems, with a few differences (due to the resource requirements of the operating systems themselves, rather than IE 4). You can even install IE 4 automatically, which makes it much easier to install IE 4 on multiple computers in a LAN.

This section will cover the following aspects of installing IE 4 on Windows 95 and Windows NT computers:

- System requirements

- Installation components

- Installation restrictions

- Active Setup

- ACME Setup

- IE service packs

- Hands-free setup

System Requirements

Running Internet Explorer 4 requires a computer that can handle the extra processing load that all the features of IE 4 place on it. Since IE 4 is extendable with plug-ins and helper applications (such as Outlook Express), the more features that you install, the more powerful computer you need. This is especially true in regards to memory and free disk space. System and disk-space requirements for IE 4 are illustrated in Tables 3.1, 3.2, and 3.3.

T A B L E 3.1	Component	Minimum Requirement
System Require-ments for a Win-dows 95 Computer	Processor	486/66
	Operating System Version	Windows 95 OSR2
	Memory	8MB without Active Desktop; 16MB with Active Desktop

T A B L E 3.2	Component	Minimum Requirement
System Require-ments for a Win-dows NT Computer	Processor	486/66
	Operating System Version	Windows NT with Service Pack 3
	Memory	16MB without Active Desktop; 32MB with Active Desktop

T A B L E 3.3	Installation Type	Size of Installation	Installation with CAB files
Free Disk Space Requirements for Internet Explorer 4 (Windows 95 and NT)	Minimal	40MB	52MB (12)
	Standard	51MB	67MB (16)
	Full	64MB	89MB (24.3)

When you install Internet Explorer 4 software, you must have room for the installation and the CAB files. However, you do not need the extra room if you are installing IE 4 from a drive letter mapped to a *NetBIOS* (Network Basic Input Output System) network share on your LAN file server. With a network-shared directory, the CAB files are not copied to your hard drive, so the extra space is not needed. After the installation, you can keep the CAB files (to reinstall components later), or you can delete them.

Internet Explorer will not run from a network disk. You must install it to the local hard disk drive of the computer that will be running IE 4.

If you are installing IE 4 to a partition other than your operating system partition (for example, if your Windows or Winnt directory resides on your C drive and you are installing IE 4 to drive D), you must have 70MB free on your operating system partition. Other factors, such as expanding swap space if you are low on memory or are running other programs, can cause your computer to use up more disk space than expected. You should add at least 5MB to the free disk space requirements for a trouble-free installation.

Installation Components

How many components of Internet Explorer you install depends on how you want to use it and how much space you have available on your system. For example, if you have a laptop and you are tight on disk space, you may want to just install the minimum components to browse the Web. If you telecommute and plan on doing a lot of Internet collaboration, you may want a full installation on your home computer. If you are distributing IE 4 to all the computers in your company, you may consider a standard installation which contains the components most people use.

A minimal installation includes the following components:

- Internet Explorer
- Java VM
- DirectShow
- Active Movie

A standard installation adds the following components to a minimal installation:

- Outlook Express
- Connection Manager
- Internet Connection Wizard
- Microsoft Interactive Music Control
- VDO Player
- Microsoft Wallet
- Web fonts

A full installation adds the following components to a standard installation:

- NetMeeting
- NetShow
- FrontPage Express
- Web Publishing Wizard
- Chat 2
- Connection Manager
- Indeo 5
- Microsoft Visual Basic 5 Runtime

Installation Restrictions

Microsoft has tried to make installing Internet Explorer 4 as easy as possible. They especially want to make it easy to migrate from other browsers to Internet Explorer.

Microsoft ✓ Exam Objective

Replace other Internet browsers. Other browsers include:

- Microsoft Internet Explorer 3.*x*
- Netscape Navigator

Before installing IE 4, you should know the following:

- IE 4 makes changes to important operating system files. When you install it to a Windows NT machine (which is persnickety about security), you must have sufficient privileges to install software. Usually, you have to use the administrator account.

- IE 3 and IE 4 will not coexist in the same installation of an operating system. You can't have multiple versions of IE 4 unless you dual boot the computer and place the versions on separate partitions. Two operating systems on the same partition (such as Windows 95 and NT) will use the same IE 4 add-ons (stored in the Program Files directory), and may get confused if you uninstall a plug-in from one of the operating systems.

- IE 4 and Netscape will coexist, and IE 4 will adopt Netscape settings when it is installed. There isn't an option to replace Netscape; the Netscape browser will still be on your computer. To remove Netscape, use the uninstall process through the Add/Remove Programs Control Panel.

- If you are reinstalling IE 4 over a previous installation of IE 4, you can't remove Windows Desktop Update as part of the reinstallation process. You will have to remove Windows Desktop Update first (see "Adding and Removing Components" later in this chapter for instructions). Additionally, later in this chapter you can not change the Setup folder the install process will use.

Active Setup

Active Setup lets you install Internet Explorer 4 over the Internet. Since many people connect to the Internet through modem lines, which are much slower than LAN connections, Active Setup will save time and money by just downloading the components that the user wants to install. In addition, Active Setup checks digital certificates on downloaded files to ensure that the Internet Explorer files aren't tampered with before they reach your computer.

Microsoft ✓ ***Exam Objective***

Specify and customize Active Setup components.

How Active Setup Works   The Active Setup program consists of a file called IE4Setup.exe, which is a self-expanding archive of files that determines (with the user's help) which Internet Explorer files to download from the Web, and then downloads those files. By default, IE4Setup.exe contacts the Microsoft Web site to download the files. If you have used the IEAK to create a custom installation of IE 4, the IE4Setup.exe you craft will point to your own setup files location. Active Setup uses Internet protocols to get the files, so it requires a TCP/IP connection to the Internet (if you are downloading from Microsoft's Web site) or to the server with the IE 4 installation files.

You don't need to have a Web browser to use Active Setup. The Active Setup Wizard is not a Web browser plug-in, nor does it send commands to another Internet tool such as FTP. The Active Setup Wizard uses the Internet protocols to download the Internet setup files. The way you get the IE4Setup.exe program itself, though, is another matter entirely. You can download it from Microsoft using Internet Explorer 3, Netscape Navigator, or any other Web browser (if the Web browser allows you to download and run executable files). You can also use the FTP tool that comes with Windows 95 and Windows NT to retrieve IE4Setup.exe. Internet service providers are allowed to distribute it on a floppy disk, and it is available on CD-ROM.

IE4Setup.exe

IE4Setup.exe is a self-extracting archive. When you run it, the contents extract to a temporary directory (C:\Temp\Ixp000.tmp), and then it runs one of the files (IE4Wzd.exe). When you start IE4Setup.exe, you can type extra command-line options that will pass to the IE4Wzd.exe program after the contents extract.

If IE4Wzd.exe runs to completion, the temporary directory will be deleted without you ever seeing it. If there is a problem before Active Setup starts, the Ixp000.tmp folder will remain. After you determine what has gone wrong, restart the Setup Wizard.

Before Active Setup can download Internet Explorer, it needs some information from you. It needs to know if you want to install or just download IE 4, what kind of installation you want, whether to include Windows Desktop Update, what language to use (English, etc.), and which site it should use to download IE 4. The section "Running Active Setup Wizard" will explore these options further.

CIF and *CAB* Files

Once IE4Wzd.exe has the information it needs from the user, it uses the Get command in the HTTP protocol to download CAB files from the Internet. CAB files are compressed archive files that the ACME Setup program will later expand and install its contents. One feature of CAB files that make them useful in an Internet setting is that they can be digitally signed, making them difficult to tamper.

The first file IE4Wzd.exe retrieves is IE40cif.cab, which is a CAB file containing a CIF file (IE40.cif). The CIF file lists what CAB files IE4Wzd.exe must download, where to put those files, and what other CAB are needed. IE40cif.cab is downloaded to the Internet Explorer 4 Setup folder, and is then copied to C:\Windows\Msdownld.tmp\Ase000.tmp where it is expanded. The CAB files listed in the CIF file are downloaded to the Internet Explorer Setup folder.

Getting *IE4Setup.exe* You need a Web browser to download IE 4 from an Internet location. Microsoft makes the IE4Setup.exe program available on its Web server, but not (for the general public) on its FTP site. The easiest way to get IE4Setup.exe is to download it from the Microsoft site using Internet Explorer 3 or Netscape Navigator.

Using IE3 to Download the Active Setup Package

If you already have a Web browser, you can use the Binary File Download option to download the IE4Setup.exe file to your hard drive from Microsoft's Web site (see Exercise 3.1). If you are using Internet Explorer 3, you may want to download the Authenticode 2 plug-in before you download IE4Setup.exe to verify that the IE4Setup.exe hasn't been tampered with.

You can download the Authenticode 2 plug-in from http://www.microsoft .com/ie/security.

EXERCISE 3.1

Downloading *IE4Setup.exe* from the Microsoft Web Site

1. Launch your Web browser.

2. Enter **http://www.microsoft.com/ie/download** in the Address field and click Enter.

3. Click the Internet Explorer 4 link.

4. Click the Windows 95 and NT 4 link.

5. Select English, and then click Next.

6. Click Next by the download site nearest you.

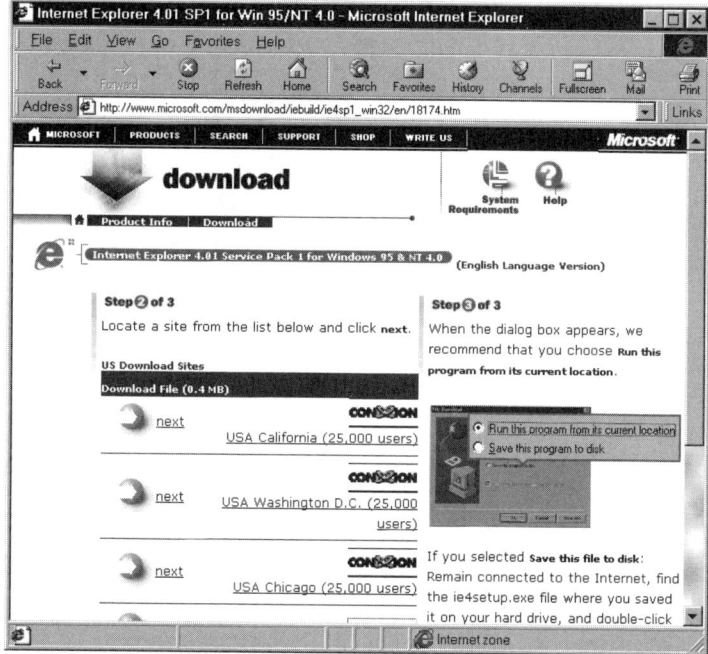

7. Select the Save This Program to Disk option, as shown below, and click OK. (Web browsers other than Internet Explorer may have different methods of saving a file to the hard drive. The methods usually involve clicking the right mouse button and selecting a Save to Disk option. Use the method appropriate to your Web browser for steps 7 through 9.)

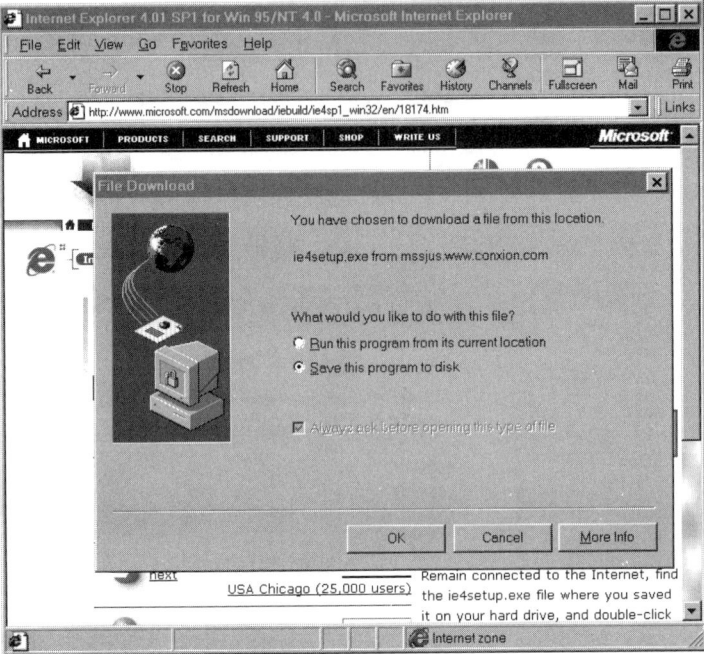

8. Enter C:\IE4Setup.exe for the location to store the file and click OK.

9. Click OK after the file has completed downloading.

Running the Active Setup Wizard Once you have the IE4Setup.exe program, you can use it to get the rest of the Internet Explorer 4 installation files. The portion of IE 4 Setup that does all of this work is the Active Setup Wizard, contained in the file IE4Wzd.exe. The default operation of the Active Setup Wizard is to ask the user for configuration options, then connect to the Microsoft site to download the files. But you can customize how it does this by passing command-line options to IE4Wzd.exe.

Command-Line Options

You can pass the command-line options to IE4Wzd.exe through the IE4Setup.exe program, in which case the options will be given to the Wizard after the initial archive is expanded. If you have already expanded the archive, you can just run the `IE4Wzd.exe` file directly, passing the options on its command line.

Some command-line options for the `IE4Setup.exe` program are shown in Table 3.4.

T A B L E 3.4	Command-Line Options	What It Means
Command-Line Options for the IE4Setup.exe Program	/q	Quiet mode.
	/t:<path>	Target folder specifies a location, other than the current directory, to expand the IE 4 Setup archive.
	/c:	Executable file to run after extraction. If no filename follows the c:, then the files will just be extracted and the process will stop. If the /c: option is not present, then the IE4Wzd.exe file will be executed after extraction.

Parameters passed to the Active Setup Wizard are typed on the command line as a part of the /c: option, surrounded in quotes, as follows:

```
Ie4setup /c:"ie4wzd.exe /m:0 /I:n"
```

The command-line options for `IE4Wzd.exe` are shown in Table 3.5.

T A B L E 3.5	Command-Line Options	What It Means
Command-Line Options for the IE4Wzd.exe Program	/qu	User Quiet mode reduces the number of dialogs to which the user must respond.
	/qa	Admin Quiet mode eliminates dialog boxes.
	/r:n	Never reboot.
	/r:I	Reboot if required.

T A B L E 3.5 *(cont.)* Command-Line Options for the IE4Wzd.exe Program	**Command-Line Options**	**What It Means**
	/r:a	Reboot after processing.
	/r:s	Reboot without prompting user.
	/n:g	Don't run GrpConv.
	/n:e	Don't extract CAB files.
	/n:v	Don't check versions while installing.
	/I:y	Retrieve Active Desktop and Windows Explorer enhancements.
	/I:n	Do not retrieve Active Desktop and Windows Explorer enhancements.
	/m:<option>	Download Set option: 0 for minimal, 1 for standard, and 2 for full installation of IE 4.
	/s:<path>	Internet Explorer destination.
	/u:	IE 4 Setup CAB files download location.

Active Setup Initialization

When you run the IE4Setup.exe program, first the Wizard performs the following system operations:

- Checks the version of the operating system

- Informs the user if the operating system version is not sufficient to run IE 4 (Windows NT 3, for example)

- Looks for a previous version of Internet Explorer and associated *Dynamic Link Libraries* (DLLs)

- Initializes *Object Linking and Embedding* (OLE), the technology that allows Web browser windows to contain other programs that extend the functionality of IE

- Checks for previous installation attempt failures
- Verifies the digital signatures on the Active Setup archive files
- Loads DLLs (Advpack.dll, W95inf16.dll, and W95inf32.dll)
- Registers and copies other DLLs to the System directory (Wininet.dll, Urlmon.dll, Jobexec.dll, and Inseng.dll)

Navigating the Wizard

When you run the Active Setup Wizard normally (i.e. not in quiet mode), the Wizard prompts you for information about how you would like to download the IE 4 CAB files. It then retrieves those files from the Internet. The first phase (prompting for information) does not require a connection to the Internet, but the second phase (retrieving) does. Exercise 3.2 walks you through the process of using the Active Setup Wizard to download IE 4.

EXERCISE 3.2

Navigating the Active Setup Wizard

Preparing for Download

1. Double-click the IE4Setup.exe icon you downloaded in Exercise 3.1.

2. Click Next on the Installation splash screen, as shown below.

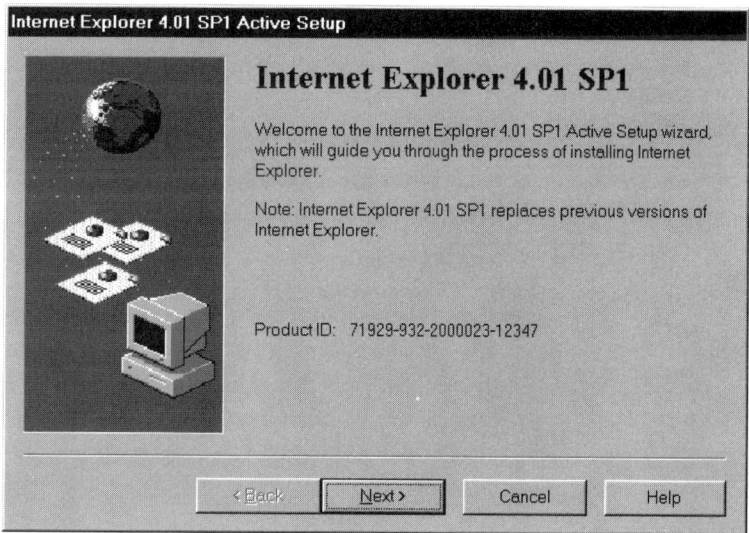

EXERCISE 3.2 (CONTINUED)

3. Click I Accept the Agreement on the License Agreement screen, and then click Next.

4. Click the Download Only option, and then click Next.

5. Select Full Installation in the drop-down list, and then click Next. If you are installing from CD-ROM, you don't have the Minimal option because the program doesn't know if the Internet Connection Wizard is already installed.

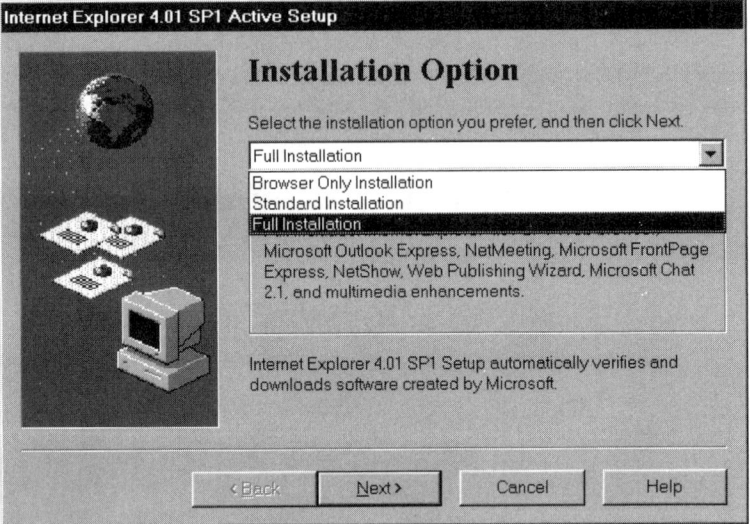

6. If Windows Desktop Update is not already installed on your computer, select Yes for Windows Desktop Update and click Next. (This option will not appear if WDU is already installed.)

7. Select your locality for Active Channel selection, and then click Next.

8. If the Setup folder does not already exist (the Setup folder remains if a previous attempt at installing IE 4 failed), accept the default path for storing the IE 4 Setup files, and click Next. You will not be prompted for a default path if the Setup folder already exists; the existing Setup folder will be used.

Retrieving *CAB* Files from Internet Source

9. If you are not already connected to the Internet, establish your connection. The Wizard will connect to Microsoft and retrieve a list of download sites.

10. If your computer must go through a proxy to get to the Internet, an error message will appear. You can click the Advanced button to set the proxy Internet name and port number.

11. Select the region nearest you, then select the site nearest you within that region. Click Next. This prompts a check for disk space against the sizes of the components listed in the IE40.cif file. C:\Windows\ Temporary Internet Files is created at this point, and the files are downloaded.

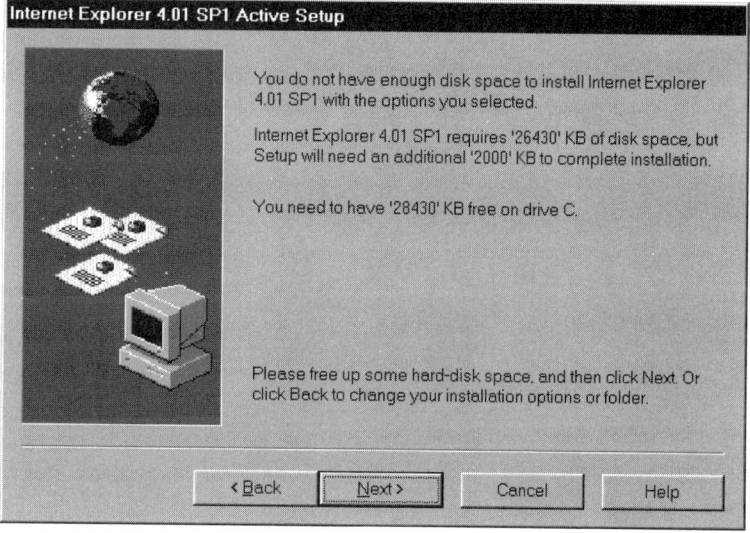

12. Click OK, or (if you did not select the Download Only option) you are asked to click the Continue button. You can disconnect from the Internet at this point.

Sometimes it is difficult to get a reliable connection to the Internet, and it can take a while to download the IE 4 Setup files. It is not uncommon for lengthy downloads to be interrupted by Internet or computer problems. Microsoft included Smart Recovery in the Download Wizard so that if the download process is interrupted, the files already downloaded won't have to be downloaded again. With Smart Recovery, the installation of IE 4 will pick up where it was interrupted.

ACME Setup

Once you have the Internet Explorer 4 installation files (on CD-ROM or downloaded to your hard disk), you can start the IE 4 installation process. IE 4 uses the same ACME interactive setup process that other Microsoft software packages use, so you should be familiar with it.

Start the ACME setup process by double-clicking the IE4Setup.exe file. If you did not select Download Only with the Download Wizard (see Exercise 3.2), the ACME Setup program will run automatically. You can also start the ACME program by inserting an IE 4 installation CD-ROM in your CD-ROM drive. A window appears, giving you the option to install IE 4, IE 4 components, or browse the CD-ROM.

If you want to use ACME setup options other than the default ones, you can start the setup program from a command prompt, as described in the next section.

Setup Options   The ACME Setup program will, by default, install files from the current directory, prompt the user for a destination directory, and record installation information to log files in default locations. You can change how ACME operates by passing command-line options to the program. You start the ACME Setup process by running the same program that you used to download the CAB files, the IE4Setup.exe program.

Command-line switches for the IE 4 ACME Setup are shown in Table 3.6.

ACME command-line options are not case sensitive, so /Q does the same operation as /q.

TABLE 3.6	Command-Line Switches	What It Means
Command-Line Switches for IE 4 ACME Setup	`/g "<file>"`	Generate log file
	`/q`	Suppress dialog boxes (/q and /q0 still present a dialog box before rebooting; /q1 suppresses the dialog box; /qT suppresses background frame and progress bar as well as the dialog box)
	`/qn`	Suppresses the reboot operation (may have a 1 or a T appended as above, e.g. /qnT to suppress dialog boxes, background frame, and progress bar)
	`/r`	Reinstall
	`/s <source directory>`	Specifies the location of the source files to install
	`/t <table file>`	Specifies the table file containing information on how to install the source files
	`/u`	Uninstall

Running ACME Setup When you restart the IE4Setup.exe program, it will continue where you left off when downloading the CAB files. Since things may have changed since downloading the files, the setup program double-checks the digital signatures and other settings (such as whether or not you have sufficient disk space) before beginning the ACME Setup process. Exercise 3.3 walks you through the ACME Setup process for IE 4.

EXERCISE 3.3

Running ACME Setup

1. Double-click the IE4Setup.exe icon.

2. Click Next at the Active Setup splash screen.

3. Accept the license agreement, and click Next.

4. Select Full Install, and click Next.

5. Accept the default location (Program Files\Internet Explorer) of IE 4, and click Next.

6. Click OK when setup has finished installing components. If you are installing on Windows NT, you will be encouraged to create an emergency boot disk.

7. Click OK to restart your computer.

8. After the restart, the setup process will finish configuring IE 4.

Internet Explorer Service Packs

No software product is perfect, Internet Explorer 4 included. Microsoft produces software patches for its operating systems and application software. In order to maintain the best security on your system and to have all the latest features and bug-fixes, you will need to install these Microsoft service packs. The latest service pack for Internet Explorer 4 (at the time of this writing) is the Internet Explorer Service Pack 1.

The latest full version of Internet Explorer 4 available to download contains the latest service pack fixes to the software. If you already have IE 4 installed, you may just want to install the changed components. Microsoft's Web site indicates that the service pack will be made available separate from IE 4 soon. For now, in order to upgrade your Web browser, you will need to download and install the full service pack version of IE 4.

Hands-Free Setup

If you need to install Internet Explorer 4 on many computers, you don't want to type in responses to prompts in setup dialog boxes for each computer. Fortunately, you can easily instruct the setup program to install everything with default settings. You can even pass along the exact settings you want all at once from the command line.

You can start an installation in hands-free mode by passing the appropriate switches from the command line, or by using the IEAK to create a custom installation of IE 4 (Chapter 6 describes how to customize a version of IE 4 for automated installation). The following is an example of starting an automatic installation from the command line (see the previous sections, "Active Setup" and "ACME Setup," for an explanation of the command-line options):

```
IE4Setup /q /c:"ie4wzd.exe /x /q1 /m:1 /I:n /r:y"
```

If you want to install IE 4 to client computers without copying the CAB files, you can create a *network share* (file server hard drive space that network clients can access using NetBIOS) on your file server with the IE4Setup.exe file and the downloaded CAB files. You can then map a drive on the client computer to the network share, then run the setup program directly from the share.

Windows 3.*x* and MacOS

Most people use Internet Explorer 4 with Windows 95 or Windows NT. Microsoft also produces versions of IE 4 for Windows 3.1, Windows for Workgroups, Windows NT (version 3.51 and earlier), the Macintosh operating system (MacOS), and some versions of Unix.

Installing IE 4 on Windows 3.1 is similar to installing it on Windows 95 and NT. Although the software looks and operates similarly, it is not the same program as the version for Windows 95 and NT. IE 4 for Windows 3.*x* is a 16-bit program, while IE 4 for Windows 95 and NT is a 32-bit program. Fortunately, you download the software from the same place (www.microsoft.com/ie/download). When you run the setup.exe file, it launches a Wizard that walks you through the installation process.

Both the installation process and the look of Internet Explorer 4 on a Macintosh are different than a Windows 95 installation and appearance. The features you have used in the Windows version (channels, favorites, etc.) are still there—just not in the places you expect. Figure 3.1 shows the Macintosh version of IE 4. Exercise 3.4 will guide you through the process of installing IE 4 on your Macintosh.

The Macintosh version of IE 4 adheres to Macintosh visual interface guidelines rather than the Windows 95 look.

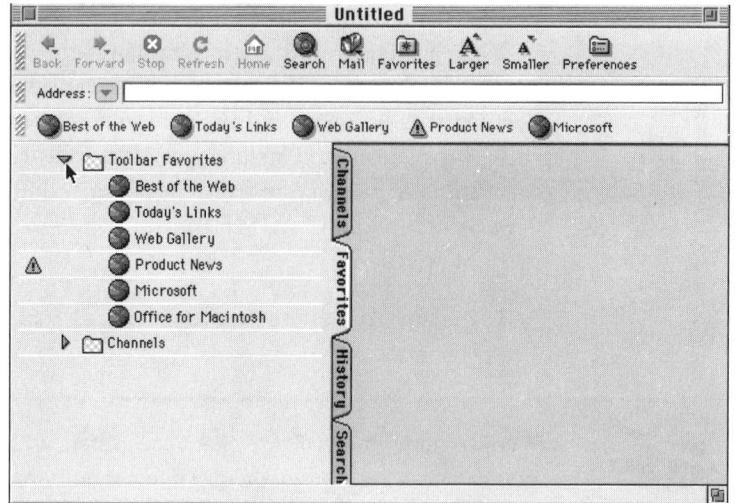

EXERCISE 3.4

Installing Internet Explorer 4 on a Macintosh Computer

1. Download Internet Explorer 4 Installer program for your Macintosh from www.microsoft.com/ie/download.

2. Run the Installer program.

3. Click the Accept button on the License Agreement screen.

4. Accept Easy Install, and click the Install button.

5. Click the Continue button to close all running applications.

6. Click Yes to make IE 4 your default Web browser.

7. Click Yes to make Outlook Express your default mail and news client.

8. After the files copy, click Restart to restart the computer.

Configuring Internet Explorer

Installing Internet Explorer is only half the job of setting it up on your computer. You still have to configure IE 4 to match your network configuration and how you plan to use the features of Internet Explorer. You need to know how to configure the following:

- Proxy settings
- Automatic Configuration options
- User profiles
- Internet Connection Wizard
- Desktop Update
- Active Setup components
- Browser options
- Active Desktop options

Configuring IE 4 to Use a Proxy Server

Many corporate and educational networks place a firewall and a proxy server between the Internet and the LAN. Computers on the LAN do not have direct access to the Internet, but must instead go through the proxy server to communicate with remote sites. This protects the LAN from intrusion from the Internet, and can also allow a LAN with a large number of computers to share a limited number of registered Internet names and addresses.

The default configuration of Internet Explorer 4 assumes that the computer it is working on has a working TCP/IP connection to the Internet. You must specify any proxy servers that IE 4 must go through to get to the Internet. Fortunately, it is easy to configure IE 4 to use a proxy, as shown in Exercise 3.5.

EXERCISE 3.5

Configuring Internet Explorer 4 to Use a Proxy Server

1. Launch Internet Explorer 4.

2. Select View ➤ Internet Options.

3. Click the Connections tab.

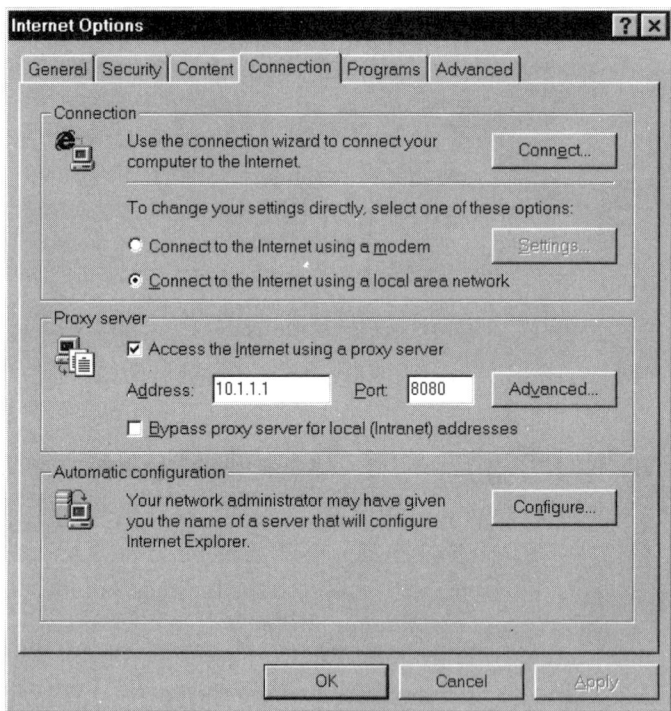

4. Select the Access the Internet Using a Proxy Server option.

5. Enter the location and port of the proxy server in the Address and Port fields.

6. Click Apply, and then click OK.

Automatic Configuration

When you are configuring a large number of computers, you don't want to configure all of the settings for each Internet Explorer installation by hand. IE 4 makes configuring large numbers of IE 4 browsers easier by supporting automatic configuration. All you have to do is supply a URL containing the automatic configuration information. In Chapter 7 you will see how to create the file for the URL containing the automatic configuration data.

With the IEAK, you can create an automatic configuration file that will be used once to set the initial state of the IE 4 browser, or you can create an automatic configuration file that the browser will periodically check for new settings or setting changes that can be downloaded to the browser automatically. Exercise 3.6 shows you how to use automatic configuration with IE 4.

EXERCISE 3.6

Using Automatic Configuration to Set Up IE 4

1. Launch Internet Explorer.

2. Select View ➤ Internet Options ➤ Connection ➤ Configure.

3. Enter the URL for the page with the configuration script or INS file. (You will learn how to create this INS file and prepare the URL in Chapter 7.)

4. Click OK.

User Profiles

One of the nice features of Internet Explorer 4 is that you can personalize it to your needs. But what if you share your computer with someone else, and that other person likes different settings than you do? Fortunately, both Windows 95 and Windows NT support user profiles, which provides a way for each user to keep their own settings for such things as favorites, background colors, Active Desktop items, and Start menu items. If you use Windows 95, you must enable the User Profiles feature before you can use it.

When you perform a full installation of Internet Explorer 4, you get a new icon (Users) in the Control Panel. Before you can use it, you must enable user profiles by selecting passwords for your Windows 95 computer (if you haven't already). Exercise 3.7 shows you how to enable profiles.

EXERCISE 3.7

Enabling Profiles in Windows 95

1. Select Start ➢ Settings ➢ Control Panel ➢ Passwords.

2. Click the User Profiles tab.

3. Select Users Can Customize button.

4. Click the Include Start Menu and Program Groups in User Settings option, and click OK.

5. Click Yes to restart your computer.

You can also enable user profiles by clicking on the Users Control Panel item. If profiles have not yet been enabled, the Users Control Panel will guide you through the enabling process.

User profiles work by providing a different place for each user's personalized settings to be stored. In Windows 95, a user's personalized settings are stored in a directory (that is named after the user's account name) in the Profiles subdirectory of the Windows directory. In Windows NT, the profiles may be stored in Winnt\Profiles. One of the files stored in the directory is User.dat (Ntuser.dat for Windows NT), which holds the contents of that user's HKEY_CURRENT_USER Registry hive.

In Windows NT, the Administrator account can create new user accounts and perform other account management operations. Since Windows 95 does not provide account security for the Windows 95 computer in isolation, all you have to do to create a new user account is provide a different user name to the Windows 95 logon window. If your Windows 95 computer participates in a Windows NT domain, you may not be allowed to do this.

To access Profile Wizard, Windows 95 requires a password for any users other than the person who installed the operating system (or the first person to start the Profile Wizard).

Since Windows 95 supports far less security than Windows NT, what you can do from the Users Control Panel is limited (see Figure 3.2). From the Users Control Panel you can:

- Create new users

- Delete users

- Copy users

- Set passwords

- Change settings (for user's profile)

FIGURE 3.2

The Users Control Panel item is where user account passwords and profile settings are established in Windows 95.

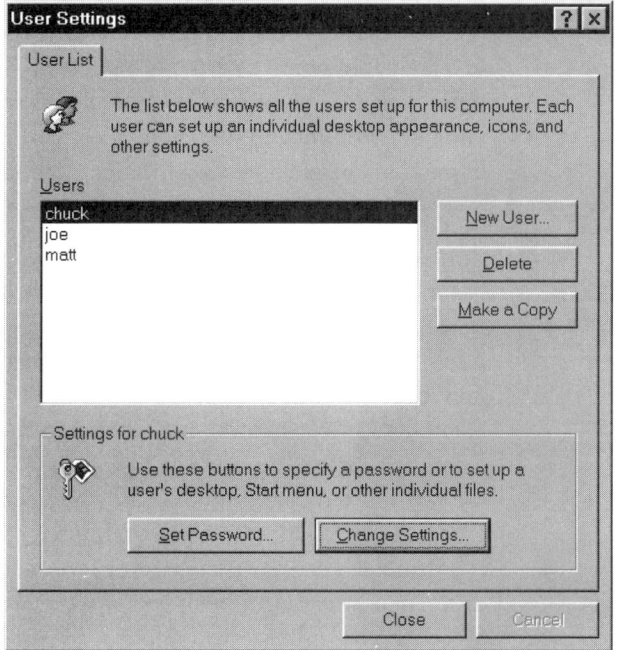

The settings for the user's profile primarily concern which user interface areas will be included in that user's private profile and which will be shared with other users of the computer. The settings can be different for each user of the computer. The computer can tell the users apart by their Windows 95 or Windows NT logon name and password, so the user doesn't have to do anything else to take advantage of private profiles. A check box in the Users Control Panel allows the user to maintain a customized version of each of the following areas:

- Desktop folder and Documents menu

- Start menu

- Favorites folder

- Downloaded Web pages

- My Documents folder

WARNING Be careful which user interface areas you make private when you enable roaming profiles on your network. Incorrectly established profiles can lead to a situation where a perfectly valid user interface change on one computer makes a profile that contains incorrect settings when transferred to another computer. For example, the user may specify a background bitmap that exists on one computer but doesn't on another.

In a network environment, you may want to give users a consistent view of the network by moving their personalized settings to whichever computer they happen to use to log on to the network. Roaming profiles provide Windows 95 and Windows NT consistent views. When the user logs on to the network, the User.dat or Ntuser.dat is copied from the network to the client computer, then the user is shown the (perhaps updated) desktop. Changes made to the user's environment (background colors, favorites, etc.) are transmitted back to the server on the network so that the next time the user logs on (no matter which computer) the changes will remain.

If the client computers on your network are configured differently or have different software installed, you will not want to include areas such as the Start Menu and Program folders in the users' profiles, because the links to the programs may differ from one computer to another. Internet Explorer 4 introduces some settings that probably should not be a part of the profile as well. Downloaded Web pages, for example, can take up a lot of space and bandwidth when copied to the network and back to the user's client computer.

The My Documents folder may contain a lot of information that may not be appropriate for the user's roaming profile.

Windows NT and Windows 95 profiles are not compatible, so changes made when logged on to a Windows 95 computer (new links in the Favorites folder, a different screen saver, and so on) will not be reflected in a Windows NT log on session and vice versa.

Using a roaming profile established on a computer using Internet Explorer 4, you can log on to a computer that uses Internet Explorer 3. Most of your settings will be understood by IE 3, but links to Active Channels will not work.

Internet Connection Wizard

In order to use IE 4 to its full potential, you need to be connected to the Internet. If you received IE 4 on CD-ROM or if it came pre-installed on your computer, however, you may need to run the Internet Connection Wizard (ICW) to connect your computer to the Internet.

The first time a fresh installation of IE 4 (not an upgrade of IE 3) starts up, the Internet Connection Wizard runs and gives you three choices for ICW configuration.

The automatic and manual options for Internet Connection Wizard installs (or reinstalls) the TCP/IP and (optionally) the Dial-Up Networking components of Windows 95. The manual configuration can be used for a connection over a phone line or over a LAN. The automatic configuration only works over dial-up phone lines.

Automatic Configuration   This selection in the ICW reinstalls your networking components from the Windows 95 installation disk(s), queries your computer for modem information, connects to the Microsoft ISP referral service, and connects you to a local Internet service provider so you can establish an Internet account. In order to use the automatic configuration in the ICW, you must have a modem attached to your computer. Automatic configuration in the ICW is best used when the user doesn't already have an Internet account with an ISP. If the user already has an account, or if the computer is on a LAN connected to the Internet, then the manual or current options in the ICW are better choices.

Manual Configuration If your Internet connection is configured, but you need to change a few settings (such as the proxy settings for IE 4), you can choose the manual option. You can also use the manual option if you still need to configure dial-up networking, but you want to use an already existing Internet service provider account instead of getting a new account referred by Microsoft.

Current Configuration This option leaves your networking settings as they are.

Using and Customizing the Internet Explorer Browser

Once you have IE 4 set up and working, you will want to configure it to suit your tastes. You need to be familiar with the customization process because the options available to the individual customization is similar to the options you will be using the IEAK to provide (or mandate) for users of your modified distribution of IE 4.

Microsoft ✓ *Exam* *Objective*	**Customize the browser.**

Capabilities and options of IE 4 that you should be familiar with include:

- Browsing Web pages
- Managing favorites
- Modifying the Search bar
- Configuring the History bar
- Configuring channels and subscribing to sites
- Browsing offline
- Changing security settings

Browsing Web Pages

Browsing Web pages is what Internet Explorer is all about. IE 4 displays a Web page, you click on a hyperlink which takes you to another page, you click on another hyperlink to go to another Web page, and so on. IE 4 typically underlines or highlights hyperlinks so you know what you can click on. The pointer icon changes from an arrow to a hand when it is on a hyperlink. Beyond this basic functionality, IE 4 includes a few features that make it easier to use than many other Web browsers and earlier versions of IE. Features just for navigating Web pages that Microsoft is particularly proud of include:

- Autocomplete and Autodomain searching
- Back and forward buttons with integrated history
- Explorer bars

Autocomplete and Autodomain Searching

URLs can be long and cumbersome to type. The Favorites feature of IE 4 makes it easier to go to the Web pages you visit often, but too many favorites can also be difficult to manage. The Autocomplete feature makes it easier to go to Web pages you've already visited by completing the URL for you.

Autocomplete works as you type a URL into the Address field of the Web browser. It matches what you have already typed with the record of all the places you've already visited. If it finds a match, it prints the remainder of the URL. If it is the correct URL, you click Enter and IE 4 will retrieve the page for you. If it isn't the URL you wanted, just keep typing. Autocomplete will keep offering complete URLs as long as there is something in the record (the IE 4 History) that matches.

Autodomain searching helps you find Web sites that you haven't previously visited. Autodomain takes advantage of the fact that most Internet sites start with www and end in .com, .org, .edu, .mil, .gov, or .net. You can type a domain name without the prefix or suffix (such as memetech rather than www.memetech.com) and IE 4 will attempt to find the site for you by trying all the domain suffixes.

Back Button, Forward Button, and History

Every user of Web browsers is familiar with the Back button, which takes you back to the Web page you viewed before the current one. If you have followed multiple links, you can click the Back button until you are back to the first page you visited when you started the Web browser. IE 4 keeps a list of all of the links used to reach the current Web page.

Internet Explorer 4 also provides you with a Forward button. This button becomes active after you click the Back button. It takes you to the page you were on before you hit the Back button. The Forward button is disabled again, until you use the Back button again.

If clicking on the Back and Forward buttons takes too much time (you may have a slow modem connection or you may want to go back to a specific page without browsing all of the intervening pages), you can click the Navigation History button (the little triangle next to the Back button). This button shows you a list of the Web sites in the order that you visited them since you started IE 4. The list is cleared every time you close the Web browser. You can select an entry to go directly to that Web page.

If you want to go to a Web location you have visited before but that is not listed in the Navigational History (which you access from the little triangle next to the Back button), you can list all of the Web sites you have visited (since the last time you cleaned out the IE 4 History) by clicking on the History Explorer bar.

Explorer Bars

Explorer bars are a new feature of IE 4. The Favorites, History, Search, and Channels buttons present Explorer bars in a new window pane to the left of the main browser view area. This area remains visible while you browse the Internet. See Figure 3.3 for a view of the Search Explorer bar.

- **Favorites**   This pane shows Web sites you have "bookmarked" for easy access.

- **History**   This pane shows Web sites you have visited.

- **Search**   This pane links you to a search engine to look for information on the Internet.

- **Channels**   This pane lists Web sites that contain time-sensitive content that IE 4 can be configured to check periodically.

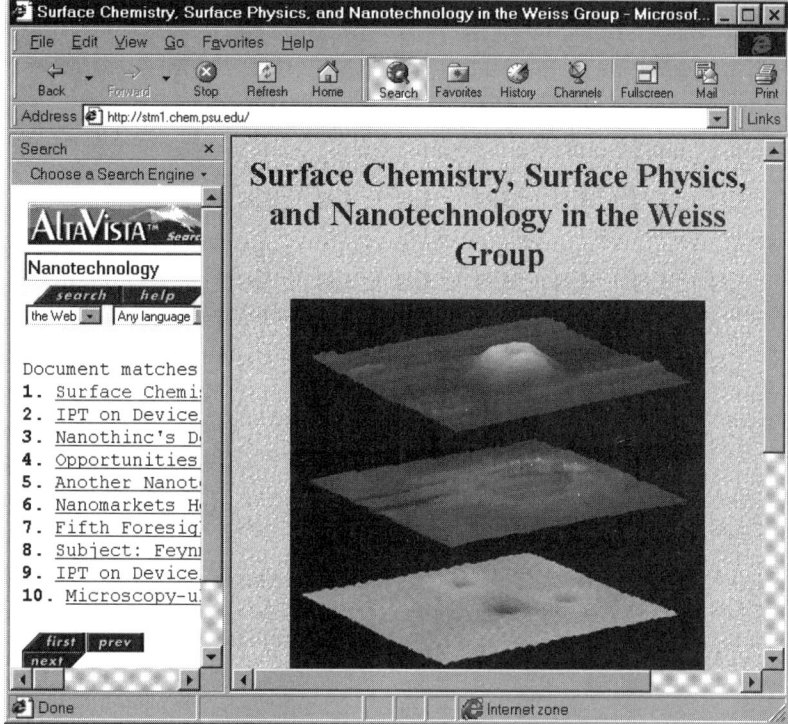

The Search Explorer
bar remains visible to
the left of the screen
while you browse
the Internet for
information.

Managing Favorites

A freshly installed version of Internet Explorer 4 comes with several entries
already installed in the Favorites channel. Fortunately, you can change what
shows up in the Favorites drop-down menu, the Favorites Explorer bar, and the
Favorites Start menu. The Favorites channel, bar, and menus are all essentially
the same thing—your favorites, just displayed differently.

By default, your favorites include:

- Channels
- Imported bookmarks
- Links
- Software updates
- My documents

Adding Links

To add a page to your list of favorites, select Favorites ➤ Add to Favorites. You can add the link to an expandable subfolder in the Favorites folder. You have the choice of just adding the link, subscribing to the page (so you will be notified if it changes), or having the page downloaded if it changes.

Adding Folders

Keeping all your favorite links in one big list makes it hard to find the exact link you want. It is more efficient to create folders for your favorite topics, and put related links in the appropriate folder.

You can organize folders of your favorite links by selecting Organize Favorites from the Favorites menu. In the Organize Favorites window, you can add, move, rename, and delete both folders and links. You can add a new folder by clicking the Create New Folder icon at the top of the window.

Moving, Renaming, and Deleting

Within the Organize Favorites window you can move the folders and links by clicking and dragging them to the desired destination. You can rename a folder or link by right-clicking the item and selecting the Rename option. You can delete items by right-clicking the item and selecting Delete.

You can also move, rename, and delete items by highlighting the item and clicking the appropriate button at the bottom of the window.

Modifying the Search Bar

When you first install Internet Explorer 4, the Search bar retrieves its information from a Microsoft ASP page (*Active Server Pages*). You can have the Search bar display your favorite Internet search engine by clicking the Choose a Search Engine button at the top of the Search bar. You will be taken to a Microsoft Web page that lists search engines that have produced search pages that conform to Microsoft's specifications (for example, it must be 200 pixels wide).

If you want to create a Search page of your own, you must use the IEAK to customize IE 4 to point to a different location than Microsoft's Web site. Also, you will need to make an HTML Search page that conforms to the requirements for an IE 4 bar. Chapter 6 explains how to use the IEAK to customize the IE 4 Search options.

Configuring the History Bar

Earlier versions of Internet Explorer kept Web files you had accessed in a directory on the hard drive. It was hard to navigate the information stored there, because many different temporary Internet files were stored together. The History bar makes it much easier to browse through where you've been because it just stores links to Web locations and organizes information by date and site. See Figure 3.4 for a view of the new History bar. The links are stored in the History directory (usually `Windows\History` for Windows 95 or `Winnt\History` for Windows NT).

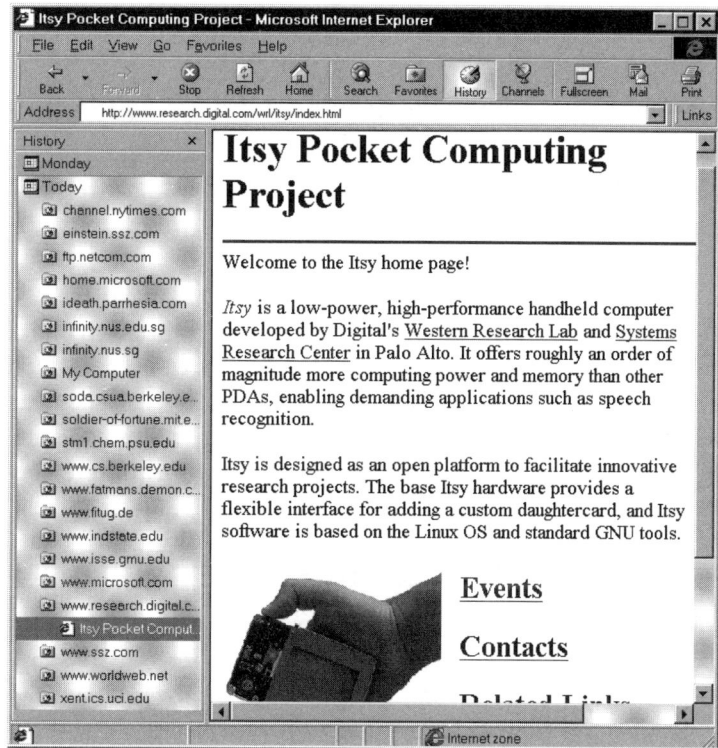

If your computer is low on disk space, you may want to reduce the number of days that IE 4 will keep the URL links in the History folder. You can set the number of days to keep links from the General tab of the Internet Options window of IE 4. You can also clear the History directory from the General tab.

Configuring Channels and Subscribing to Sites

One of the advantages of the Internet over traditional media, such as magazines and books, is how easy it is to publish and update information. This can be cumbersome, however, if you are using the Internet to stay current—especially if you get your information from multiple Web sites. With traditional Web browsers the only way to stay current is to frequently visit the Web sites to see if anything has changed. However, Microsoft has introduced a concept called Active Channels to help overcome this "deficiency" of the World Wide Web. You can configure your Web browser to periodically check a Web site and download any changes since the last time you visited it.

Microsoft
✓ *Exam*
Objective

Configure channels, software distribution channels, and site subscriptions.

An Active Channel is a Web site with a special file describing its contents and instructing the Web browser how often to check for new information on specific sites. The special file is called a *Channel Definition Format files,* or CDF. CDFs make subscribing to Web sites easy. You can also subscribe to Web sites that don't have CDF files by configuring the frequency of IE for checking the site and *link crawl depth* (how far IE will follow links in the pages it retrieves) manually.

Using the Channel Bar

You open the Channel bar (like the History bar or Search bar) by clicking the Channel bar icon in the Web browser window. If you have installed Active Desktop, you can also click on the Channel bar icon in the Status bar. A list of channels will appear on the left side of the Web browser in a pane 200 pixels wide (see Figure 3.5).

IE 4 ships with a list of pre-configured channels. You can change this list and create your own channels with the IEAK. When you click a channel, it opens a list of sub-channels. When you click a sub-channel, it takes you to the default Web page for that sub-channel.

FIGURE 3.5

Microsoft ships IE 4 pre-configured with several channels in the Channel bar.

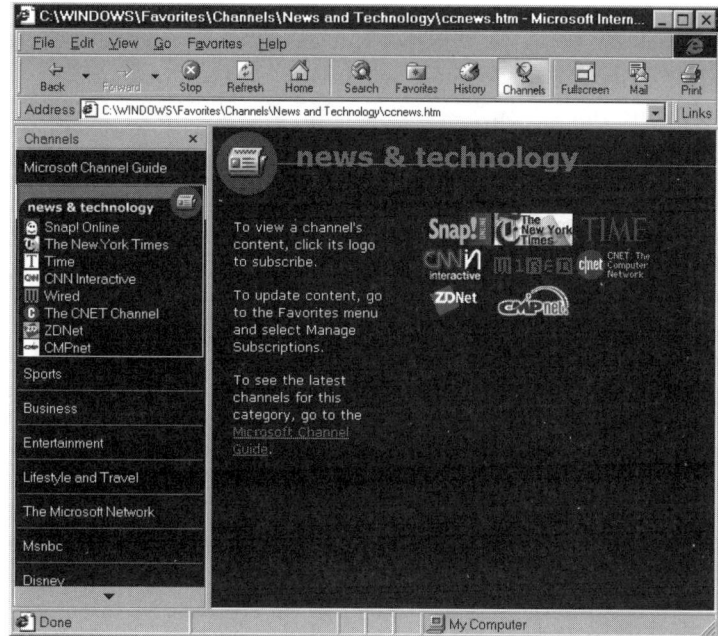

You can remove channels and sub-channels by right-clicking on that item in the Channel bar and then selecting the Delete option from the menu. You can create new channels and sub-channels by dragging folders into the Channel bar and dropping them there. You can re-arrange the channels by dragging them from one spot to another within the Channel bar.

Subscribing

When you see a Web page with a Channel icon on it, you can subscribe to that Web site by clicking on the Channel icon (see Figure 3.6). The CDF file for the channel will be sent to the Web browser and the new channel will be installed in the Channel bar. Microsoft has provided a list of channels you may like to subscribe to in the Channel bar.

FIGURE 3.6

You can click on the Active Channel graphic on a Web page to subscribe to that Web page and insert a reference to it in your Channel bar.

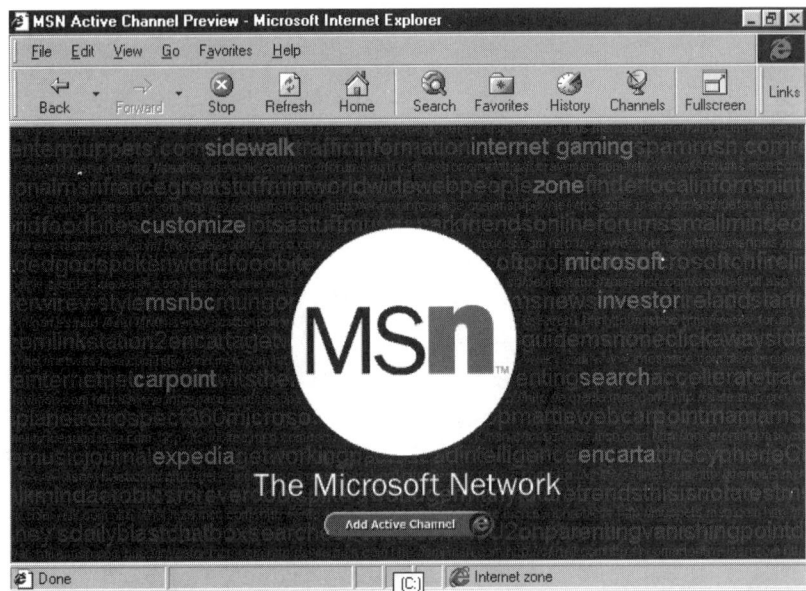

Just because channels show up in the Channel bar, doesn't mean you've subscribed to them. IE 4 will periodically check subscribed channels for new information. If you want to subscribe to one of the channels Microsoft has placed there for you, right-click on that channel and select Subscribe from the menu.

You can subscribe to Web sites that don't have CDF files by selecting the Add to Favorites option from the Favorites menu. Exercise 3.8 shows you how.

EXERCISE 3.8

Subscribing to a Web Site

1. Launch Internet Explorer 4.

2. Type **http://www.starlingtech.com/quotes/qotd.html** into the Address field, and click Enter.

3. Select Favorites ➤ Add to Favorites.

4. Check Yes, Notify Me of Updates and Download the Page for Offline Viewing options.

5. Click Create In.

6. Highlight the Channels entry.

7. Click the OK button.

Customizing Subscriptions

If the page you are subscribing to is an index page and you want to retrieve it's sub-pages, you can modify the subscription properties for your new channel to make it retrieve more than one page at a time. The link-crawl setting for the subscription specifies how "deep" IE 4 will go in following links from the top level page. You can change the link-crawl setting for a subscribed channel by right-clicking the channel in the Channel bar and then selecting Properties ➤ Receiving ➤ Advanced, then entering the depth in the Download Linked Pages box.

Other properties you can change include the types of objects that will be downloaded (graphics, sounds, ActiveX controls, etc.), the maximum amount to download, the username and password to use to access the pages, and the frequency and times to check for new data on the site.

Browsing Offline

The subscription feature of Internet Explorer 4 makes browsing offline more than just rummaging through your Temporary Internet Files folder. You can now configure IE 4 to grab information from the sites you are interested in while you are doing other things (such as sleeping or actually working in the office instead of browsing the Web). You can view those pages later, without being connected to the Internet. Browsing offline is especially useful for people with laptops or people who regularly download a great deal of information over a slow modem connection.

You can browse offline by selecting File ➤ Work Offline in the Internet Explorer window. You can view any page listed in the History bar. Instead of being retrieved from the Internet, that page will be loaded from the Windows\Temporary Internet Files directory. You can follow links on that page if those links also reside in the History folder. The shape the cursor takes as you move it over a hypertext link will tell you if the link still resides in the History folder. If the cursor turns into a hand with a little NOT sign, then the page is no longer in the cache. If you click on a link that is not in the cache, IE 4 will ask you if you want to connect to the Internet to retrieve the page.

Customizing Windows Explorer and Active Desktop

One of the features that Internet Explorer 4 can give you that no other Web browser can is complete integration with your Windows 95 or Windows NT operating system. With IE 4, you can put Web pages in your Start menu, applets on the desktop, links in the Taskbar, and hypertext customization in your hard drive folders. Every Desktop Explorer window is now a Web browser.

Microsoft ✓ *Exam* *Objective*	**Customize the browser.**

Microsoft ✓ *Exam* *Objective*	**Customize Active Desktop items and Active Channels.**

Configuring and Using the Start Menu and Favorites

With Internet Explorer 4 you can rearrange programs by clicking the programs in the Start menu and dragging them to your desired location, similar to rearranging the Favorites menu in earlier versions of Internet Explorer. This is much easier than opening up the properties page for the Start menu and rearranging them.

The favorites in IE 4 also appear as a sub-menu in the Start menu. You don't have to start Internet Explorer to access your favorites—you can just click the favorite from the Start menu, and IE 4 will launch and load that page for you.

Although the favorites portion of the Start menu is the usual location for links to Internet sites, you don't have to leave them there. You can place links elsewhere in the Start menu, even at the top level or in the Programs section. You can also place links to Web pages on the desktop.

In addition to the Favorites menu, IE 4 adds more items to the Start menu. The following three new items are part of the Find feature:

On the Internet   This takes you to the search engine you have configured IE 4 to use in the Search bar.

Using Microsoft Outlook   This uses the features of Microsoft Outlook to browse the contents of files on your hard drive to help you find specific information.

People   This retrieves your default address book so you can quickly retrieve contact information.

The following are new items in the Settings menu:

Taskbar and Start Menu   This is where you can create new toolbars for the Taskbar, make toolbars that reside on the desktop, and modify existing toolbars.

Folder Options   This gives you control over how the Desktop Explorer displays folder information.

Active Desktop   This is where you control how Active Desktop places Internet information on your screen backdrop and screensaver.

Configuring the Taskbar

Prior to the Active Desktop Update in Internet Explorer 4, the Taskbar just displayed which programs you were running and the status of a few services (such as the fax service or printing) in the bottom-right corner of the screen.

Active Desktop Update now allows you to add toolbars to the Taskbar. It comes with the following four default toolbars:

Address   You can type a URL in the Address text field and IE 4 will load the page. As you click hyperlinks and go to different pages, the URL of the page currently displayed will appear in this field.

Links   This is the same as the Links section of the Favorites menu in IE 4.

Desktop   This toolbar places all of the links on your desktop (such as My Computer, Network Neighborhood, etc.) on the Taskbar.

Quick Launch   This toolbar gives you quick access to Internet Explorer, Outlook Express, Show Desktop, and Show Channels.

You can select which toolbars will show up on the Taskbar by right-clicking on a blank area in the taskbar and selecting Toolbars in the pop-up menu. You then place a check mark by each toolbar you want to appear in the Taskbar. You can create new toolbars from Web pages or folders on your hard drive by right-clicking on a blank area in the Taskbar and then selecting Toolbar ➤ New Toolbar.

To rearrange the toolbars on the Taskbar, drag them to the desired location. You can also drag them off the Taskbar onto the desktop, and vice versa.

The Quick Launch toolbar draws its contents from the Application Data\Microsoft\Internet Explorer\Quick Launch subdirectory of the Windows or Winnt directory. You can place new Quick Launch items there, or simply drag the item My Computer or Windows Explorer and drop the item on the Quick Launch toolbar.

Configuring the Desktop Explorer

When you install Internet Explorer 4, you have the option of installing Windows Desktop Update. One part of this component makes browsing your hard drive look and behave like browsing the Internet (except it is much faster). Directory windows look like Web pages, and a single click will launch an application. When the directories of your hard drive are presented in this manner, you have Web Style selected.

Web Style is a new, but optional, way of viewing the contents of folders. You can also choose to have the folders displayed in the classic style of Windows 95 and NT prior to IE 4. You can specify that all folders are displayed one way or the other, or you can specify that only those directories that contain HTML content be displayed as Web pages.

Web View

Showing your file system folders as Web pages gives you a consistent way of viewing resources, whether they be on your LAN or on the Internet. It also gives you the ability to customize how the folders look. You have a richer set of tools to work with, including icons, hypertext links, and scripting languages. See Figure 3.7 to see how folder looks using the default Web View.

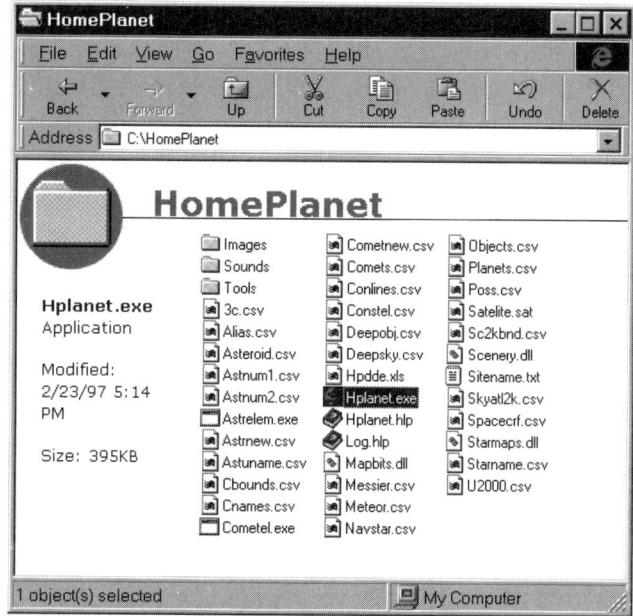

With Web View, how the information in a folder is displayed depends on the contents of a hypertext template file, or HTT file. The file `folder.htt` contains the default look for folders that have not been customized, and a `folder.htt` file in a directory is the template file for that directory, overriding the default `folder.htt` for all directories. Each customized directory also has a `Desktop.ini` file describing the location and layout of the desktop folders in Web View. The specific HTT files installed for IE 4's Web View are as follows:

Mycomp.htt   The Web View for My Computer

Controlp.htt   The Web View for the Control Panel

Deskmovr.htt   The Web View for the Active Desktop

Folder.htt   The Web View for default folders

Printers.htt   The folder for print devices

Safemode.htt   The look of a system that has been shut down unexpectedly and then restarted

You can change the appearance of a folder by editing the HTT file for that folder using an HTML editor or a text editor. The Web View Wizard automates customization of Web pages. The Web View Wizard helps you create an HTT file for a folder, edit that HTT file using your favorite HTML editor, and save the customization to a `Folder.htt` file within the folder. You can also use the Web View Wizard to remove customization from a folder, returning it to the default Web View or Classic View state.

Configuring Active Desktop

The Web View of folders is nice, but the characteristic feature of Windows Desktop Update is Active Desktop, which makes it possible for you to put Web content (including HTML pages and applets) directly on the desktop and in the screen saver. Now, instead of a passive bitmap or randomly shifting graphics, you can have periodically updated Internet information (such as stock quotes, breaking news, or cartoon panels) displayed on the desktop or as the screen saver.

Internet Explorer 4 stores Active Desktop configuration in the `Desktop .htm` file, which consists of HTML tags for images or frames with X and Y coordinates, an ActiveX control for managing the images and frames, and a link to the background image and text.

Wallpaper

You enable Active Desktop wallpaper from the Properties window for the desktop (right-click on the desktop and select Properties from the pop-up menu). Internet Explorer 4 adds a Web tab to the familiar tabs. In the Web tab, you can select the View My Active Desktop as a Web page option. In the Background tab, you can select which HTML document to make your background.

Active Desktop Items

There are two ways of adding items to your Active Desktop. You can add items from the Properties window of the desktop. The New button in the Web tab allows you to specify a URL that references the item. The second way, which only works for Web objects specifically designed to be Active Desktop items, is to use Internet Explorer 4 to click on a link in a Web page that refers to a CDF file that specifies a desktop component. IE 4 can then update your Active Desktop to include the item referenced in the CDF file.

In the same manner as you added Active Desktop items, you can disable or remove items from your screen using the Web tab in the Properties window for the desktop. To disable the item, clear the check box next to the entry describing the item, or select that entry and click the Delete. See Figure 3.8 for a view of the Web tab in Display Properties.

FIGURE 3.8

The Web tab in Display Properties shows you the Active Desktop items and allows you to disable or delete them.

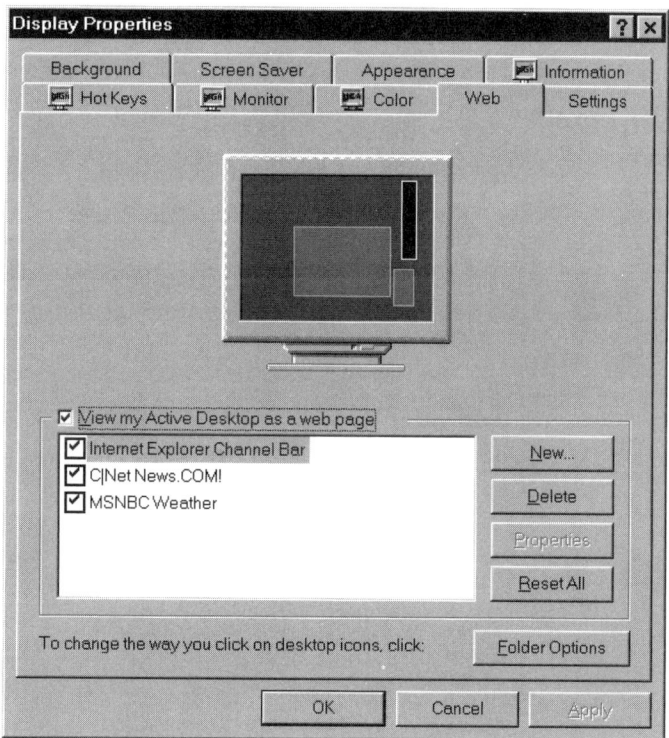

Channel Screen Saver

Active Desktop Update in Internet Explorer 4 adds a new screen saver to the list of screen savers in the Desktop Properties window. The Channel screen saver will cycle through Active Channels you to which you have subscribed in Internet Explorer. When you subscribe to an Active Channel that supports the Channel screen saver, a new entry will appear in the list of channels for the screen saver to cycle through. You can choose not to have a channel appear in the cycle by removing the check mark next to the channel from the screen saver's Configure button in the Screen Saver tab.

Adding and Removing Components

After installing Internet Explorer 4, you may discover that you want more functionality (maybe you would like to view VRML data) or perhaps less functionality (you might not like the memory and processing power consumed by Windows Desktop Update). You can use the Add/Remove Programs item in the Control Panel to change your installation of IE 4 by installing new components (sometimes called plug-ins) or removing IE 4 components.

The Add/Remove Programs feature only controls components that were registered by the original installation program. With this feature you are limited to adding or removing components that were downloaded by IE4Setup .exe or that came with IE 4 on the CD-ROM. If you want to add a component from Microsoft's Web site, you should use the ACME Maintenance mode in IE4Setup.exe. To completely remove IE 4 or to remove the Windows Desktop Update, you should run the IE4Setup.exe program to activate the ACME Maintenance mode.

Add/Remove Programs in the Control Panel

You should be familiar with the Add/Remove Programs feature of the Control Panel because it is the way Microsoft manages the modification and removal of all Microsoft software. The software packages installed by the Setup Wizard are added to the list of installed software that the Add/Remove

Program feature can manage (see Figure 3.9). Components you should look for from a full installation of IE 4 include:

- Microsoft Chat 2
- Microsoft FrontPage Express
- Microsoft Internet Explorer 4
- Microsoft Internet Explorer 4 Setup Files
- Microsoft NetMeeting 2.1
- Microsoft NetShow Player 2
- Microsoft Wallet
- Microsoft Web Publishing Wizard 1.51

FIGURE 3.9

The Add/Remove Programs window allows you to select which registered components you want.

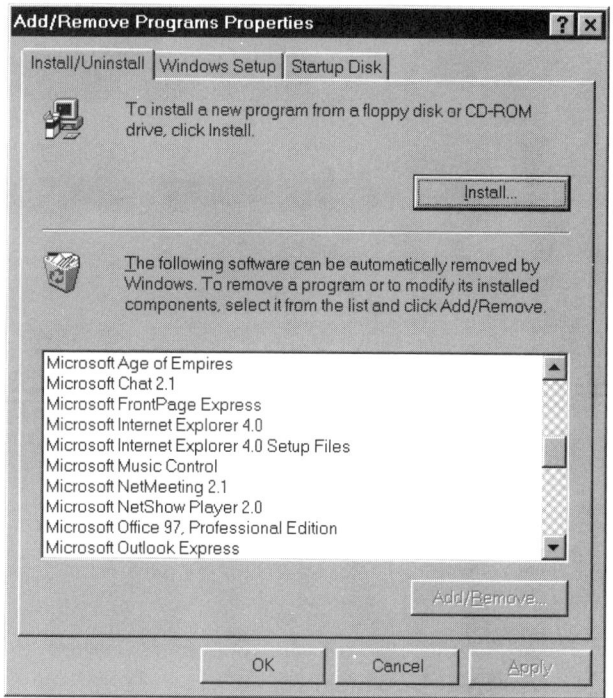

You can add and remove a component by placing or removing the check mark next to that component. When you exit the Add/Remove Software window, the features you selected will be modified.

When Add/Remove Programs removes a software component, the CAB files are left in the Setup folder so you can add them again later.

ACME Maintenance Mode

When you run the IE4Setup.exe program on a computer that already has Internet Explorer 4 installed, the program gives you the option of reinstalling IE 4 or of going into ACME Setup mode to add or remove components to IE 4. Your three initial options (see Figure 3.10) are the following:

- Uninstall IE 4 and all its components
- Add a component to IE 4 (adds from Internet)
- Remove Desktop Update component, but leave IE 4

FIGURE 3.10

In ACME Maintenance Mode you can remove IE 4 components or add new components from the Internet.

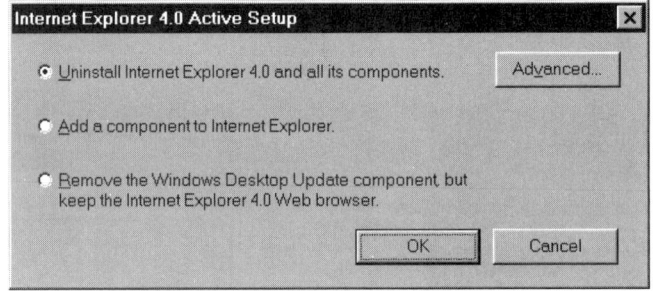

You can also add new components to IE 4 by inserting the Internet Explorer 4 installation CD-ROM. The Autorun feature of the CD-ROM will make similar options available to you, and will have many of the components available on Microsoft's download site, although the components on CD-ROM may not be as recent as the ones on their Web site.

Uninstalling Internet Explorer

Some people want to remove Internet Explorer once it has been installed. While Microsoft has a hard time understanding why anyone would want to do this, they have provided a way to remove IE 4 from your Windows computer. You can use either the Add/Remove Software feature of the Control Panel or you can run the IE4Setup.exe program to uninstall IE 4 as described in the previous section.

IE 4 makes quite a few changes to your operating system—so many, in fact, that if you try to reinstall Windows 95 or OSR2 on an operating system that already has IE 4 installed, you will have difficulties. You can't reinstall Windows 95 or OSR2 without uninstalling IE 4 first.

Don't be surprised when you uninstall Internet Explorer 4 and you don't get back all of the disk space used by IE 4. The uninstall process removes the Windows enhancements and removes the IE 4 program files, but it does not remove many of the DLL files and resource files (bitmaps, sounds, etc.) that come with IE 4. The list of files left behind after a deinstallation of IE 4 is considerable.

If the Add/Remove Programs feature runs into difficulty removing Internet Explorer 4, and the IE4Setup.exe program can't handle it, you can run the emergency removal program IERemove.exe. IERemove.exe will attempt to place core components of your Windows 95 computer to the way it was before you installed IE 4.

Be very careful using IERemove.exe—it should be your last resort when no other method works. Because it does not cleanly uninstall the IE 4 components from your system, your operating system may be left in an unstable condition.

Summary

In order to effectively customize and deploy Internet Explorer 4 to a large number of computers, you need to know how it will be used and how to configure it for individual computers. The Custom installation process controlled by the IEAK is just a modification of the regular installation process described in this chapter, and the features governed by the IEAK are the Internet Explorer, Web View, and Active Desktop features. You should be very familiar with how the IE4Setup.exe program and associated files work, because the purpose of the IEAK is to create a custom installation by modifying those files.

This chapter showed you how to install and configure IE 4 and the modifications it makes to your Windows environment, but the IE 4 Web browser is just one of the components downloaded when you perform a full installation, and just one of the components you can configure with the Internet Explorer Administrator's Kit. In the next chapter you will see how to install and configure the components most often used with IE 4 (Outlook Express, NetShow, NetMeeting, and Microsoft Chat).

Review Questions

1. You have Internet Explorer 3 installed on your Windows 95 computer. You want to upgrade to IE 4. How can you get IE 4? Choose all that apply.

    A. Purchase it on CD-ROM from your local computer software store.

    B. Install it from the Windows 95 installation CD-ROM.

    C. Download it from Microsoft's Web site (www.microsoft.com/ie/download) using IE3.

    D. Download it from Microsoft's FTP site (ftp.microsoft.com/ie/download) using FTP.

2. You want to use Microsoft NetMeeting. Which form of installation should you use?

   A. None. It comes with Windows 95 and Windows NT.

   B. Minimal.

   C. Standard.

   D. Full.

3. You want to use Outlook Express. Which form of installation should you use?

   A. None. It comes with Windows 95 and Windows NT.

   B. Minimal.

   C. Standard.

   D. Full.

4. You want to use IE 4 on a laptop that has very little free disk space. Which form of installation should you use?

   A. None. It comes with Windows 95 and Windows NT.

   B. Minimal.

   C. Standard.

   D. Full.

5. You want to have the Internet FTP protocol on your desktop as well as IE 4. Which form of installation should you use?

   A. None. It comes with Windows 95 and Windows NT.

   B. Minimal.

   C. Standard.

   D. Full.

6. You want to remove Microsoft Chat from your Windows 95 computer. How should you do it? Choose all that apply.

   A. Locate the Microsoft Chat executable file and delete it using the Desktop Explorer.

   B. Launch Add/Remove Programs from the Control Panel and remove the check next to Microsoft Chat.

   C. Run `IE4Setup.exe` and remove the Microsoft Chat component.

   D. Type **IERemove.exe /app:Chat** at the command prompt.

7. You have performed a full installation of IE 4 on your Windows 95 OSR2 computer. You want to reinstall Windows 95 OSR2. What must you do first?

   A. Remove IE 4 and Windows Desktop Update.

   B. Format your hard drive.

   C. Install Windows Desktop Update.

   D. Remove the Program Files/Internet Explorer folder.

8. You want to change the appearance of a folder on your hard drive in Web View. Which file should you modify?

   A. `Mycomp.htt`

   B. `Webview.htt`

   C. `Folder.htt`

   D. `Controlp.htt`

9. You have configured Windows 95 to use Active Desktop. You have installed several Active Desktop components, and you want to disable one. How do you disable an Active Desktop component?

   A. Disconnect from the Internet.

   B. Open the Web tab of the Display Properties page and remove its check mark.

   C. Left-click on that component and select Unsubscribe from the pop-up menu.

   D. Remove Windows Desktop Update using the ACME maintenance mode.

10. How do you subscribe to an Active Channel? Choose all that apply.

    A. Click on a link that refers to a CDF file.

    B. Click on a link that refers to a HTT file.

    C. Select Add to Favorites in the Favorites menu, then choose one of the two page subscription options.

    D. Drag a link to the page into the Channel bar.

11. You want to install IE 4 with minimal prompting during the installation. You have downloaded the IE4Setup.exe program already. What command will achieve your goal?

    A. IE4Setup /quiet

    B. Setup.exe /quiet

    C. IE4wzd.exe /q /c:/x /m:1 /I:n /r:y

    D. IE4Setup /q /c:"IE4wzd.exe /x /q1 /m:1 /I:n /r:y"

12. You have downloaded the IE4Setup.exe program for your Windows 95 and NT computers. You also have an older computer running Windows 3.1 on which you want to install IE 4. What should you do?

    A. Use the IE4Setup.exe program.

    B. Download the Setup.exe program that will install IE 4 on Windows 3.*x* computers.

    C. Download the IE4Win3.exe program that will install IE 4 on Windows 3.*x* computers.

    D. Download IE3, because IE 4 only runs on Windows 95 and Windows NT.

13. How can you get Internet Explorer 4 for Macintosh?

    A. IE 4 is not supported on the Macintosh platform.

    B. www.microsoft.com/ie/download

    C. www.microsoft.com/apple/IE4

    D. ftp.apple.com/microsoft/ie

14. You want to enable passwords so that several people can use the same Windows 95 computer and each have their own set of favorites. How do you enable profiles?

   A. Select Start ➣ Settings ➣ Control Panel ➣ Passwords.

   B. Select Start ➣ Settings ➣ Control Panel ➣ User Manager.

   C. Select Start ➣ Programs ➣ Administrative Tools ➣ User Manager.

   D. Profiles are automatically enabled in Windows 95 when more than one unique password is used to log on.

15. What can't you do in ACME maintenance mode?

   A. Remove IE 4.

   B. Remove an IE 4 component.

   C. Customize IE 4 for distribution.

   D. Add an IE 4 component.

16. You have downloaded IE4Setup.exe to a network share to which the client computers on your network have a drive mapped. You want to install the software without many user interactions. You would like to install Windows Desktop Update and you want it to reboot automatically without prompting the user.

   Required Result: Install IE 4.

   Optional Result 1: Install without many user interactions.

   Optional Result 2: Reboot automatically.

   Suggested Solution: Issue the command IE4Setup.exe /q / c:"ie4wzd.exe /x /qa /m:1 /I:y /r:s".

Which of the following is correct?

A. The suggested solution accomplishes the required result and both optional results.

B. The suggested solution accomplishes the required result and just one optional result.

C. The suggested solution accomplishes the required result only.

D. The suggested solution does not accomplish the required result.

17. Your Intranet Web site uses an ActiveX control that only runs in IE 3. You discover this after upgrading to IE 4. You want to revert back to IE 3 on the computer you use to access the Intranet Web site.

Required Result: Remove IE 4 from the computer.

Optional Result 1: Cleanly uninstall any DLLs installed by IE 4.

Optional Result 2: Restore the previously installed Web browser.

Suggested Solution: Run the IERemove.exe program on the computer.

Which of the following is correct?

A. The suggested solution accomplishes the required result and both optional results.

B. The suggested solution accomplishes the required result and just one optional result.

C. The suggested solution accomplishes the required result only.

D. The suggested solution does not accomplish the required result.

CHAPTER

4

Configuring Custom Components

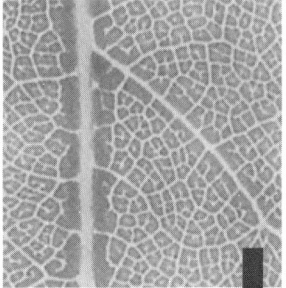

Internet Explorer 4 gives you a powerful interface to the Internet, but there is more to the Internet than just Web pages. You can also exchange e-mail, chat with other Internet users, participate in newsgroups, watch video presentations, and even collaborate on shared projects over the Internet connection. All of these activities require additional Internet tools. Microsoft has provided additional custom components that you can download and use with Internet Explorer 4 to perform these expanded Internet activities.

You need to know what the custom components are and how they are used to effectively customize and troubleshoot their installation. This chapter will describe the following custom components:

- Microsoft Outlook Express

- Microsoft Chat

- Microsoft FrontPage Express

- Microsoft Web Publishing Wizard

- Microsoft NetShow Player

- Microsoft NetMeeting

Microsoft
✓ *Exam*
Objective

Configure Outlook Express for custom installations of Internet Explorer 4.0.

Microsoft Outlook Express

The World Wide Web gets all the Internet hype, but another Internet service, electronic mail (e-mail), has been around for decades longer and is still used more by most Internet users. While the Web turns the Internet into your library, yellow pages, and shopping center, e-mail turns the Internet into your lightning-fast post office. Just as the Web speeds information retrieval tremendously, e-mail speeds correspondence between people.

Microsoft has a number of software products for handling e-mail. Outlook is the latest incarnation of Microsoft's full-featured mail package. In addition to accessing LAN and Internet mail boxes, it integrates personal information management, fax reception, and scheduling. You must purchase Outlook, however, and there are many free e-mail packages available on the Internet.

In order to compete with the free e-mail packages and newsreaders, Microsoft has made a feature-reduced version of Outlook, called Outlook Express, available. (Express, presumably, because it *expresses* less features, not because it runs faster.) When you perform a full installation of Internet Explorer 4, Outlook Express is installed on your computer (see Figure 4.1). You may want to have Outlook Express in addition to Outlook because Outlook Express, unlike Outlook, can handle more than one Internet mail account.

FIGURE 4.1

Outlook Express gives you quick and easy access to Internet mail and newsgroups.

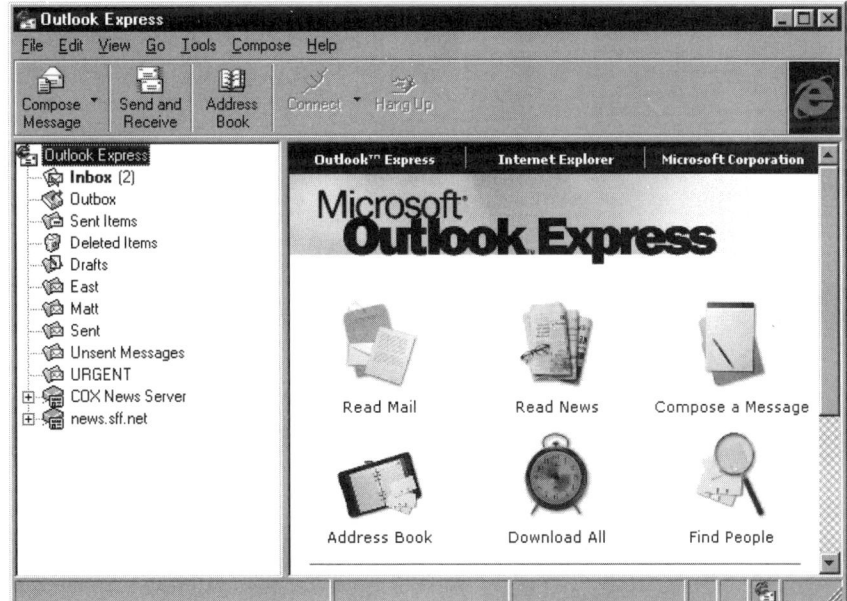

 Outlook Express looks significantly different than Outlook, Microsoft's full-featured e-mail package.

How E-Mail Works

Getting a mail message from your computer to the destination computer across the Internet is an involved procedure. Many different pieces of software and hardware have to cooperate or the message will arrive garbled, go to the wrong place, or not arrive at all. Each component performs a specific and simple task, as follows:

1. You compose the message in a text window. You type the recipient's e-mail address, the subject, and the body of the message. Then you click Send.

2. The e-mail package sends the text message via SMTP to a mail host. Usually all outgoing e-mail from one personal computer is sent to the same mail host, no matter where the eventual destination. On LANs, the PC may first send the message via IMAP to a LAN mail host, which will recognize that the message should go out over the Internet. That IMAP mail sender forwards the message via SMTP (Simple Mail Transfer Protocol) to an Internet mail host. (Some people are lucky enough to have more than one e-mail address. People with mail accounts at work may configure their e-mail software at home to check both their ISP mail host and their work mail host over the Internet. Outlook Express makes it easy to check multiple e-mail accounts.)

3. The Internet mail host looks at the To field in the message to determine its final destination. If it doesn't already know where to send the message (by having sent a message there before or having the destination explicitly specified in its setup), the mail host asks the Internet Domain Name System where to send the message.

4. If the Internet mail host can open a direct connection to the specified mail destination, it sends the message to the destination computer via SMTP. If the mail host must send the message to an intermediate mail

host (one that bridges Internet mail to an Intranet mail system or a LAN e-mail system), the mail host sends it to the intermediate host, which will then forward it to the destination (there may be multiple intermediate mail hosts).

5. If the mail host cannot determine where to send the mail, it returns the mail to the sender. If the destination or intermediate host is unavailable, the mail host will periodically try to send the message and then return the message to the sender.

6. The destination mail host holds the message in a mailbox until the recipient uses a client mail package to retrieve the message using *POP3* (Post Office Protocol 3) or IMAP. Depending on the configuration of the mail package, the retrieved message may be left on the mail host or it may be deleted.

Internet mail was originally designed just to transfer simple text messages. Since computer users often have to exchange more than just text messages, clever programmers soon found ways to encode other kinds of files so that pictures, sound files, and programs could be sent through e-mail as text messages. The early encoding and decoding programs were clumsy to use.

Modern e-mail packages automatically encode and decode other kinds of files and include them in text messages. Other files included in a mail message in this manner are called attachments. MIME (Multipurpose Internet Mail Extensions) is a popular method of constructing mail messages with attachments. The MIME standard describes exactly how to encode the attachments, how to inform the recipient mail package what attachments are included in the message, and what are the contents of those attachments.

E-mail is sent over the Internet as clear text, which means that any intermediate computer can easily read the contents of the message. Another encoding standard, S/MIME (Secure Multipurpose Internet Mail Encoding), describes how a mail package can encrypt a message so that the destination mail package (and only the destination mail package) can decrypt and read the message. S/MIME also provides for digital signatures, which provides assurances that the message actually came from the apparent sender and was not forged or modified through an intermediate computer.

Outlook Express Features

Protocols are how Outlook Express communicates with other mail software. Outlook Express is a full-featured mail package, supporting all of the common protocols used to exchange e-mail on the Internet, including the encryption and HTML protocols. Supported protocols of Outlook Express include:

Simple Mail Transport Protocol (SMTP)   This protocol is used to deliver Internet mail to intermediate mail hosts and to electronic mailboxes.

Post Office Protocol version 3 (POP3)   This protocol is used by mail clients to check Internet mail.

IMAP4   This protocol is used to check LAN-based mail services.

HyperText Markup Language (HTML) Mail   Outlook Express mail messages can contain HTML tags which describe how the mail message should be presented to the user.

MIME HTML (MHTML)   This protocol describes how hypertext referenced content can be embedded directly in the mail message rather than requiring the recipient to retrieve graphics, sound files, and so on separately over the Internet.

Secure Multipurpose Internet Mail Encoding (S/MIME)   This specifies how encrypted and digitally signed mail should be structured and exchanged.

Lightweight Directory Address Protocol (LDAP)   This Internet directory protocol stores lists of people and their Internet addresses, and allows users who connect to the LDAP service to browse the shared list.

NetNews Transport Protocol (NNTP)   This is how Internet News is exchanged between news servers.

The e-mail user is usually more concerned with the features of Outlook Express that make it easy to use. The features include:

- Multiple mailbox support
- Multiple mail server support
- Integration with other Windows software (IE 4 specifically)
- Encryption and authentication support

- The ability to handle rich messages (with graphics and sound), as well as attachments

- Inbox Assistant, which allows the user to set rules that Outlook Express will follow to automatically manage incoming e-mail

Configuring Outlook Express

A full installation of Internet Explorer 4 includes Outlook Express. If you selected an installation of IE 4 that does not include Outlook Express, you can use the steps outlined in Chapter 3 to add it.

Every organization and Internet service provider has a different Internet mail host computer. When installing Outlook Express, you need to specify the host computer you want Outlook Express to check for mail. Likewise, if you are going to use Outlook Express as your newsreader, you must specify the host computer you want Outlook Express to check for news. Outlook Express comes configured with a number of LDAP locations; however, if your organization has its own LDAP directory, you'll need to insert that also.

Selecting the Mailbox and Establishing Servers

You can find most configuration options for Outlook Express under the Tools menu. You set up which servers Outlook Express will connect to from the Accounts menu. You can have separate mail accounts that use different servers and mailboxes for each account, allowing several people to use the same computer to check their mail.

Outlook Express can import many configuration settings from other e-mail packages. In which case, you won't need to configure mail and news server locations, just import the information. Exercise 4.1 walks you through the process of setting up Outlook Express for a user's e-mail and news use.

The first time you run Outlook Express the Internet Connection Wizard may ask you how you want to connect to the Internet. Before you can use Outlook Express you must configure your connection (by giving it dial-up networking settings, LAN settings, or instructing the Wizard to use your current networking settings).

EXERCISE 4.1

Establishing Servers for Outlook Express

Connecting to the Internet

1. The first time you run Outlook Express the Internet Connection Wizard will start. Use the Internet Wizard to configure your current networking connection by following the prompts. Select Next ➤ I Already Have ➤ Next ➤ Finish.

2. Click OK to accept the current location for the Outlook Express mail folder.

Configuring E-Mail

1. Launch Outlook Express by choosing Start ➤ Program Files ➤ Internet Explorer ➤ Outlook Express.

2. Open the Internet Accounts window by choosing Tools ➤ Accounts.

3. Click the Mail tab, and then click Add ➤ Mail.

4. Enter your name as you would like it to appear in the From field of e-mail messages, and then click Next.

5. Enter your e-mail address in the Address field, and click Next.

6. Select POP3.

7. Enter the Internet host name of the POP3 server.

8. Enter the Internet host name of the SMTP server (this may be the same or may be different from the POP3 Internet host), and click Next.

9. Enter the password for the POP3 mail account, and click Next.

10. Enter a name for this mail account.

11. Select an Internet connection method, and click Finish.

Configuring News

1. Click the News tab in the Internet Accounts window (Tools ➤ Accounts).

2. Click Add ➤ News.

EXERCISE 4.1 (CONTINUED)

3. Enter your name as you would like it to appear in the From field of news messages, and click Next.

4. Enter your e-mail address, and click Next.

5. Enter the Internet host name of the news server, and click Next.

6. Enter a name that you can remember for this server, and click Next.

7. Choose an Internet connection method, and click Next.

8. Click Finish.

You can set Outlook Express for more than one user or for more than one e-mail account for each user. Repeat Exercise 4.1 to add more e-mail accounts for a Windows 95 or Windows NT user (a user may have more than one Internet mail account, such as a home account provided by the user's ISP and another account provided by the user's company). If several people use the same Windows 95 or Windows NT computer to check their mail, set up their separate e-mail accounts by logging on to the computer using the user's account name and password, then repeating the process described in Exercise 4.1.

Importing Messages and Address Information from Other Mail Packages

Microsoft Exam Objective

Replace other Internet mail clients. Other mail clients include:

- Internet Mail and News
- Netscape Mail
- Eudora

When you installed Internet Explorer 4 (including Microsoft Outlook Express), your computer may already have had other e-mail clients installed.

Active Setup does not remove these other mail and news packages. Outlook Express will import mail and news settings from the more popular packages. If you would like to remove these other mail and news packages, you'll have to follow the instructions provided with the individual package. You may want to wait to remove these packages until after you have imported their settings into Outlook Express, or you can leave these packages on your computer and set Outlook Express as your default mail and news package.

Outlook Express will import configuration settings from Microsoft Exchange and Microsoft Outlook. Outlook Express will also import connection settings from the following mail packages if it detects them when it is installed:

- Microsoft Exchange

- Microsoft Outlook

- Microsoft Windows Messaging

- Eudora Pro

- Eudora Light

- Netscape Communicator

- Netscape Mail

In addition to migrating connection settings, Outlook Express will also attempt to transfer the saved mail in personal mailboxes established by these software packages. Outlook Express only attempts to do this automatically when it is first installed. However, if later you use these packages and want to transfer the Address Book or saved mail, you will have to use the Outlook Express Import tool or the Address Book Import tool. The Address Book Import tool can import address information in the following formats:

- Eudora Pro or Eudora Light

- LDAP Data Interchange Format

- Microsoft Exchange Personal Address Book

- Microsoft Internet Mail for Windows 3.1 Address Book

- Netscape Address Book

- Netscape Communicator Address Book

- Text File (comma separated)

Engaging LDAP

The Lightweight Directory Access Protocol makes it easier to send messages to other people. LDAP makes it so that you don't have to remember and type the entire e-mail address to send mail to that person. You can type something simpler, such as the person's name, and Outlook Express will look for that name in the directory and retrieve the actual e-mail address.

To the Outlook Express user, LDAP is a lot like a personal address book, except that it is shared with other people on the local network or even with others over the Internet. Many organizations use LDAP to provide a centrally managed list of e-mail addresses and contact information for employees. When an individual's e-mail address changes, the address only needs to be updated once. People sending e-mail to that individual may not even be aware of the change.

Outlook Express comes preconfigured with a number of LDAP servers already installed. You can add a new server to those Outlook Express will check by adding it to the list in the Directory Services tab of the Internet Accounts window.

Configuring Multiple E-Mail and News Accounts

Many people have more than one e-mail account. They may have an e-mail account at work and a personal account at home. In addition, many people are members of service organizations, are going to school, or have other hobbies that warrant a dedicated mail account.

Outlook Express makes it easy to check multiple mail accounts. All you have to do is create another mail account in the Internet Accounts window. You can perform Exercise 4.1 as many times as you have e-mail accounts. Similarly, you can configure Outlook Express to access newsgroups on several different news servers. When you read news, you choose from which server to draw the news.

Navigating Outlook Express

Outlook Express has a visual format that you may recognize from other Microsoft products. A menu at the top of the window with a context-sensitive toolbar underneath gives you access to the tools and functions of the program. The main window is divided into two vertical panes. On the left is a hierarchical view of the folders managed by Outlook Express, and the right pane displays the contents of the folders, with the list of contents on top and an individual entry displayed underneath. See Figure 4.2 for a view of the Outlook Express main program.

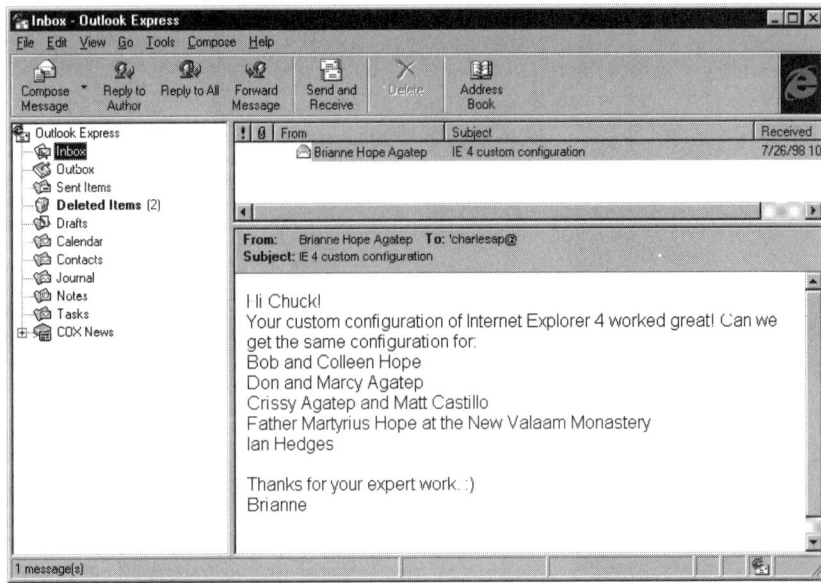

The hierarchical view of the folders displays various mailboxes (Inbox, Outbox, Sent Items) that contain e-mail messages, as well as entries for each of the news servers Outlook Express is configured to use. You navigate through mailboxes and news servers by clicking the entries in the left window pane.

The right window pane displays the contents of the folder selected in the left window pane, and will change to reflect what folder you have selected in the left pane. To view messages you've sent to others, for example, you can click on the Sent Items entry. In the right pane at the top, a list of messages you've sent will be displayed. The highlighted message will be displayed for you to read in the lower portion of the pane. If you want to read news postings in the `comp.os.windows.misc` newsgroup (to which you have subscribed), you can double-click your news server in the left pane and select the newsgroup from the expanded tree. The right window pane will display a list of postings in the newsgroup, and one posting will be displayed in the rest of the pane.

Sending and Receiving Mail

You compose mail by clicking on the Compose Message button in the toolbar of Outlook Express or by selecting Compose ➣ New Message from the Outlook Express menu. Alternatively, you can send messages using

HTML stationery, by selecting Compose ➤ New Message Using, and then selecting Stationery.

When you send an e-mail message, you must specify a recipient. You can type the e-mail address of the recipient directly in the To field of the message, or you can click the Contact Card button next to the field to select from the addresses in your Address Book. You should also enter a short description of what the message is about in the Subject field (this helps the recipient identify the message).

In addition to the text you type into the main area of the text message, you can also use Outlook Express to send attachments. The paper clip icon on the toolbar will allow you to insert a file, as will the Insert menu at the top of the window. When you are done composing the message, you can click the Send button on the toolbar, or from the File menu select Send Message Using or Send Message Later Using. The Send Message Using and Send Later Using options allow you to select which e-mail account to use to send the message, if you have more than one account.

When you send a message, a copy of the message is stored by default in the Sent Items folder. If you have chosen to have the message sent later, when you connect to the Internet, the message will wait in the Outbox until Outlook Express has a chance to send it. New received messages appear in the Inbox.

EXERCISE 4.2

Sending Mail

1. Launch Outlook Express.

2. Click the Compose Message button.

3. Type **SNPIEAK@aol.com** in the To field.

4. Type **Chapter 4 Exercise 2 Completed!** In the Subject field.

5. Type **I have completed Exercise 2 in Chapter 4. I will have my Internet Explorer Administration Kit Certification soon.**

6. Click Send.

Using the Address Book

The Address Book is where you keep e-mail addresses of people with whom you frequently exchange mail. You can create easily remembered aliases such as "mom" or "boss" which Outlook Express will expand to a full e-mail address. In addition, you can create mailing lists that allow you to send the same message to everyone on the list. This way you can send mail to all of the members of your work team, everyone in the Finance department, or all of your friends and relatives without having to type or select all of the recipients individually.

In Outlook Express, you can add entries to the Address Book and edit existing entries by clicking the Contact Card button when composing a message. Or you can add and edit entries by opening the Address Book from the Tools menu by selecting Tools ➤ Address Book. You can add new individual contacts or new groups, add contacts to existing groups, and search for addresses in the Address Book. A contact can have more than one e-mail address, and you can select which address should be used by default.

You can store more than e-mail addresses in the Address Book. Contact information such as mailing addresses, phone numbers, birth dates, Web page URLs, NetMeeting contact information, and digital IDs for authentication and secure communication can be stored in the Address Book.

Managing Mailboxes and Using the Inbox Assistant

New mail arrives in your Outlook Express Inbox by default. In time, if you do nothing but read the messages, messages will pile up in the Inbox, making it difficult to navigate through them. It is good practice to create additional folders and to move mail messages you've read into the appropriate folder or to delete the message to make your mailboxes manageable.

In Outlook Express, you create folders by selecting File ➤ Folder ➤ New Folder. You can also add a folder by right-clicking the entry in the left window panel in which you would like the folder inserted and then selecting New Folder from the pop-up window. You must name the new folder. After you have created the new folder, you can select e-mail messages in the right window pane, drag them to the left pane, and drop them in the newly created folder. Outlook Express will then move the mail message from the Inbox to the new folder.

If you receive a lot of mail from many different sources, moving messages from one folder to another and deleting inappropriate messages can be tedious. More importantly, e-mail messages that you really want to read can get lost in all the unwanted messages. Outlook Express has a feature called the Inbox Assistant that can do much of the work for you. And it can bring important messages to your attention.

From the Tools menu, select Inbox Assistant to create *rules* that Outlook Express can use to determine what mailbox a message should go in and which ones to delete. A rule has two parts: the criteria and the action.

The criteria that must be met before a rule will take effect consists of text to be matched in the To, CC, From, and/or Subject fields. A rule can be in effect for all accounts you have established in Outlook Express, or just for messages larger than a specified size. Alternatively, you can create a rule that will apply for all e-mail messages—this is most useful when you need to forward all your mail to a new address, or when you want everyone who sends you mail to receive an automatically generated reply.

WARNING   Be careful when enabling automatically generated replies to e-mail—if the recipient of the reply also automatically generates a reply you could create an endless exchange of replies, swamping both mailboxes and eating up network capacity.

The action portion of the rule can consist of a number of operations, including:

- Moving the message to a specific folder
- Copying the message to a specific folder
- Forwarding the message to an e-mail address
- Replying to the sender of the message with a generic reply
- Leaving the message on the POP or IMAP server
- Deleting the message from the POP or IMAP server

In Exercise 4.3 you will create a folder called URGENT and create a rule that will automatically move messages with URGENT in the Subject field to that folder.

EXERCISE 4.3

Creating a Folder and Establishing a Rule

1. Launch Outlook Express.

2. Right-click on the root Outlook Express item in the left window pane.

EXERCISE 4.3 (CONTINUED)

3. Select New Folder in the pop-up menu.

4. Enter **URGENT** in the name field, and click OK.

5. Select Tools ➤ Inbox Assistant.

6. Click Add.

7. Type **URGENT** in the Subject field.

8. Select the Move To check box.

9. Click the Folder tab next to the Move To check box.

10. Select the URGENT folder.

11. Click OK in the Move window, and then click OK in the Properties window.

Reading News

Outlook Express must be configured with the location of a news server before you can use it to read news postings (see Exercise 4.1). Once it is configured with the location of a news server, you can subscribe to newsgroups and read the news postings. Different news servers may have different newsgroups available, so Outlook Express can be configured to connect to many different news servers.

Many organizations have news servers that serve only specialized newsgroups for that organization, called private newsgroups. These private newsgroups offer a forum to support collaboration among a widely dispersed group. These private newsgroups are often password protected so only members of the organization can read and post messages.

When you first click on a new news server, Outlook Express will ask you if you want to download a complete list of newsgroups hosted on that server. You can then select and subscribe to specific newsgroups. The groups you subscribe to will show up under the news server entry in the left panel. When you are done subscribing to newsgroups, you can highlight one in the left panel. Messages for that group will appear in the right panel and the text of the selected message will be displayed at the bottom of the right panel.

After reviewing messages in a newsgroup you can post your own replies by clicking on the Compose Message button in the toolbar or selecting New Message from the Compose menu. Describe the contents of the message in the Subject field, and type the text of the message in the text window. You can send it when you are ready by clicking the Post button or selecting Send Message from the File menu. See Figure 4.3 to see a new message being composed.

FIGURE 4.3

You can post messages to Internet newsgroups using Outlook Express.

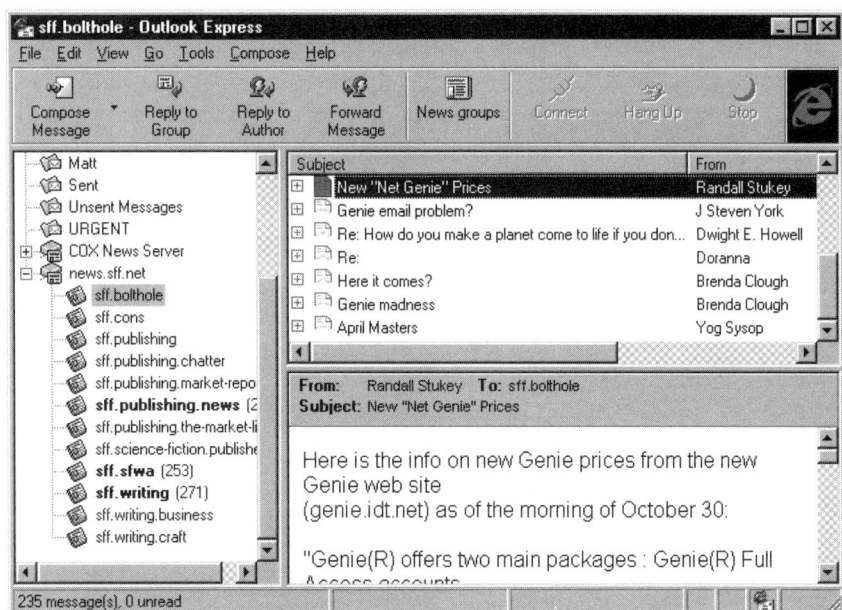

Configuring Filters

Millions of Internet news messages are posted every day. Many individual groups have hundreds of postings daily, and it can be difficult to sort through all of them. Internet news is an anarchy (nobody is really in control), which makes it easy for some individuals to abuse it by posting indiscriminately, or by posting annoying or offensive messages. Fortunately, you don't have to waste time on messages you're not interested in—you can configure Outlook Express to make it appear (on your computer) that those postings don't even exist! (They're still there on the server, but you don't have to look at them.)

You can filter news messages by the person posting the message, the topic(s) of the message, by message length, or by how long the message has been posted. You can have more than one filter, and you can have different filters for different newsgroups. Exercise 4.4 shows you how to configure an e-mail filter.

EXERCISE 4.4

Configuring a Newsgroup Filter

1. Select Tools ➤ Newsgroup Filters.

2. Click Add.

3. Select the newsgroup you want to filter, or leave the Groups field at its default All Groups setting.

4. In the From field, enter the e-mail of the person whose postings you do not want to view, or in the Subject field enter the subject about which you do not want to view postings.

5. Click OK in the Properties window, and click OK in the Newsgroup Filters window.

Setting Security

Sending a message via e-mail is a lot like sending a postcard to someone in another city. Anyone along the way, including the postal workers and the people who share the mailbox at the destination, can read what you have written. Also, the recipient has no way of being sure that you are the person who sent it.

Outlook Express can help you secure your e-mail by using encryption to protect your mail message from being read as it makes its way from your computer to the recipient's computer, much like an envelope protects regular mail letters from being read as they make their way from your mailbox to your mother's. Only the recipient can decrypt and "open" the envelope. With Outlook Express you can digitally "sign" your mail messages so the recipient can be sure that you are the person who sent it. Outlook Express uses the S/MIME protocol and digital IDs to perform both these functions.

Obtaining a Digital ID

Before you can encrypt or sign mail you must receive a digital ID. A digital ID is similar to a driver's license or other personal identification in that it provides assurance that you are who you say you are. Rather than special papers, metal strips, or holography, Outlook Express uses mathematics (prime numbers and public key cryptography) to create digital IDs that are difficult to forge. A computer can check your identity by performing mathematical operations on the digital ID.

You obtain a digital ID from a Certificate Authority (much like you obtain a driver's license from the Department of Motor Vehicles or a credit card from a bank). Exercise 4.5 shows you how to get a trial digital ID.

EXERCISE 4.5

Getting a Trial Digital ID from VeriSign

1. Launch Internet Explorer.

2. Type **www.microsoft.com/ie/ie40/oe/certpage.htm**.

3. Click the VeriSign button.

4. Enter your name in the Name In Digital ID field.

5. Enter your e-mail address in the E-mail Address field.

6. Enter a *challenge phrase* that you can use to revoke your digital ID. (A challenge phrase is a special password that you can provide to revoke your digital ID in case it is later compromised by a hacker or another network miscreant.)

7. Enter your country, zip code, date of birth, and gender.

8. Select the 60-day free trial ID.

9. Read the terms of the trial agreement, and click Accept.

10. Launch Outlook Express.

11. Click the Send and Receive Mail button.

12. Open your Inbox, and select the mail message from VeriSign.

13. Go to the IE 4 window, and click the Install button.

14. Go to Outlook Express, and click Tools ➤ Accounts.

EXERCISE 4.5 (CONTINUED)

15. Select the mail account you want to use for secure mail, and then click the Properties button.

16. Select the Security tab.

17. Select the Use a Digital ID check box.

18. Click the Digital ID button.

19. Select the certificate you just received, and click OK.

20. Click Apply, and then click OK.

Sending Signed Mail

Once you have a digital ID installed in Outlook Express, you can send digitally signed mail and encrypted mail. Mail recipients can verify your digital signature by checking with the Certificate Authority from which you received the ID (such as VeriSign). You can send your digital ID to others by sending a signed message.

To send a signed message, compose the message just as you would any other message. But before you send the message, select Tools ➤ Digitally Sign in the Message window, or click the signature icon in the toolbar. A small ribbon will appear at the end of the Subject line, indicating that the message has been signed.

If you have several mail accounts defined in Outlook Express, you must use one that has been configured for digital ID. You can have different digital IDs for separate e-mail accounts, and a single e-mail account can have several digital IDs.

Receiving Signed Mail

Digitally signed mail will show up in your inbox just like any other mail message. You can tell that a message is digitally signed because it has a small ribbon on it in the list view and a larger ribbon icon in the expanded view of the mail message. You can examine the certificate by right-clicking the ribbon icon. From the pop-up menu you can verify the digital signature and establish whether or not you trust that digital ID. A digital ID that uses Veri-Sign as a Certificate Authority is probably trustworthy, but you should think twice about using software that has been signed with a digital ID that uses an unfamiliar Certificate Authority, such as NoGoodNiks Inc.

The first time you receive a digitally signed e-mail, Outlook Express will present you with a message informing you that the e-mail is signed. You can select to disable the message so that it will not appear with subsequent digitally signed e-mail messages.

When you receive a digitally signed message you can add the digital signature to your Address Book by opening the Properties window for that message, selecting the Security tab, and then clicking the Add Digital ID button.

Sending and Receiving Encrypted Mail

Sending encrypted mail is similar to sending digitally signed mail, except that both you and the recipient must have digital IDs, and the sender must have the public portion of the recipient's digital ID.

A digitally signed e-mail message contains the public portion of the signer's ID. This means that for someone to send you an encrypted message, you need to send them a digitally signed message first, and vice versa.

You send an encrypted message just as you would a signed message, by composing the message, and then clicking the Encrypt Message button, or by selecting Tools ➤ Encrypt Message from the New Message window.

Encrypted messages will show up in your Inbox like any other message, except there will be a little lock icon next to the message in the message list, and a larger lock icon will appear in the top portion of the message itself. (The first time you receive an encrypted message Outlook Express will give you helpful instructions for handing encrypted messages.) Outlook Express handles the details of encrypting and decrypting the mail messages. You can send and receive messages as usual, except for the act of specifying that encryption take place.

Security Zones

Since Outlook Express mail and news messages can contain active HTML data, such as Java applets and ActiveX controls, you have to be careful about the origin of those applets and ActiveX controls. A malicious individual could conceivably create applets or controls that do damage to your file system or operating system, or that retrieve information from your hard drive and send the data onto the Internet.

To help combat this problem Outlook Express lets you define security zones and control what kinds of active HTML features will be allowed in each security zone. (See Chapter 3 for an overview of the security zones, and Chapter 8 for a more detailed exploration of security, including zones. The options in Outlook Express for mail and news are the same as for Internet Explorer 4 active HTML features.

Microsoft Chat

The Web is similar to a library, a place you can get information about just about anything. Internet mail is similar to paper and postal worker–based mail in that it enables people to exchange messages over great distances. Internet news is similar to a great big cork bulletin-board to which anyone can post messages. Is there an Internet-based communications service that is like the telephone, allowing immediate communication between people? Of course there is!

Internet Relay Chat (IRC) is similar to a conference call by allowing real-time conversations over channels. IRC gives each Internet user a text console which receives and displays what each user has typed. Some IRC clients even allow users to be graphical cartoon characters, with the dialog arranged in a layout similar to a comic strip. Conversations over IRC are arranged into "channels," like citizen-band (CB) radio, except that each channel has a name rather than a number. Everyone in a channel can see what is "said" by other people in the channel. Channels in IRC are very much like "rooms" in online service–based systems such as America Online or CompuServe.

How Do You Use Microsoft Chat?

Microsoft Chat is Microsoft's implementation of an Internet Relay Chat client. A full installation of Internet Explorer 4 includes Microsoft Chat. If you did not select a full installation of IE 4, you can add Microsoft Chat by following the instructions for adding components in Chapter 3.

When you first launch Microsoft Chat, you are requested to specify a chat server to which it should connect. Microsoft Chat requires a server to coordinate the messages of multiple chat clients and to provide a listing of channels in which the clients participate. The default server is `mschat.msn.com`, but you can enter almost any IRC server because Microsoft Chat uses the IRC protocol to exchange chat information.

In the server selection screen, you are also given the option of going to a specific channel (also called a chat room) or of seeing a listing of all the rooms supported by that chat server. From the list you can select the channel that interests you.

Once you are in a chat room, you can choose to view conversations in text mode or in cartoon mode (see Figures 4.4 and 4.5). You can leave the chat room and enter other chat rooms, or even enter other chat rooms without leaving the first chat room. Microsoft Chat's tabs allow you to follow multiple conversations at one time. A small right panel shows which people are listening or talking in the currently selected chat room.

FIGURE 4.4

Microsoft Chat gives you a forum for immediate conversation.

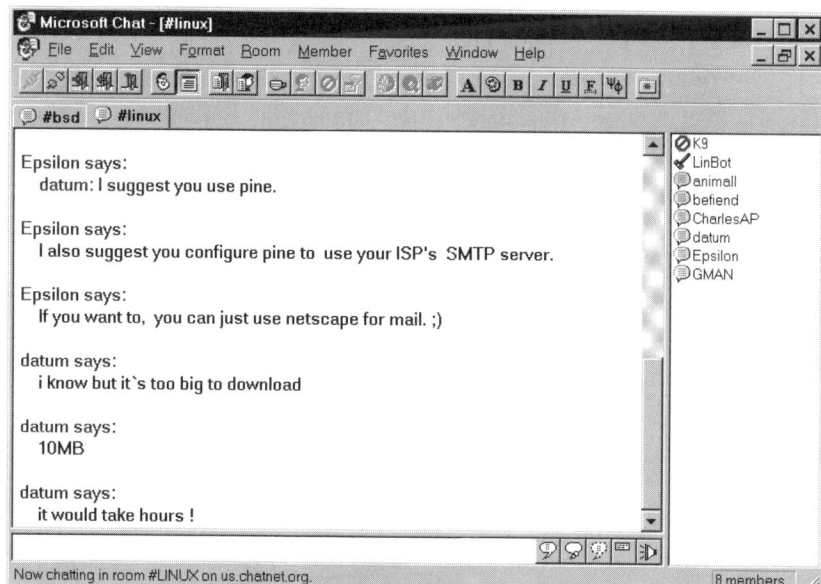

Microsoft Chat gives you a graphical view of the conversation in cartoon-strip format.

When you first begin using Microsoft Chat, you may want to configure your chat profile so that people who talk with you can know a little bit about you. You can view the profile of a person in the chat room by selecting that person's name on the list of participants and clicking the Get Profile button. Likewise, people in the chat room can also view your profile.

With Microsoft Chat, you can also select which cartoon character will represent you in the cartoon view of the chat room. As the conversation progresses, you can change the character's expression from neutral to happy, happy to angry, angry to surprised, and...

Microsoft Chat allows you to do more than just send messages for everyone to read in chat rooms. You can also "whisper" messages to specific individuals in the room, create new chat rooms, kick people out of chat rooms (if you have sufficient privilege to do so), and invite people who have logged on to that IRC server but haven't entered the room to come to the private chat room and join in on the conversation.

Microsoft FrontPage Express

Creating simple Web pages manually with a text editor is easy. However, graphically rich pages and pages with complicated *markups* (HTML tags) are more difficult, and they can be arduous to debug manually.

Without specialized Web development tools (whether the page is simple or complex), you must use a text editor to create the HTML and a Web browser to view your pages.

Microsoft provides a professional quality Web site creation tool called FrontPage to address the need for automated Web page editing and link maintenance. FrontPage is a commercial product, but Microsoft provides FrontPage Express with Internet Explorer 4 at no additional cost. FrontPage Express is a version of FrontPage with less functionality. FrontPage Express consists of what is the FrontPage Editor in the full software, but it does not include tools to help you view and manage the network of links that bind entire Web sites together.

Web site creation tools, such as FrontPage and FrontPage Express (see Figure 4.6), are to Web creation what Word is to word processing. With FrontPage Express, or a similar tool, creating Web pages is nearly as simple as using a word processor to write a brochure.

FIGURE 4.6

FrontPage Express is a useful tool for Web page creation.

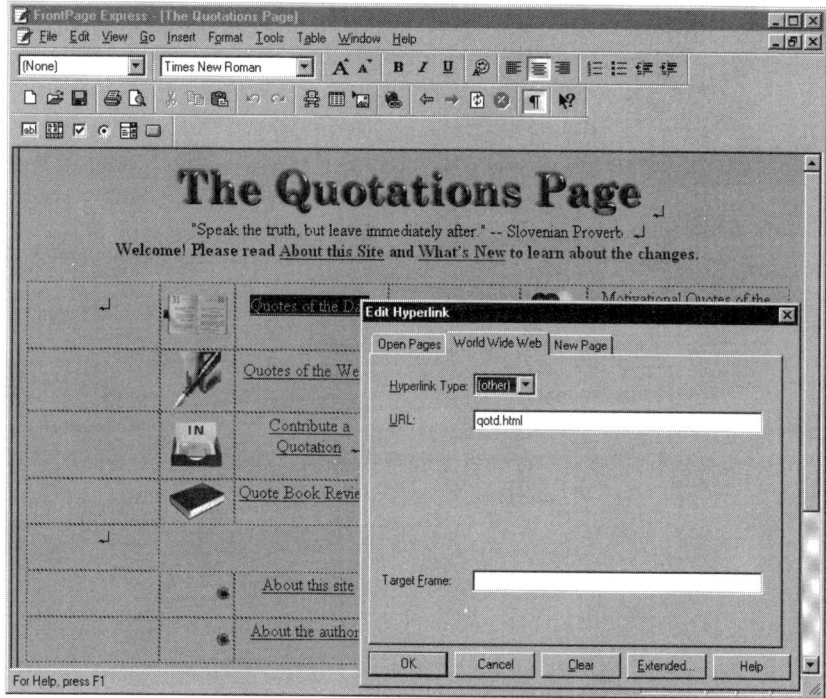

FrontPage Express is missing an important component. It does not have a built-in utility to create, convert, or manage graphics. It will allow you to assign a default graphical editor, but the editor has to conform to the way FrontPage launches external software programs in order to work correctly. Many popular graphics editors don't work correctly with FrontPage, so when you double-click a graphics file, the editor will not open a file.

Creating Webs with FrontPage Express

Working with FrontPage Express is easy. FrontPage Express organizes your work into *webs,* collections of HTML pages and files that combine to accommodate a specific purpose. You should think of each web as a separate project.

FrontPage uses the templates similar to the templates used in the other Office applications to help jump-start your project. Microsoft has incorporated typical Web-site requirements into these templates so you can put together a Web site by simply filling in content unique to your organization.

Web templates are great for getting information onto the Internet in a hurry—but don't expect your site to look distinctive or unique. Web sites obviously based on FrontPage templates are cropping up all over the Net. If you want your site to be memorable, you'll have to do the hard work of designing the Web site yourself.

Exercise 4.6 shows you how to create a new Web site based on one of the built-in Web templates.

EXERCISE 4.6

Creating a Web Site with FrontPage

1. Select Start ≻ Programs ≻ Internet Explorer ≻ FrontPage Express ≻ File ≻ New.

2. Select Personal Home Page Wizard, and then click OK.

3. Select Personal Interests, and click Next.

4. Type **home1.htm** in the Page URL input box and **My Home Page** in the Page Title input box, and click next.

5. Clear all check marks except for Job Title, and click Next.

6. Select Bullet List, and click Next.

7. Enter several items of interest to you, and click Next.

8. Enter your e-mail address, URL, and phone number, and click Next.

9. Select Use Link, enter your e-mail address again, and then click Next.

10. Accept the order of home page sections, and click Next.

11. Click Finish.

Now that you have a template Web site in place, you're ready to work with FrontPage to modify the site for your requirements. Exercise 4.7 shows you how to work with the Web site you created in Exercise 4.6. You can finish working with this Web site at your leisure.

EXERCISE 4.7

Working with FrontPage

1. Launch FrontPage Express, and open the demo page you created.

2. Highlight Home Page 1, and replace it with your name.

3. Highlight the Employee Information section, and delete it.

4. Right-click the link to Sample Site 1, and select Hyperlink Properties from the pop-up window.

5. In the World Wide Web tab, replace the Page URL with www.altavista .digital.com, and click OK.

6. Select Files ➤ Save As ➤ As File ➤ Save to save your Web page.

In Exercise 4.6, you edited the Web page using FrontPage Express, which does not always display the information the way a Web browser displays it. You should always check your work in a browser before you post it for public display. Although the FrontPage Express display is similar to that of a Web browser, many minute differences can affect the way your page is viewed. Contrast the page shown in Figure 4.7 with Figure 4.8 to compare a Web page shown in FrontPage Editor with the same page shown in Internet Explorer. Notice that the spacing of the text differs slightly. You should always preview your site in all available Web browsers and platforms so that you know how your site will look to your audience.

FIGURE 4.7

A Web page previewed In FrontPage Express

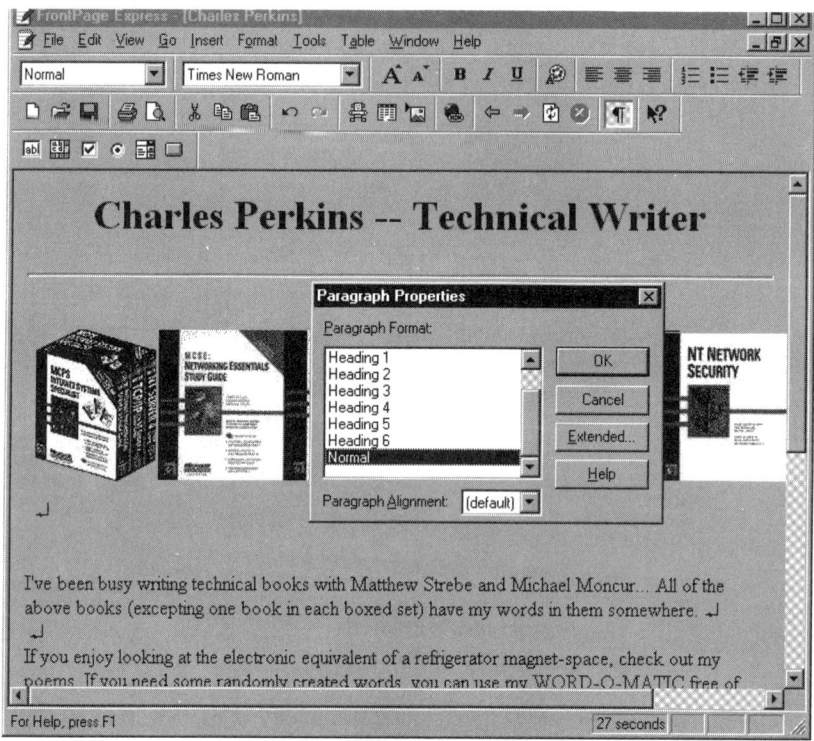

FIGURE 4.8

The same Web page
(as Figure 4.7) pre-
viewed in Internet
Explorer

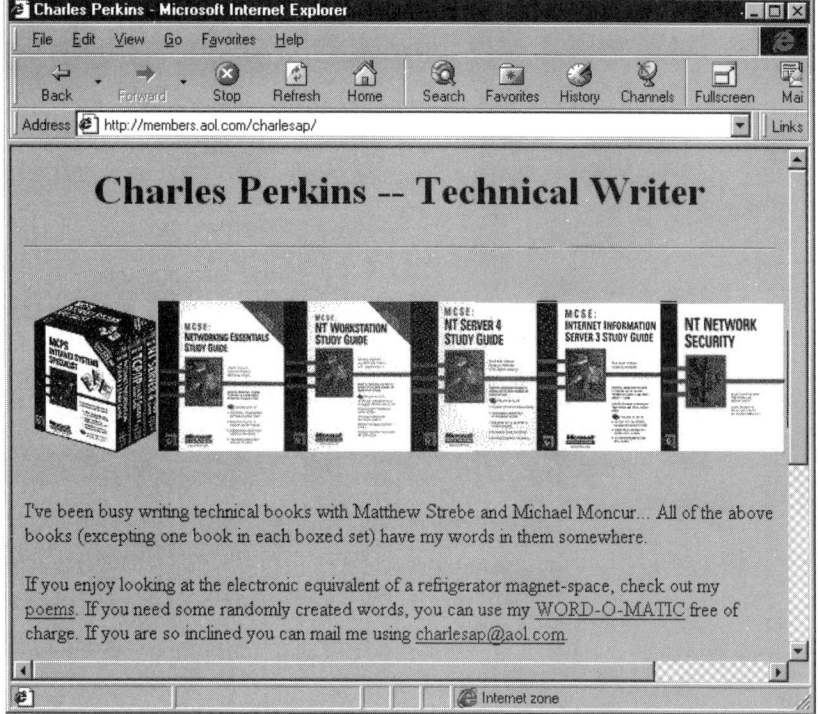

Microsoft Web Publishing Wizard

Once you have created several Web pages, you will want to make those pages available on a Web server or Internet service. The Microsoft Web Publishing Wizard will help you "post" your pages to your Internet Web server.

Most Internet service providers allow for clients to use FTP to update their own Web pages. Some Internet Web servers require special protocols or additional information in order to post Web pages to the server. The Web Publishing Wizard has configuration information for the following Web page services (more configuration information is available on Microsoft's Web site):

- America Online
- America Online Primehost
- CompuServe
- GNN
- Sprynet

Exercise 4.8 walks you through the process of posting the Web page you created to a Web service. Some steps may vary when you upload the Web page since some services are configured differently for Web page update.

EXERCISE 4.8

Publishing a Web Page with the Web Publishing Wizard

1. Launch the Web Publishing Wizard (click Start ➤ Programs ➤ Internet Explorer ➤ Web Publishing Wizard), and click Next.

2. Enter the directory path of the page you created in Exercise 4.6, and click Next.

3. Enter a name for the Web site, and click Next.

4. Enter the URL where the HTML files will be placed.

5. Enter the location on your hard drive where the local copy of the files is stored (this location must already exist), and click Next.

6. Enter the FTP server name and personal subfolder where your HTML files are stored on the remote Web server, and click Next.

7. Click Finish.

8. Enter your ISP account name and password, and click Next for FrontPage Express to upload the Web files.

Microsoft NetShow Player

With Internet Explorer 4 you have a library, with Outlook Express you have a post office, with News you have a bulletin board, and with Chat you have a telephone. But what about television? Is there an Internet counterpart to TV? Yes there is!

Microsoft's NetShow Player lets you watch audio-video streams over the Internet. You can launch NetShow from the Start menu (Start ➤ Programs ➤ Internet Explorer ➤ NetShow Player), or you can open a Web page that contains an Active Streaming Format item (the embedded version of NetShow player will display the video and audio in the browser).

Like the other components described in this chapter, a full installation of Internet Explorer 4 includes NetShow Player. After the initial installation, there is little configuration for you to do in NetShow Player, except perhaps to specify a proxy server address and port if a proxy server resides between your computer and the Internet.

Microsoft Wallet

With Internet Explorer 4, buying products over the Internet has never been easier. Microsoft has integrated a virtual extension of your wallet into IE 4. It stores purchasing information such as your name, mailing address, phone number, and credit card numbers. Whether or not this is a good thing is open to debate. At your direction, IE 4 can automatically present the purchasing information to remote Internet servers so that you can buy things over the Internet by just clicking on a link.

There is no separate program to manage Microsoft Wallet. You will find the Wallet information in View ➤ Internet Options ➤ Content in Internet Explorer 4. Two new buttons, Addresses and Payments, allow you to enter the information for commercial Internet transactions.

From the Addresses button you enter contact information just as you do in the Address Book. In fact, if you already have an entry for yourself in the Address Book, you can simply select that entry, and it will be imported into the Addresses window.

You can store several credit cards in the Payment Options window. The four types of cards supported by Microsoft Wallet are Visa, MasterCard, American Express, and Discover. You can supply credit card numbers for several of each card.

Microsoft NetMeeting

Microsoft NetMeeting, similar to Microsoft Chat, provides for real-time communications between individuals, but NetMeeting goes beyond simple text or cartoon graphics. With NetMeeting, two people can share applications and documents, send files to each other, draw on a shared whiteboard, and even view each other using real-time video streams from one computer to the other.

Microsoft Exam Objective

Choose the appropriate configurations for the NetMeeting client. Configurations include:

- Internet Locator Service (ILS) server connectivity
- IP connectivity
- Peer-to-peer networking
- Proxy server settings
- Proxy client settings

Microsoft Exam Objective

Configure NetMeeting for various tasks. Tasks include:

- Multi-point application sharing
- Transferring files
- Videoconferencing

The primary use for NetMeeting is Web videoconferencing using video cameras and microphones. In order to operate with other videoconferencing equipment and software, NetMeeting complies with videoconferencing standards, including the H.323 standard for audio support and the T.120 standard for video. In order to allow people who want to videoconference to find each other, NetMeeting also supports the LDAP protocol for communicating with *Internet Locator Servers* (ILS), which are Internet servers that provide directory services for Internet users much like phone books do for telephone users.

Configuring NetMeeting

The first time you start NetMeeting after it has been installed on a computer, the NetMeeting Configuration Wizard will prompt you for information that is needed for NetMeeting to run. You will be asked which ILS server NetMeeting should connect to when it is launched. The Wizard will ask you for your own contact information (so other users of the ILS server can find you), and you will be asked to identify the speed of your connection to the Internet. If NetMeeting detects a sound card, the NetMeeting Configuration Wizard will call up the Audio Tuning Wizard to configure the NetMeeting audio parameters. Exercise 4.9 walks you through the process of setting up NetMeeting.

EXERCISE 4.9

Configuring NetMeeting

1. Launch Microsoft NetMeeting.

2. Click Next in the introduction screen.

3. Select the Log On to a Directory Server option.

4. Leave the directory server location at its default value, and click Next.

5. Enter your contact information (first name, last name, etc.), and click Next.

6. Select the For Personal Use option, and click Next.

7. Select the option reflecting your Internet connection speed, and click Next.

8. If you have a sound card, configure your audio settings using the Audio Tuning Wizard.

9. Click Finish.

Microsoft NetMeeting uses the Internet Protocol (IP) to make the connection to the ILS server and also to make the conferencing connection to the other computer(s) in the meeting. NetMeeting does not have a configuration option for going through a traditional proxy server like Internet Explorer 4 does—NetMeeting expects to connect directly to the ILS server and to the other meeting participants. In addition, for audio and video conferences, NetMeeting opens TCP ports that may not be determined in advance. This means that in order to allow videoconferencing, you have to open up all the ports in your firewall. This greatly weakens the ability of the firewall to protect your network from intrusion from the Internet.

Normal proxy servers will not correctly handle the H.323 and LDAP protocols, so if you want to perform videoconferencing through a strict firewall or isolate computers on your LAN by hiding their network addresses, you will need to use a specialized proxy server that supports the H.323 and LDAP (for ILS) protocols. There is no special proxy client software to use—you configure the NetMeeting software to access the videoconferencing proxy server rather than the LDAP server and it redirects the IP connections.

Establishing a Meeting

When you launch NetMeeting and it connects to an ILS server using the LDAP protocol, the main window will show a list of users (hosting and participating) in NetMeeting sessions on that server. You can host a meeting yourself by selecting Call ➢ Host Meeting in the Microsoft NetMeeting window, or you can join another meeting by selecting Call ➢ New Call.

The Internet Locator Server acts as a general meeting point and contact reference for NetMeeting and Outlook Express users (to Outlook Express users the ILS server looks like an address book that is shared by everybody on the network). The contact information in the server is supplied by the clients when they connect to the server, so all a user has to do is connect to the server to be visible to other users.

Although NetMeeting is set up for you to connect to an ILS server when you start the program, you don't have to connect to a user registered on the ILS server. When you select New Call, you can enter the ILS entry (for registered users) or enter the Internet address or telephone number of users for peer-to-peer NetMeeting conferencing that is not mediated by the ILS server.

The NetMeeting window for an in-progress meeting consists of audio and recording volume levels, a small video display area, and a list of users. From the Tools menu, you can display a shared whiteboard on which the meeting participants can draw, a Microsoft Chat session so participants can type messages to each other, and file transfer directory options for exchanging files. The Options window allows you to change your personal profile as well as the calling, audio, and video settings.

Configuring NetMeeting Options

As an administrator of NetMeeting software (or as a NetMeeting user), you may want to configure the behavior of NetMeeting to match your conferencing needs. The Options window (select Tools ➤ Options in the NetMeeting window) contains the following six tabs for configuring various aspects of NetMeeting behavior:

General   This tab configures how NetMeeting starts up, how it handles incoming calls, how much bandwidth it can expect to have available, and where to put transferred files.

My Information   This tab holds your contact information (including your name, address, and e-mail address).

Calling   This tab defines the default ILS server that NetMeeting will connect to and whom NetMeeting will attempt to automatically connect to (using speed dial).

Audio   This tab can launch the Audio Tuning Wizard, control microphone sensitivity, and configure an H.323 gateway.

Video   This tab configures whether videoconferencing automatically starts when you establish a meeting, controls the size and quality of video images, and selects the video-capture device to be used.

Protocols   This tab is where you can enable or disable conferencing over a direct serial cable or over the Internet (TCP/IP).

Sharing and Conferencing

Conferencing requires two or more participants. Microsoft Chat (described earlier in this chapter) is useful when several people want to converse (textually) over the Internet. NetMeeting goes beyond multiparty text conversations—with NetMeeting, several people can talk to each other (audio conferencing), exchange audio as well as video (videoconferencing), and even cooperatively work on shared documents, drawings, programs, and shared windows or programs (multipoint data conferencing).

Before you can exchange audio and video, both parties must have appropriately configured audio and video hardware. Unfortunately, there is no standard audio or video hardware or software distributed with every PC. Most PC-compatible audio and video hardware comes with drivers for Windows 95, 98, or NT, and NetMeeting will use standard Windows audio devices and most video devices that capture the video to main memory in a standard frame buffer format rather than using special video overlay modes (which bypass main memory). How these devices are configured are detailed in their own manuals, of course.

Sharing the whiteboard, file sharing, and sharing applications that are NetMeeting enabled does not require special hardware support (other than having a working network connection, of course). First a NetMeeting meeting must be established, and then users can join the meeting and share the whiteboard, chat sessions, files, or applications. Exercises 4.10 and 4.11 show a conferencing session. Exercise 4.10 you will establish a NetMeeting session, and in Exercise 4.11 you will connect to an already established NetMeeting session.

EXERCISE 4.10

Establishing a Call, Receiving a File, and Using the Whiteboard

1. Start Microsoft NetMeeting.

2. Connect to the Internet Locator Server ils.microsoft.com.

3. Select Call ➤ Host Meeting.

4. Wait an appropriate length of time for the other user to send a file, and then select Tools ➤ File Transfer ➤ Open Received Files.

EXERCISE 4.10 (CONTINUED)

5. Double-click the file to open it.

6. Select Tools ➤ Whiteboard.

7. Draw a happy face.

EXERCISE 4.11

Connecting to a Meeting and Sending a File

1. Launch Microsoft NetMeeting.

2. Connect to the Internet Locator Server ils.microsoft.com.

3. Select Call ➤ New Call.

4. Enter the e-mail address or LDAP name of the individual performing Exercise 4.10, and then click Call.

5. Select Tools ➤ File Transfer ➤ Send File.

6. Select a file to send, and then click Send.

Summary

For Internet collaboration, e-mail exchange, news reading, Web publishing, purchasing products, and video watching, Microsoft has supplied some additional software packages to accompany Internet Explorer 4. The component that receives the most use is Outlook Express, for reading e-mail and news postings.

Now you have a good feeling for the components that come with Internet Explorer 4, and how to configure and use these components. In Chapter 5, you will plan how to customize and provide these components to your organization or customers.

Review Questions

1. You want to send encrypted mail over the Internet. What do you need in order to configure Outlook Express to encrypt and decrypt the mail for you?

    A. A hardware encryption dongle

    B. The Pretty Good Privacy encryption tool suite

    C. A digital ID from a Certificate Authority

    D. The Microsoft Encryption Client software package

2. You have performed a full installation of IE 4. You want to watch ASF video streams over the Internet. What additional tool do you have to install?

    A. Microsoft NetMeeting

    B. Nothing, because Microsoft NetMeeting is already installed.

    C. Microsoft NetShow

    D. Nothing, because Microsoft NetShow is already installed.

3. Which component does not come as a separate program, but is available as a part of Internet Explorer 4?

    A. Microsoft NetShow

    B. Microsoft Wallet

    C. Microsoft Chat

    D. Microsoft Outlook Express

4. You routinely send identical status update e-mail messages to everyone in your department. You want to do this with minimal effort. What is the most efficient way to send the message to each of your coworkers?

    A. Type the message once, copy it to the clipboard, and paste it into a message for each recipient.

    B. Type the message once. Type the e-mail address of each recipient into the To field.

    C. Create a group in the Address Book. Add each coworker to the group. Send the message to the group.

    D. Send the message to the first person in the group with a note at the bottom requesting them to forward it to the next person in the group.

5. You see a little ribbon next to an e-mail message you have received in Outlook Express. What does the ribbon mean?

    A. The message is important.

    B. The message is an award winner.

    C. The message is encrypted.

    D. The message is digitally signed.

6. You don't want to see any Internet news messages from a particularly offensive newsgroup member. What can you do so that you never view messages from this person?

    A. E-mail the person, and ask them to stop being offensive.

    B. E-mail the person's Internet service provider and ask that their account be terminated.

    C. Create a filter that blocks posts from that user.

    D. Create a filter that removes posts from that user from Internet news servers.

7. Which of the following is not a field that you can base a mail rule in Outlook Express?

   A. Subject

   B. To

   C. From

   D. Date Sent

8. You have a video camera that you want to use for videoconferencing over the Net. What package should you use?

   A. Microsoft NetMeeting

   B. Microsoft NetShow

   C. Microsoft Exchange

   D. Microsoft Outlook Express

9. Which of the following e-mail packages will Outlook Express import mail messages from? Choose all that apply.

   A. Outlook

   B. Netscape Communicator

   C. Eudora Light

   D. Microsoft Exchange

10. Which credit cards is Microsoft Wallet configured to handle? Choose all that apply.

   A. Visa

   B. MasterCard

   C. American Express

   D. Discover

11. What Microsoft tool helps you manage your personal Internet mail?

    A. Inbox Assistant

    B. Web Publishing Wizard

    C. Exchange Server

    D. Microsoft Bob

12. You maintain a copy of your personal Web site on your computer. You make changes to your Web pages on your computer and then upload them to your Web space on your Internet service provider. You have been using FTP to copy the files one by one. What tools can help you manage and move the Web pages more efficiently?

    A. Inbox Assistant

    B. Web Publishing Wizard

    C. FrontPage Express

    D. Personal Web Server

13. How do you configure Microsoft Wallet with your financial and Contact information?

    A. Select Start ➤ Programs ➤ Internet Explorer ➤ Microsoft Wallet, and enter the information in the Contacts and Payments tabs.

    B. Enter the information in the Addresses and Payments sections by selecting View ➤ Internet Options ➤ Content.

    C. Enter the information in the Addresses and Payments tabs by selecting View ➤ Microsoft Wallet.

    D. Enter the information by selecting File ➤ Security ➤ Financial.

14. You want to edit your home page on your Internet service provider. What tool that comes with IE 4 can you use?

A. Outlook Express

B. FrontPage Express

C. FrontPage

D. Web Publishing Wizard

15. You want to talk with other people over the Internet using IRC. What program that comes with IE 4 can you use?

A. Microsoft NetMeeting

B. Microsoft Chat

C. Microsoft IRC

D. Outlook Express

16. You want to encrypt the communications between your sales people (who have laptops and use the Internet to communicate with the main office) and the office. You also want the sales force to be certain that e-mail messages they receive from the home office actually came from the home office and were not forged by a hacker. You would also like to provide for encrypted file transfers.

Required Result: Establish encrypted e-mail exchange.

Optional Result 1: Provide for e-mail authentication.

Optional Result 2: Encrypt FTP data transfers.

Suggested Solution: Install Outlook Express on all of the sales laptops and on the main office computers. Obtain digital certificates for each and install them. Send a digitally signed message from the main office to the sales force, and reply to the main office with a digitally signed message.

Which of the following is correct?

A. The suggested solution accomplishes the required result and both optional results.

B. The suggested solution accomplishes the required result and just one optional result.

C. The suggested solution accomplishes the required result only.

D. The suggested solution does not accomplish the required result.

17. As the network administrator, you have to deal with a tremendous amount of e-mail. You want to prioritize the e-mail so that you can deal with urgent messages first, routine e-mail later, and UFO-interest-L mailing list mail at your leisure. You also want to discard all mail that comes from the `spam.net` domain.

Required Result: Route urgent mail to the URGENT folder.

Optional Result 1: Delete mail originating from the `spam.net` domain.

Optional Result 2: Move mail from the mailing list to the LIST folder.

Suggested Solution: In Outlook Express create two new folders— URGENT and LIST. Create three rules: 1) move mail containing URGENT in the subject field to the URGENT folder; 2) move mail containing UFO-interest-L in the source field to the LIST folder; 3) delete mail containing `spam.net` in the source field. Inform network users that priority mail should contain URGENT in the subject field.

Which of the following is correct?

A. The suggested solution accomplishes the required result and both optional results.

B. The suggested solution accomplishes the required result and just one optional result.

C. The suggested solution accomplishes the required result only.

D. The suggested solution does not accomplish the required result.

CHAPTER

5

Planning for Deployment

A little bit of planning can save a lot of effort when you build a custom version of Internet Explorer 4 for your LAN, ISP, or software package. You need to know the customization options and the settings required for your situation before you can begin, otherwise you may end up with an inappropriate or unusable custom IE 4 package.

In planning the deployment of Internet Explorer 4, you need to select your licensing mode for the Internet Explorer Administration Kit—that choice limits the options you have in the IEAK and puts legal restrictions on how you can deploy IE 4. You must decide whether Windows Desktop Update will be installed automatically, how much customization you will perform on the browser (with or without ADU), and what you intend to do with other clients and browsers that may already be installed on the computer. Finally, you must plan whether and how you will install additional Internet software such as Outlook Express and NetMeeting.

Planning Overview

This chapter will help you develop a plan for deploying Internet Explorer 4 to computers in your network or to customer computers (if you manage an Internet service provider or develop Internet content). To plan the successful deployment of Internet Explorer 4 you need to do the following:

1. Assemble your deployment team.

2. Evaluate the capability of computers on your network to run the new software.

3. Identify the settings and features needed by prospective users.

4. Anticipate compatibility issues and deployment hurdles.

5. Choose a distribution strategy.

6. Identify security hazards, establish a security policy, and determine security settings for software.

7. Identify groups of users and computers with different software settings requirements. Establish which groups merit customized configurations.

8. Create a schedule with milestones and responsibilities.

The Deployment Team

Your deployment team will need to include professionals who can develop and test the deployment plan, train the users, deploy the software, and provide support after the software is installed. The size of your team will depend upon support-staff resources as well as the size and complexity of your organization. Corporate administrators of large networks or administrators for ISPs and ICPs with a substantial customer base will need people with a wide variety of skills, including software installation and configuration, troubleshooting, hardware upgrading, and personable customer/user support.

Hardware Capability

For you to deploy Internet Explorer 4 to computers in your organization, you must make sure that the computers are capable of running the software. You should be familiar with the memory, disk space, operating system, and processing requirements of IE 4 as outlined in Chapter 3. Record the CPU type, disk capacity, OS type and service pack level, and amount of memory of each of the computers. Your team should gather information and make preparations to upgrade any computers that don't meet the minimum requirements.

Needed Settings and Features

Before deciding to fully implement Internet Explorer 4, the needs of your organization and users must be clearly identified. For the ICP or ISP the options are limited—the custom Internet Explorer 4 package must be able to operate on personal computers that have been configured in ways you cannot foresee. An ICP or ISP will primarily be interested in expanding the capability of IE 4 and customizing IE 4 to more closely tie it with the product or service of that ICP or ISP. See the "Planning the Deployment for Internet Service Providers" section in this chapter for specific features of IE 4 that an ICP or ISP may want to use.

A corporate administrator, on the other hand, has more leeway for making changes to the basic Internet Explorer 4 configuration, because the corporate administrator has more control over how the computer will be used. However, the corporate administrator isn't free to do just anything—the computers must remain useful so that the users can do their jobs. The primary purpose of the administrator is to provide the software and hardware tools, as well as network environment, that makes the user's job easier. Otherwise, why have computers and corporate administrators?

As a corporate administrator you have quite a few options when you customize Internet Explorer 4 and deploy it on your network. As with any change on the user desktop, there are trade-offs between the options. Different groups within your organization will have different needs, and it is essential that you talk to the various managers and their power users to accurately access their needs. The IS manager is responsible for your long-term desktop strategy, but to make that strategy succeed, it is essential to get the buy-in and cooperation of internal customers. The feedback you get from your user community will help you select the appropriate deployment strategies. See the section "Planning Deployment in the Corporate Environment" in this chapter for a discussion of how you can customize IE 4 for your network.

Distribution Strategy

In advance you need to think about how you will get the custom Internet Explorer 4 package to your users or customers. Again, ICPs and ISPs have limited choices (Internet distribution, CD-ROM, or floppy disk), although the ISP has the special option of creating a single floppy disk distribution. Very few ICPs or ISPs will establish a NetBIOS connection with their clients that a file server shared-directory distribution would require.

Corporate administrators have the choice of performing any form of distribution with the exception of creating a single floppy disk. Though few corporate administrators will go to the trouble of creating a custom CD-ROM, many will use the Web site distribution method to make Internet Explorer 4 available on their Intranet, and will place IE 4 on a network share for easy distribution over a LAN.

Security

An important aspect of planning your Internet Explorer 4 package is deciding how security should be configured for your users or your customers. The default security settings work well for ISPs and ICPs, with the exception of an ICP that provides a service over the Internet that requires enhanced security. A bank that uses IE 4 for online bill paying or account viewing, for example, may want to establish more stringent security settings than the default setting. The more stringent settings may include preconfiguring trusted hosts settings and preinstalling digital certificates to make confidential information exchange more difficult to intercept.

A corporate administrator should determine what security settings match the security philosophy and practices of the corporate network. Some networks contain more sensitive information than others (a public access library network may contain personal e-mail, an academic network may contain student grades, a product distributor network may contain credit card numbers, and a military network may contain national security information), and the security settings for Internet Explorer 4 should match the justified paranoia security requirements of the network. See Chapter 8 for a deeper examination of the network security features of IE 4.

Custom Configurations

If you have several kinds of computers (such as Windows 95, Windows 98, Windows NT, and MacOS) and several groups of computer users that require different configuration settings (for example, engineers, data entry clerks, and corporate officers), you may want to establish custom configurations for each group. For example, the engineers can have their Active Desktops display current industry news, public access lab computers can be configured to use a special proxy server, and corporate officers can automatically subscribe to relevant financial and corporate data sources. Later, you can make changes for one group of users while leaving settings alone for other groups.

Schedule

A good deployment plan will follow a timeline. The timeline should establish dates for completing the following major tasks of creating and distributing Internet Explorer 4:

- Team Selected
- IEAK and IE 4 software collected
- End user PC survey completed
- Hardware and operating systems upgraded

- Custom files created and collected

- Distribution site(s) prepared

- Preliminary IE 4 package produced and tested (repeat until the package installs and operates properly on test computers)

- Final IE 4 package produced and verified to work properly

- Deployment media prepared

- Deployment completed

The next sections of this chapter explore planning issues and alternatives in more detail.

IE 4 Deployment Considerations and Strategies

Installing Internet Explorer 4 on a hundred computers is a little different from installing it on one computer. When you work with many computers, you want the installation process to be as automated as possible. Also, if you are installing IE 4 to a LAN, you may want to preset certain IE 4 settings to match your networking environment. If you are making IE 4 available to people who use your product or people who connect to your ISP service, you will want to customize IE 4 to reflect your company's image, and you'll want to refer to your company's services.

Microsoft ✓ *Exam* *Objective*	**Develop custom installation strategies for Internet Explorer 4.0.**

Microsoft ✓ *Exam* *Objective*	**Develop a configuration plan for Active Setup components.**

Considering the Windows Desktop Update

One of the first things to decide is whether you will include Windows Desktop Update in your custom distribution of Internet Explorer 4. Windows Desktop update makes considerable changes in the appearance of Windows to users. If you include WDU, you must be prepared to help users adapt to the new environment. A distribution that contains Windows Desktop Update will also use more memory in the destination computer (16MB instead of 8MB is required for Windows 95, and 24MB instead of 16MB for Windows NT). WDU does require more customization settings in the IEAK, and it can complicate future reinstallation of the operating system (see Chapter 3 for details).

Microsoft
Exam
Objective

In corporate administrator mode or Internet service provider mode, choose the appropriate installation of Internet Explorer 4.0, with or without the Windows Desktop Update.

Planning Deployment in the Corporate Environment

You should choose the corporate licensing mode when you are preparing to install Internet Explorer 4 on computers in your LAN. The Corporate mode is also appropriate for other users of IE 4, including public kiosks (networked or displaying information from stored HTML files) and end-user locations where IE 4 is used by the customer to access information that is presented in Web format.

The difference between the corporate license of IEAK and the ISP or ICP license is that with the corporate license you have control of the computer on which Internet Explorer 4 will be installed. The configuration and correct operation of the PC is your responsibility whether the computer is a general-use PC on your corporate LAN, a kiosk displaying company advertising to passersby, or a PC that is used by customers and dedicated to the task of accessing your company Intranet data.

Microsoft
Exam
Objective

In corporate administrator mode, develop appropriate security strategies for using Internet Explorer 4.0 for various sites. Sites include:

- Public kiosks
- End-user sites
- Business sites

The decisions you make when planning to deploy Internet Explorer 4 on your network touch almost every aspect of your network, from the hardware and software already installed to which IE 4 features you want your users to have and whether the users should be able to change what you've installed. Considerations for corporate deployment of IE 4 include:

Client hardware   The computers on which IE 4 will be deployed must meet minimum hardware requirements (which are explored in greater detail in Chapter 3). You may need to add memory or hard drive space to some computers in your network before you install IE 4.

Client operating system   IE 4 runs on Windows 95, Windows 98, Windows NT, MacOS, and Solaris. If you are installing IE 4 on Windows NT computers, they must have Service Pack 3 installed (you may have to upgrade the operating system software on some Windows NT computers).

Installed client software   The installation process will migrate settings if the computers in your network already have Web browsers installed, such as IE 3 or Netscape. (See Chapter 3 for more information on installing over other Web browsers.) Settings that IE 4 will adopt from other Web browsers include:

Proxy settings

Favorites (also called bookmarks)

Cookies

IE 4 will not include Web browser extensions (plug-ins) that were installed in earlier Internet Explorer browsers (or any other browsers for that matter) but do not come with IE 4. You must include in your custom configuration of IE 4 all plug-ins that you want your IE 4 Web browsers to use.

Distribution media   In corporate administrator mode, you have the choice of distributing the custom configuration of IE 4 from a download location, on CD-ROMs, or on multiple floppy disks. You do not have the option of creating a single floppy disk that will download and install IE 4 from the network. If you select the CD-ROM option from the IEAK Wizard, you can also create a custom autorun screen to automatically appear when the CD-ROM is inserted in the drive of a computer.

Download sites   For the option of distributing IE 4 from a Web site, the IEAK allows you to specify up to 10 Web sites from which the user can download your custom version of IE 4. You should prepare those Web sites to host the IE 4 distribution files (Internet Information Server (IIS) on Windows NT works well).

Network settings   In advance, you should know the network settings IE 4 will need to operate on your network, especially the domain name, proxy server address, name server address, and default gateway.

Network security   You should determine what will be the custom browsers' security settings. You should arrange the site certificate and Authenticode settings for the browser, as well as determine the security level (low, medium, high) for each security zone (local Intranet, Internet, etc.). See Chapter 7 for more information on IE 4 security.

Package selection   You must decide which components you want to install in your custom configuration of IE 4. You may specify up to 10 installation options that include Outlook Express, Microsoft Chat, and additional software that you provide (as many as 10 custom components).

Browser settings   You can preconfigure the browser to operate on your network. You will need to gather the appropriate settings for your network, including:

The browser Start and Search pages

The browser Support page

Browser favorites

IE 4 Welcome page and desktop wallpaper

Active Channels

HTML templates for Windows Desktop Update (the My Computer and Control Panel Web views, for example)

User Agent string

Proxy settings

Automatic browser configuration   Determine the frequency you want the autoconfiguration to check for updates and URLs for Internet settings (INS files) and autoproxy settings (JS or PAC files). If autoconfiguration is enabled, it will check for updates at least as often as the browser is started.

Language versions   Decide in advance which languages your custom version of IE 4 will support.

Branding   You can set the title bar text of the browser as well as the bitmap used in the background. You can also specify a custom browser logo. In addition, you can customize the Setup Wizard to display your company's name and logo. If you use these branding options, you will want to prepare the logos and the caption text prior to running the IEAK.

System policies   In a corporate environment you may want to limit users' abilities to change the configuration of their Web browser, Internet software, and operating system. Configurable settings for the users are stored in the User's Profile (described in Chapter 3). With the IEAK you can set or "lock down" settings in such areas as:

Microsoft NetMeeting

Active Desktop

Internet Properties

Outlook Express

Shell (Microsoft's term for Desktop Explorer settings)

Channels and Subscriptions

Microsoft Chat

Internet Explorer 4

Internet code download

Custom installation package version   You must specify a version number and configuration identifier for your packaged version of IE 4.

Planning Deployment for Internet Service Providers

Planning an Internet Explorer 4 deployment for the ISP licensing mode is a little simpler than for the corporate mode, because an ISP has less control of the computer on which IE 4 will be installed. The ISP is not responsible for upgrading the customer's operating system with the latest version or installing more memory. The ISP can simply let the customer know the hardware and software requirements and let the customer do the necessary upgrades.

One area in which ISP use of the IEAK can be more complex than corporate use is when the ISP specifies custom settings for the Internet Connection Wizard. ISP users can use the Connection Manager Administration Kit and create custom Signup Server options so that a first-time user of the Internet can quickly and easily have service established with an Internet service provider.

An ISP has one additional distribution-media option that the ICP and corporate user of the IEAK don't have—the single floppy disk. The single floppy disk option makes installing IE 4 easier for computer users that don't have a CD-ROM drive and don't yet have an Internet connection. It connects the user's computer to the ISP and downloads the IEAK from a location specified with the IEAK. This is the only distribution option that does not require that the entire IE 4 package be delivered as a single unit.

You need to plan how you will customize Internet Explorer 4 and deliver the custom Web browser. You should consider the following:

Client hardware   The computers that use IE 4 must meet certain minimum requirements (which are explored in Chapter 3). You should make the customer aware of the IE 4 hardware and software requirements.

Distribution media   In ISP mode, you have the choice of distributing the custom configuration of IE 4 in its entirety from a download location, on CD-ROM, or on multiple floppy disks. In addition, you may distribute the IE4Setup.exe program on a single floppy disk (that will connect to the network to get the rest of IE 4). If you select the CD-ROM option from the IEAK Wizard, you can also create a custom autorun screen to automatically appear when the CD-ROM is inserted in the drive of a computer.

Download sites   For the option of distributing IE 4 from a Web site, the IEAK allows you to specify up to 10 Web sites from which the user can download your custom version of IE 4. You should prepare those Web sites to host the IE 4 distribution files (IIS on Windows NT works well).

Connection Manager settings   If you plan to customize the Internet Connection Wizard, you must have information available, such as a list of potential ISP phone numbers in geographic regions, signup server information for each location, and custom signup files for your service (including HTML pages and CGI or ASP scripts to perform the signup service).

Network settings   You should know the network settings IE 4 will need to operate on your network, especially the domain name, proxy server address, name server address, and default gateway.

Network security   The default settings of IE 4 as supplied by Microsoft are appropriate for end-user general purpose Internet browsing and should not be changed for an Internet service provider scenario. Changes could either weaken the security of the user's computer or (by tightening security) remove functionality (compared to uncustomized versions of IE 4). See Chapter 7 for more information on IE 4 security.

Package selection   You must decide which components will be the default components installed to the computers in your custom configuration of IE 4. You may specify up to 10 installation options, including Outlook Express, Microsoft Chat, and additional software that you provide (as many as 10 custom components).

Package options   You can preconfigure the browser to operate in the network environment established by the ISP. You will need to gather the appropriate settings for the ISP network, including:

The browser Start and Search pages

The browser Support page

Browser favorites

IE 4 Welcome page and desktop wallpaper

Active channels (an ISP can add just one active channel to the Channel bar and can only remove channels that directly compete with services of the ISP)

User Agent string

Proxy settings

Automatic browser configuration   Determine how frequently you want the autoconfiguration to check for updates to IE 4 settings. When you run the IEAK you will need to know the autoconfigure URLs for Internet settings (INS files) and autoproxy settings (JS or PAC files). If autoconfiguration is enabled, it will check for updates at least as often as the browser is started. If the settings stored at the URL have changed, then IE 4 will update its own settings to match.

Language versions   You should decide in advance which languages your custom version of IE 4 will support.

Branding   You can set the title bar text of the browser as well as the bitmap used in the background. You can also specify a custom browser logo. In addition, you can customize the Setup Wizard to display your company's name and logo. If you use these branding options, you will want to prepare the logos and the caption text prior to running the IEAK.

Custom Installation Package version   You must specify a version number and configuration identifier for your version of IE 4.

It is not appropriate for an ISP to configure system *policies* (policies is Microsoft's term for operating system restrictions applied to user accounts or computer configurations) for customers, so a custom-configured IE 4 package built by an ISP may pre-configure IE 4, Outlook Express, and Active Desktop Update settings, but may not restrict the user from changing those settings later.

Planning for Automatic Signup Using the Internet Connection Manager

For many home computer users, the first time they connect to the Internet will be when they install and run Internet Explorer 4. If you are an ISP, you can make connecting to your service much easier by creating a custom IE 4 package that also customizes the Internet Connection Manager.

Microsoft ✓ *Exam* *Objective*	**Develop strategies for using the Internet Connection Wizard in the Internet service provider mode. Elements include:** • Modem detection • Stack installation • Configuration of dial-up connections

The Internet Connection Manager (ICM) runs on top of the dial-up networking software of Windows 95 and NT. The Internet Connection Manager recognizes when a software package (such as Internet Explorer 4 or Outlook Express) wants to connect to an Internet service (such as a Web site or mail host) and, using the Internet Connection Wizard, guides the computer through the process of dialing and connecting to an Internet service provider. If there is no established ISP for the Connection Manager to connect to, the ICM will guide the user through the process of selecting and subscribing to an ISP.

The Internet Connection Wizard (ICW) comes configured by default with phone numbers for some Internet service providers, arranged geographically. In ISP mode, you can configure the ICW to connect to your own service and start the subscription process automatically (the user, of course, must confirm the subscription and arrange payment for services as appropriate).

An ISP who is distributing a custom Internet Explorer 4 package must prepare the software to be installed on computers that may not already have networking or TCP/IP installed. The Internet Connection Wizard will detect which networking stack is installed, and prompt the user to insert the Windows 95 or NT operating system installation disks to load the TCP/IP protocol and networking components if necessary.

Also, users must be informed that they will need some physical connection to the Internet—usually via modem or via a direct (LAN) connection. If the user does not specify that Internet Explorer 4 should use the LAN, or specify that the ICW should leave the network settings alone, then the ICW will attempt to use a modem to connect to the Internet (and will attempt to auto-detect a modem if it finds no modems have been preconfigured).

The tool an ISP uses to configure Internet connections for Internet Explorer 4 is the Connection Manager Administration Kit. In addition, in the IEAK an ISP must configure the location of the customized Connection Manager file, as well as enter the automatic sign-up server location and network information (such as phone number, authentication options, encryption choices, and gateway settings).

Planning to Support Multiple Platforms

Many networks include computers with operating systems other than Windows 95 or Windows NT. Many home and home-office users prefer the ease of use of the Mac operating system, or the specialized software support of UNIX. And some users still have computers running the Windows 3.1 operating system. When you plan your custom IE 4 packages you should keep these users in mind. There is still competition to Windows, and many users are staunch in their support of these other platforms.

You can use the IEAK to create custom Internet Explorer 4 packages for Windows 3.1, Macintosh, and Unix (Solaris) operating systems in addition to Windows 95 or NT. The custom packages for these operating systems must be created separately from the Windows 95/NT packages, but you have many of the same customization options as you do for Windows 95/NT.

Because each operating system is different, some IEAK customization features are not supported for each package. As you plan your deployment of IE 4 you should be aware of the limitations of the IEAK on each operating system, as outlined in Table 5.1.

T A B L E 5.1: Availability of IEAK Customized Features in Various Operating Systems

Custom Settings	Available for Windows 95/NT	Available for Windows 3.1	Available for Macintosh	Available for UNIX
Active Desktop Component	Yes	No	No	No
Active Setup Wizard	Yes	Yes	No	No
Authenticode	Yes	No	No	Yes
Automatic Version Synchronization	Yes	Yes	No	Yes
Browser Title	Yes	Yes	Yes	Yes
CD	Yes	Yes	Yes	Yes
CMAK	Yes	No	No	No
Delete Competing Channel	Yes	Yes	Yes	No
Desktop Wallpaper	Yes	No	No	No
Download URL's Version Information	Yes	Yes	No	Yes
Favorites	Yes	Yes	Yes	Yes
Import Channels	Yes	Yes	Yes	No
Import Software Updates	Yes	No	No	No

T A B L E 5.1: Availability of IEAK Customized Features in Various Operating Systems *(Cont.)*

Custom Settings	Available for Windows 95/NT	Available for Windows 3.1	Available for Macintosh	Available for UNIX
LDAP Settings	Yes	Yes	Yes	No
License Agreement	No	No	Yes	No
Mail/News Settings	Yes	Yes	Yes	No
Multiple Floppies	Yes	Yes	Yes	No
Outlook Express	Yes	Yes	Yes	No
Package Title	Yes	Yes	No	No
Packaged Files	Yes	Yes	No	Yes
Proxy Settings	Yes	Yes	Yes	Yes
Select a Download Site	Yes	Yes	No	No
Select Channel or Category	Yes	No	Yes	No
Sign Up Server Options	Yes	Yes	Yes	No
Signature	Yes	Yes	No	No
Single Floppy	Yes	No	No	No
Site Certificate	Yes	Yes	No	Yes
Software Update Channels	Yes	No	Yes	No
Start and Search Page	Yes	Yes	Yes	Yes

T A B L E 5.1:   Availability of IEAK Customized Features in Various Operating Systems *(Cont.)*

Custom Settings	Available for Windows 95/NT	Available for Windows 3.1	Available for Macintosh	Available for UNIX
Support Page	Yes	Yes	Yes	Yes
System Policies & Restrictions	Yes	Yes	No	Yes
User Agent	Yes	Yes	Yes	Yes

Preparing Icons for Branding

There are several ways you can use the IEAK to customize Internet Explorer 4. To make your organization more visible, you can replace several of the bitmaps used by IE 4, Active Setup, and Outlook Express with your own corporate or organizational logo. If you want to take advantage of this option you should prepare bitmaps of your own logos for the following IE 4 items:

- The icon used for the Active Setup Wizard

- The toolbar bitmap that provides a backdrop for buttons and menus in IE 4

- The background bitmap for the CD-ROM autorun screen

- The CD-ROM button image

- Channel bar icons and graphics (for your own channels)

- An LDAP icon (if you provide an LDAP server)

Planning for Automatic Configuration and Active Setup

If you are distributing IE 4 to a large number of customers or employees, you will want to make it easy for you to update the software settings (such as changing the network address of the ISP proxy server or the security settings for browsers in your LAN) at a later date.

Microsoft
Exam
Objective

In corporate administrator mode or Internet service provider mode, choose strategies for managing automatic configuration by using the IEAK Profile Manager. Methods include:

- Microsoft JScript autoproxy
- .ins files
- .adm files

Internet Explorer 4 enables you to automatically and centrally configure the browser. Through the browser you can configure other software, including some parts of the operating system. IE 4 has two mechanisms for autoconfiguration: JScript autoproxy files (JS or PAC files), which were used with IE 3 and Netscape Navigator, and autoconfiguration files (INS files), which are easier to work with because they don't require programming.

When you plan how you will support autoconfiguring the Web browsers (whether you are working with corporate client computers or computers that belong to ISP customers) you will need to decide what to do in three areas: the initial IE 4 browser settings (especially the location the browser will turn to for the autoconfiguration files), the contents of the autoconfiguration files, and the location and access of the autoconfiguration files hosted on the network.

Since each user of an installed IE 4 Web browser can have their own settings, you may want to create several different autoconfiguration files, one for each group of users that need similar IE 4 configurations. For example, in your network you may want to establish different Active Channel settings for people in Engineering than for Sales and Marketing. You may want to establish a third configuration for company executives (perhaps with an automatic stock ticker showing the company's performance on their desktops). You will still want to maintain central control over the configuration of the browsers on all three sets of users. You can choose to lock-down IE 4 settings on the computers of users in selected groups.

You can use the IEAK to create autoconfiguration files (which have the .ins extension). One file is created for each group of users you specify. When the INS file is created, the necessary Internet Explorer 4 files for that configuration are collected into CAB files. When it is time for a Web browser with autoconfiguration enabled to check for updates, the browser contacts the preconfigured location and retrieves the INS file. If there are changes in the IE 4 setting, the INS file instructs the browser which CAB files to download. The downloaded CAB files are expanded. Then the INF files are examined, and updated files are installed to the Web browser, add-on programs, or operating system.

For Internet Explorer 4 to update itself or install packages automatically by downloading CAB files, you will have to take steps to ensure that security is not compromised and that IE 4 will accept the new CAB files. Depending on the security settings established in the IEAK, IE 4 will check the digital signature of the CAB files it has downloaded and will not install them if they do not contain a signature that IE 4 trusts. You will have to configure security zones in IE 4 so that it will allow the files to be retrieved, and you should get a digital certificate from a certificate authority so that you can digitally sign the CAB files. See Chapter 7 for more information on digital certificates and IE 4 security.

Your autoconfiguration options in the IEAK are not limited to IE 4 or add-on components. You can autoconfigure other aspects of Windows 95 or Windows NT by importing ADM files that are more commonly used by the Policy Editor (`poledit.exe`) to create policy (POL) files.

Importing ADM files may create duplicate keys, so you should use the Check for Duplicate Keys option after importing the policy template.

Windows 95 and Windows NT desktop settings for the Policy Editor are different. Windows 95 policy files will not necessarily work on Windows NT, and vice versa. Use extreme caution when modifying operating system settings, because changes you make on one operating system may conflict with changes you make for another system.

Replacing Other Browsers

The Internet Explorer 4 Setup program will not automatically remove other Web browsers and third-party Internet client tools. Depending on what you specify in the IEAK, it may not even make itself the default Web browser. It is your decision to remove this software. The exception is IE 3, which will automatically be upgraded to IE 4. IE 3 and IE 4 cannot coexist within the same operating system.

Microsoft ✓ ***Exam*** ***Objective***

Develop strategies for replacing other Internet browsers. Other browsers include:

- Microsoft Internet Explorer 3.*x*
- Netscape Navigator

When you plan to upgrade computers that already have other Web browsers, you should determine what you will need to do to ensure that Internet Explorer 4 will provide the users with the same level of functionality. IE 4 will import many of the Web browser settings of IE 3 and Netscape, but it will not import plug-ins from these or other Web browsers. If the Web browsers on your network use plug-ins that are not distributed by default with IE 4, you should locate versions of these plug-ins that work with IE 4 and include them as custom components in your distribution of IE 4. However, be careful that you don't violate the licensing agreements for these software components.

Your customers may be accustomed to the helper applications of other Web browsers. You can configure IE 4 to use these same helper applications by placing their MIME types and file extensions in IE 4's configuration. When planning to migrate from these other Web browsers to IE 4, you should determine which helper applications are important to your users and collect the MIME and file type information.

Planning the Deployment of Built-In and Custom Components

In addition to creating a plan to install the Web browser, you should plan how you will configure the related Internet services that come with Internet Explorer 4, especially Outlook Express and Microsoft NetMeeting.

Outlook Express

To send and receive mail, Outlook Express must be provided with the network location of an IMAP server, or POP and SMTP servers. If you want users to be able to participate in Internet newsgroups, you will also need to have the news server Internet address to provide to the IEAK Wizard.

Microsoft ✓ *Exam* *Objective*	**Choose the appropriate configuration strategy for Microsoft Outlook Express.**

If the computers you are working with already have e-mail and news clients installed, Outlook Express will take most of the settings from the previously-installed packages. If the computers do not have e-mail and news clients installed, you will have to determine the e-mail and news settings when you run the IEAK so that you can preconfigure Outlook Express for your network.

Microsoft ✓ *Exam* *Objective*	**Develop strategies for replacing other Internet mail clients. Other mail clients include:** ▪ Internet Mail and News ▪ Netscape Mail ▪ Eudora

---

Outlook won't import settings from every mail software package, but it will import from some of the most popular ones. Outlook Express is designed to import from Netscape Mail, Eudora, Eudora Light, Microsoft Exchange, and Microsoft Outlook. Settings Outlook Express will import include the following:

- SMTP and POP server locations

- Names, organizations, addresses, reply addresses, and signatures for the mail users

- Address book information of mail recipients

- Mail attachment (MIME) settings

- Automated mail-checking schedule

- Domain name servers

- News servers

- Secure Password Authentication

- LDAP settings

- Infopane and Welcome messages for Outlook Express

- Default signature files for outgoing e-mail and news messages

If mail packages other than Outlook Express already exist on the computers, you should decide which should be the default mail and news client. The IEAK gives you the option to make Outlook Express the default or to leave the existing default settings.

You can customize Outlook Express to create an *infopane* (the bottom right pane in the Outlook Express window) that contains an HTML file that shows information and links related to your organization. You will want to prepare this page prior to running the IEAK Wizard.

You can also prepare a welcome message as the first screen the users see as they open Outlook Express for the first time. That message can introduce them to the features of Outlook Express, provide company policy on e-mail use, or provide any other information you would like to include.

Many organizations require a signature with a legal disclaimer on all outgoing mail from its employees. Other organizations use the Signature feature (not to be confused with digital signatures) as free advertising. You should consider (or have the management in your organization consider) whether your organization should have a common signature at the bottom of all e-mail messages and news postings, and establish what will be said in the signature.

For Outlook Express to be an effective tool, your organization must be able to connect to mail and news servers. Microsoft Exchange, running on Windows NT Server, is Microsoft's recommended e-mail server package for corporate administrators that have the hardware resources and the need to maintain their own mail servers. If you are a corporate administrator of a smaller network, you can usually connect your users to your ISP's news server, and if you are an ISP you probably already have news and mail servers established.

NetMeeting

Microsoft NetMeeting (as described in Chapter 4) is a tool for online real-time collaboration. You can exchange text, audio, video, and even work on shared documents simultaneously with NetMeeting. NetMeeting uses video-conferencing protocols over TCP/IP to exchange the data, and it uses LDAP servers to find other NetMeeting users.

Microsoft NetMeeting is easy to configure and use. It comes configured, by default, with a set of Microsoft LDAP servers so that your users can find each other. However, you may want to establish your own LDAP server if you don't want to rely on Microsoft's service. If you provide your own LDAP server, you will have to specify the location of your own LDAP server in the System Policies and Restrictions portion of the IEAK.

Potentially, NetMeeting can place a much greater demand on network bandwidth than Internet Explorer 4 or Outlook Express, because streaming audio and video contains much more information than e-mail messages and Web pages. If you have a slow network connection to the Internet, or if you fear that bandwidth charges may grow excessively, you can restrict audio and video uses of NetMeeting. You should evaluate the needs of your organization for audio and video conferencing and set the NetMeeting restrictions accordingly.

Microsoft NetMeeting (unlike Outlook Express) does not have a sequence of IEAK screens set aside for configuring it. If you need to change the Net-Meeting settings in your custom package from their defaults, you do so in the System Policies section of the IEAK Wizard or the IEAK Profile Manager. Specific settings you may want to customize include:

- The location of the default directory server
- The NetMeeting home page

Other information, such as the personal information of NetMeeting users (name, e-mail address, etc.), must be provided to NetMeeting after it has been installed on the destination computer—you can't provide that information using the IEAK Wizard or the IEAK Profile Manager. Similarly, audio and video hardware configuration is also performed after the software is installed on the destination computer. See "Microsoft NetMeeting" in Chapter 4 for more information on configuring and using NetMeeting.

NetMeeting restrictions are established using the IEAK Wizard (when you build your custom Internet Explorer 4 package) or using the IEAK Profile Manager if you have autoconfiguration enabled for your deployed IE 4 browsers. The restrictions you enable should reflect the security and network performance concerns of your network.

If you are concerned about network users consuming too much network bandwidth, you should establish a maximum value for the following System Policy settings:

- Limit for audio/video throughput

- Prevent the user from sending video

- Prevent the user from receiving video

If you are concerned about hackers exploiting NetMeeting to attack computers on your network, you should consider enabling the following Net-Meeting restrictions:

- Disable all application sharing features

- Prevent the user from sharing the clipboard

- Prevent the user from sharing MS-DOS windows

- Prevent the user from sharing Explorer windows

- Prevent the user from collaborating

- Disable TCP/IP

- Disable null modem

On the other hand, you may be more concerned about keeping users of general-access computers from changing NetMeeting settings on those computers (and thereby confusing other users of NetMeeting on that computer or causing NetMeeting not to work properly). To restrict users from making changes, you should consider enabling the following System Policy restrictions for NetMeeting:

- Disable the General Options page

- Disable the My Information Options page

- Disable the Calling Options page

- Disable the Audio Options page

- Disable the Video Options page

- Disable the Protocols page

Planning Checklist

The following checklists of configuration settings will help you plan your version of Internet Explorer 4 and gather needed information for running the IEAK. The lists are of settings that are those commonly provided or modified by administrators or service providers who are making a custom version of IE 4.The checklists are in order of the IEAK installation process, which is divided into five stages: gathering information, specifying Active Setup parameters, customizing Active Setup, customizing the browser, and component customization.

Each stage lists the following:

- Installation decisions you must make

- Information you need to complete that stage of the installation

Stage 1: Gathering Information

This stage gathers basic information about how you will use the IEAK. The information you must have for this section includes the following:

Decisions

Which IEAK role do you need?

❑ ICP

❑ ISP

❑ Corporate

Do you want to provide Automatic Version Synchronization support?

❏ Yes

❏ No

Which method of distribution do you want to use?

❏ CD-ROM

❏ Multiple floppy disks

❏ Single floppy disk (ISP Only)

Information

Company name

_____

Customization code

_____

Target language

_____

Path to destination folder

_____

Stage 2: Selecting Active Setup Parameters

For this stage of the IEAK, you need information about how you will con-figure Active Setup for your custom version of Internet Explorer 4. You need to specify which Microsoft site you will synchronize the IE 4 software with (if you chose to use AVS in Stage 1) and what components you will synchro-nize. You can synchronize any or all of the components in the "Decisions" section of Stage 2 (you should synchronize all of the components that you will include in your custom IE 4 package). In addition, you should know which custom components (up to 10) you want to install and have them ready.

Active Setup will only install packages that are digitally signed by organi-zations it has been configured to trust. If you have included components that are not supplied and signed by Microsoft, you must know which digital signatures to configure Active Setup to trust.

Decisions

Which of the following components would you like to synchronize?

❏ Microsoft Internet Explorer 4

❏ Microsoft Internet Explorer Core Fonts

❏ Microsoft NetMeeting

❏ Microsoft Outlook Express

❏ Microsoft Chat 2

❏ Microsoft NetShow

❏ Intel Indeo 5

❏ VDOLive Player

❏ Microsoft Interactive Music Control

❏ Microsoft Internet Explorer Sound Pack

❏ Macromedia Shockwave Director

❏ Macromedia Shockwave Flash

❏ RealPlayer by Progressive Networks

❏ Microsoft FrontPage Express

❏ Microsoft Web Publishing Wizard

❏ Microsoft Visual Basic Run Time

❏ Microsoft Wallet

❏ Task Scheduler

❏ Microsoft Internet Explorer Supplemental Fonts

Information

AVS synchronization download site

Custom Components (up to 10)

1. _____
2. _____
3. _____
4. _____
5. _____
6. _____
7. _____
8. _____
9. _____
10. _____

Trusted Publishers

_____

_____

_____

_____

_____

Custom Component Information (Required for Each Component)

Name of component

_____

Location or path to component

_____

CAB files command to perform the extraction

_____

Global Universal Identifier (GUID)

EXE files parameter necessary for the installation

Version number of component

Size of the package

Uninstall key to remove the package

Stage 3: Customizing Active Setup

As described earlier in this chapter, you can brand your version of Internet Explorer 4 by providing custom icons and title bar text. You can supply up to 10 configuration options for your users to choose from (such as IE 4 only, standard, or full) or you can specify a silent install (in which you specify only one configuration option).

With each configuration option you can specify which of the standard Microsoft components (that you chose to synchronize in Stage 1) to install, as well as up to 10 custom components. You also can specify up to 10 download locations for the user to visit to download the IE 4 package files.

You must prepare a version number for your custom version of Internet Explorer 4. If you are preparing multiple configurations of IE 4, you also need a configuration identifier. In either case, you should provide the URL for the site where users may obtain product updates.

If you are using the IEAK in ISP or ICP mode you can make it easier for first-time users of the Internet to connect to your service by establishing a custom Internet Connection Manager profile. You use the Connection Manager Administration Kit to develop the custom profile. You must also create custom HTML pages and CGI or ASP scripts to support automatic signup of first-time users.

Decisions

Which button style do you want?

- ❏ Standard

- ❏ 3-D

- ❏ Custom

Do you want Silent Install?

- ❏ Yes

- ❏ No

Would you like to install Windows Desktop Update?

- ❏ Yes

- ❏ No

- ❏ User's choice

Would you like to use a custom profile for the Internet Connection Manager (ISP and ICP only)?

- ❏ Yes

- ❏ No

Information

Title bar text for the autorun page

_____

Location of the autorun Custom Background bitmap

_____

Standard text color

_____

Background text color

_____

Path to the custom bitmap file

_____

Active Setup Wizard title bar text

_____

Active Setup Wizard bitmap path

_____

Custom components installation title text

_____

Configuration options (up to 10)

1. _____
2. _____
3. _____
4. _____
5. _____
6. _____
7. _____
8. _____
9. _____
10. _____

Package download locations

_____

_____

_____

_____

_____

_____

_____

_____

IE 4 version number

_____

IE 4 configuration identifier

_____

IE 4 product update URL

_____

IE 4 installation location

_____

Path to Internet Connection Manager custom profile

_____

Information Required for Each Configuration Option

Option name

_____

Option description

_____

List of components that option will install (select from standard and custom packages you chose in Stage 2)

_____

Information Required for Each Download Location

Site name

_____

Site URL

_____

Site region

_____

Stage 4: Customizing the Browser

In this customizing the browser stage, you have branding options, as well as a choice of what to place in the favorites, in the Explorer bars, in the channels, on the Active Desktop, and in the custom Web View folders. In addition, you can set the Internet settings for Internet Explorer 4 including the proxy, autoconfiguration, security, and user agent string values.

If you are going to customize the toolbar, you must provide a toolbar title and the location of a custom bitmap for the toolbar background. You should supply default Web pages for Start Up, Search, and Help. You should prepare a list of URLs of Web pages that will appear by default in the Favorites folder.

You must also decide if you are going to modify the Active Channels that Microsoft provides by default. If you want to modify the Active Channel settings you will have to select the channels you want to include in Internet Explorer 4 and import those channel settings into the IEAK. You can do the same for Software Distribution channels.

Similarly, you can customize the Active Desktop and toolbar settings of your custom Internet Explorer 4 package by configuring the Active Desktop of the Web browser on the same computer as the IEAK and then importing those settings. You should choose which (if any) Active Desktop or toolbar settings you want to change.

You can change the appearance of the Windows Desktop Update Web View of the My Computer folder and Control Panel folder. You can, for example, place your logo in the corner, or you can use your corporate bitmap as a backdrop to the windows. If you want to do this, you will need to know the locations of the modified HTT files.

A custom User Agent string can uniquely identify your modified Internet Explorer 4 Web browser to Web sites. If you would like to use this feature, you should prepare a string to append to the regular User Agent string.

You will have to collect autoconfigure and proxy information if you choose to enable the autoconfigure and proxy mechanisms, and if you want to change security settings (certificate authorities, Authenticode security, security zones, or content ratings). You will have to make those changes in Internet Explorer 4 and import them into the IEAK. See Chapter 8 for more information on these security settings.

If you are an ISP you should consider establishing a sign-up server for your service so that your customers can get connected with the least amount of effort on their part. If you choose to use the automatic sign-up features of the Internet Connection Manager, you will have to prepare a sign-up Web site and collect the sign-up information that the ICM will need.

Decisions

Do you want to customize the title bar?

❏ Yes

❏ No

Do you want to customize the Welcome page?

❏ Display default Welcome page

❏ Do not display Welcome page

❏ Use custom Welcome page

Do you want to disable the IE 4 Welcome window?

❏ Yes

❏ No

Do you want to import the current channel configuration for Active Channels?

❏ Yes

❏ No

Do you want to delete the existing IE 4 channels?

❏ Yes

❏ No

Do you want the Channel bar to appear by default (NT 4 only)?

❏ Yes

❏ No

Would you like to import software distribution channels?

❏ Yes

❏ No

Which software distribution channel schedule would you like to use?

❏ None

❏ Auto

❏ Daily

❏ Weekly

❏ Monthly

Would you like to import Active Desktop components from IE 4?

❏ Yes

❏ No

Would you like to import Desktop toolbar settings from IE 4?

❏ Yes

❏ No

Do you want to enable Automatic Browser configuration?

❏ Yes

❏ No

Do you want to enable Proxy settings?

❏ Yes

❏ No

Would you like to import Certificate Authorities from IE 4?

❏ Yes

❏ No

Would you like to import Authenticode security information from IE 4?

❏ Yes

❏ No

Do you want to import Security Zone settings from IE 4?

❏ Yes

❏ No

Which Local Intranet Zone setting do you want to use?

❑ High

❑ Medium

❑ Low

❑ Custom

Which Trusted Sites Zone setting do you want to use?

❑ High

❑ Medium

❑ Low

❑ Custom

Which Internet Zone setting do you want to use?

❑ High

❑ Medium

❑ Low

❑ Custom

Which Restricted Sites Zone setting do you want to use?

❑ High

❑ Medium

❑ Low

❑ Custom

How do you want IE 4 to handle scripts?

❑ Enable

❑ Prompt

❑ Disable

How do you want IE 4 to handle running controls?

❑ Enable

❑ Prompt

❑ Disable

How do you want IE 4 to handle downloading signed controls?

❏ Enable

❏ Prompt

❏ Disable

How do you want IE 4 to handle downloading unsigned controls?

❏ Enable

❏ Prompt

❏ Disable

How do you want IE 4 to handle initializing unsigned controls?

❏ Enable

❏ Prompt

❏ Disable

Which Java restrictions do you want?

❏ Low

❏ Medium

❏ High

❏ Disable

How do you want IE 4 to handle Active Scripting?

❏ Enable

❏ Prompt

❏ Disable

How do you want IE 4 to handle Java applets scripting?

❏ Enable

❏ Prompt

❏ Disable

How do you want IE 4 to handle file download?

❏ Enable

❏ Disable

How do you want IE 4 to handle font download?

❏ Enable

❏ Disable

Which User Authentication do you want to use?

❏ Anonymous

❏ Prompt

❏ Automatic in Intranet

❏ Automatic

How do you want IE 4 to handle submitting non-encrypted data?

❏ Enable

❏ Prompt

❏ Disable

How do you want IE 4 to handle launching applications from IFRAME?

❏ Enable

❏ Prompt

❏ Disable

How do you want IE 4 to handle installation of desktop items?

❏ Enable

❏ Prompt

❏ Disable

How do you want IE 4 to handle drag-and-drop or copy-and-paste of files?

❏ Enable

❏ Prompt

❏ Disable

What safety level do you want for software channel permissions?

❏ Low

❏ Medium

❏ High

Do you want to import Content Ratings settings from IE 4?

❑ Yes

❑ No

What content rating do you want to establish for language?

❑ 0 (none)

❑ 1

❑ 2

❑ 3

❑ 4 (explicit)

What content rating do you want to establish for nudity?

❑ 0 (none)

❑ 1

❑ 2

❑ 3

❑ 4 (explicit)

What content rating do you want to establish for sex?

❑ 0 (none)

❑ 1

❑ 2

❑ 3

❑ 4 (explicit)

What content rating do you want to establish for violence?

❑ 0 (none)

❑ 1

❑ 2

❑ 3

❑ 4 (explicit)

Do you want users to have the ability to see sites that have no rating?

❏ Yes

❏ No

Do you want to require a supervisor password (not the same as the network supervisor password) on the user computer that will allow users to view restricted content?

❏ Yes

❏ No

How do you want automatic sign-up to be configured?

❏ Sign-up server

❏ Serverless

❏ No sign up

Do you want to use a custom profile for the Internet Connection Manager? (Sign-up server and serverless only)

❏ Yes

❏ No

Do you want to use Static DNS Address for the sign-up server? (Sign-up server and serverless only)

❏ Yes

❏ No

Do you want to use IP Header Compression for the sign-up server? (Sign-up server and serverless only)

❏ Yes

❏ No

Do you want to encrypt passwords for connections to the sign-up server? (Sign-up server and serverless only)

❏ Yes

❏ No

Do you want to use Default Remote Gateway to connect to the sign-up server? (Sign-up server and serverless only)

❑ Yes

❑ No

Do you want to use Software Compression for the connection to the sign-up server? (Sign-up server and serverless only)

❑ Yes

❑ No

Information

Title bar text

_____

Toolbar background bitmap path

_____

Start page URL

_____

Search page URL

_____

Online Support page URL

_____

Name and URL of Favorites (no limit)

_____

_____

_____

_____

_____

_____

Custom Welcome page URL

_____

Path to custom Desktop Wallpaper file

_____

Active Channels to add to the Channel bar (ISP and ICP limited to one, no corporate limit)

_____

_____

_____

_____

Software distribution channels to add (no set limits)

_____

_____

_____

_____

Path of My Computer (`Mycomp.htt`)

_____

Path of Control Panel (`Controlp.htt`)

_____

Custom String to Be Appended to User Agent

_____

Autoconfigure URL (`INS` file)

_____

Autoproxy URL (`JS` or `PAC` file)

_____

Autoconfigure every _x_ minutes

_____

HTTP address and port

_____

Secure address and port

_____

FTP address and port

_____

Gopher address and port

_____

Socks address and port

_____

Exceptions to proxy server

_____

Root Certificates to import for Certificate Authorities (no set limits)

_____

_____

_____

_____

Trusted Sites (no set limits)

_____

_____

_____

_____

Restricted Sites (no set limits)

_____

_____

_____

_____

Supervisor's password for overriding content restrictions

_____

Ratings Bureau URL

_____

Path for the Internet Connection Manager connection profile (Sign-up server and serverless only)

_____

Path of the folder that contains the sign-up files (Sign-up server and Serverless only)

_____

URL of the CGI or ASP script that generates the sign-up INS file (Sign-up server only)

_____

Choices and Information for Sign-Up Connections

Sign-up server connection name

_____

Sign-up server area code

_____

Sign-up server phone number

_____

Sign-up server country code

_____

Sign-up server primary DNS address

_____

Sign-up server alternate DNS address

_____

Logon script path

Stage 5: Customizing Components

In this stage of Internet Explorer 4 customization, you should be prepared with configuration information needed by the custom components and Internet tools that extend the functionality of IE 4. You will need to prepare network information about the services (mail, news, etc.) that these tools will need to participate on the network.

Decisions

Do you want to make Outlook Express the default mail client?

❏ Yes

❏ No

Do you want to make Outlook Express the default news client?

❏ Yes

❏ No

Do you want to use Secure Password Authentication?

❏ Yes

❏ No

Do you want to check names against this server when sending mail?

❏ Yes

❏ No

Which authentication type would you like to use?

❏ Anonymous

❏ Secure Password

❏ Password

Which path to the Outlook Express Infopane do you want to use?

❏ URL

❏ Local file path

Do you want to append a signature to mail messages?

❏ Yes

❏ No

Do you want to use the mail signature as the news signature?

❏ Yes

❏ No

Do you want to append the news signature to news postings?

❏ Yes

❏ No

Information

Incoming (POP3 or IMAP) Server

_____

Outgoing Mail (SMTP) Server

_____

Internet News Server

_____

Friendly (easy-to-remember) Name for the LDAP server

_____

Directory Service

_____

Home Page

_____

Search Base

_____

Service Bitmap

_____

Path to Infopane

_____

Custom Welcome Message HTML Path

_____

Custom Welcome Message Sender

_____

Custom Welcome Message Reply-To

_____

Mail Signature

_____

News Signature

_____

Establishing System Policies and Restrictions

You can do more to customize Internet Explorer 4, both to restrict users' ability to change the configurations and to customize the operation of IE 4 and associated components.

The following settings are different from the settings in the previous sections of the checklist because the following settings should be left alone unless you have a reason to change them (for example, to lock-down settings on public access computers). If you do not make changes in the following settings, then the default settings will be used and the user can change the settings. See Appendix B for more information on what each policy setting does. You can make these settings take effect either using the IEAK or the System Policy Editor in Windows NT (see Figure 5.1), which is explored further in Chapter 6. Scan through the following settings and check the settings that you feel would be appropriate for your custom version of Internet Explorer 4.

FIGURE 5.1

You can also use the
System Policy Editor
in NT to make
system policies
and restrictions.

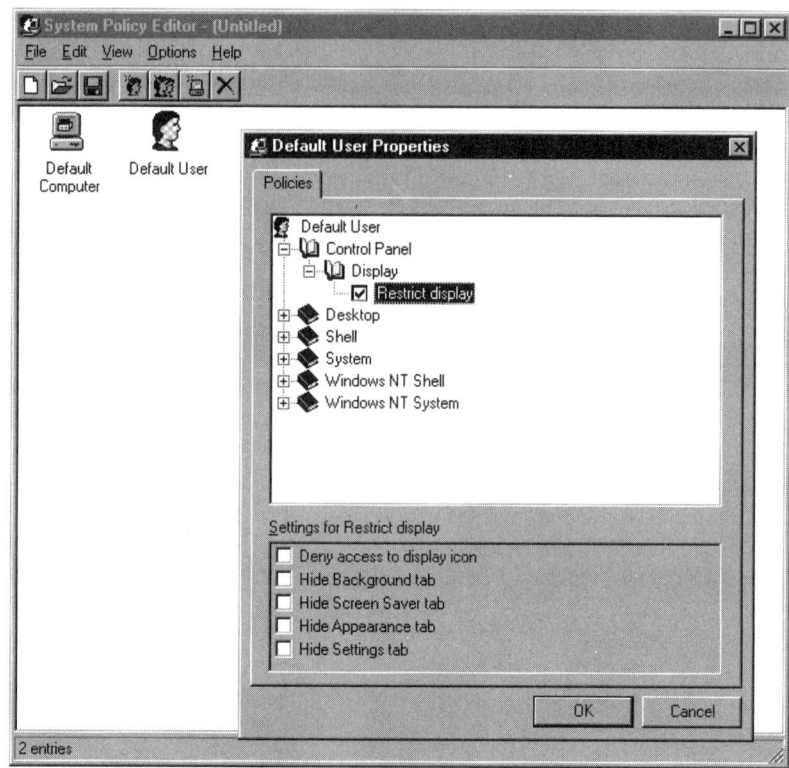

Microsoft NetMeeting Settings

Restrict the Use of File Transfer

  ❑ Prevent the user from sending files.

  ❑ Prevent the user from receiving files.

Restrict the Use of Application Sharing

  ❑ Disable all application sharing features.

  ❑ Prevent the user from sharing the Clipboard.

  ❑ Prevent the user from sharing MS-DOS windows.

  ❑ Prevent the user from sharing Explorer windows.

  ❑ Prevent the user from collaborating.

Restrict the Use of the Options Dialog

❑ Disable the General Options page.

❑ Disable the My Information Options page.

❑ Disable the Calling Options page.

❑ Disable the Audio Options page.

❑ Disable the Video Options page.

❑ Disable the Protocols Options page.

❑ Prevent the user from answering calls.

❑ Prevent the user from using audio features.

Restrict the Use of Video

❑ Prevent the user from sending video.

❑ Prevent the user from receiving video.

❑ Prevent the user from using directory services.

❑ Set the default Directory server.

❑ Set Exchange Server property for NetMeeting address.

❑ Preset User Information category.

NetMeeting Defaults

Set the default directory server.

_____

Set Exchange Server property for NetMeeting address.

_____

Preset User Information category.

_____

Set NetMeeting home page.

_____

Set limit for audio/video throughput.

_____

Microsoft NetMeeting Protocols

❑ Disable TCP/IP.

❑ Disable null modem.

Web Desktop Settings

Desktop

❑ Disable Active Desktop.

❑ Do not allow changes to Active Desktop.

❑ Hide Internet Explorer icon.

❑ Hide Network Neighborhood icon.

❑ Hide all items on Active Desktop.

Active Desktop Items

❑ Disable all Desktop items.

❑ Disable adding any Desktop items.

❑ Disable deleting any Desktop items.

❑ Disable editing any Desktop items.

❑ Disable closing any Desktop items.

Desktop Wallpaper

❑ Disable HTML wallpaper.

❑ Disable changing wallpaper.

Desktop Toolbars Settings

❑ Disable dragging, dropping, and closing all toolbars.

❑ Disable resizing all toolbars.

Start Menu

❑ Remove Favorites from Start menu.

❑ Remove Find from Start menu.

❑ Remove Run from Start menu.

❑ Remove Documents from Start menu.

❑ Do not keep history of recently opened documents.

❑ Clear history of recently opened documents.

❑ Disable Logoff.

❑ Disable Shut Down.

❑ Disable Changes to Printers and Control Panel settings.

❑ Disable Changes to Taskbar and Start menu settings.

❑ Disable Context menu (right-click) for Taskbar.

❑ Hide custom programs folders.

❑ Hide common program groups in Start menu (Windows NT only).

Shell Settings

❑ Enable Classic Shell.

❑ Disable File menu in Shell folders.

❑ Do not allow customization of folders in Web View.

❑ Disable Context menu in Shell folders.

❑ Only allow approved Shell extensions.

❑ Do not track Shell shortcuts during roaming.

❑ Hide floppy drives in My Computer.

❑ Disable Net Connections/Disconnections.

Printer settings

❑ Hide General and Details tabs in Printer Properties.

❑ Disable Deletion of Printers.

❑ Disable Addition of Printers.

System

❑ Run only specified Windows applications.

❑ Do not allow computer to restart in MS-DOS mode.

Internet Settings

Colors

General colors

❑ Background color (0,0,0 through 255,255,255)

_____

❑ Text color (0,0,0 through 255,255,255)

_____

❑ Use Windows colors.

Link colors

❑ Link color (0,0,0 through 255,255,255)

_____

❑ Visited Link color (0,0,0 through 255,255,255)

_____

❑ Use Hover color (0,0,0 through 255,255,255)

_____

Fonts

Font Size

❑ 0 (smallest)

❑ 1

❑ 2

❑ 3

❑ 4 (largest)

Languages

Choose the default language preferences

_____

Modem Settings—Dial-Up Networking Connection

❏ Enable Autodialing.

❏ Number of times to attempt connection

❏ Number of seconds to wait between attempts

❏ Connect without user intervention.

    ❏ Yes

    ❏ No

❏ Disconnect if idle after specified number of minutes.

    ❏ Yes

    ❏ No

❏ Minutes to wait before disconnecting

❏ Perform system security check before dialing.

Programs

Program to use for Calendar

Program to use for Contacts

Program to use for Internet call

Browsing

    ❏ Disable Script Debugger.

    ❏ Launch Channels in Full Screen mode.

    ❏ Launch Browser in Full Screen mode.

❏ Use Autocomplete.

❏ Show Friendly URLs in Status Bar.

❏ Enable Smooth Scrolling.

❏ Enable Page Transitions.

❏ Browse in a new process.

❏ Enable Page Hit Counting.

❏ Enable Scheduled Subscription Updates.

Underline Links

❏ Always

❏ Never

❏ Hover

Multimedia

❏ Show pictures.

❏ Play animations.

❏ Play videos.

❏ Play sounds.

❏ Enable Smart image dithering.

Security

❏ Enable Profile Assistant.

❏ Delete saved pages when browser is closed.

❏ Do not save encrypted pages to disk.

❏ Warn if forms you submit are being redirected to a different Web site.

❏ Warn if changing between Secure and Insecure mode.

Cookies

❏ Always accept

❏ Prompt

❏ Disable

Java VM

❏ JIT Compiler Enabled.

❏ Java Logging Enabled.

Printing

❏ Print background colors and images.

Searching

Autoscan common root domains.

❏ Search when URL fails.

❏ Always search.

❏ Always ask.

❏ Never search.

Toolbars

❏ Show Font button.

❏ Use Small icons.

HTTP 1.1 settings

❏ Use HTTP 1.1.

❏ Use HTTP 1.1 through proxy connections.

Outlook Express Settings

General Settings

Mail and News Security Zones

❏ Put mail and news in the Restricted Sites zone (instead of the Internet zone).

HTML Mail and News Composition Settings

❏ Mail: Make Plain Text Message Composition the Default for Mail Messages (instead of HTML mail).

❏ News: Make HTML Message Composition the Default for News Posts (instead of plain text).

❏ View Customization folder and message navigational elements.

❏ Turn on Outlook Bar.

❏ Turn off Folder List (tree view of folders).

❏ Turn on Folder Bar (horizontal line displaying folder names).

❏ Turn off the Tip of the Day.

Channels and Subscriptions Settings

❏ Maximum KB of site Subscriptions (zero disables restriction)

_____

❏ Maximum KB of channel Subscriptions (zero disables restriction)

_____

❏ Maximum number of site subscriptions that can be installed (zero disables restriction)

_____

❏ Minimum number of minutes between scheduled subscription updates (zero disables restriction)

_____

❏ Beginning of range in which to exclude scheduled subscription updates. Minutes from midnight (zero disables restriction)

_____

❏ End of range in which to exclude scheduled subscription updates. Minutes from midnight (zero disables restriction)

_____

❏ Maximum site subscription crawl depth

_____

Internet Explorer Properties

General Tab Settings

- ❏ Disable Changing Home Page settings.
- ❏ Disable Changing Cache settings.
- ❏ Disable Changing History settings.
- ❏ Disable Changing Color settings.
- ❏ Disable Changing Link Color settings.
- ❏ Disable Changing Font settings.
- ❏ Disable Changing Language settings.
- ❏ Disable Changing Accessibility settings.

Security Tab Settings

- ❏ Use only machine settings for security zones.
- ❏ Do not allow users to change policies for any security zone.
- ❏ Do not allow users to Add/Delete sites from a security zone.

Content Tab Settings

- ❏ Disable Changing Ratings settings.
- ❏ Disable Changing Certificate settings.
- ❏ Disable Changing Profile Assistant settings.
- ❏ Disable Changing Microsoft Wallet settings.

Connection Tab Settings

- ❏ Disable Calling Connection Wizard.
- ❏ Disable Changing Connection settings.
- ❏ Disable Changing Proxy settings.
- ❏ Disable Changing Automatic Configuration settings.

Programs Tab Settings

❏ Disable Changing Messaging settings.

❏ Disable Changing Calendar and Contact settings.

❏ Disable Changing Internet Explorer Default Browser settings.

Advanced Tab Settings

❏ Disable Changing Settings on Advanced tab.

Code Download

❏ Internet Search path

Channels Settings

❏ Disable Channel User interface.

❏ Disable Adding and Subscribing to Channels.

❏ Disable Editing Channel Properties and Channel Subscriptions.

❏ Disable Removing Channels and Subscriptions to Channels.

❏ Disable Adding Site Subscriptions.

❏ Disable Editing Site Subscriptions.

❏ Disable Removing Site Subscriptions.

❏ Disable Channel Logging.

❏ Disable Update Now and Update All for Channels and Subscriptions.

❏ Disable All Scheduled Channel and Site Subscriptions.

❏ Disable Unattended Dialing by Subscriptions.

❏ Disable Password Caching for all channel or site subscriptions.

❏ Disable Downloading of Channel Subscription Content (change notification will still function).

❏ Disable Downloading of Site Subscription Content (change notification will still function).

❏ Disable Editing and Creating of Schedule Groups.

Microsoft Chat Settings

❏ Chat Server List (separated by semicolons)

_____

❏ Default Chat server

_____

❏ Default Chat room

_____

❏ Default Chat character

_____

❏ Default backdrop

_____

❏ User Profile string

_____

Do you want to show only the registered rooms in Room List?

❏ Yes

❏ No

Summary

Planning makes building your custom version of Internet Explorer 4 easier and gives you software that is better configured for your network environment. Gathering all of the information in one place in advance also provides you a record of your configuration of IE 4. This record is necessary so that later you can debug your IE 4 setup, create a new version of IE 4 with updated components, and make incremental changes to your established configurations.

Of the three IEAK licensing modes (Internet content provider, Internet service provider, and corporate administrator), the most often used mode will be corporate administrator. The corporate mode is also the mode that gives the user of the IEAK the most freedom for modifying Internet Explorer 4. However, corporate mode does not allow a single-floppy distribution (that option is reserved for ISPs only).

After evaluating your network needs and proceeding through the checklists of information required for the IEAK, you can move on to Chapter 6, where you will use the IEAK to build your custom version of Internet Explorer 4.

Review Questions

1. Which licensing mode allows you to create single floppy disk distributions?

   A. ISP

   B. ICP

   C. CORP

   D. MCP

2. Which licensing modes allow you to create multiple floppy disk distributions?

   A. ISP

   B. ICP

   C. CORP

   D. MCP

3. Which licensing modes allow you to create CD-ROM distributions?

   A. ISP

   B. ICP

   C. CORP

   D. MCP

4. What kind of server does NetMeeting use to find other users of NetMeeting?

    A. LDAP

    B. ICQ

    C. Windows NT

    D. TCP/IP

5. You are replacing IE 3 browsers that use the JScript autoproxy feature. You want to have the same functionality in the new IE 4 browsers, and you want to exert the least amount of effort possible. What must you do?

    A. Create equivalent INS files for IE 4.

    B. Import the JC files into your custom IE 4 browser using the IEAK.

    C. Nothing, IE 4 will import the IE 3 autoproxy settings.

    D. IE 4 does not support autoproxy.

6. Which of the following will IE 4 import automatically from Netscape Navigator?

    A. Proxy Settings

    B. Bookmarks

    C. Plug-ins

    D. Helper applications

7. Your network users are accustomed to the helper applications (not plug-ins) set up in Netscape Navigator. What must you do to enable IE 4 to use these same helper applications?

    A. Nothing, IE 4 will import them automatically.

    B. Import equivalent helper applications from the Microsoft Web site.

    C. Configure the MIME types and file extensions for the helper applications in the Web browser.

    D. IE 4 will not use Netscape helper applications.

8. You want to include a software package as a custom component in your version of IE 4. What form must the custom component take in order to be included by the IEAK and expanded by Active Setup? Choose all that apply.

   A. CAB files

   B. ZIP files

   C. A self-extracting EXE archive

   D. An ISAPI DLL

9. You have created CAB files for custom component, digitally signed them, and included them in your distribution with the IEAK. However, Active Setup refuses to install them. What might be the problem?

   A. The software must be in the form of a self-extracting EXE archive.

   B. You must have Microsoft digitally sign the software for Active Setup to accept the signature.

   C. You must configure Active Setup to accept the digital signature that you used to sign the component.

   D. Only Internet content providers can provide custom components.

10. You want to use IE 4 autoconfiguration to manage Windows 95 settings that are not in the IEAK. How can you lock-down the settings (such as Dial-Up Networking, Desktop icons, and Start menu items) for a group of users?

   A. You cannot use IE 4 autoconfiguration to modify Windows 95 User Profile or policy settings.

   B. Create an autoproxy JScript applet that manipulates the users' profile settings upon start-up of IE 4.

   C. Create a CAB archive of the users' mandatory User Policy directory and include it as a custom component in the IEAK.

   D. Create an ADM file of policy settings with poledit, and import the file into the IEAK.

11. You want to brand the CD-ROM autorun screen. What options does the IEAK give you to customize the screen that appears when you put the CD-ROM in the drive? Choose all that apply.

   A. The background bitmap

   B. The CD-ROM button image

   C. The window title text

   D. The text and highlight colors

12. You want your Web servers to be able to identify when users of your custom Web browser access your Web sites. What customization feature can you use to achieve this?

   A. The version number

   B. The Configuration Identifier

   C. The User Agent string

   D. The customization code

13. Which IE 3 plug-ins will IE 4 import automatically? Choose all that apply.

   A. Shockwave

   B. RealAudio Player

   C. QuickTime Player

   D. None

14. You do not have an LDAP server on your network, and you want to use NetMeeting for collaboration over the Internet. You need an LDAP server so users can find each other and establish connections. What must you install in addition to installing IE 4 with NetMeeting on client computers?

    A. Install an LDAP server on a Windows NT computer in your network.

    B. Install Microsoft Exchange on a Windows NT computer in your network.

    C. Install an ICQ server on a Windows NT computer in your network.

    D. Nothing, you can use LDAP services provided by Microsoft.

15. You have installed IE 4 on a computer that previously had Netscape Navigator installed. You notice that Navigator is still present on the desktop and in the Start menu. Why is this?

    A. You must specify Remove Navigator in the IEAK to remove the software when IE 4 is installed.

    B. Your Microsoft license agreement restricts you from removing competing browser software.

    C. You must create a custom uninstall autoconfiguration (INS) file to remove Netscape.

    D. The IE 4 installation process will not automatically remove competing browsers.

16. You manage a large network that contains Windows 95 and 98 computers (browsing the Internet using IE 4), Windows 3.1 computers (browsing the Internet using IE 3), and Linux computers (browsing the Internet using Netscape). You want to automatically configure all of these Web browsers to find and use the proxy server. You would like the Web browsers to bypass the proxy server if the connection is made using the HTTPS protocol. You would like to use a single file for managing automatic proxy configuration.

Required Result: Establish automatic proxy configuration for all the browsers in the network.

Optional Result 1: Bypass the proxy server for HTTPS traffic.

Optional Result 2: Use a single automatic proxy configuration file.

Suggested Solution: Create a JS autoproxy file that checks to see if the access is via HTTPS. If so, it returns the location of the destination resource; otherwise, it returns the address of the proxy server.

Which of the following is correct?

A. The suggested solution accomplishes the required result and both optional results.

B. The suggested solution accomplishes the required result and just one optional result.

C. The suggested solution accomplishes the required result only.

D. The suggested solution does not accomplish the required result.

17. You manage a large network that contains Windows 95 and 98 computers (browsing the Internet using IE 4), Windows 3.1 computers (browsing the Internet using IE 3), and MacOS computers (browsing the Internet using Netscape). You want to automatically configure how all of these Web browsers find and use the proxy server. You don't want to do any programming and you want to lock-down browser security settings.

Required Result: Establish automatic proxy configuration for all the Web browsers in the network.

Optional Result 1: Avoid programming.

Optional Result 2: Lock-down security settings.

Suggested Solution: Install IE 4 on the Windows 3.1 and MacOS computers. Configure all IE 4 browsers to use autoconfiguration. Use the IEAK Profile Wizard to create an INS file, specifying the proxy server location and locking-down security settings.

Which of the following is correct?

A. The suggested solution accomplishes the required result and both optional results.

B. The suggested solution accomplishes the required result and just one optional result.

C. The suggested solution accomplishes the required result only.

D. The suggested solution does not accomplish the required result.

CHAPTER

6

Customizing and Deploying
Internet Explorer

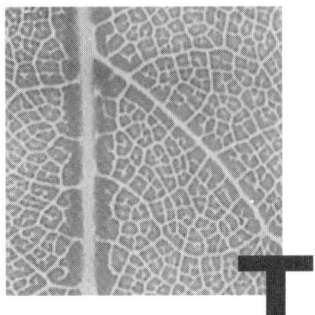

This chapter shows you how to use the Internet Explorer Administration Kit. By now you should know what Internet Explorer 4 can do and have an idea about how you would like to customize it. In Chapter 5 you should have filled out the planning checklist for the IEAK. Now you will go through the steps of making those custom changes to IE 4, including preparing custom bitmaps, creating custom packages, customizing Active Setup, and customizing IE 4 itself.

If you are going to brand your version of Internet Explorer 4 (in other words, if you are going to put your own icons, bitmaps, and title bar text in the software), then you need to have these custom bitmaps and texts prepared. If you want to include a custom component with the IE 4 package, you will have to create and digitally sign that component so that the Active Setup program can download and install it. In this chapter you will:

- Prepare customized files

- Create a custom IE 4 package with the IEAK

- Deploy the custom IE 4 package from a URL, a CD-ROM, and floppy disks

Preparing Customized Files

Before you run the IEAK you may need to create or acquire custom files. If you want to brand your version of Internet Explorer 4, you will need to make bitmaps. If you want to use the automatic update feature of IE 4, you will need to allocate Web server space for autoconfiguration (INS) files. A few custom files are:

- CAB or EXE custom component files
- Autorun screen bitmap
- Autorun buttons bitmap
- Active Setup bitmap
- Toolbar bitmap
- Default home page
- Search page
- Help Web pages
- Additional Favorites Web pages
- Welcome page
- Windows Desktop Update background HTML document
- Company- or organization-specific Active Channel files, including channel icons
- Software Distribution Channel files
- LDAP button bitmap
- Outlook pane HTML page

After completing the checklist in Chapter 5, you should have a good idea which of the above resources you need for your custom version of Internet Explorer 4. Some of the files require more effort to create than others—Active Channels and Software Distribution Channels, for example, require expertise in HTML, programming, and Web publishing, which is beyond the scope of this book. You are shown how to work with INS files in Chapter 7. Generating bitmaps and creating custom components are described below.

Creating or Locating Custom Graphics

By replacing the standard icons and buttons of Active Setup and Internet Explorer 4, you create a visual link between the Internet Explorer software and your company, product, or service. Although you could just throw together some images in the right format with a paint program, you should, instead, have professionals prepare your graphics for you. A visual artist has the skills to make visually appealing graphics that present the image you want your custom product to convey (which, presumably, is not: "I threw this together in a weekend using Microsoft Paint").

The IEAK requires the images to be in specific formats, as shown in Table 6.1.

T A B L E 6.1 Custom Images and Their Formats	**Images**	**Formats**
	Autorun screen bitmap	540x357 256-color BMP file
	Autorun buttons bitmap	177x118 256-color BMP file
	Active Setup bitmap	120x239 256-color BMP file
	Toolbar bitmap	Not specified, but from 64x64 up to 1280x64 would be appropriate with light colors so that black buttons show up well
	Channel icons	32x32 icon in BMP format, 80x32 graphic and 192x32 image in GIF, BMP, or JPG format
	LDAP button bitmap	134x38 in 16-color BMP file

The 256-color custom bitmaps you create will only be in effect on computers that are configured to use 256 colors or greater. On computers that use standard VGA (which supports only 16 colors), the default bitmaps will be displayed instead of your custom bitmaps.

You will want to have these bitmap files accessible when you run the IEAK. You should copy them to your hard drive or a network share that has a drive letter mapped to it. If these files fit on a floppy disk, you can insert that disk when you run the IEAK, and give the path to the floppy when prompted for the files.

Creating Custom Components

The Active Setup program will only install software that is contained in a self-extracting executable (EXE) or cabinet (CAB) file. If you have files you want to distribute with Internet Explorer 4 (whether they are programs or data files), you must collect them into either the EXE or CAB format. Most Microsoft software uses the CAB format, and Microsoft distributes a tool (IExpress.exe) with the IEAK that will put installable software into a package for you. See Figure 6.1 for a view of IExpress.exe.

F I G U R E   6.1

IExpress.exe guides you through the process of creating CAB files for your custom components.

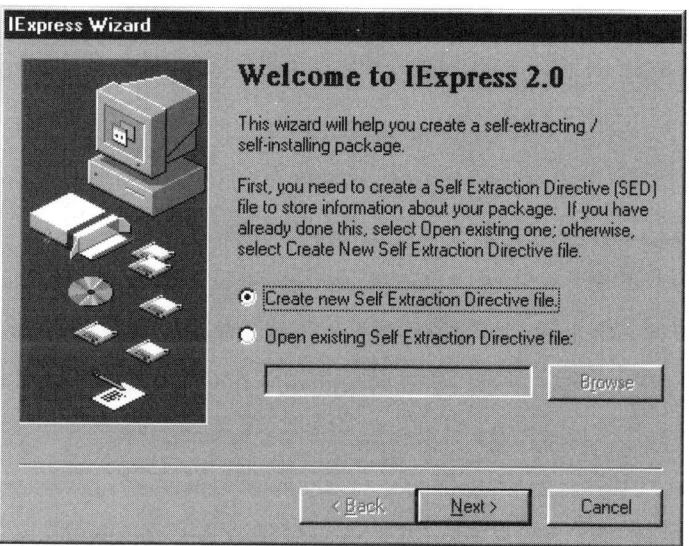

What you include in a custom component is up to you and the licensing agreements of your software (most commercial software restricts being redistributed in this manner). Exercise 6.1 shows you how to create a cabinet file using the IExpress program.

EXERCISE 6.1

Creating a Custom Component *CAB* File

1. Open the IEAK (double-click My Computer, double-click the C drive, double-click Program Files, and double-click IEAK). Select Tools ➤ IExpress.exe.

2. Select Create New Self Extracting Directive File. Click Next.

3. Select Extract Files, and run installation command. Click Next.

4. Enter **TestComp** as the name of the custom component, and click Next.

5. Select Prompt User With, and type **Install Test Component?** in the text field. Click Next.

6. Select Do Not Display a License, and click Next.

7. Click Add. Then insert the Sybex CD-ROM in your CD-ROM drive, and browse to the Examples subdirectory. Select TestComp.exe, and click Next.

8. Type **TestComp.exe** in the Install Program field, and click Next.

9. Select Default, and click Next.

10. Select Display Message, type **Test Component Installed**, and click Next.

11. Enter **C:\Component\TestComp** for the target path, and click Next.

12. Select No Reboot, and click Next

13. Select Don't Save, and click Next.

14. Click Next, and click Finish.

Signing Components

When you break the seal on the software package you bought from a software store, you know who to blame if the software doesn't work. If there is a virus on the CD-ROM, the publisher of the CD-ROM must have put it there (or allowed it to get there due to lax security when preparing the software package). When you download software from the Internet, you don't have that physical assurance that someone hasn't tampered with the software on its way from the publisher to you.

Since there may not be any physical packaging for the Internet Explorer 4 components, Active Setup provides another way to be sure that the software came untampered from the software manufacturer. Active Setup requires that the components it installs be digitally signed. A digital signature contains information about the signer and a hash of the item being signed. It can't be forged without the signer's private key. A digital signature can be verified by anyone with the signer's public key, so a digital signature assures that the signed software came from the software manufacturer and hasn't been modified since the signature was applied to the software.

Active Setup checks to see if a file has been modified by looking at the hash of the file. A hash of a file is like a fingerprint of a person—each file produces a unique hash when it passes through the hashing function. To check to see if a file has been modified, you can pass it through the hashing function again—if it has been changed, the new hash (fingerprint) won't match the old one.

Since Active Setup requires that the components it installs are digitally signed, you will need to acquire public and private keys (in the form of a digital certificate) to sign your packages. Digital certificates are created by certificate authorities (such as VeriSign), which, for a fee, will create a digital certificate for you and will verify the information you give them after they perform some basic checks.

In addition to identifying the item being signed and verifying the identity of the signer, a digital signature also identifies which certificate authority gave the signer the certificate with the public and private keys. This enables you to be sure (if you trust the organization that gave the certificate) that the software publisher signing the software is reputable.

If you are developing software to be distributed over the Internet (in other words, if you are an Internet content provider or an Internet service provider), you will want to get a digital certificate from a reputable certificate authority (such as Verisign) so that your customers can be assured that you are a legitimate company, and not a front for hackers or other mischievous individuals. If, however, you are distributing your custom components in a closed environment, and you trust yourself not to introduce any viruses or security breaches, you can use the tools provided with the IEAK to create a test certificate to sign your software. Exercise 6.2 shows you how to do this.

You have to sign the components that the IEAK creates for you. After running the IEAK, you need to sign the following files: Branding.cab, Desktop .cab, Ie40cif.cab, IE4setup.exe, all CAB files beginning in Chl, and any custom components you create.

EXERCISE 6.2

Creating Test Certificates and Signing a Component *CAB* File

1. Go to the command prompt (select Start ➢ Programs ➢ MSDOS Prompt).

2. Type **cd\"Program Files"\IEAK\Reskit\Addons\Tools**, and click Enter.

3. Type **Setreg 1 true**.

4. Type **makecert u:testkey –k:test.pvk -n:"CN=UnverifiedSoftware" testcert.cer**, and click Enter.

5. Type **cert2spc testcert.cer cert.spc**, and click Enter.

6. Type **signcode –spc cert.spc –v test.pvk c:\components\"Test Component.exe"**, and click Enter.

Collecting Network Information

In order to customize Internet Explorer 4 for a network, you must know about the network. You need to know server names, proxy server addresses, proxy server ports, and automatic update URLs. Exactly what information you need will depend on how your network is configured—if there is no proxy server on your network, for example, you won't need to know the proxy server address and ports. In Chapter 5 you gathered the information you need for your network. The exercises in this chapter assume a specific network configuration, described below, and illustrated in Figure 6.2. Your own network will be different, and you should adapt the specifics of the exercises to match your network.

FIGURE 6.2

Fictional network used
in Exercises 6.3–6.8

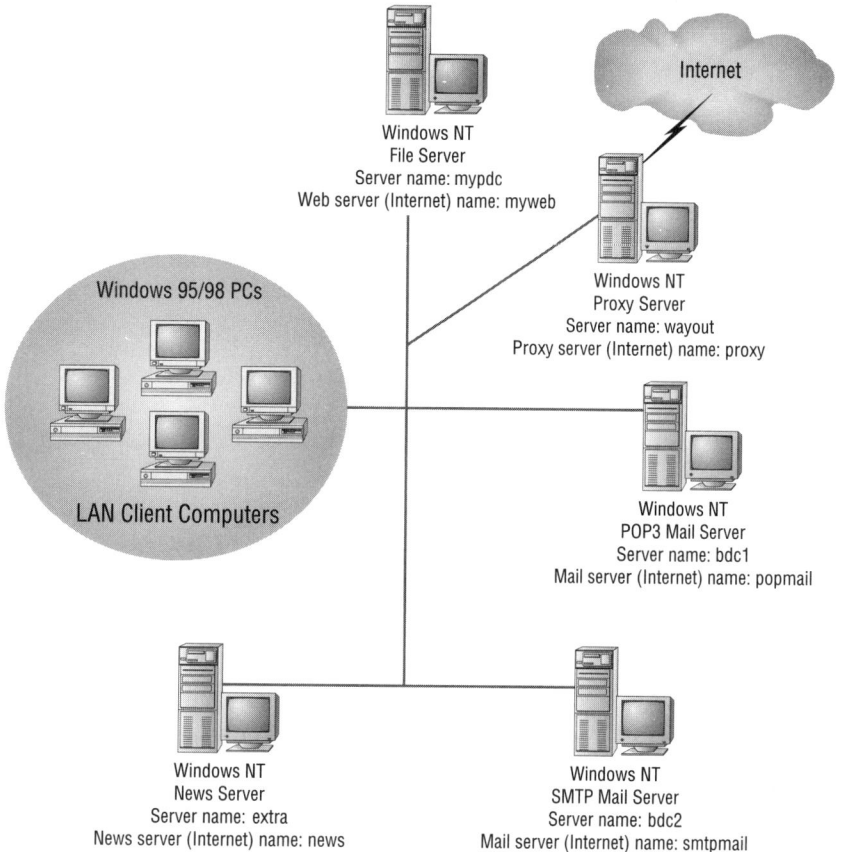

Salient features of the fictional network are as follows:

Distribution Web server: myweb

File Server: mypdc

Proxy server: proxy (port 8080)

POP3 mail server: popmail

SMTP mail server: smtpmail

News server: news

Create a Custom IE 4 Package with the IEAK

Once you have collected the custom files and identified the necessary Internet software settings for your network, you are ready to create your custom Internet Explorer 4 package using the IEAK. The IEAK Wizard will present a series of screens, each giving you a section of IE 4 to customize or preconfigure. The IEAK Wizard screens are divided into the following five stages:

1. Gathering Information

2. Specifying Active Setup Parameters

3. Customizing Active Setup

4. Customizing the Browser

5. Component Customization

There are five exercises for using the IEAK (6.3 through 6.7), one for each stage of the IEAK Wizard. You should perform each exercise to create your custom Internet Explorer 4 package. Each exercise begins with an introduction where you will learn more about your options and the consequences of choices.

IEAK Stage 1: Gathering Information

First, the IEAK Wizard needs some basic information about how you will use the Wizard and how you will distribute the IEAK. You need to provide your company name and customization code, as well as the licensing mode (ISP, ICP, or corporate), which is described in greater detail in Chapter 5(see Figure 6.3). You should also decide if you want to use AVS (described in more detail in Stage 2), the location for the custom package(s) you are creating, and which language the resulting Internet Explorer 4 package should use.

Getting the Customization Code

If you downloaded the IEAK by following Exercise 2.1 in Chapter 2, you should already have the customization code. If you obtained the IEAK on CD-ROM (in the Microsoft Internet Explorer Resource Kit, for example) you still need to go to the Microsoft Web site (`http://ieak.microsoft.com`) to get a password and a customization code. Exercise 6.3 shows you how to download the IEAK.

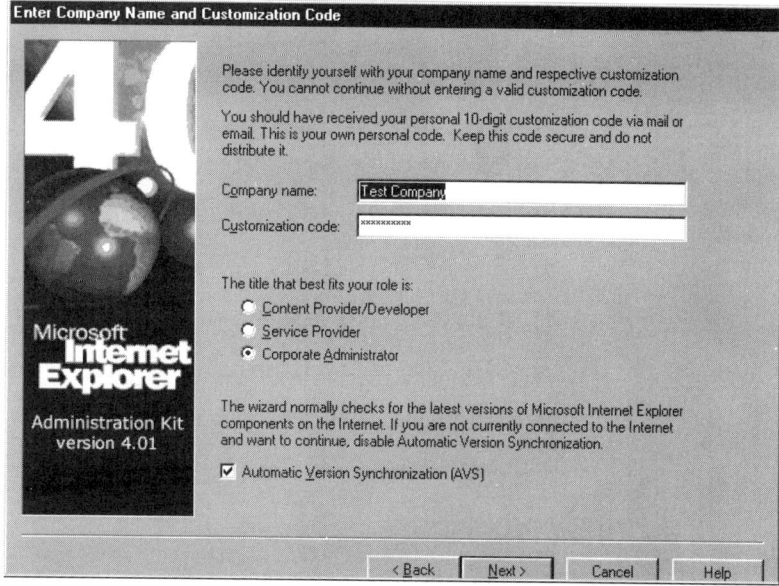

F I G U R E   6.3

You can use the IEAK in Content Provider/ Developer (ISP) mode, Service Provider (ISP) mode, or Corporate Administrator mode.

EXERCISE 6.3

Downloading the IEAK from Microsoft's Web Site

1. Launch Internet Explorer 4.

2. In the Address field, type **http://ieak.microsoft.com/gettheieak.asp**, and click OK.

3. Click New Registration in the left-hand column.

4. Enter your e-mail address, name, and company, then click Enter.

5. Go to your e-mail program, and get the password from the e-mail message from Microsoft.

6. Go to Internet Explorer, and click the Login link at the bottom of the page.

7. In the Password field, enter your password, then click OK.

8. Enter your job title, address, telephone number, fax number, and corporate URL. Click Next.

9. Select Both ➤1-100 for IE, NetMeeting, and Outlook Express. Click Next.

10. Select Other, click Next, click Proceed, and then click the License Agreement Wizard link at the bottom of the page.

11. Select To Companies Within Your Organization, and click Next.

12. Select Yes. Click Next.

13. Read the license agreement, then click I Accept.

14. Click Review Your Licenses.

15. Note the customization code for IEAK 4.

What Is AVS?

When you build your custom version of Internet Explorer 4, you need to ensure that you are using the latest versions of all the IE 4 components. If you enable Automatic Version Synchronization, the IEAK will take over the chore of checking version numbers for your components and comparing them with the latest versions available for those components. This process is explained in the next section, where you specify the location for AVS to search for components and specify what AVS should do with them.

If you have a good connection to the Internet, you should leave AVS turned on. If you prepare the custom version of Internet Explorer 4 on an isolated machine, or if you have just downloaded the components and have a very slow network connection, you can turn AVS off. You cannot turn off AVS the first time you run the IEAK, because the IEAK must download the components of IE 4 at least once!

Where Can You Store the Custom Package?

You must specify a location for the IEAK to store the custom package(s) of Internet Explorer 4. The hard drive must have enough free space for the downloaded CAB files and additional space for the configuration files that the IEAK will create to guide Active Setup as it installs your custom IE 4 package.

What About Languages?

Most people who create custom versions of Internet Explorer 4 will create English custom versions. However, Microsoft provides files for supporting IE 4 in over 20 languages, and if your product, service, or network environment is used by people who speak more than one language, you may want to prepare additional versions of IE 4 to support those languages.

You must run the IEAK again for each additional language you want to support. Each language-differentiated version of Internet Explorer 4 resides in a different subdirectory under the folder you specify in this stage, and, therefore, each language-differentiated version takes up additional space. For example, to support both English and Spanish, the combined packages will use approximately twice the space as just English.

If you prepare multiple language versions of Internet Explorer 4, you should take care that the custom packages, branding bitmaps, and text match the language you are configuring IE 4 to use. You wouldn't want the browser to use Swahili, but the CD-ROM autorun bitmap to be in English, would you?

Exercise 6.4 will get you started using the IEAK. Exercises 6.4 through 6.8 must be performed in order to produce a custom IEAK package.

EXERCISE 6.4

Using the IEAK to Gather Information (Stage 1)

1. Select Start ➤ Programs ➤ Microsoft IEAK ➤ IEAK Wizard.

2. Click Next, and click Next again to get past the main introduction and Stage 1 Introductory screens.

3. Enter **Test Company** in the Company Name field.

4. In the Customization Code field, enter the customization code you received from the Microsoft Web site.

5. Select the Corporate Administrator radio button.

6. Make sure that the Automatic Version Synchronization box is selected, and click Next.

7. Select English, and click Next.

8. Enter **c:\IEAKCustom** as the destination folder for the customized packages.

9. Select the CD-ROM option.

10. Select the Multiple Floppy Disks option, and click Next to proceed to Stage 2.

IEAK Stage 2: Specifying Active Setup Parameters

In the second stage of the IEAK, you configure which of the usual components Active Setup will install and which software publishers it will trust. All of the components that are in your custom Internet Explorer 4 package must be on your hard drive in order for the IEAK to create a custom IE 4 package. With the IEAK, you can use AVS to automatically retrieve newer versions of standard components. You must provide the paths to any custom components that you want to include in your version of IE 4.

Using AVS

If you enabled AVS in Stage 1, the IEAK will automatically check the versions of the components Microsoft distributes with Internet Explorer 4. You specify the location for the IEAK to look for new components (you will want to select the Microsoft site nearest you). You will see a list of components the first time you run the IEAK, and a red X icon will appear next to any of the components that you don't have. Subsequently, after you run the IEAK and have synchronized the components at least once, you should see green check marks indicating that you have the latest version or yellow caution icons informing you that Microsoft has updated the component since the last time it was downloaded (as shown in Figure 6.4).

If you disable AVS, all of the components in the component list will show up with yellow caution icons. These yellow caution icons indicate that the IEAK is unable to determine if the components are the latest versions, and you will not be able to synchronize the components.

F I G U R E   6.4

AVS automatically synchronizes your components for IEAK with the components available from Microsoft's download site.

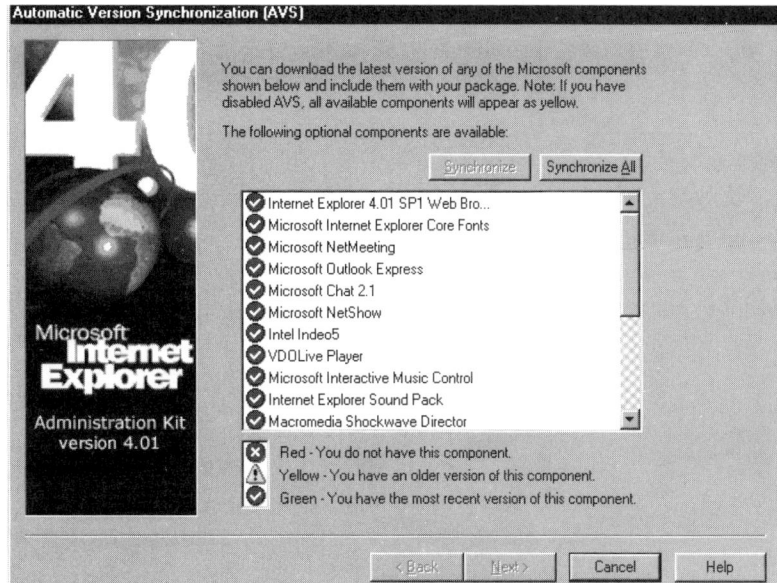

If you have a slow network connection, you may want to download only the components that you intend to include in your custom Internet Explorer 4 package. You can do this by selecting each component and clicking the Synchronize button. If you have a fast network connection, you can click the Synchronize All button.

Custom Component Information

When you create a custom component you must inform the IEAK. You need to give the custom component a name and location, as well as establish a *GUID* (globally unique identifier) and version number. The GUID distinguishes that component from all other components, even components that have the same name. The Generate button will automatically make a unique GUID for you (as shown in Figure 6.5).

The version number is used by Active Setup and Internet Explorer 4's autoconfiguration mechanism to ensure that your custom version of IE 4 has installed the latest version of the custom component. If you want users of your custom component to be able to cleanly remove it from their computers, you should provide a unique uninstall key. If the component is a self-extracting EXE file, you can also supply any necessary parameters for expanding and installing the component.

F I G U R E 6.5

Using the IEAK, you must specify the custom components you want to install in your version of IE 4.

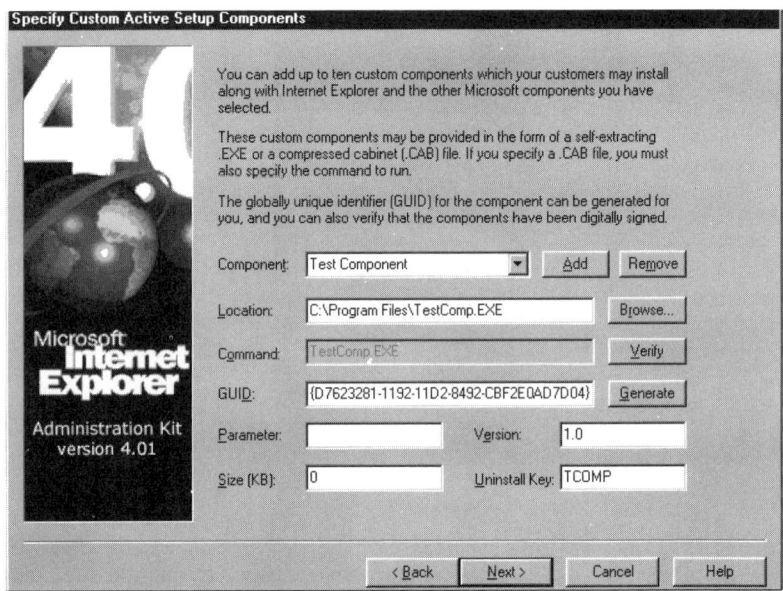

Active Setup and Certificates

As described earlier in this chapter, Active Setup will only install components that have been digitally signed by organizations it trusts. That means that Active Setup must have a list of trusted organizations that it can check the digitally signed CAB files against. The final step in Stage 2 is to specify which organizations your version of Active Setup should trust by selecting those certificates from the list.

Like many of the other settings, the IEAK takes its list of certificates from the Internet Explorer 4 browser of the computer you are using to run the IEAK Wizard. To add certificate choices to the IEAK, you must add the certificates in the Content tab of the IE 4 browser. Exercise 6.5 guides you through Stage 2 of the IEAK.

EXERCISE 6.5

Using the IEAK to Collect Setup Components (Stage 2)

1. At the introductory screen to Stage 2 of the IEAK Wizard, click Next.

2. Select the Microsoft download site nearest you, and click Next.

3. Using the IEAK Wizard, specify that the computer should trust Microsoft by selecting Always Trust Content From the Microsoft Corporation, and clicking Yes. Do the same for the producers of other software packages included with IE 4 (such as Shockwave, produced by Macromedia).

4. Click the Synchronize All button.

5. Click the Next button in the AVS screen.

6. Click Add in the Specify Custom Active Setup Components screen.

7. Type **Test Component** in the Component field.

8. Type **C:\Components\TestComp.EXE** in the Location field.

9. Click the Generate button to automatically generate a GUID.

10. Type **1.0** in the Version field.

11. Type **TCOMP** in the Uninstall Key field, and click Next.

12. Highlight the root entry, and click Next to proceed to Stage 3.

IEAK Stage 3: Customizing Active Setup

In this stage, you configure how Active Setup looks and which options (for how this custom Internet Explorer 4 package will behave during installation) will be presented to the user. You choose the bitmap images, the title bar text, the available setup options (standard, full, or enhanced), the location to which users can download the CAB files for the custom IE 4 package, the destination folder on the computer for the CAB files, and whether to include Windows Desktop Update.

If you are using the IEAK in ISP mode, you have the option in this stage of specifying a custom profile for the Internet Connection Manager. That profile can configure your custom Internet Explorer 4 package to connect directly to your ISP using a modem and a local phone number. You can create a custom ICM profile using the Connection Manager Administration Kit, which comes with the IEAK on the IE 4 Resource Kit CD-ROM.

Microsoft
✓ *Exam*
Objective

Specify and customize Active Setup components.

Branding Options for Active Setup

The branding options for Active Setup are more useful to an Internet service provider or Internet content provider than a corporate administrator. This is because the corporate administrator (or someone working for the corporate administrator) will most likely be the person installing Internet Explorer 4 on the computers in the corporate network. For the ISP and ICP, however, it will be the customer performing the installation, and to the ISP and ICP, that installation process is one more opportunity to increase product visibility. The ISP and ICP will want to use the branding options for Active Setup (see Figure 6.6). You should have the bitmap files and title bar text prepared in advance.

FIGURE 6.6

You can customize how Active Setup looks to users installing your custom IE 4 package.

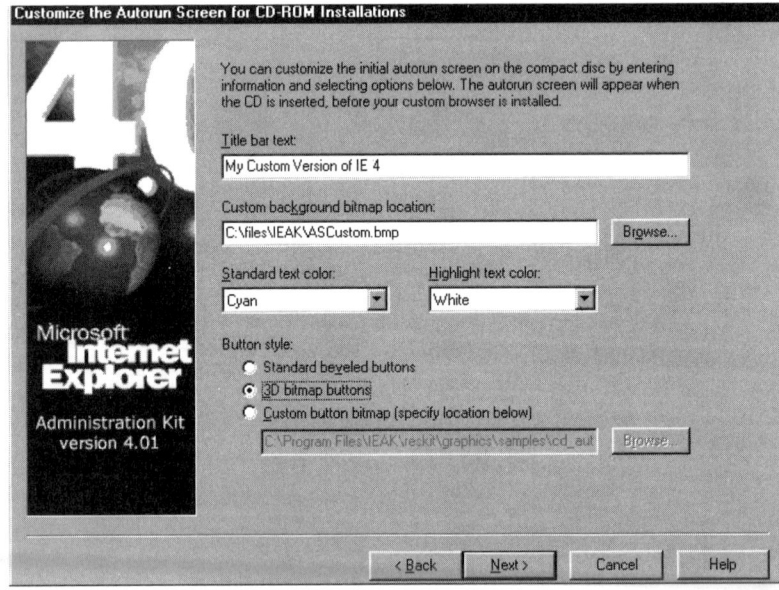

You have the following options for branding Active Setup:

- Specify a custom CD-ROM autorun bitmap and button image
- Configure a custom autorun window title bar text
- Specify a custom Active Setup bitmap
- Configure a custom Active Setup window title bar text

Silent Installation

In this stage you can choose to silently install this version of Internet Explorer 4 on destination computers. A silent installation happens without user inter-action. Be aware that the system may reboot at the end of the installation process, catching the user by surprise. If you choose the silent install option, the following IEAK choices are restricted:

- You cannot give the user the choice of installing Windows Desktop Update (you have to decide while creating the custom package whether WDU will be installed or not).
- You can have only one installation option.
- You can have only one site for downloads.

If you want to perform silent installations at separate locations with dif-ferent download sites for each location, you will need to run the IEAK as many times as you have locations because you can specify only one down-load site in a silent installation.

Creating Multiple Setup Options

Internet Explorer 4 has three setup options (see Figure 6.7): Minimal, Stan-dard, and Full. The Minimal option just installs the IE 4 browser. Standard installs Outlook Express as well, and Full installs all of the commonly dis-tributed components supplied by Microsoft. (See the Installation Compo-nents section in Chapter 3 for a complete list of what is installed for Minimal, Standard, and Full installation options). You can create your own IE 4 instal-lation options (in addition to or replacing the Microsoft options). Each of your custom options will have its own list of components to install. You can specify up to 10 installation options for your custom IE 4 package.

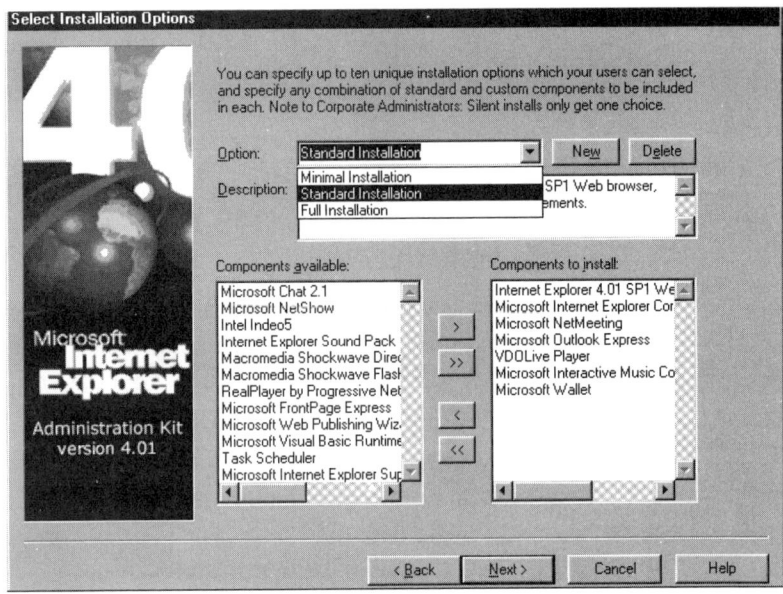

FIGURE 6.7
Using the IEAK, you
can specify up to 10
installation option
configurations for IE 4.

When you create multiple installation options, you do not need to reserve space for each option independently. Instead, you only need to reserve space for the sum of all of the components used in all of the installation options. For example, if Option 1 includes components A and B, while Option 2 includes components A and C, then you need space for components A, B, and C for building your custom Internet Explorer 4 package.

Creating Multiple Download Sites

You can specify up to 10 download sites for your custom Internet Explorer 4 package. If your users will be downloading your version of IE 4 over the network, you need to specify at least one location. Specifying additional locations is a good idea if you manage a large or geographically distributed network. The locations you specify in this stage are the Web site locations (URLs) where you put the custom package you are creating.

Version Numbers, Configuration Identifiers, and the Component Page URL

You should supply a version number to keep track of changes you make to your custom Internet Explorer 4 package. If you make multiple versions (for example, one version including a custom component and another without that component), you should give each version a unique configuration identifier.

Users may want to extend the functionality of the custom Internet Explorer 4 package by downloading additional components. The URL of Add-on Component Page field points the browser to a location for additional components. You can leave this field blank (in which case the user will be directed to the Microsoft site) or you can provide your own location.

Choosing Where to Put IE 4 on the Destination Computers

Internet Explorer 4 goes in the C:\Program Files\Internet Explorer folder by default. However, you can specify an alternate location in this stage of the IEAK. Since the Program Files folder and Windows System folder may not be in their standard locations on the C drive, you can specify the folder name and put the package in one of those two folders, or you can specify a complete file path for your version of IE 4.

Selecting Windows Desktop Update

Your last option for this stage is the installation of Windows Desktop Update. You must decide whether you want to install Windows Desktop Update, or let the user decide to install it. Windows Desktop Update makes significant changes in the appearance of the Windows operating system, and it requires more RAM than Internet Explorer 4. Before you set Windows Desktop Update to always install, you should ensure that the computers it will be installed on can handle the increased load and that the users are prepared for the change in how their computers work.

In Exercise 6.6 you customize Active Setup for your Internet Explorer 4 package.

EXERCISE 6.6

Using the IEAK to Customize Active Setup (Stage 3)

1. At the introduction screen to Stage 3, click Next.

2. Type **My Custom Version of IE 4** in the title bar text field.

3. Enter the location of the ASCD.bmp file on the Sybex CD-ROM (e.g., D:\examples\ASCD.bmp).

4. Click the Custom Button Bitmap option.

EXERCISE 6.6 (CONTINUED)

5. Enter the location of the ASBtn.bmp file on the Sybex CD-ROM (e.g., D:\examples\ASBtn.bmp), and click Next.

6. Type **Custom IE 4 Install** in the Active Setup Wizard Title Bar Text field.

7. Enter the location of the ASCustom.bmp file on the Sybex CD-ROM (e.g., D:\examples\ASCustom.bmp).

8. Type **Customized Components,** and click Next.

9. Select Install Packages Silently, and click Next.

10. Select Standard Installation.

11. Highlight the words Test Component you added in Exercise 6.5.

12. Click the Right Arrow (>) button to add the component to the list of components available for the Customized Components option.

13. Highlight the Microsoft NetMeeting component, and click the Right Arrow (>) button.

14. Click Next to proceed to the Specify Download URLs screen.

15. Click Add.

16. Type **My Test Download Site** in the Site Name field.

17. Type **http://myweb:8080** in the URL field, and click Next.

18. Type **justtest** as the configuration identifier, and click Next.

19. Select the Program Files folder option, type **Internet Explorer (Custom)** in the Folder Name field, and click Next.

20. Click Yes to integrate the Windows Desktop Update in your package, and click Next to proceed to Stage 4.

IEAK Stage 4: Customizing the Browser

In this stage of the IEAK you preconfigure the browser for your network environment and brand the browser to match your company's image. Before you perform the exercise for this stage, you should understand where the IEAK gets its browser settings.

Importing Current Web Browser Settings

The IEAK does not include screens that allow you to manipulate the Internet Explorer 4 settings for the Active Channels, Software Distribution Channels, Active Desktop, Desktop Toolbars, Security Zones, or Content Ratings. These settings are either left at their default values or are taken from the IE 4 that is installed on the computer running the IEAK. The IEAK does include screens that allow you to import these settings from IE 4. In the case of the Internet Explorer 4 Security Zones, the IEAK will open the configuration windows in IE 4 for you to make changes before you import them.

Branding

You are allowed to change the appearance of elements in Internet Explorer 4 to promote your company or product. Specifically, you can change the toolbar background bitmap, the title bar text, and the home page URL. If you manage a public access computer lab, provide dial-up (ISP) services, or provide Internet services that can be accessed via a Web browser, you might like to have an ever-present reminder on the user's screen of whose services they are using. You might like the default home page to be the home page of your service. The branding options of the IEAK can help you do that.

Default Settings

The default settings of Internet Explorer 4 establish the initial Web browsing environment that the user will have, including the first Web page that will appear in the browser window, the initial favorites and channel settings, which search engines and on-line support pages the user will be provided, and how the Windows Desktop Update will be configured. You can customize all of these settings to make an initial environment appropriate to how your custom IE 4 package will be used. You can make your own home page the default, include a channel of your own, add components to the Active Desktop, and even preload the favorites menu with your own sites. You will want to configure proxy server settings for how your network is configured if you have a proxy server on your network as well. You can change the following default settings in this stage of the IEAK:

- Home page URL

- Search and online support URLs

- Favorites

- Welcome messages

- Desktop wallpaper

- Active Channels

- Software Distribution Channels

- Active Desktop settings

- Toolbar settings

- Web View settings

- Autoconfiguration

- Proxy settings

- Security settings

Figure 6.8 shows you the IEAK screen for preconfiguring the links and Favorites menus in your custom Internet Explorer 4 package.

Making changes in this stage only establishes the initial settings of IE 4—the user can change the settings after IE 4 is installed on the user's computer. To make setting changes that the user cannot modify, you can establish system policies in Stage 5 of the IEAK or establish system policies using the IEAK Profile Manager, described in Chapter 7.

FIGURE 6.8

You can add additional URLs to your list of favorites using the IEAK.

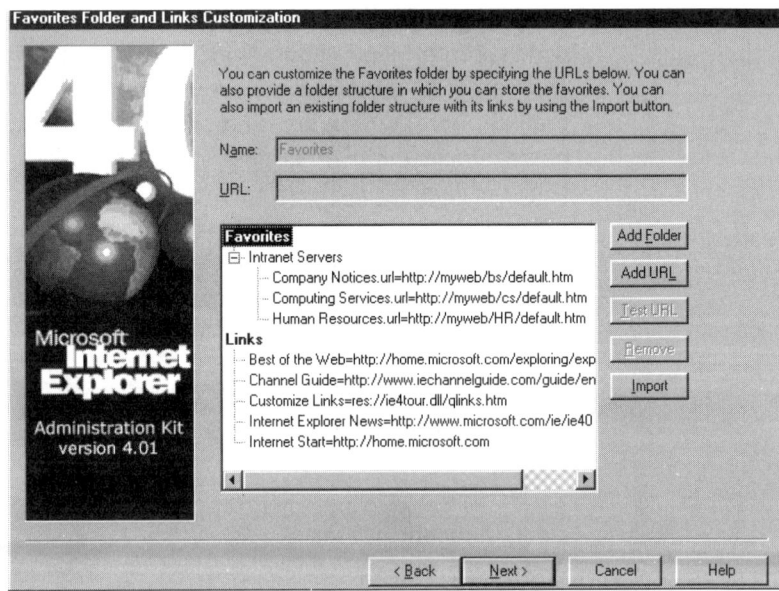

An Internet service provider may want to have the default page displayed by Internet Explorer 4 be the service's home page. An Internet content provider, on the other hand, will want to point the Web browser to the company's products or services home page. A corporate administrator may configure the Web browser to load an Intranet Web page, or perhaps an external Web page appropriate to what the users need (for example, a news service, a weather page, or a stock ticker).

Microsoft strongly recommends that you create an online support page and configure your custom Internet Explorer 4 package to point to it, so that your customers or users have an easy way to get information and resolve problems with the custom software.

You can preconfigure the favorites and Active Channels to include Web sites or channels appropriate to your business or product. You should certainly include links to Web sites you maintain. If you include links to Web sites you do not maintain, you should frequently check to make sure that the links are still valid (Web sites can change addresses or disappear entirely). If you are using the IEAK in ISP or in ICP mode, you can add one Active Channel and delete Active Channels that directly compete with your service.

Active Desktop Settings

You can place what will be automatically on your users' desktops when they turn on their computers, such as Microsoft's Channel Guide. In order for the IEAK to import Active Desktop settings, you must configure the settings for Internet Explorer 4 on the IEAK computer. You can, of course, leave the Active Desktop settings at their Microsoft defaults.

Security Settings

In a corporate environment, you may want to change the default security settings for Internet Explorer 4. You will want to establish trusted sites and certificates, mark restricted sites, set allowed levels for rated content, and allow or not allow unrated content. Depending on your security needs, you may want to disable scripting, ActiveX control downloads, Java applet downloads, and even file downloads of any type.

Autoconfigure

With a little bit of preparation, you can use the Autoconfigure mechanism of Internet Explorer 4 to vastly ease your Internet management burden. With careful use of the ADM File Import function (merging Windows policy files with IE 4 autoconfiguration files), you can extend the reach of centralized management to other aspects of the Windows operating system.

One of the files produced when you use the IEAK is an INS file containing the configuration settings for your custom Internet Explorer 4 package. When Active Setup installs IE 4 on a computer it parses the INS file for IE 4 configuration settings, Active Desktop settings, and component settings. If you import ADM policy settings (as in Stage 5 of the IEAK), Active Setup will even make changes to operating system settings.

Autoconfigure works by checking an INS file to see if there are any settings changes. You can configure the autoconfigure mechanism in Internet Explorer 4 to look for changes on a regular basis while IE 4 is open, or just when IE 4 starts (if autoconfigure is turned on, it will automatically check for new settings whenever IE 4 is started). You can make changes to INS files using the IEAK Policy Editor.

Internet Explorer 4 also supports the autoproxy files (JS or PAC) used by Internet Explorer 3. If you already have autoproxy files configured for your network, you might want to use them instead of the autoconfiguration files. However, autoconfiguration files do not require programming and are easier to use.

Proxy Settings

While you can leave most of the Internet Explorer 4 configuration settings alone (they will simply adopt the Microsoft default settings), you will need to configure the proxy settings to match the configuration of your network. Otherwise, users may not be able to access the Internet using your custom IE 4 package. If you have a proxy server on your network, you should preconfigure IE 4 with the proxy address and port number for each of the protocols you have proxies for (they may all be the same address and port, or may be different, as shown in Figure 6.9).

For computers connected to a LAN and for computers connected to an ISP, there are often several locations that should not go through a proxy server. If you are configuring Internet Explorer 4 for a LAN, you should list Intranet sites on your LAN that should not go through the proxy server. If you manage an ISP with a proxy server, you may also have servers (mail, news, local Web, etc.) that are on the subscriber's side of the proxy, and therefore shouldn't use the proxy service—you will need to list these addresses so that IE 4 will not use a proxy to access them.

FIGURE 6.9

You should preconfig-
ure your version of IE 4
with proxy server set-
tings for your network.

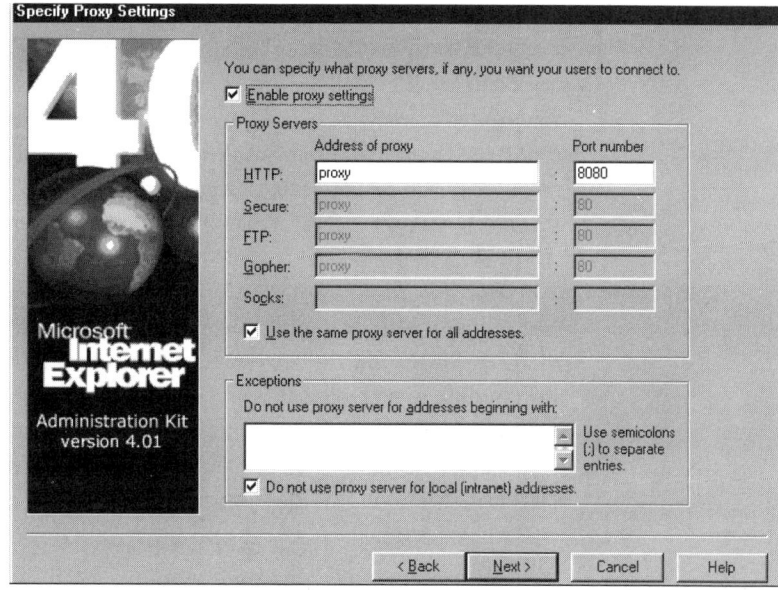

Signup Server, Serverless Signup, and No Signup

If you are using the IEAK in ISP mode, you can configure the options the
Internet Connection Manager has for establishing an account with the ISP
you manage. The three options are Internet Signup Server, Serverless Signup,
and No Signup. These options do not appear if you are using the IEAK in
Corporate mode.

Microsoft
✓ *Exam*
Objective

**Develop strategies for using the Internet Connection Wizard
in Internet service provider mode. Elements include:**

- Modem detection

- Stack installation

- Configuration of dial-up connections

Using the Internet Signup Server option requires that you run a server program that the Internet Connection Wizard can connect to in order to open an account for the user. Most ISPs implement the signup server using CGI scripts on the ISP Web server. In addition to establishing a signup server, you will have to supply an HTML page that describes the service and an Internet signup file (named `signup.isp`) that is used to dial the modem and reach the Internet signup server. The signup server gives the Internet Connection Wizard the rest of the information it needs to open an account with the ISP and to establish a network connection once the account is opened.

If your ISP docs not maintain a signup server, you can enter the information, which would otherwise be provided by the signup server, directly into the IEAK and select the Serverless Signup option. If you use the Serverless Signup option, you need to provide an INS file (which the ISP file must refer to) that contains network settings (such as the proxy server location, news server addresses, and mail server addresses) in addition to providing an HTML file and an ISP file (as with the Signup Server option).

For both the Signup Server and Serverless options, you can provide a custom Internet Connection Manager profile and static Domain Name Server addresses, configure header compression, encrypt passwords, define gateways, and establish software compression for the connection. These settings configure how the connection will be made between the user's computer and the dial-up server so that the Internet Connection Wizard can get the connection settings it needs to establish a regular dial-up Internet connection.

If you select the No Signup option, the user is expected to either have an Internet connection already established or have some other method of opening an account with an ISP. Many ISPs use their own signup methods which differ from the method established by Microsoft. These ISPs should create a custom Internet Explorer 4 package using the IEAK that uses the No Signup option.

In Exercise 6.7 you will use the IEAK to customize the browser settings of your Internet Explorer 4 package.

EXERCISE 6.7

Using the IEAK to Customize the Browser (Stage 4)

1. In the introduction screen to Stage 4, click Next.

2. Check the Customize Title Bars option, and type **Test Company** in the title bar text field.

3. Enter the location of the Toolbar.bmp file on the Sybex CD-ROM (e.g., D:\examples\Toolbar.bmp), and click Next.

4. Click Next to accept the default home page and search page.

5. Type **http://myweb/help.html** in the URL field, and click Next.

6. Click Add Folder, and type **Intranet Servers** in the Name field.

7. Click Add URL, type **Human Resources** in the Name field, and type **http://myweb/HR/default.html** in the URL field.

8. Click Add URL, type **Computing Services** in the Name field, and type **http://myweb/CS/default.html** in the URL field.

9. Click Add URL, type **Company Notices** in the Name field, and type **http://myweb/BS/default.html** in the URL field.

10. Click Next to go to the next screen.

11. Select Do Not Display a Welcome Page.

12. Select the Disable Internet Explorer 4.0 Welcome Window option.

13. Enter the location of the WDUBack.bmp file on the Sybex CD-ROM (e.g., D:\examples\WDUBack.bmp), and click Next.

14. Click the Launch Channel Guide button.

15. Click the Science Channel link on the left side of the Web page.

16. Click Add Active Channel button, and click OK.

17. Click No to keep your current screen saver, and then switch back to the IEAK Wizard.

18. Select the Import Current Channel Configuration option, and click Next.

19. Select the Import Current Software Distribution Channel Configuration option.

20. Set the schedule to Auto, and click Next.

21. Select the Import the Current Active Desktop Settings option.

22. Click the Modify Settings button, and click the Web tab.

23. Click the Folder Options button, and click Yes to go to the folder options panel.

24. Select the Classic folder view option. Click Apply, and click OK.

25. Click Next to exit the Specify Active Desktop Components screen. Click Next to leave the Custom Desktop Toolbars at the Microsoft defaults. Click Next to leave the My Computer and Control Panel Web View features at the Microsoft defaults.

26. Type **TestBrowser** for the Custom User Agent string,and click Next.

27. Select the Enable Automatic Browser Configuration box.

28. Type **http://myweb/auto/test.ins** into the autoconfigure (INS) URL field, and click Next.

29. Type **proxy** for the proxy server name and **8080** for the port address, then click Next.

30. Leave Certificate Authority and Authenticode settings at their defaults, and click Next.

31. Leave Security Zones and Content Ratings at their defaults, and click Next to go on to Stage 5.

IEAK Stage 5: Component Customization

In the final stage of the IEAK, you customize the components that come with Internet Explorer 4 and establish policies to "lock-down" IE 4 settings. To accomplish this, you will need all the network settings (server names, server addresses, and port numbers).

In the previous stage, you configured security settings to protect network users from Internet intruders, and in the Policies portion of this section you can lock-down Internet Explorer 4 settings to protect them from the users themselves. You need to know that some users will not appreciate being kept from "fiddling" with their computer.

Microsoft
✓ *Exam*
Objective

Configure built-in and custom components of Internet Explorer 4.0 by using the IEAK wizard. Components include:

- Microsoft Outlook Express
- Microsoft NetMeeting

Outlook and LDAP

One nice feature of Outlook Express is how it can use LDAP servers as a common network repository of e-mail addresses, phone numbers, and other contact information. If common contact information is stored on the LDAP server, a change to an address is instantly available to everyone, mailing lists are easily updated, and users have a consistent view of contact information no matter what computer in the network they happen use.

In order for Outlook Express to connect to an LDAP server, you need to supply an easy-to-remember name, the Internet address of the directory service, a home page, a search base, and a bitmap for Outlook Express to display. The search base can be base, one, or sub. You should select base (the default) unless the LDAP server contains an immense amount of contact information divided into many organizational groupings. In that case, sub will instruct the server to search a portion of the contacts, and one will interrogate just one organizational level.

Uses for Signatures

Most organizations that configure standard signatures for their employees or customers use the signature to append a legal disclaimer to outgoing messages. You should consider whether your organization could be held responsible for something one of your users writes, and if a disclaimer would be appropriate. Of course, you should consult the Legal department or a legal consultant that understands your organization for the wording (and appropriateness) of such a disclaimer.

The Registry, Customization, and ADM Files

In the final section of Stage 5, you can establish system policies and restrictions to lock-down Internet Explorer 4, Outlook, and Microsoft NetMeeting settings. From this screen you can also import policy settings for the Windows operating systems (the policies are stored in an ADM file for each operating system).

The System Policies and Restrictions window has two panes you can work in, as shown in Figure 6.10. On the left is a tree view with seven top level entries. You can click on an entry (folder) to "expand" it and show you the folder contents (settings categories). These settings appear on the right pane when you select a setting category in the left pane. The following are the top level options:

- Microsoft Chat
- Microsoft NetMeeting
- Internet Restrictions
- Internet Settings
- Outlook Express
- Web Desktop
- Subscriptions

FIGURE 6.10

You can lock-down IE 4 browser settings by establishing system policies and restrictions in the IEAK.

 **NOTE** You can learn more about the System Policy options for Internet Explorer 4, Windows 95, and Windows NT in Appendix B.

In Exercise 6.8 you will use the IEAK to configure mail and news and to set system policies for NetMeeting.

EXERCISE 6.8

Using the IEAK to Customize Internet Components and Establish System Policies (Stage 5)

1. In the introduction screen to Stage 5, click Next.

2. Check the options to make Outlook the default Mail and News client, and click Next.

3. Type **TestDirectory** for the easy-to-remember name of the LDAP server.

4. Type **directory.testcompany.com** in the Address field.

5. Type **http://www.directory.testcompany.com** in the Home Page field.

6. Type **base** in the Search Base field.

7. Enter the location of the LDAP.bmp file on the Sybex CD-ROM (e.g., D:\examples\LDAP.bmp), and click Next.

8. Type **http://myweb/outlook/pane.html** in the Outlook URL field, and click Next.

9. Select the Append the Following Signature to Outgoing Mail Messages option and the Use Mail Signature Also as News Signature option.

10. Type **This message does not necessarily represent the views or opinions of Test Company, a wholly owned subsidiary of Fictional Corp.** in the text box, and click Next.

11. Click the Microsoft NetMeeting folder in the components tree view.

12. Select the NetMeeting Settings entry.

EXERCISE 6.8 (CONTINUED)

13. In the right panel, scroll down to Restrict the Use of Video, and select the first two options.

14. Scroll down to Set the Default Directory Server, type **directory .testcompany.com** in the text field, and click Next.

15. Click Finish to have the IEAK create the IE 4 package in the directory you specified in Stage 1 of the IEAK.

Deploying the Custom IE 4 Package

Once you have built a custom version of Internet Explorer 4 the hard part is over. However, you're not quite done yet. You also have to make the custom software available to your users or customers. You have the following distribution options:

- Network share

- CD-ROM

- URL

- Floppy disk

Microsoft ✓ *Exam Objective*

In corporate administrator mode or Internet service provider mode, deploy a preconfigured version of Internet Explorer 4.0 by using the IEAK. Distribution methods include:

- Download

- CD-ROM

- Floppy disk

Deploying from a Network Share

An easy way to install Internet Explorer 4 on a computer is to map a drive to a network share that contains the custom IE 4 package. However, this option is only appropriate for corporate administrators, because few Internet service providers will take the security risk of providing NetBIOS access to their file and print servers. Nevertheless, this is a good way to install IE 4 when the destination computer doesn't have a Web browser already installed, and when you don't want to create a custom CD-ROM or load all those installation files onto floppy disks. Exercise 6.9 shows you how to install IE 4 on a computer by mapping a drive to a network share.

Another advantage of deploying from a network share is that Active Setup doesn't copy the CAB files to a temporary location on the destination computer's local hard drive (it does expand the CAB files to a temporary location, though). This is because (as far as Active Setup is concerned) the files just need to be accessible from a drive letter. A network drive is just as good as a local one for containing the setup files, but you can't run Internet Explorer 4 from a network drive, because parts of IE 4 (particularly Windows Desktop Update) must be available to the operating system before networking starts.

The folder you should share on the server to make Internet Explorer 4 available over the network is the directory containing the CD-ROM distribution files. You don't have to digitally sign these files because they won't be downloaded using Active Setup. Instead, you run the installation program directly.

Deploying from a CD-ROM

Deploying from a CD-ROM is similar to deploying from a network share. Active Setup doesn't have to copy the CAB files because they are locally available (however, it will expand them to a temporary location). It takes a bit more effort and some special hardware and software to burn a CD-ROM, but installation is easier because you can speed the installation by using the autorun feature. And you don't have to map a drive letter to a network share and find the IE4Setup.exe file. Instead, you just insert the disk and click Install.

Deploying from CD-ROM is most appropriate for Internet content providers and Internet service providers who need to get the Internet Explorer 4 software to people who may not have an Internet setup yet and who may not be connected to a LAN. The additional expense of a CD-ROM writer and software, or of sending the custom IE 4 package to a commercial CD-ROM production service, can be amortized across a much wider customer base. Also, deploying from CD-ROM for ICP and ISP customers avoids long download times for those with slow modems.

The files for distributing Internet Explorer 4 on CD-ROM are contained in the CD directory of the custom package folder you specified at the beginning of the IEAK Wizard. You don't have to digitally sign these files because they won't be downloaded using Active Setup. Instead, you run the installation program directly from the CD.

Deploying from a URL

Deploying from a URL is a method appropriate for ISPs, ICPs, and corporate administrators alike. In order to deploy Internet Explorer 4 over the network, you must have a Web server to host the files. Unlike hosting the files on a network share, you don't have to worry as much about file server security, and setting up a Web site is much easier than creating a CD-ROM. See Exercise 6.9 to deploy from a URL using Internet Information Server (IIS) on a Windows NT Server computer.

There are two prerequisites for deploying from a URL: the destination computers must be connected to the Internet (or Intranet), and the destination computers must have a Web browser already installed.

The Internet Explorer 4 files for Internet distribution are contained in the IE 4 site directory of the custom package folder you specified at the beginning of the IEAK Wizard. These cabinet files must be digitally signed before you run Active Setup.

Deploying from Floppy Disks

Working with floppy disks can be slow, and the disks don't contain much information (compared to CD-ROMs and hard drives), so deploying from floppy disks should be your last resort. Fortunately (for older computers that do not have CD-ROMs, are not connected to a LAN, and don't have Web browsers already installed), the floppy disk will work in almost any computer. But be prepared to swap disks frequently while installing the browser.

Exercise 6.9 assumes that you have a Windows NT 4.0 file server which is also running Internet Information Server 4. In the exercise you will sign the

CAB files IEAK has created, create a network share containing the IE 4 distribution files, create distribution floppy disks, and create a URL containing the files.

The files for distributing Internet Explorer 4 on floppy disks are contained in the MFloppy directory of the custom package folder you specified at the beginning of the IEAK Wizard. You don't have to digitally sign these files because they won't be downloaded using Active Setup. Instead, you run the installation program directly from the floppy disks.

EXERCISE 6.9

Deploying the IEAK

1. Go to the command prompt by selecting Start ➤ Programs ➤ MSDOS Prompt.

2. Type **cd\"Program Files"\IEAK\Reskit\Addons\Tools,** and click Enter.

3. Type **Setreg 1 true.**

4. Type **makecert u:testkey –k:test.pvk -n:"CN=UnverifiedSoftware"** **testcert.cer,** and click Enter.

5. Type **cert2spc testcert.cer cert.spc,** and click Enter.

6. Type **copy cert.spc c:\IEAKCustom\IE4Site\en** and click Enter.

7. Type **copy test.pvk c:\IEAKCustom\IE4Site\en** and click Enter.

8. Type **cd \IEAKCustom\IE4Site\en** and click Enter.

9. Type **signcode –spc cert.spc –v test.pvk Branding.cab** and click Enter.

10. Repeat Step 9, replacing **Branding.cab** with **Desktop.cab.**

11. Repeat Step 9, replacing **Branding.cab** with **IE40cif.cab.**

12. Repeat Step 9, replacing **Branding.cab** with **IE4setup.exe.**

13. Repeat Step 9 for each CAB file beginning with CH, replacing **Branding.cab** with the name of the CAB file. Delete cert.spc and test.pvk.

EXERCISE 6.9 (CONTINUED)

14. On the Windows NT file server that is running IIS, copy the entire contents of the `C:\IEAKCustom\IE4Site\` folder to the folder on the file server located at `C:\InetPub\IE4Distrib`, creating the folder if necessary.

15. Start the Microsoft Management Console by selecting Start ➢ Programs ➢ Windows NT 4.0 Option Pack ➢ Microsoft Internet Information Server ➢ Internet Service Manager.

16. Click the + next to the Internet Service Manager icon to expand it.

17. Select the IIS server computer in the list of servers (click it once).

18. From the Action button select New ➢ Web Site.

19. Type **IE4 Distribution Web site** in the Web site description field, and then click the Next button.

20. Type **8080** in the field for the TCP port value for the Web site. Click the Next button to continue.

21. Type **C:\InetPub\IEDistrib** in the Path field, and click Next.

22. Click Finish to create the distribution Web site. The custom distribution files can now be accessed by going to the new Web site you have just created.

Summary

Using the IEAK is straightforward once you have gathered the information and files you need (the checklist at the end of Chapter 5 should guide you through obtaining that information). If you have set up the Internet Explorer 4 Web browser on the IEAK computer the way you want the custom Web browsers to operate (as far as Active Channels, Security, Content Ratings, and the Active Desktop), then all you have to do is import those settings when you run the IEAK. Once you have created a custom IE 4 package, you must digitally sign the CAB files and make them available to your users or customers. How you deploy IE 4 will depend on your specific network situation. You may place it on a network share if you manage a LAN, you may create CD-ROMs if you create Internet content, or you may provide a URL and floppy disks if you are an Internet service provider.

The autoconfigure INS files are a powerful way to centrally control the configuration of Internet Explorer 4 browsers and, by extension, the computers they run on (if you import ADM files into the INS file). Corporate administrators will find this feature useful. Chapter 7 will explore managing deployed browsers in this manner.

Review Questions

1. You want to add an Active Channel to your custom IE 4 package. You are using the IEAK in corporate administrator mode. How do you add the channel?

   A. You are not allowed to add channels to the IEAK in corporate administrator mode.

   B. Select the Add Channel button on the Configure Channels screen of Stage 4 of the IEAK.

   C. Configure Active Channels in your IE 4 Web browser, then import the channel configuration in the IEAK.

   D. Configure the Active Channels using the Policy Editor, then import the channel configuration in the IEAK.

2. The first time you run the IEAK all of the components in the AVS screen show up with red X icons next to them. What is wrong?

   A. The IEAK cannot contact the Microsoft Web site.

   B. The components have not been digitally signed by Microsoft.

   C. You have not digitally signed the components.

   D. Nothing is wrong. The first time you run the IEAK you need to synchronize all the components.

3. You see yellow caution symbols next to several components in the AVS screen. What do these caution symbols mean?

    A. You have older components. You should synchronize those components to get the latest versions.

    B. The components have not been digitally signed. You should get a digital certificate and sign these components.

    C. The IEAK cannot find these components. You need to download them again.

    D. The components are present and up-to-date but have not yet been selected for inclusion in your custom IE 4 package.

4. What restrictions does selecting Silent Install place on your version of IE 4? Choose all that apply.

    A. You can specify only one download location.

    B. You can specify only one installation option.

    C. You can specify only one Active Channel.

    D. The installation process must not reboot the computer.

5. You want to make English, Spanish, German, and French custom versions of IE 4. How many times must you run the IEAK?

    A. One

    B. Two

    C. Three

    D. Four

6. You installed your custom IE 4 package on an older computer. Instead of your custom bitmaps you see the default IE 4 bitmaps displayed at a lower resolution. What is the problem?

   A. You have included your bitmaps in the wrong format. They must be 256-color BMP images.

   B. You have not digitally signed the images. Active setup has rejected them and replaced them with 16-color standard bitmaps.

   C. The computer is only configured to support 16-color images (standard VGA), so your bitmaps can't be displayed. The default bitmaps are displayed instead.

   D. Windows 3.1 does not support 256-color images. You must upgrade to Windows 95 or Windows NT.

7. You are creating your custom IE 4 package on a Laptop that is not currently connected to the Internet. (You previously ran the IEAK while connected to the Internet and synchronized all the components.) You run the IEAK again with AVS turned off. In the AVS screen all of the components show up with yellow caution icons. What is wrong?

   A. Microsoft has updated all of the components. You must synchronize components to get the latest versions.

   B. You do not have any of the components necessary to build a custom IE 4 package. You must connect to the Internet and download the components.

   C. You must digitally sign all of the components.

   D. Nothing is wrong. The IEAK is indicating that it can't verify whether or not the components are the latest versions.

8. You need a certificate to digitally sign your custom components and the components that IEAK prepares for you. You just want a test certificate for in-house testing of your version of IE 4. Which tool will generate test certificates for you?

    A. `IExpress.exe`

    B. IEAK

    C. `Makecert.exe`

    D. `Signcode.exe`

9. You have received a certificate from Verisign, and now you want to sign the IE 4 CAB files. What tool can you use to sign the files using that certificate?

    A. `IExpress.exe`

    B. `Signcabs.exe`

    C. `Makecert.exe`

    D. `Signcode.exe`

10. You have auto-proxy files already created for the IE 3 computers in your network. You want the same functionality in IE 4, but want to expend a minimum of effort. What can you do?

    A. Translate the autoproxy JS file into an autoconfiguration INS file using the IExpress Wizard. Configure your custom IE 4 package to use the autoconfiguration file.

    B. Translate the autoproxy JS file into an autoconfiguration INS file using the IEAK Profile Manager. Configure your custom IE 4 package to use the autoconfiguration file.

    C. Configure your custom IE 4 package to use the autoproxy JS file.

    D. Create a new INS file that has the equivalent functionality of the autoproxy JS file.

11. How do you configure your custom version of IE 4 to trust specific software publishers when downloading ActiveX controls?

    A. Add the publisher's certificate to those trusted in the Content tab of IE 4. Import the settings into the IEAK.

    B. Add the publisher's Internet address to the trusted sites list in the Security tab of IE 4. Import the settings into the IEAK.

    C. Add the publisher's certificate to the list of certificates at the end of Stage 2 (Customizing Active Setup) of the IEAK.

    D. You cannot preload IE 4 with trusted certificates. The user must choose to accept the certificate the first time he or she downloads the ActiveX control.

12. The IEAK does not provide you with an option to change one bitmap for branding purposes. Which bitmap is it?

    A. CD-ROM autorun bitmap

    B. Toolbar background bitmap

    C. Explorer spinning "e" bitmap

    D. Active Setup bitmap

13. You want to provide a custom Active Channel for news about your company. You need to prepare bitmaps for the channel. What sizes should they be? Choose all that apply.

    A. 32x32

    B. 80x32

    C. 64x64

    D. 192x32

14. What formats can the large (192x32) bitmap image for a custom Active Channel be? Choose all that apply.

   A. GIF

   B. BMP

   C. JPG

   D. TIFF

15. You want to include your own custom component with your custom IE 4 package. Your component consists of several program files, a dozen or so data files, and a `setup.exe` program that installs the component. What archival formats can you put this component into so that Active Setup will download and install it? Choose all that apply.

   A. ARC

   B. CAB

   C. ZIP

   D. EXE

16. You are creating a custom IE 4 package to enable customers to easily connect to the ISP you manage. You want to include a custom software component that keeps track of the connection time that will be displayed and billed to the user. You want the user to be able to download and install the custom IE 4 package using the Active Setup program and the single floppy distribution process. You would like the user to be assured that the custom package was produced by a reputable firm, and that the software has not been tampered with.

   Required Result: Create distribution files that Active Setup can download and install.

   Optional Result 1: Assure the user that your company is reputable.

   Optional Result 2: Assure the user that the files have not been tampered with.

   Suggested Solution: Digitally sign the files with the test root certificate using the `makecert`, `cert2spc`, and `signcode` programs.

Which of the following is correct?

A. The suggested solution accomplishes the required result and both optional results.

B. The suggested solution accomplishes the required result and just one optional result.

C. The suggested solution accomplishes the required result only.

D. The suggested solution does not accomplish the required result.

17. You manage Windows NT Workstation computers and Windows 95 computers in a public access computer laboratory at your college. Guests use the GUEST_STUDENT account. You want to lock-down settings in IE 4 so that students have a consistent IE 4 configuration no matter what computer they use and no matter who has used the computer previously. In addition to locking-down IE 4 settings, you would also like to restrict the operating system options (including desktop settings) that the user is allowed to modify. You also want to create one custom IEAK package for both Windows 95 and Windows NT.

Required Result: Lock-down IE 4 settings.

Optional Result 1: Lock-down desktop settings for Windows 95 and Windows NT Workstation.

Optional Result 2: Create just one custom package for both Windows 95 and Windows NT.

Suggested Solution: Run the IEAK twice. Lock-down the IE 4 settings in both, but only import the Windows NT ADM file to one custom IE4 package and import the Windows 95 ADM file to the other custom IE4 package in order to lock-down operating system settings.

Which of the following is correct?

A. The suggested solution accomplishes the required result and both optional results.

B. The suggested solution accomplishes the required result and just one optional result.

C. The suggested solution accomplishes the required result only.

D. The suggested solution does not accomplish the required result.

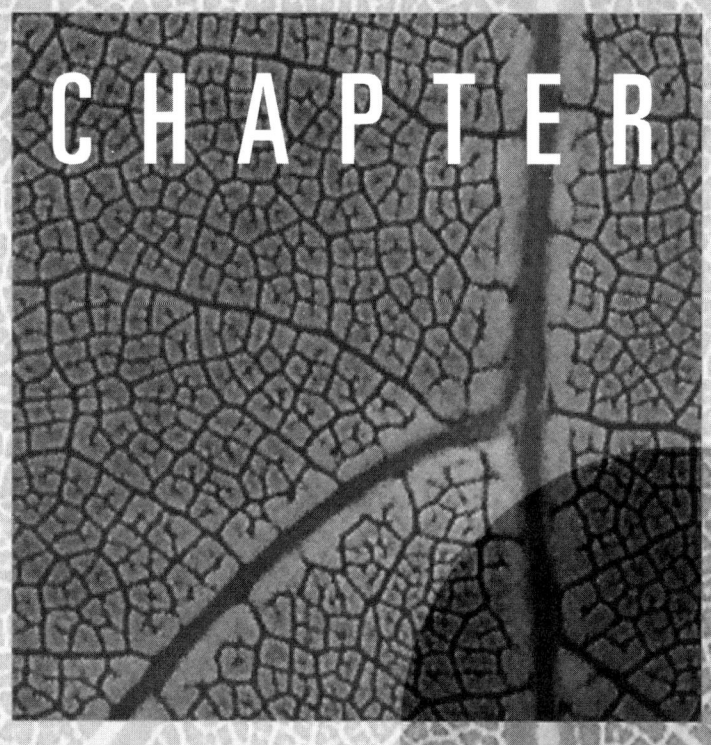

CHAPTER

7

Managing and Updating
Deployed Browsers

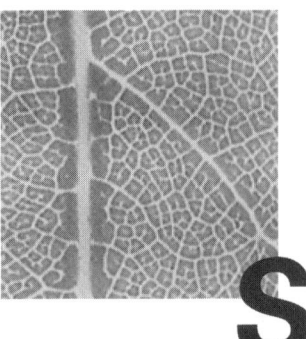

Some corporate network administrators will install Internet Explorer 4 on the computers in their networks and then try to forget about those computers. Those administrators quickly discover that IE 4 is not so easily forgotten, especially when businesses are increasingly dependent on services delivered over the Internet. After IE 4 is deployed, it is often the case that Intranet servers move from one machine to another, proxy servers change their port numbers and Internet address locations, LDAP servers come and go, and all those installed Web browsers must be updated to reflect the changes in the network. On the Internet, just as it is in the real world, the only constant is change.

Clever network administrators prepare for the changes by making it easy for themselves to make changes in software settings later. They take advantage of the autoconfiguraton mechanisms of Internet Explorer 4 and prepare INS files so that when proxy server settings change, all of the browsers can be updated by making one change, in just one place.

In addition, network administrators that are concerned about the future will examine the security needs of their network and configure the software to keep hackers and other Internet miscreants out.

Automatic Configuration

The automatic configuration mechanisms in Internet Explorer 4 are not entirely new—Microsoft is merely extending the functionality of features that are already in place. When you create a custom IE 4 package, you specify how IE 4 and its associated components should be configured. When Active Setup downloads the IE 4 components, it also downloads those settings. ACME Setup then applies those settings to your operating system and software when it installs the components.

The key to understanding the autoconfiguration feature is to realize that you can apply the configuration settings that were created in the IEAK even after the software is installed. You can make changes to the configuration later, and reapply the settings to already installed software. You can even configure Internet Explorer 4 to automatically check for configuration changes and apply them.

Microsoft ✓ *Exam* *Objective*	**Manage autoconfiguration by using the IEAK Profile Manager. Methods include:** • JScript autoproxy • .ins files • .adm files

The Internet Explorer 4 autoconfiguration mechanism works for all IE 4 settings including proxy server settings. IE 3 used a different mechanism primarily for proxy server settings called autoproxy, which is also used by Netscape Web browsers. Autoproxy files used JScript routines to determine proxy server settings when the Web browser attempted to make Internet connections. If you have a mixed IE 3 or Netscape and IE 4 network (or if you just don't want to change something that works just fine), you can continue to use the JS or PAC autoproxy files because IE 4 supports them as well.

How Automatic Configuration Works

The autoconfiguration feature of Internet Explorer 4 is just a reapplication of the software installation configuration mechanism. When you use the IEAK to make a custom IE 4 package, the IEAK creates an INS configuration file for ACME Setup to apply to IE 4 and components. The IEAK also creates component installation and policy information files for the IE 4 and its components (with INF extensions), which are included in the CAB component files. A brief recap of how the installation process works is in order:

1. The user obtains and runs the IE4Setup.exe Active Setup program.

2. Active Setup uses the INS file to determine which components to download as CAB files.

3. Active Setup starts ACME Setup to install the downloaded software on the destination computer.

4. ACME Setup uses the INS and INF files to install and configure the downloaded components.

Autoconfiguration uses those same INS and INF files to make changes to already installed software. Internet Explorer 4 can be configured to check for updated INS and INF files every time IE 4 starts or periodically (while IE 4 is running). You can, of course, configure IE 4 to never check for new configuration files.

Internet Explorer 4 autoconfiguration will look for an INS file in the location you specify in the IEAK or in the Connection tab of the Internet Settings window. That INS file will identify CAB files containing the INF files. (The CAB files contain the IE 4 component software as well.) IE 4 doesn't have to download all the CAB files for every configuration change—just ones that contain updated software or changed INF files.

Version information is contained in the configuration files. The autoconfiguration mechanism keeps the old files, so that Internet Explorer 4 can distinguish which files have changed and apply updated changes only.

How JScript Autoproxy Works

Instead of the automatic configuration feature of Internet Explorer 4, IE 3 used a mechanism called autoproxy to automatically configure itself to work in a network environment. Autoproxy is limited in what you can use it for (you can't use it to install software, for example), but it is very handy for finding an appropriate proxy server address and port number. Autoproxy files are an excellent way of centrally controlling network connections in a multi-browser environment because they are supported by most browsers.

Autoproxy files are small JScript programs. You don't need any special tools to create autoproxy files—a simple text editor such as Notepad will work. Because the autoproxy files are programs and can interrogate their environment, you can do some things that the Internet Explorer 4 autoconfiguration mechanism can't do. Autoproxy files allow you to see if a domain is local and the proxy should be bypassed, and to see if the type of document specified in the URL is usually bandwidth intensive and should go through a proxy. In comparison, with autoconfiguration files you would have to explicitly change the INS and INF files to reflect network accessibility changes, and there is no way for autoconfiguration to separate JPG traffic from HTML or TXT traffic.

Autoproxy files contain one or more JScript routines, one of which Internet Explorer 4 calls when it tries to make an HTTP connection. One routine must have the name FindProxyForURL. The FindProxyForURL function receives the URL and host name for the resource IE 4 is attempting to access. It then returns instructions on how to access that resource to the Web browser. It must return a string containing either "DIRECT", "PROXY <host>:<port>", or "SOCKS <host>:<port>" (you would of course replace <host> and <port> in those strings with the Internet address and port number of the proxy server or socks server).

The autoproxy routines are written in JScript, but they are not complete JScript applets. They may not use objects to open windows or interact with the user or operating environment. If you include such a function in your autoproxy file, the routine will quietly fail. The JScript program, on the other hand, may use regular JScript language functions and have access to a few routines with which the JScript program can query the environment.

Browsers that support autoproxy must provide JScript routines that the autoproxy program can use to determine how the Web browser should access a resource. Internet Explorer 4 allows autoproxy programs to refer to the following functions (you can refer to Microsoft's Web site or Netscape's autoproxy programming documentation for function descriptions, programming examples, and required parameters for each of the functions):

- isPlainHostName( )

- dnsDomainIs( )

- localHostOrDomainIs( )

- isInNet( )

- dnsResolve( )

- myIpAddress( )

- dnsDomainLevels( )

- shExpMatch( )

- weekdayRange( )

- dateRange( )

- timeRange( )

Learning to program in JScript is a topic worthy of a book of its own (and you can find Sybex titles on that very subject at a bookstore near you), but the following example of an autoproxy function should help you understand what is going on:

```
function FindProxyForURL(url, host)
{
    if (url.substring(0, 5) == "http:") {
    if (shExpMatch(url, "*.jpg*") {
     return "PROXY jpgproxy.testco.com:8080";
    }
    else {
     return "PROXY webproxy.testco.com:8080";
    }}
    else if (url.substring(0, 4) == "ftp:") {

     return "PROXY ftpproxy.testco.com:2121";
    }

    else {

        return "DIRECT";
    }
}
```

In the above example, the autoproxy file first checks to see if the URL is for a Web location. If so, it checks to see if it refers to a JPG image. If it is a JPG image, Internet Explorer 4 is instructed to use a special proxy server, otherwise it uses a different proxy server. On the other hand, if the request is for a file via FTP, IE 4 is directed to use the FTP proxy server, and for all other URLs, IE 4 will go directly to the destination.

Since autoproxy files are simple text files that contain programs, and since Web browsers configured to use autoproxy automatically download the PAC or JS files from a Web location when the browser starts, you should consider automatically generating PAC or JS file with an Active Server Page or CGI program. That way you can provide each Web browser with an autoproxy file specifically tailored to the computer or user requesting the autoproxy file. You could, for example, provide a different autoproxy file to users on your engineering *subnet* (communication subnetwork) than you do to users on your marketing subnet.

Using the IEAK Profile Manager

While you can edit autoproxy files with any text editor, the IEAK Profile Manager is the tool you use to manage Internet Explorer 4 autoconfiguration settings (see Figure 7.1). With the Profile Manager, you can read and edit INS and ADM files (which contain IE 4 configuration and policy settings) and create new INS and INF files for groups of users that need different IE 4 configurations. You can also import ADM files created with the Policy Editor for Windows 95 or NT, which allows you to use the autoconfiguration mechanism to manage more than just IE 4 and its related Internet components.

F I G U R E   7.1

You can use the IEAK Profile Manger to modify INS and INF files created by the IEAK.

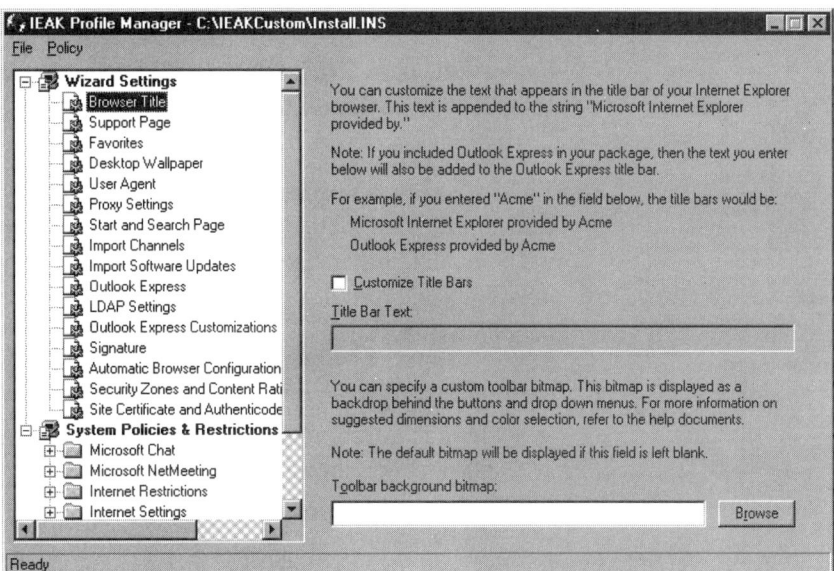

IE 4 and Components Management

When you run the IEAK Profile Manager, you see a main window divided into two frames (a tree view on the left and settings on the right) and a menu across the top. The tree and settings frames are inactive (grayed-out) until you open an existing INS file from the File menu or create a new INS file (also from the File menu).

You can find the INS file that the IEAK creates in the language subdirectory (usually under *en* for English) of the directory you specify to contain the custom version of IE 4. For example, if you specify `C:\CustomIE4` for the location of the destination folder of customized packages in the IEAK, and you select English for the IE 4 language, then you will find `install.ins` in the location `C:\CustomIE4\en\`.

There are two major branches in the tree view of the left panel:

Wizard Settings   Contains settings you can change in Stages 4 and 5 of the IEAK Wizard. You cannot add and remove components (such as Outlook Express), but you can configure information that the components may need (such as POP and IMAP server locations). The Wizard settings are stored in the INS file.

System Policies and Restrictions   Gives you the same options for locking-down IE 4 features and restricting options as the System Policies and Restrictions portion of Stage 5 of the IEAK Wizard.

While the Wizard settings are read and stored in the INS file, the options you can choose for System Policies and Restrictions are not. Instead, they are drawn from ADM files and stored to INF files that are then packaged in CAB files. Each ADM file contains restrictions for a corresponding program or function, as shown in Table 7.1.

The ADM files can be found in the appropriate language subfolder (such as *en* for English) in the Policies subfolder of the IEAK folder.

T A B L E 7.1	ADM File	Restrictions It Contains
ADM Files and Restrictions	Chat.adm	Microsoft Chat
	Conf.adm	Microsoft NetMeeting
	Inetres.adm	Internet Restrictions

T A B L E 7.1 *(cont.)* ADM Files and Restrictions	**ADM File**	**Restrictions It Contains**
	Inetset.adm	Internet Settings
	Oe.adm	Outlook Express
	Shell.adm	Web Desktop
	Subs.adm	Subscription

When you save the autoconfiguration settings, the Profile Manger creates INF files from the ADM files. INF files describe to ACME Setup which components to install and which Registry settings to create or change in order to support the installed software. The Profile Manager fills the Registry settings portion of the INF files with Registry key changes (taken from the ADM files) that lock-down IE 4 settings.

The INF files are packaged as CAB files for the Internet Explorer 4 autoconfiguration mechanism or for Active Setup to download. You must specify the location for Profile Manager to store the INS files and the CAB files containing the INF files. You must also specify the URL for the IE 4 package CAB files, and you can change the names of the INS files and CAB files containing the INF data (see Figure 7.2).

Importing Policy Files

One nice feature of the IEAK Policy Editor is that you can import policy options (registry key changes that you make that lock-down settings) from other ADM files. ACME Setup and the autoconfiguration mechanism of Internet Explorer 4 don't care what kind of policy settings they find in an INF file; any policy settings found in the INF file will be applied if ACME Setup or the autoconfiguration mechanism is allowed to make the changes.

With Windows NT, you may not be able to change some policy settings if the user is running the install software or is running IE 4 and is not logged on with sufficient privileges.

FIGURE 7.2

When saving your
modified INS file, you
also specify the
location and names
of the CAB files
that contain modified
policy information.

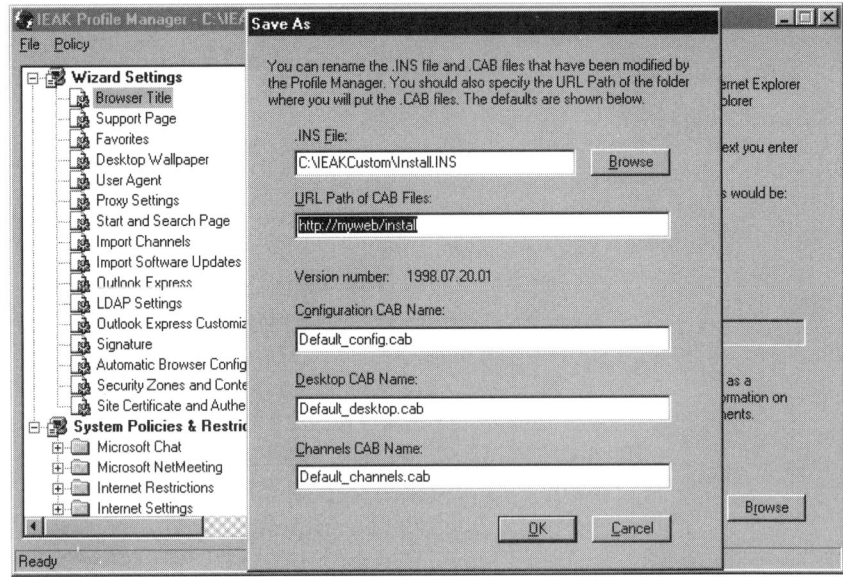

To create and edit Windows 95–specific policy settings, you can use the
Admin.adm file that comes on the Windows 95 installation CD-ROM (found
in the Admin\Apptools\Poledit directory), and you can use the Admin.adm
file from Windows NT to edit Windows NT policy settings. When you
import either ADM file into the IEAK Policy Editor, some Registry keys will
overlap—make sure that you don't establish conflicting values. When the
ADM file is imported, it will display duplicate keys (see Figure 7.3). You can
request to see the list of duplicate keys later by selecting Check Duplicate
Keys from the Policy menu.

The default IEAK Policy Editor ADM files only give options for Registry keys
that work for Windows NT or Windows 95. If you import a Windows 95 ADM
file, you will end up with autoconfiguration files that only work for Windows 95, and if you import a Windows NT ADM file, you will end up with
autoconfiguration files that only work for Windows NT. You should not
import ADM files for both operating systems. If you have both Windows 95
and Windows NT computers on your network, you should create two sets
of autoconfiguration files—one for each platform.

F I G U R E   7.3

If you import
additional ADM files
into the IEAK Policy
Editor, you must be
careful not to establish
conflicting settings
in keys that are
duplicated.

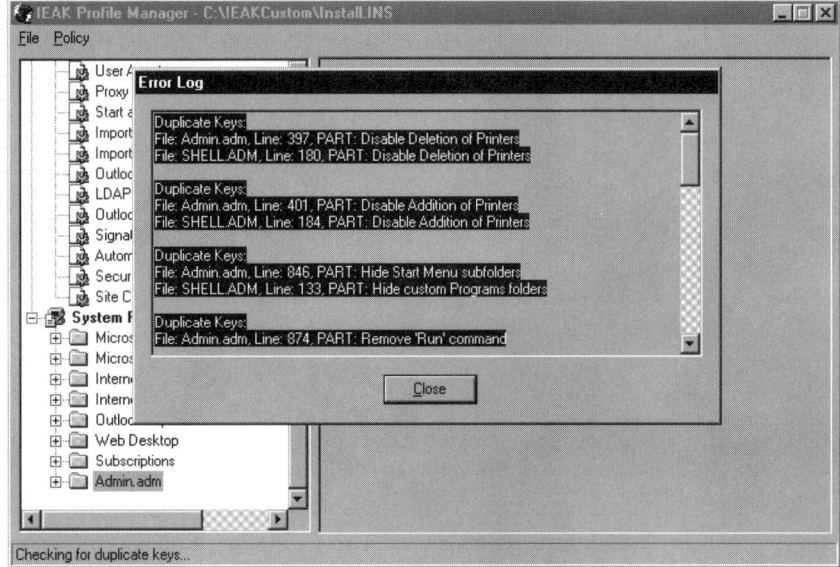

The typical use of ADM files is for network administrators to create policy files (which have the POL extension) to be stored on the file server and automatically downloaded when the user logs on to the network. Network administrators use the Poledit program (on the Windows 95 installation CD-ROM) or the System Policy Editor (in the Windows NT Administrative Tools) to create the policy files using options listed in the ADM files.

Policy files stored on a file server may contain settings that conflict with policies you establish with the IEAK Policy Editor. Be very careful that you don't establish conflicting settings when using both system policies on your network and autoconfiguration policies with IE 4.

One way to resolve conflicts between the Internet Explorer 4 autoconfiguration policies and Windows 95/NT system policies is to import the ADM files into the IEAK Policy Editor and make policy changes there. This method does not require users to log on to the network for changes in policy to take effect. It does, however, require them to run IE 4 for the changes to take effect.

Another way to resolve conflicts is to import the IEAK Policy Editor ADM files into the System Policy Editor program (click the Add button in Policy Template options), and make policy changes from there. Rather than having the policy changes made when the user runs Internet Explorer 4, you can use the network logon method of having Windows 95 or Windows NT policies updated, using the `config.pol` or `NTConfig.pol` files. This method requires users to log on to the network for changes in policy to take effect and bypasses the autoconfiguration mechanism of IE 4.

Managing Multiple *INS* files

Different groups of users may have different Internet Explorer 4 configuration needs, and therefore should have different autoconfiguration files established for them. For example, you may want to establish very restrictive policy settings for the computers in a public-access computing lab, but place only minimal restrictions on the Web browsers used by the accounting staff. If you have imported operating-system specific ADM files into your Policy Editor, you will want to have separate INS files for your Windows NT and Windows 95 users.

You should save the modified INS files and associated CAB files under distinctive names. The distinctive names ensure that that your different Internet Explorer 4 configurations will not conflict and that each autoconfiguration file can be retrieved from a separate URL by IE 4 Web browsers.

Establishing Autoconfiguration on Previously Installed IE 4 Browsers

If you already have Internet Explorer 4 browsers installed on computers in your network and you want to use the autoconfiguration feature, you don't have to replace the browsers with a custom IEAK-configured package. You only have to go to the Connection tab in the browser's Internet Options window. The Configure button will allow you to enter the URL to your autoproxy or autoconfiguration (INS) file. If you want IE 4 to immediately download any new configuration settings, you can click the Refresh button, and it will retrieve any new settings. Follow Exercise 7.1 to establish autoconfiguration on a previously-installed IE 4 browser. (Exercise 7.1 assumes that your autoconfiguration file is called `default.ins` and is stored on the myweb Web server. You should make appropriate changes to Step 3 to match your network.)

EXERCISE 7.1

Establishing Autoconfiguration on a Previously Installed IE 4 Browser

1. Launch Internet Explorer 4.

2. Select View ➤ Internet Options ➤ Connection ➤ Configure.

3. Enter **http://myweb/autoconfig/default.ins** in the URL field, and click OK.

4. Click Apply for the changes to take effect.

Using Autoconfiguration to Change Proxy Server Settings

One of the most frequently changed network settings for Internet Explorer 4 is the setting that determines how the proxy server is configured. The proxy servers come and go, the port addresses for each proxy protocol move around, and the network administrator has to update the installed Web browsers to reflect the new changes. With autoconfiguration, the process is much easier. All you have to do is make the changes in one Web browser, and then use the IEAK Profile Manager to update all the other browsers through the updated INS file. Exercise 7.2 shows you how to update the settings.

Microsoft ✓ *Exam Objective*

In corporate administrator mode, manage proxy server support for custom installations of Internet Explorer 4.0.

EXERCISE 7.2

Updating Proxy Server Settings Using the IEAK Profile Manager

1. Launch the IEAK Profile Manger program by selecting Start ➤ Programs ➤ Microsoft IEAK ➤ IEAK Profile Manager.

2. Open the INS file for your custom version of IE 4 by selecting File ➤ Open, browse to IEAKCustom, select Install.INS, and click Open.

3. Open the Wizard Settings branch in the left tree view, then select Proxy settings.

4. In the panel on the right, select the Enable Proxy Settings box .

5. Type **myproxy** in the Address of Proxy HTTP field, and type **8080** in the Port Number field.

6. Select the Use the Same Proxy Server for All Addresses box.

7. Select File ➢ Save.

8. Enter **http://myweb/install/** in the URL Path of CAB Files field.

9. Click the OK button to save the file.

Locking-Down IE 4 Settings for Public Web Browsing

Corporate administrators of large networks often manage groups of computers that are available for any user to use. Maintaining consistency in these computers is important because if one user customizes the settings in the computer, the next user may not be able to figure out how to use the computer or may have to spend time putting the settings back so that the user can work comfortably.

By locking-down settings, you can maintain a standard browser setup for users, and you can also keep inquisitive or careless users from circumventing network security. A large fraction of the policy settings you can configure in the IEAK Policy Editor consist of Internet Explorer 4 settings you can lockdown. Some settings you might want to restrict are described in the next several pages, grouped according to the IE 4 system policies section they reside in.

NetMeeting Policy Restrictions   The restrictions you may want to make in NetMeeting are all on the Options page. You can disable the whole page, or just some of the options as follows:

- Disable the General Options page

- Disable the My Information Options page

- Disable the Calling Options page

- Disable the Audio Options page

- Disable the Video Options page

- Disable the Protocols Options page

Web Desktop Policy Restrictions   This is where you can get really draconian on your Internet Explorer 4 policies. The Web Desktop policy settings control what users can configure in a Windows 95 or Windows NT computer that has been enhanced with Windows Desktop Update.

You can lock everything down, or just a few things that you don't want users meddling with. Stopping people from changing the background pattern really doesn't accomplish much, other than to make sure the company logo stays in the screen background. Keeping people from deleting desktop items, changing the Taskbar or Start menu, or deleting printers, however, are policies you should seriously consider if you intend to allow unsupervised public use of your network computers. Policy settings you can lock-down for the Web desktop include the following:

- Do not allow changes to Active Desktop

- Hide Network Neighborhood icon

- Disable Adding Any Desktop Items   .

- Disable Deleting Any Desktop Items

- Disable Editing Any Desktop Items

- Disable Closing Any Desktop Items

- Disable Changing Wallpaper

- Disable Dragging, Dropping, and Closing All Toolbars

- Disable Resizing All Toolbars

- Remove Favorites from Start menu

- Remove Find from Start menu

- Remove Run from Start menu

- Remove Documents from Start menu

- Disable Logoff

- Disable Shut Down

- Disable Changes to Printers and Control Panel settings

- Disable Changes to Taskbar and Start menu settings

- Disable Context menu (right-click) for Taskbar
- Hide custom programs folders
- Hide Common Program Groups in Start menu (Windows NT only)
- Disable File menu in Shell folders
- Do not allow customization of folders in Web View
- Disable Context menu in Shell folders
- Only allow approved Shell extensions
- Do not track Shell shortcuts during roaming
- Hide General and Details tabs in Printer Properties
- Disable Deletion of Printers
- Disable Addition of Printers
- Run only specified Windows applications
- Do not allow computer to restart in MS-DOS mode

Internet Explorer Policy Restrictions   Internet Explorer policy restrictions control what users can change in Internet Explorer itself. In a general-use computer, a user should have a lot of leeway to customize the browser to his or her preferences. A general-use computer, on the other hand, should not be customized to what one user likes because you can be certain that some other user will hate it. In addition, you want users to have a consistent environment, and you don't want users changing the basic network settings (such as the location of the proxy server in an attempt to circumvent network security).

As with the Web View settings, some of the following settings (such as colors, fonts, history, and Microsoft Wallet—nobody is putting their credit card numbers in a general-use computer) don't significantly change the behavior of Internet Explorer 4. The proxy, Security Zone, and certificate settings, however, do significantly impact how IE 4 operates. The results of misconfiguring these settings can range from users having too much access to the Internet to not being able to access the Internet at all. IE 4 policies you can establish include the following:

- Disable Changing Home Page settings
- Disable Changing Cache settings

- Disable Changing History settings

- Disable Changing Color settings

- Disable Changing Link Color settings

- Disable Changing Font settings

- Disable Changing Language settings

- Disable Changing Accessibility settings

- Use Only Machine settings for Security Zones

- Do not allow users to change policies for any Security Zone

- Do not allow users to Add/Delete sites from a Security Zone

- Disable Changing Ratings settings

- Disable Changing Certificate settings

- Disable Changing Profile Assistant settings

- Disable Changing Microsoft Wallet settings

- Disable Connection Tab settings

- Disable Calling Connection Wizard

- Disable Changing Connection settings

- Disable Changing Proxy settings

- Disable Changing Automatic Configuration settings

- Disable Changing Messaging settings

- Disable Changing Calendar and Contact settings

- Disable Changing Internet Explorer Default Browser settings

- Disable Changing Settings on Advanced Tab

Channels Policy Restrictions   Your users work with Active Channels through the browser, but the channels can be displayed either in the browser or on the Active Desktop. The IEAK Profile Manager lets you edit Channels policies separately from the Web View or Internet Explorer policies.

You should first decide if you want users of restricted Web browsers to use Active Channels at all. If so, you will want to establish the channels that

Internet Explorer 4 will subscribe to in the IEAK, and disallow any changing of those channels on general-use computers. You have the following policy options to help you:

- Disable Channel User Interface

- Disable Adding and Subscribing to Channels

- Disable Editing Channel Properties and Channel Subscriptions

- Disable Removing Channels and Subscriptions to Channels

- Disable Adding Site Subscriptions

- Disable Editing Site Subscriptions

- Disable Removing Site Subscriptions

- Disable Editing and Creating of Schedule Groups

In Exercise 7.3 you will modify your autoconfiguration file to restrict changes to Internet Explorer 4, Active Desktop, and Active Channels. You can later configure general-use computers to use this autoconfiguration setup rather than the INS file you created with the IEAK.

EXERCISE 7.3

Restricting Changes to IE 4 Using Autoconfiguration Files

1. Start the IEAK Profile Manger program by selecting Start ➤ Programs ➤ Microsoft IEAK ➤ IEAK Profile Manager.

2. Open the INS file for your custom version of IE 4 by selecting File ➤ Open, browse to IEAKCustom, select Install.INS, and click Open.

3. Open the System Policies and Restrictions branch in the left tree view.

4. Open the Internet Restrictions subbranch in the left tree view.

5. Select the General item in the left tree view.

6. Select all of the check boxes in the panel on the right.

7. Repeat steps 5 and 6 for the Security, Content, Connection, Programs, Advanced, and Channels settings subbranches.

8. Open the Web Desktop subbranch in the left tree view.

9. Select the Desktop item in the left tree view.

10. Select the Do Not Allow Changes to Active Desktop check box.

11. Select File ➤ Save.

Blocking Access to Unapproved Sites

Most network administrators manage computers that are used by adults or other (supposedly) responsible individuals. Most network users can be trusted not to connect to unsafe Internet sites (sites that might contain dangerous Web content (Trojan horse ActiveX controls, downloadable files with viruses, and so on). However, some network administrators are not so lucky, and must "protect" users (children, students, the morally indignant, etc.) from offensive material, or must keep adventurous users from burning their fingers (and corrupting their hard disks) through accessing Internet sites with dangerous files or Web pages.

You can use the IEAK Profile Manager to keep your users from contacting dangerous Internet sites and to set content ratings limitations that users can't change. Exercise 7.4 shows you how to restrict access to these sites.

Restricting Access to Specific Internet Sites and to Sites with Registered Offensive Material

1. Launch the IEAK Profile Manger program by selecting Start ➤ Programs ➤ Microsoft IEAK ➤ IEAK Profile Manager.

2. Open the INS file for your custom version of IE 4 by selecting File ➤ Open, then browse to IEAKCustom, select `Install.ins`, and click Open.

3. Open the Wizard Settings branch in the left tree view.

4. Open the Security Zones and Content Ratings subbranch in the left tree view.

5. Select the Customize Security Zones settings radio button.

EXERCISE 7.4 (CONTINUED)

6. Click the Modify Settings button.

7. Select Restricted Sites Zone from the Zone drop down box.

8. Click the Add Sites button.

9. Type **http://www.hakerz-r-us.com** in the Add field, and then click the Add button.

10. Click the OK button to close the Restricted Sites Zone window.

11. Click the OK button to close the Security window.

12. Select File ➢ Save.

Signing the Autoconfiguration *CAB* Files

Since the autoconfiguration CAB files are downloaded and expanded in the same manner the Internet Explorer 4 installation files are downloaded and installed, you have to sign the autoconfiguration CAB files the same way. You need to use a digital certificate that the installed IE 4 browsers are already configured to use. Refer to Exercise 6.2 in Chapter 6 to see how to sign the files you have created in the last few exercises.

Software Distribution Channels

Centrally configuring the Internet Explorer 4 browsers in your network and automatically downloading and installing new software can save you a lot of administrative hassle as your network changes and grows. Microsoft has utilized the autoconfiguration mechanism and Active Channels technology to allow you to update existing software and install new software on computers that have IE 4 installed.

Microsoft ✓ *Exam Objective* | **Choose Active Desktop items and develop Active Channels.**

Microsoft ✔ ***Exam Objective***

Customize Active Desktop items and Active Channels.

How Software Distribution Works

Distributing software is a tricky business, and many network administrators prefer to distribute software the old-fashioned way, package-by-package, one computer at a time. Although, installing software by hand can take a lot of time on a big network, some software packages lend themselves to automatic distribution. So careful packaging of the software and judicious use of the Software Distribution Channel technology can save network administrators a lot of time and give software publishers a new and compelling way to distribute their programs.

Software Distribution Channels can help network administrators install some software, but the software channels are most useful to software developers (because the software must be packaged in a format that can be downloaded and installed by Internet Explorer 4). Software developers can package the software more easily, and a software developer that can deliver their programs over the Web (as well as update that software automatically) has a very real advantage over software companies that must rely on traditional retail distribution channels (such as your local software store).

To distribute software automatically over the Web you need to do the following:

1. Allocate server resources for software distribution.

2. Create a Channel Distribution Format Specification file.

3. Create Open Software Distribution (OSD) files and software distribution CABs for software updated using Microsoft Internet Content Distribution (MSICD).

4. Create updated IE 4 CAB files for software that was updated using Active Setup.

5. Sign the software distribution packages and make them available on the Software Distribution Channel.

6. Subscribe installed IE 4 browsers to the Software Distribution Channel and modify the custom IE 4 package to include the Software Distribution Channel for new IE 4 installations.

Allocating Server Resources

To distribute software over the Web you need a Web server. The Software Distribution Channel that contains your software is just a Web site with a special file (a Channel Distribution Format file) that describes the software to be downloaded. Internet Information Server on Windows NT Server, of course, makes an excellent platform for hosting a Software Distribution Channel, but any Web server will do.

If you manage network services for a company that has computers in more than one location (a company with branch offices or factories in other cities, for example), you may want to set up several Web locations that mirror (maintain copies of) the Software Distribution Channel. That way users can update their software from an Intranet site on their local LAN rather than over a slower and more expensive WAN link. Similarly, if you manage computing services for an Internet content provider that uses Internet Explorer 4 autoconfiguration to distribute software, you might want to establish several Internet servers with the Software Distribution Channel around the world so that Internet customers can update their software from a site reasonably close to them.

If you are delivering software over the Internet, you don't necessarily have to have your own Web server hardware. There are many Internet service providers who will be happy to host your Web files for you, including Software Distribution Channel files, which look just like any other kind of file to an ISP.

Creating a CDF File for Software Distribution

Channel Distribution Format files (CDF files) tell browsers how to download information automatically from Web sites. CDF files make Active Channel technology more than just a Web page, because they outline the active contents of a Web site, provide channel graphics and information (for the Internet Explorer 4 Channel bar), suggest download intervals, and indicate when site content has changed. Since program files on a Web server are just another form of Web content, the Active Channel CDF file can notify the browser when a program file has been updated, just as easily as it notifies the browser when a Web page graphic has changed.

The easiest way to create Channel Distribution Format files is with the Microsoft CDF Generator that comes in the Internet Client Software Development Kit (SDK). The CDF generator guides you through the process of building a generic Active Channel. The process includes specifying the location of the Channel content (the HTML pages), the Channel Bar icons, and the optimum interval for subscribing the browser to check for new content.

The files CDF Generator makes are adequate for most Web content, but Internet Explorer 4 needs more information to automatically update software. A CDF that distributes software needs one or more SOFTPKG tags that identify the software locations and versions that are available to be downloaded. You can add SOFTPKG tags to an existing CDF file using a text editor, or you can edit an existing software CDF file (such as the one displayed below) to meet your needs.

Each Software Distribution Active Channel includes or refers to the following:

- A CHANNEL HREF that includes a URL to a Web page that is to be displayed in the users' browser window when the users click that Active Channel

- An (optional) desktop Channel bar logo, browser Channel bar logo, and browser Channel bar icon

- A title and abstract for the Active Channel

- A usage value (Software Update causes the channel to appear in the Software Update section of the Favorites menu rather than in the Channel bar)

- A schedule for the browser to check for updates

- One or more SOFTPKG items describing software to be distributed

Each SOFTPKG item contains the following information that Internet Explorer 4 uses to distinguish when to install or update software:

- A name uniquely identifying the software package.

- A version number that IE 4 checks to see when newer software is available.

- An autoinstall flag (yes or no) that tells IE 4 whether or not to automatically install the software or just to inform the user that there is new software available.

- A Style field, which should be MSICD for software installed using the Internet Content Distribution method, or ActiveSetup for IE 4 components included in a custom IE 4 configuration. For MSICD, IE 4

must be told in the CDF file where to find the software to install—
a CODEBASE tag in the file contains the location information. OSD
files further specify how IE 4 should install the software. `ActiveSetup`
does not use the CODEBASE tag nor does it use OSD files. Instead the
custom package is sought among the IE 4 CAB files built with the IEAK.

- A precache flag, which tells IE 4 to download the files to the computer's hard drive before installation.

- One or more IMPLEMENTATION tags, which specify an operating
system (such as Windows 95 or Windows NT) and a CODEBASE
location to find the distribution CAB or EXE files.

The example CDF file that follows shows you how a Software Distribution Channel is constructed:

```
<?XML version="1.0"?>
<!DOCTYPE Channel SYSTEM "http://www.w3c.org/Channel.dtd">
<CHANNEL HREF="http://myweb/distrib/hello.htm">
     <TITLE>Test Software Distribution Channel</TITLE>
     <LOGO HREF="http://myweb/distrib/hello.ico"
STYLE="icon"/>
     <USAGE VALUE="SoftwareUpdate"/>
     <SOFTPKG NAME="{55272F7E-1B37-11D1-8933-00805F8A4D63}"
          VERSION="0,1,0,1"
          AUTOINSTALL="No"
               STYLE="MSICD"
               PRECACHE="yes">
          <TITLE>Hello</TITLE>
          <ABSTRACT>Abstract: Hello Green v2.0
application installed via Active Channel</ABSTRACT>
          <IMPLEMENTATION>
               <OS VALUE="Win95" />
               <CODEBASE HREF="http://myweb/distrib/
hello.cab">
          </IMPLEMENTATION>
     </SOFTPKG>
</CHANNEL>
```

Since you can only specify the update schedule at the top level of the CDF file, all of the channels in the CDF file will have the same schedule. You can't specify different schedules for different subchannels. Also, the red gleam on the Channel bar icon that indicates a change in the Active Channel is the same gleam that appears for changes, and it only notifies the user of top level changes. The user only gets notified of changes in subchannels if the user elects to use e-mail notification of changes.

After you have created the Active Channel CDF file, you place the file (along with any icon, graphic, or explanatory HTML files) on the Web server that is used to download updates for users.

Creating OSD Files

If you are using MSICD to update software on users' computers, you may also have to create an Open Software Distribution (OSD) file for each of the software packages. The OSD must be contained in a CAB file in order for Internet Explorer 4 to trust it. The OSD file specifies how the other contents of the CAB file should be installed (or it can, optionally, specify how the contents of another CAB file that is referenced by a URL should be installed).

Active Setup packages don't need OSD files, and neither do MSICD files that are packaged in EXE format rather than CAB format. The OSD file is similar to the SOFTPKG portion of a CDF file, as you can see in the following example listing:

```
<?XML version="1.0" ?>
<!DOCTYPE SOFTPKG SYSTEM
"http://www.microsoft.com/standards/osd/osd.dtd" >
<?XML::namespace href="http://www.microsoft.com/standards/
osd/msicd.dtd" as="msicd"?>
<SOFTPKG NAME="{55272F7E-1B37-11D1-8933-00805F8A4D63}"
     VERSION="0,1,0,1"
     STYLE="MSICD">
     <TITLE>Hello</TITLE>
     <ABSTRACT>Abstract: Hello Green v2.0 application
installed via Active Channel</ABSTRACT>
     <msicd::NATIVECODE>
          <CODE NAME=hello.exe"
               CLASSID="{55272F7E-1B37-11D1-8933-
00805F8A4D63}"
```

```
                    VERSION="3,43,243,0" >
                    <IMPLEMENTATION>
                    <OS VALUE="Win95" />
                    <CODEBASE HREF="http://myweb/distrib/
hello.CAB">
                    </IMPLEMENTATION>
            </CODE>
        </msicd::NATIVECODF>
    </SOFTPKG>
```

You can learn more about OCD files and Internet software distribution in the Internet Client Software Development Kit, which is included in the Internet Explorer 4.0 Resource Kit. You can also learn more about OCD files and CDF files from Microsoft's home page (www.microsoft.com).

Signing Software

Internet Explorer 4 will not trust any CAB or EXE files it downloads if they are not digitally signed, so you will have to sign these CAB and EXE files just like you did with the IEAK-created CAB files. Follow the same steps outlined in Exercise 6.2 in Chapter 6 to digitally sign the files.

When signing the software, be sure to use a certificate that your custom version of IE 4 has been configured to trust. This way, any CDF packages you have configured to be automatically installed will not have to stop to ask the user if that certificate can be trusted.

Subscribing Browsers

The final step to automatically distributing software is to subscribe the browsers to your Software Distribution Active Channel. If you included a sufficient number of Active Channels in your custom Internet Explorer 4 package, you can just use one of those channels. If you have configured your custom IE 4 package to install with autoconfiguration turned on by default, all you have to do is use the IEAK Profile Manger to update the Active Channels, and the installed browsers will import the new channel automatically.

You subscribe Internet Explorer 4 browsers to software update channels by clicking on links to CDF files in the Web browser. You then have the option of accepting the default schedule or changing it, and you can choose whether you will be notified of changes or just have the changes happen automatically. You can go through the process for each Web browser in your network, or you can use the IEAK or the IEAK Profile Manager to import those settings so that all your Web browsers can be updated automatically.

Summary

Internet Explorer 4 autoconfiguration can reduce the amount of effort required to manage a network full of IE 4 browsers. Autoconfiguration makes it easy to change network settings when network resources (such as proxy servers, mail servers, and news servers) move. Also, autoconfiguration can preconfigure and lock-down browser settings such as the Content Advisor restrictions and which computers will be included in the Restricted Sites zone.

Internet Explorer 4 also supports autoproxy, which was used in IE 3 and Netscape to automatically configure proxy settings, but did not automatically configure other settings (such as security zones or system policy settings). Autoproxy files are JScript programs that, when the user asks the Web browser to retrieve a resource, determines at that time where to look for the resource. Autoproxy files are more flexible than autoconfiguration files, but autoconfiguration files can manage much more of the browser's behavior.

Internet Explorer 4 uses Active Channel technology to automatically check for newer versions of software. Software Distribution Channels use Channel Distribution Format files to identify software packages that are either distributed as a part of the IE 4 package (and are updated using Active Setup) or are distributed separately and are defined using Open Software Distribution files.

This chapter has shown you the features Internet Explorer 4 and the IEAK give you for managing deployed IE 4 browsers. The next chapter will show you how to secure a single IE 4 browser and how to secure browsers in your LAN from Internet intruders.

Review Questions

1. You want to modify your autoconfiguration (INS) file to reflect the latest proxy server settings for your network. What tool is most appropriate for this purpose?

   A. The IEAK Wizard

   B. The IEAK Profile Manager

   C. The IEAK INS Editor

   D. A text editor

2. You want to modify your autoproxy (PAC) file to reflect the latest proxy server settings for your network. What tool is most appropriate for this purpose?

   A. The IEAK Wizard

   B. The IEAK Profile Manager

   C. The IEAK INS Editor

   D. A text editor

3. You have created new INS and INF files using the IEAK Profile Manager, and you have placed them in the appropriate locations on your Web server. Your IE 4 users complain that their browsers are not being updated to reflect the changes you have made. What might be the problem? Choose all that apply.

   A. You have not digitally signed the new CAB files generated by the IEAK Profile Manager.

   B. You have not installed Windows Desktop Update.

   C. You have not enabled Roaming Profiles on the client computers.

   D. The Web browsers have not been configured to use autoconfiguration.

4. You want to manage proxy settings for all of the Web browsers in your network. Some network users insist on using Netscape instead of IE 4 software. What automatic configuration mechanism is most appropriate in this situation?

   A. Autoconfiguration INS files

   B. Automatically downloaded batch files

   C. PAC Autoproxy files

   D. There is no common method for automatic configuration that works for both IE 4 and Netscape Navigator.

5. You want to import policy settings for the Windows 95 operating system into the IE 4 autoconfiguration files for your network. What file should you import into the IEAK Profile Manager?

   A. `Config.pol`

   B. `Autoexec.bat`

   C. `Admin.adm`

   D. `Admin.ins`

6. You import policy settings from Windows 95 into the IEAK Profile Editor, but the Editor informs you that there are duplicate keys. What have you done wrong?

   A. You have not digitally signed the resulting INS file.

   B. You have imported the wrong file.

   C. You need to convert the file before importing it with the `IE4Convert.exe` program.

   D. You have done nothing wrong. The IE 4 policy settings already contain some operating system Registry keys.

7. You manage Windows 95 computers on a Windows NT–based network domain. You already use system policies to control some aspects of Windows desktop behavior for network users. You use IE 4 auto-configuration to lock-down many browser, Active Desktop, and Shell settings. Users note inconsistent operating system behavior. What is the problem?

A. System policies and IE 4 policies are conflicting, so users get different behavior when they log on to the network and when they start IE 4.

B. Windows NT policy settings are being applied to Windows 95 computers, which has confused the Registry.

C. You have imported Windows NT policy information into the IEAK Policy Editor, and the duplicate keys are causing problems.

D. You have imported Windows 95 policy information into the IEAK Policy Editor, and the duplicate keys are causing problems.

8. What is the most efficient way to support different groups of users that have different IE 4 Active Desktop Update configuration settings needs?

A. Create multiple custom IE 4 packages using the IEAK.

B. Create multiple custom autoproxy files using a text editor.

C. Create multiple custom autoconfiguration files using the IEAK Profile Manager.

D. Create multiple custom system policy files using the System Policy Editor.

9. You need to establish autoconfiguration in an already installed Web browser. How do you do it?

    A. Select View ➤ Internet Options ➤ Connection ➤ Configure.

    B. Select File ➤ Internet Options ➤ Advanced ➤ Autoconfigure.

    C. Select File ➤ Preferences ➤ Connection ➤ Configure.

    D. Select View ➤ Internet Options ➤ Advanced ➤ Autoconfigure.

10. What is the easiest way to stop users from changing their Active Desktop settings in previously-installed IE 4 Web browsers?

    A. Select Do Not Allow Changes to Active Desktop in the System Policy Editor, and save the policy to a `config.pol` file.

    B. Select Do Not Allow Changes to Active Desktop in the IEAK Policy Editor, and save the policy to an `INS` file. Configure browsers to use the autoconfiguration file.

    C. Select Do Not Allow Changes to Active Desktop in the Policies section of the IEAK Wizard.

    D. Select Do Not Allow Changes to Active Desktop in the Advanced tab of the IE 4 Internet Options window.

11. How do you input restricted Web sites into IE 4 policy files?

    A. Enter the restricted sites into the IE 4 Web browser, then import the settings into the Security Zones and Restrictions portion of the IEAK Profile Manager.

    B. Enter the settings into the Security Zones and Content Ratings section of the IEAK Profile Manager.

    C. Edit the `INF` files with a text editor.

    D. You can't. Blocking Web sites is a function of a firewall not a Web browser.

12. You want to distribute software over the Web and use Active Channel technology to have updates to it automatically installed by IE 4. However, you want to distribute the software separately from your custom IE 4 package. What distribution method should you use?

   A. Shrink-wrap

   B. Active Setup

   C. MSICD

   D. FTP

13. What two packaging options do you have for distributing MSICD (and Active Setup) software?

   A. .ZIP

   B. .PKG

   C. .EXE

   D. .CAB

14. You must create an Active Channel that contains the scheduling information for browsers to check for software updates, the location of the software, and icons for the Channel bar, menu, and Explorer bar. What file do you need to create?

   A. An HTML file

   B. An OSD file

   C. A CDF file

   D. An INF file

15. You are using the CAB distribution format for your Software Distribution Channel. You have already created a Channel Distribution Format file. What additional file do you need to create ?

   A. An OCD file

   B. An SID file

   C. An EXE file

   D. A TXT file

16. You manage the computers used by children in a grade school. You are required to restrict the Web browsers on the computers from accessing Web sites that are rated to have explicit sexual, vulgar, violent, or pornographic content. In addition, you would like to keep the users from downloading files from specific computers or Internet domains that you know contain files with viruses, Trojan horses, and pirated software. You want teachers to be able to override these restrictions.

Required Result: Prevent browsing of sites with content ratings beyond what is acceptable to your school.

Optional Result 1: Block software downloading from known hacker sites and networks.

Optional Result 2: Provide a method for teachers to override the restrictions.

Suggested Solution: Configure browsers to use profiles. Use the IEAK Profile Manger to create an INS file that includes Content Ratings restrictions and lists known hacker sites and networks in the Restricted Sites zone. Assign a supervisor password for the Content Advisor and give that password to the teachers in the school.

Which of the following is correct?

A. The suggested solution accomplishes the required result and both optional results.

B. The suggested solution accomplishes the required result and just one optional result.

C. The suggested solution accomplishes the required result only.

D. The suggested solution does not accomplish the required result.

17. You manage the computers used by children in a grade school. You are required to restrict the Web browsers on the computers from accessing Web sites that are rated to have explicit sexual, vulgar, violent, or pornographic content. In addition you would like to keep the users from downloading files from specific computers or Internet domains that you know contain files with viruses, Trojan horses, and pirated software. You want teachers to be able to override these restrictions.

Required Result: Prevent browsing of sites with content ratings beyond what is acceptable to your school.

Optional Result 1: Block software downloading from known hacker sites and networks.

Optional Result 2: Provide a method for teachers to override the restrictions.

Suggested Solution: Configure browsers to use profiles. Use the IEAK Profile Manger to create an INS file that includes Content Ratings restrictions and lists known hacker sites and networks in the Restricted Sites zone. Modify the security settings to disable downloading software from the Restricted Sites zone.

Which of the following is correct?

A. The suggested solution accomplishes the required result and both optional results.

B. The suggested solution accomplishes the required result and just one optional result.

C. The suggested solution accomplishes the required result only.

D. The suggested solution does not accomplish the required result.

CHAPTER

8

Network Security

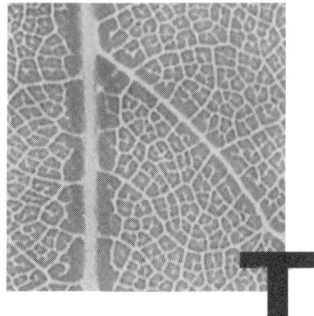

The Internet is a dangerous place. Hackers, crackers, virus creators, and other rapscallions abound. Only vigilance will keep your data truly safe, but some Internet Explorer 4 safety features will help by locking some obvious doors and windows to your digital home.

In order to protect yourself from Internet dangers, you need to know what threats the Internet presents. You must also understand the tools you have to protect yourself and the security trade-offs of using those tools. In a corporate network setting, you need to know how to efficiently manage the security of a large number of computers, so that lack of vigilance (or intentional security laziness) on the part of network users doesn't leave your whole network open to intrusion. This chapter helps you secure Internet Explorer 4 by covering the following topics:

- Security threats

- Security zones

- Security levels

- Digital certificates

- Content Advisor

- Secure communications

- Network security considerations

Security Threats

The first rule in any adversarial conflict is to know your enemy. What are the threats to your computer? What are the threats to your network? Just who is trying to break in, steal your data, or format your hard drive? There are several kinds of Internet bad guys and, to be fair, bad girls—each has a different intent and different method of attack. Internet threats include the following:

- Network Intruders
- Vandals
- Eavesdroppers

Related but different are internal security concerns:

- Users (such as minors) that increase the organization's liability for computer use (or misuse)

Network Intruders

There are people on the Internet who try to break into computers electronically. These people are commonly called hackers, although some old-school computer enthusiasts complain that hacking used to mean benign but clever use of computers (these people prefer the term "crackers" for people who break into computers).

Network intruders have many varied reasons for breaking into computers. Some hackers do it for the thrill of the attempt, others do it to show their mastery of operating systems and networks. Few do it for financial gain (to steal software, credit card numbers, or other valuable data files), although some break into computers to place files on the penetrated computers—usually using the computers as a temporary repository for pirated software or pornographic images.

Vandals

Most network intruders try not to disrupt the computers that they compromise, because once the owners of the computers realize what's happened, they lock the hackers out and establish stricter security measures to keep the hackers from coming back.

Vandals, on the other hand, want all the notoriety they can get. A vandal isn't stashing away files or snooping through files—the vandal wants to cause the maximum disruption possible, and doesn't mind crashing computers or disrupting information services to do it. Some vandals use hacking skills to break into computers in order to change Web pages to reflect their own agenda. Some vandals exploit networking weaknesses to crash the computers. Other vandals create viruses and release them to do indiscriminate and widespread damage.

Eavesdroppers

Your computer may be impervious to network attack, protecting you from vandals and network intruders, but no (useful) computer is an island these days. When you connect your computer to the Internet, you do it for the purpose of exchanging information over the Internet, and that exchange of information (whether it be private e-mail messages or credit card numbers for online purchases) is vulnerable to "eavesdropping" by people personally interested in you (however unlikely that is) or just interested in the commercial value of the data you transmit.

Minors and Users of Enhanced Liability Computers

In a reversal of normal security concerns (preventing outsiders from viewing internal information), you may have to restrict what outside material your internal users can view. If you manage computers used by minors, or if misuse of the computers you manage may expose your organization to lawsuits, you may want to restrict the kind of Internet information those computers can access. A fifth-grade teacher, for example, would want to keep students from viewing pornographic Web pages, and a manager of an Internet coffee shop may want to lock out obvious hacker sites.

Security Zones

Not all computers that you connect with using the Internet protocols are equally risky. You can probably trust the Internet Web and FTP servers for your own organization. Most commercial software publishers are trustworthy as well. If all you know about a Web site is its URL, however, you should think twice about trusting software downloaded from that location, even simple Java applets, because the program code can contain viruses or a Trojan horse.

Internet Explorer 4 uses security zones to partition the Internet into zones of increasing risk (see Figure 8.1). A zone is a computer or group of computers that have a distinct set of security settings that IE 4 observes when communicating with the computer(s). IE 4 recognizes the following zones:

- Local machine

- Trusted Sites zone

- Local Intranet zone

- Internet zone

- Restricted Sites zone

F I G U R E 8.1

IE 4 divides computers it communicates with into security zones.

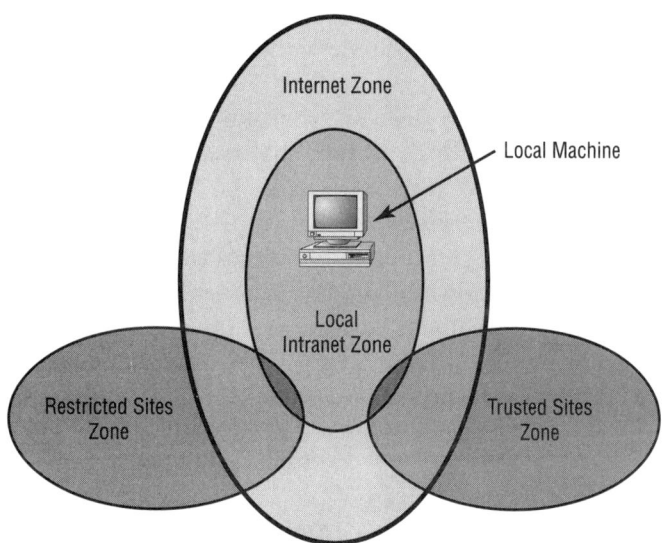

Microsoft
✓ Exam
Objective

In corporate administrator mode, create and assign various levels of security for security zones.

Local Machine

The Local Machine zone consists of just one computer—the one running Internet Explorer 4. IE 4 trusts this zone, because if viruses have already infected the computer IE 4 is running on, or hackers have already obtained its password lists, then there is nothing IE 4 can do about it. This zone is not configurable through the security options of IE 4.

Trusted Sites

Trusted sites are computers that you know you can trust. Your own company's Web site, for example, should be placed in this zone, especially if you are using it for autoconfiguration of Internet Explorer 4 browsers in your LAN. Sites on the Internet that you are confident do not threaten your computer or your network, and that merit a low-security level also may be listed in Trusted Sites. Sites that may merit a low-security level include those from which you want your browsers to automatically download signed ActiveX controls, run Java applets at low safety, or install desktop items automatically. (See "Security Levels" later in this chapter for more information on security levels.)

You configure the Trusted Sites through the Security tab of the Internet Options window in Internet Explorer 4. You can set the zone to the High, Medium-, Low-, or Custom-security level, and you can explicitly list the computers that should be trusted (see Figure 8.2) through the Add Sites button.

Since URLs to Internet sites can refer to a computer either by its Domain Name System (DNS) name or by its numerical IP address, you should enter trusted sites twice into the Trusted Sites list—once by the DNS name and again by the IP address of the trusted computer. Otherwise users may get inconsistent behavior from their Web browser—sometimes accessing the site at medium- or high-security levels, and other times accessing the site (correctly) at a low-security level.

Since the Trusted Sites list consists of URLs to Internet sites, you can limit how Internet Explorer 4 trusts a site by the type of connection (such as HTTP or HTTPS), the port number (if specified), and by the path on that site. In short, if what you enter in the Trusted Sites list matches the first part of the URL, then IE 4 will access that site as a trusted site.

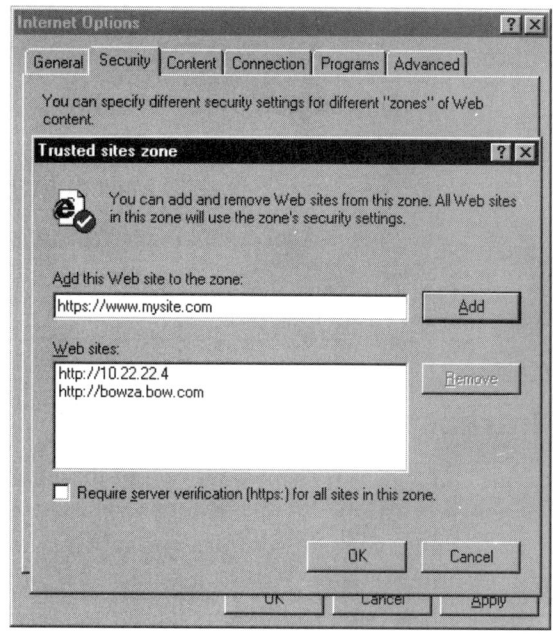

F I G U R E 8.2

You configure and add trusted sites through the Security tab of the Internet Options window.

If you want all communications with trusted sites to use the Hypertext Transport Protocol Secure (HTTPS) method of encrypted communication, then you can select the Require Server Verification check box at the bottom of the Trusted Sites zone window. While this box is selected, Internet Explorer 4 requires any additional trusted sites entered to have the `https://` protocol specification.

EXERCISE 8.1

Adding Sites to the Trusted Sites List

1. Launch Internet Explorer 4.

2. Select View ➢ Internet Options ➢ Security.

3. Select Trusted sites zone in the Zone drop-down box.

4. Click the Add Sites button.

5. Enter **http://www.mysite.com** in the text field, and then click the Add button.

6. Enter **http://10.22.22.1** in the text field, and then click the Add button.

7. Enter **https://www.mysite2.com** in the text field, and then click the Add button.

8. Enter **https://10.22.22.2** in the text field, and then click the Add button.

9. Click the OK button in the Trusted Sites zone window.

10. Click the OK button in the Internet Options window.

Local Intranet Zone

This zone is intended for all of the computers on the same Local Area Network as the computer running Internet Explorer 4. As with the Trusted Sites zone, you can specifically list Intranet locations that should be in the Intranet zone, but you also have the following three options (see Figure 8.3) for automatically including sites:

- **Include all local (Intranet) sites not listed in other zones.** A local (Intranet) site, according to Microsoft, is any site accessed by its DNS name that has no dots in the name. MyWeb, for example, is a local (Intranet) site, while www.myWeb.com isn't. Since official and complete domain names always have .com, .org, .us, or some other top-level domain name appended to the root, it is usually safe to assume that a DNS name without dots is for internal use only, and therefore local.

- **Include all sites that bypass the proxy server.** If computers on your network use a proxy server to access the Internet, computers that are on the same side of the proxy as you (i.e. on the same LAN) can be considered local (Intranet) sites. This option is only useful if your IE 4 browser uses a proxy server, though. This option also lists the sites that IE 4 should bypass the proxy server to access.

- **Include all network paths (UNCs).** On Microsoft LANs, resources are referenced by UNC (Universal Naming Convention) paths, which indicate the NetBIOS share and the path to the resource on that share (for example, \\sally\hplj4 refers to a shared printer on Sally's computer, and \\memetech\secret\world_domination .doc refers to the world_domination document on the memetech file server). If a Web page or other resource is referred to by a UNC path, you can usually assume it is stored on your LAN somewhere, otherwise your computer won't be able to find it.

F I G U R E 8.3

IE 4 lets you decide
what sites qualify as
being part of your local
Intranet.

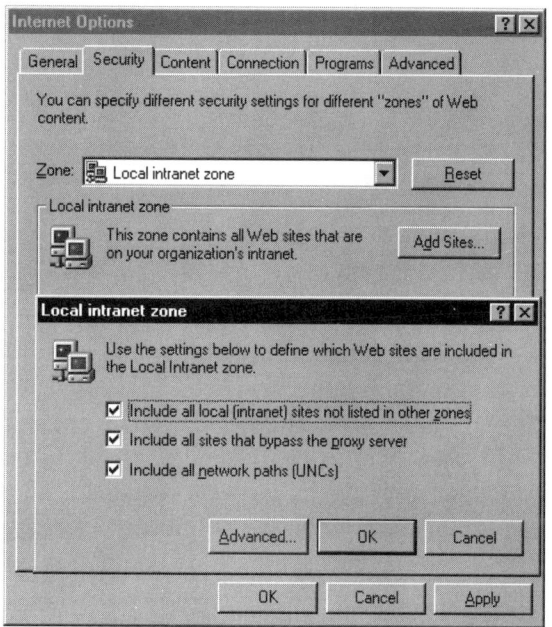

Just because a computer is on the Local Intranet zone doesn't mean that Internet Explorer 4 completely trusts that computer. The default security level for the local (Intranet) zone is medium—the same, in fact, as the IE 4 security level for the Internet zone. Many home computers connect directly to an Internet service provider via dial-up modem connections, ISDN, or (for the lucky few) cable modems; they share their Local Intranet zone with hundreds or thousands of absolute strangers. The default IE 4 settings reflect the need to provide protection for these users from each other.

If you are confident that the users of computers in your network don't provide the same level of threat as Internet users, you can reduce the security level of Internet Explorer 4 browsers in your network. You might want to do this so that users can collaborate, make their own Web pages, and not have security warnings and download prompts get in their way. Exercise 8.2 shows you how to lower the security level.

EXERCISE 8.2

Changing the Security Level of the Local Intranet Zone

1. Launch Internet Explorer 4.

2. Select View ➢ Internet Options ➢ Security.

3. Select Local Intranet zone in the Zone drop-down box.

4. Click the Low Radio button.

5. Click the OK button in the Internet Options window.

Internet

Almost all sites a Web browser accesses will be a part of the Internet zone. If a site is not in the Restricted Sites list, the Trusted Sites list, or part of the Local Intranet zone, then it is a part of the Internet zone. You can't add sites to the Internet zone; you can only remove sites (by adding them to other zones). Your only configuration option for the Internet zone is to set its security level (to low, medium, high, or custom). You might want to set the security level of the Internet zone to high if your network contains especially sensitive information or the computer you are browsing the Internet with should not be exposed to even a minimum degree of threat from the Internet.

Restricted Sites

Restricted sites are not banned sites—they are sites that you may view with Internet Explorer 4, but that you do not trust for anything else. Specifically, Restricted sites are sites from which you don't want IE 4 users to download any kind of file or active content. The default security level for Restricted sites is high.

You have the same security options for the Restricted Sites zone as you do the Local Intranet Sites zone; you can set the security level to high, medium, low, or custom, and you can add or remove specific Internet locations to or from the list of sites. The same caution for entries to the zone applies—you should make two entries for each Restricted site, one referring to the site by its DNS name and the other referring to the site by its numerical IP address. In Exercise 8.3 you will restrict several sites in your Internet Explorer 4 Web browser.

EXERCISE 8.3

Restricting Sites

1. Launch Internet Explorer 4.

2. Select View ≻ Internet Options ≻ Security.

3. Select Restricted Sites zone in the Zone drop-down box.

4. Click the Add Sites button.

5. Enter **http://www.badsite.com** in the text field, and then click the Add button.

6. Enter **http://10.99.99.1** in the text field, and then click the Add button.

7. Click the OK button in the Restricted Sites zone window.

8. Click the OK button in the Internet Options window.

Security Levels

The point of having security zones is so that you can establish different (and appropriate) security levels for each zone. Internet Explorer 4 has three security levels defined by default, and a fourth setting that lets you specify individual security settings such as file download permissions and what to do with ActiveX controls. The following four security levels are available:

- Low

- Medium

- High

- Custom

Default Security Levels

The **Low**-security level should be selected when Internet Explorer 4 browsers connect with sites that you trust and when you don't want IE 4 to prompt users that the site contains otherwise risky content such as unsigned ActiveX controls or desktop items to install. If you trust the users on your own network, you can place the Local Intranet zone at this security level. The Trusted Sites zone has the Low-security level by default, and your own Web sites (especially ones containing IE 4 distribution files and autoconfiguration files) should be listed in the Trusted Sites zone.

The **Medium**-security level is for sites of which you don't control the content. This means that most of the Internet should be browsed with a medium level of security. This level of security requires that the user be prompted as to whether Internet Explorer 4 should perform potentially risky operations such as downloading unsigned code or submitting non-encrypted form data to a Web site. The user can then decide if the site should be trusted.

The **High**-security level is for sites that you do not trust at all. Any active content downloading (such as ActiveX controls or Java applets) is disabled, and users are not allowed to download any files, even to store them to their hard drives. Table 8.1 describes what the security options are for Low-, Medium-, and High-security levels.

TABLE 8.1 Security Options for Low-, Medium-, and High-Security Levels	**Security Option**	**Low**	**Medium**	**High**
	Script ActiveX controls marked safe for scripting	Enable	Enable	Enable
	Run ActiveX controls and plug-ins	Enable	Enable	Disable
	Download signed ActiveX controls	Enable	Prompt	Disable
	Download unsigned ActiveX controls	Prompt	Disable	Disable
	Initialize and script ActiveX controls not marked as safe	Prompt	Prompt	Disable
	Java permissions	Low safety	High safety	High safety
	Active scripting	Enable	Enable	Enable
	Scripting of Java applets	Enable	Enable	Enable
	File download	Enable	Enable	Disable

Implementing and Supporting Microsoft® Internet Explorer 4.0 by Using the Microsoft® Internet Explorer Administration Kit

Exam 70-079: Objectives

Exam objectives are subject to change at any time without prior notice and at Microsoft's sole discretion. Please visit Microsoft's Training & Certification Web site (www.microsoft.com/Train_Cert) for the most current listing of exam objectives.

TABLE 8.1 *(cont.)* Security Options for Low-, Medium-, and High-Security Levels	**Security Option**	**Low**	**Medium**	**High**
	Font download	Enable	Enable	Prompt
	User Authentication—Logon	Automatic	Automatic in Intranet	Prompt
	Submit non-encrypted form data	Enable	Prompt	Prompt
	Launch applications and files from an Iframe	Enable	Prompt	Disable
	Drag-and-drop or copy and paste files	Enable	Enable	Prompt
	Software Channel permissions	Low safety	Medium safety	High safety

Custom Settings

Sometimes the default security levels are not appropriate for your specific use of Internet Explorer 4. For example, you may want to use Anonymous Logon Authentication only for the Local Intranet zone (while leaving the other security settings alone), or you may want to disable scripting for accesses to sites in the Restricted Sites zone. The Custom security level lets you pick and choose among security settings, and establish your own security level for each of the Trusted Sites, Local Intranet, Internet, and Restricted Sites zones (see Figure 8.4). There are six general areas for which you can customize security settings:

- ActiveX controls and plug-ins
- User Authentication
- Downloads
- Java
- Miscellaneous
- Scripting

F I G U R E 8.4

You can create your own custom security level in IE 4.

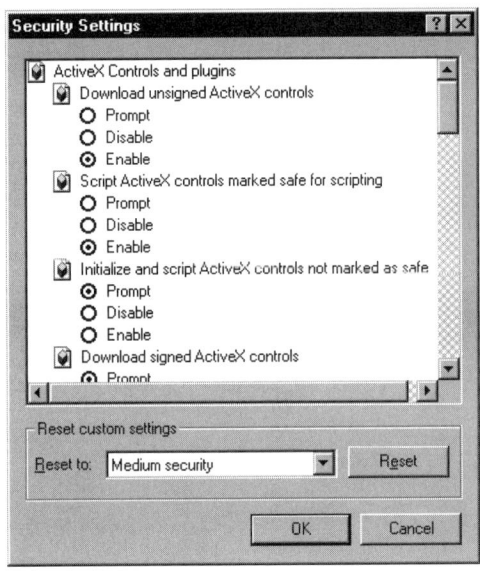

ActiveX Controls and Plug-Ins

Some people want to view other kinds of data besides just HTML and graphics (GIF or JPG) files in their Web browser. Microsoft distributes some additional components (such as the RealAudio plug-in) that allow the browser to play audio files. The technology to extend Internet Explorer 4 to handle new kinds of data is called ActiveX, and many companies provide ActiveX controls so that IE 4 can view information stored in their proprietary formats. Adobe Acrobat is an ActiveX control—it extends IE 4 to be able to view files stored in the PDF format, which gives the creators of the documents much more control over how the document is displayed than HTML does.

The problem with downloading new controls into your Web browser is that the control may do more than you expect it to—it may search your hard drive for information, it may interfere with other running programs, or it may be designed to crash your computer. A digitally-signed ActiveX control gives you some assurance that the control can be trusted, but the truly paranoid may not want to take even the small risk that an otherwise trustworthy software company may have, themselves, been compromised by hackers.

Some ActiveX controls interact with scripts stored in the Web page. The danger a script poses directly corresponds to the power the ActiveX control gives it. An ActiveX control that will only allow a script to list items to display in the Web browser window is relatively safe, while an ActiveX control that gives scripts functions for accessing the hard drive can be dangerous. Some ActiveX controls are marked safe for scripting; you must determine if you agree with that marking. A suspicious administrator may disable this feature, while an Intranet manager who has developed custom ActiveX controls may depend on this feature being enabled. The five ActiveX security options you have in Internet Explorer 4 are as follows:

- Download unsigned ActiveX controls (Prompt, Disable, Enable)
- Script ActiveX controls marked safe (Prompt, Disable, Enable)
- Initialize and script ActiveX controls (Prompt, Disable, Enable)
- Download signed ActiveX controls (Prompt, Disable, Enable)
- Run ActiveX controls and plug-in (Prompt, Disable, Enable)

 Since one Web site can refer to control or plug-in stored on another Web site, and each site may reside in a different security zone, IE 4 will use the most restrictive setting of the two zones.

User Authentication

In the Logon item of the User Authentication section you can choose one of four options for this custom security level:

- Automatic logon with current username and password
- Automatic logon only in Intranet zone
- Prompt for user name and password
- Anonymous logon

The User Authentication section governs how Internet Explorer 4 will log on to sites that require logon authentication in the current zone. The first option (automatic logon with current username and password) will attempt to log on to password-protected sites in the zone using Windows NT Challenge and Response. If Windows NT Challenge and Response is not supported by the Web server, the user is queried for a username and password to supply to the Web server.

The second option (automatic logon only in Intranet zone) will attempt to use the username and password for local sites, and will prompt for a username and password for other sites. Anonymous logon never prompts the user for a username and password—the guest account is used instead. Internet Explorer 4 will remember the username and password after it has been entered the first time, and will supply the username and password without prompting the user when the site is accessed again.

Downloads

Two things (besides active content such as ActiveX controls or Java programs) that users can download from Web sites are fonts (for Internet Explorer 4) and files. Web page designers may want to provide fonts for download so that they can have more control over how their Web sites are viewed on the Web browser. The only conceivable way it could be dangerous to download a font is if the font file were so large that it took up all the free hard drive space on the user's computer—and with the size of hard disks today, such a font could take weeks to download over a regular modem (if such an immense font actually exists)—so this security option is not very useful.

Files, on the other hand, can contain all sorts of nasty stuff, including viruses, Trojan horses, and software that is simply buggy or inappropriate for the users to install on their computers. The user is always prompted about whether to run the file (if it is an executable) and/or where to store it. Only the Restricted Sites zone disables file downloads by default. The two Internet Explorer 4 download options are

- Font download (Prompt, Disable, Enable)
- File download (Disable, Enable)

Java

The Java portion of Custom Settings controls the permissions that are granted to Java applets when they are downloaded from a site in the security zone. The permissions can be set to allow any Java operation (low safety), require Java applets to operate in a *sandbox* (a sandbox is a restricted memory area that limits the operations a Java program can perform) with a *scratch space* (a scratch space is a safe storage area on the computer for the applet) and limited I/O (medium safety), or require Java applets to operate in the sandbox only (high safety). Two additional options are to disable Java altogether, or to set custom permissions for Java in this zone. The Internet Explorer 4 security levels for Java are:

- Low safety

- Medium safety

- High safety

- Disable Java

- Custom

As with ActiveX controls, a Java applet may be downloaded from a different site than the HTML page that refers to the applet, and each site may be in a different security zone. The most restrictive of the two security zones' settings will be used.

Miscellaneous

There are several miscellaneous security settings that you can custom configure for a zone. For software channels, you can disable the notification and downloading of packages (high safety); allow notification and downloading, but prevent automatic installation (medium safety);or allow notification, downloading, and automatic installation (low safety).

You can also configure how Internet Explorer 4 handles launching applications from IFRAMEs, control whether users can install desktop items in the zone, and control whether users can drag-and-drop or cut and paste files from the security zone. The Submit Non-encrypted Form Data setting controls how form data is sent to a Web site in the zone—unencrypted data can be intercepted by other computers in the zone, so some sites (trusted sites accessed over the Internet that contain sensitive data, for example) may require that this option be set to Disable. IE 4 gives you the following miscellaneous security options:

- Software channel permissions (Medium safety, Low safety, High safety)

- Launching applications and files in an Iframe (Prompt, Disable, Enable)

- Installation of desktop items (Prompt, Disable, Enable)

- Submit non-encrypted form data (Prompt, Disable, Enable)

- Drag and drop or copy and paste files (Prompt, Disable, Enable)

Scripting

Internet Explorer 4 supports JavaScript (called JScript by Microsoft) and VBScript programs in HTML pages. JScript and VBScript are less powerful programming languages than Java, but can use Java applets to do more complicated things. You have the following options of allowing the scripts to call Java applets and disabling scripting entirely for sites in the zone:

- Scripting of Java applets (Prompt, Disable, Enable)
- Active scripting (Prompt, Disable, Enable)

In Exercise 8.4 you will customize the local Intranet Zone to allow Internet Explorer 4 to download and execute unsigned ActiveX controls.

EXERCISE 8.4

Customizing Local Intranet Zone Security Settings

1. Launch Internet Explorer 4.

2. Select View ➤ Internet Options ➤ Security.

3. Select Local Intranet zone in the Zone drop-down box.

4. Select the Custom radio button, and click the Settings button.

5. Select Enable Download Unsigned ActiveX Controls.

6. Select Enable Initialize and Script ActiveX Controls Not Marked as Safe.

7. Select Low Safety for Java Permissions.

8. Click OK in the Security Settings window.

9. Select OK in the Internet Options window.

Java Security

Trust-based security is Microsoft's term for its Java security model. It uses the security zones (described in the previous section) along with Java-specific permissions and digitally-signed CAB files to create a secure environment for your computer to run Java programs developed by people that you don't necessarily trust. (Perhaps this security technology should be called Distrust-based security.)

It is more difficult to make Java applets secure than most other Web content because there is no way of knowing in advance just what a Java applet will do. The advantage of Java is the flexibility it gives Web designers. It is a complete programming language in which developers can write any sort of program, from a little Web-based interest calculator all the way to a full-featured word processor and spreadsheet. Unfortunately, it is just as easy to use Java to create Trojan horse applets that appear to have some useful function but instead search your hard drive for information or attempt to crash your computer.

Despite the dangers of Trojan horses, Java was designed with security in mind. Features such as the Sandbox environment, scratch pads, and limited I/O help you run programs for which you can't verify the safety level. The Java security features of Internet Explorer 4 tie into the other security features, including security zones and checking digitally signing code to ensure that downloaded applets have not been tampered with.

Java and Zones

Internet Explorer 4 uses security zones to give appropriate security settings to different Web sites. You might want to configure the Web browser to download and execute unsigned Java programs from the Trusted site zone. This allows those programs to access computer resources and other networks in your LAN, but you don't want to give applets from the Restricted site zone those abilities. In fact, you might not want to run unsigned applets from the Restricted site zones at all.

The security zones for Java are the same security zones defined for Internet Explorer 4 as a whole. Table 8.2 shows the default Java settings for the security zones.

T A B L E 8.2 Default Java Settings for Security Zones	**Security Zone**	**Default Java Settings**
	Local Machine	Low Safety
	Trusted Sites	Low Safety
	Local Intranet	High Safety
	Internet	High Safety
	Restricted Sites	High Safety

Java and Permissions

There are quite a few Java security settings you can modify in Internet Explorer 4, but there are only four general types of sites—those you must trust, those you trust a lot, those you trust a little bit, and those you don't trust at all. Microsoft has made configuring Java security easier by collecting common security settings for each level of trust. The first level of trust is just for the computer you are running IE 4 on. There are no settings (it is assumed to be safe) for that computer. When the applet comes from another computer, however, one of the following three safety levels usually applies:

High Safety   Creates a safe environment to run untrusted programs (that kind of environment is often called a sandbox, because the program is allowed to play inside the sandbox, but is not allowed outside the sandbox). The applet can do the following:

- Open network connections only to the machine that supplied the applet

- Warn user before operation

- Read system properties

- Access reflection APIs for classes from the same loader

Medium Safety   Includes the ability to store information on the Web browser computer in additon to the options that High safety provides. The applet can do the following:

- Store persistent data in a scratch space

Low Safety   Gives the applets all the permissions of High and Medium safety, but also allows the computer to run Java applets. The Low safety applet can do the following:

- Perform file I/O to the hard drive or network

- Launch other programs

- Open windows and dialog boxes

- Perform thread management

- Open network connections to locations other than the origin of the applet

- Load libraries

- Call native operating system functions

- Run without warning the user

- Modify the Registry

- Print

If one of the above three standard settings doesn't fit your needs for running Java applets (for example, if you want an applet to print and do network I/O, but not file I/O or launch other programs), you can customize the Java safety permissions for a zone (see the section "Custom Permissions" in this chapter).

You can disable Java for a zone if you think Java is too much of a risk for your computer.

Signing Java Code

You should feel safer when Internet Explorer 4 is running Java applets that have been digitally signed by a trusted software distributor than when it is running unsigned Java applets. Signing a Java applet does not prove that the applet will do no harm to your computer, but it does prove that a (allegedly) responsible party has vouched that the applet is safe to run, and that somebody has vouched for that software publisher. The applet may still have bugs, of course. Also, just because the applet has been signed doesn't mean that the signer is trustworthy—you have to use your judgment about which software publishers you feel are really responsible. Code signed by FlyBy-Night, Inc. may be less trustworthy than code signed by Microsoft.

When Java code is signed (you can use tools provided with the Microsoft Internet Client Software Development Kit or the Microsoft SDK for Java), the signer includes the default safety level expected by that applet in the signature. Before a Java applet is run, Internet Explorer 4 uses this information to present a warning dialog box, listing the level of risk that running the applet presents to the computer. The user can then decide whether to run the applet.

Custom Permissions

If one of the three standard safety levels doesn't suit your needs for a zone (for example, if you want your unsigned Java applets in your Intranet to be able to access other network addresses), then you can customize the Java permissions for that zone. All the computers included in that zone will have the custom permissions, so you should make sure that any changes that you make are appropriate for the zone as a whole.

At first, it isn't at all obvious how you go about creating custom security settings, because the Java Custom Settings button doesn't show up in the Security Settings window until you select the Custom Java Permissions item (see Figure 8.5). When you select Custom and click the Java Custom Settings button, a window will appear that will allow you to view and edit Java security permissions.

FIGURE 8.5

You must select Custom in Java Permissions before the Java Custom Settings button will appear.

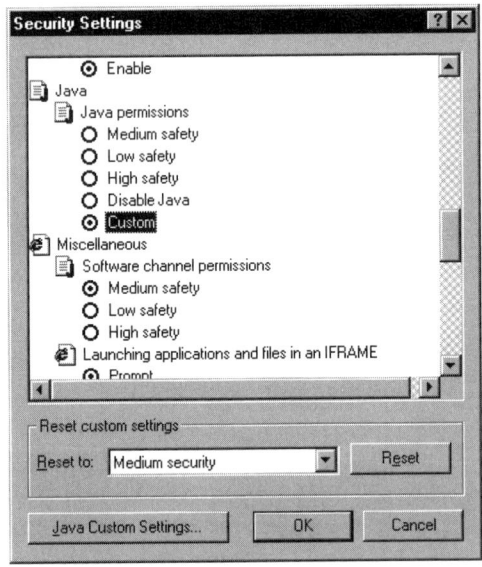

In the Java Security Permissions window there are two sets of permissions available to you—those for unsigned Java applets and those for digitally-signed Java applets. The permissions you can change are listed in the Tables 8.3 and 8.4. Making appropriate settings changes will require a good understanding of Java programming and the effects of each feature—refer to the documentation in the Microsoft Internet Client Software Development Kit or the Microsoft SDK for Java for more information on the effects of changing specific Java permissions in a zone. Exercise 8.5 shows you how to customize Java permissions.

T A B L E 8.3: Default Java Safety Settings for Unsigned Content

Unsigned Content Permission	Possible Settings	High Safety	Medium Safety	Low Safety
Run unsigned content	Run in sandbox, Disable, or Enable	Run in sandbox	Run in sandbox	Run in sandbox
Access to all files	Disable or Enable	Disable	Disable	Disable
Access to all network addresses	Enable or Disable	Disable	Disable	Disable
Execute	Enable or Disable	Disable	Disable	Disable
Dialogs	Enable or Disable	Disable	Disable	Disable
System information	Enable or Disable	Disable	Disable	Disable
Printing	Enable or Disable	Disable	Disable	Disable
Protected scratch space	Enable or Disable	Disable	Disable	Disable
User-selected file access	Enable or Disable	Disable	Disable	Disable

T A B L E 8.4: Default Java Safety Settings for Signed Content

Signed Content Permission	Possible Settings	High Safety	Medium Safety	Low Safety
Run signed contract	Prompt, Disable, or Enable	Prompt	Prompt	Enable
Access to all files	Prompt, Disable, or Enable	Prompt	Prompt	Enable
Access to all network addresses	Prompt, Disable, or Enable	Prompt	Prompt	Enable
Execute	Prompt, Disable, or Enable	Prompt	Prompt	Enable

T A B L E 8.4:   Default Java Safety Settings for Signed Content *(Continued)*

Signed Content Permission	Possible Settings	High Safety	Medium Safety	Low Safety
Dialogs	Prompt, Disable, or Enable	Prompt	Prompt	Enable
System information	Prompt, Disable, or Enable	Prompt	Prompt	Enable
Printing	Prompt, Disable, or Enable	Prompt	Prompt	Enable
Protected scratch space	Prompt, Disable, or Enable	Enable	Enable	Enable
User-selected file access	Prompt, Disable, or Enable	Enable	Enable	Enable

EXERCISE 8.5

Customizing Java Permissions for the Local Intranet Zone

1. Launch Internet Explorer 4.

2. Select View ➤ Internet Options ➤ Security.

3. Select Local Intranet zone in the Zone drop-down box.

4. Select the Custom radio button, and click the Settings button.

5. Select Custom for Java permissions.

6. Click the Custom Java Settings button.

7. Click the Edit Permissions tab.

8. Click the Enable button to run unsigned content.

9. Click OK in the Local Intranet Zone window.

10. Click OK in the Security Settings window.

11. Click OK in the Internet Options window.

Digital Certificates

Digital Certificates are Microsoft's answer to the age-old question: whom do you trust? One answer is, of course, Microsoft. But then, how do you know if a software package really came from Microsoft rather than from a hacker who has programmed the computer to tell you it is from Microsoft? Digital Certificates use a technology called Public Key Cryptography to create unforgeable patterns, or signatures, in the programs.

A person's signature is (usually) the person's name, written by that person's hand. Two important properties of signatures that make them useful in the modern world of contracts and affidavits:

- Only the signer can create the signature on a document (or, rather, it is very difficult for anyone other than the signer to create the signature on the document).

- Anyone can verify that the signature was made by the signer and not by some other person by examining the signature (by comparing the signature to another document the signer has signed).

If you look at a paper certificate, you can usually find a signature on it somewhere, and the same is true for digital certificates. A certificate attests to some fact (a birth, marriage, achievement, or change of status), and an authority of some kind signs the document, affirming that the certificate is correct. Of course, the validity of the certificate is directly related to the authority and trustworthiness of the signer—not just anyone can sign a marriage certificate for example, and those who can (accredited ministers, justices of the peace, or other authority recognized by the state) are expected to be careful about signing only valid marriage certificates.

Computer certificates are similar to paper certificates in that they have one or more signatures included on them, and their validity is dependent on those signatures. They also include information that the signer attests is true, including:

- The owner's public key

- The owner's name or alias

- An expiration date

- A serial number

- The name of the certificate authority that issued the certificate

- The authority's digital signature

A digital signature can also include other information. Commonly, a certificate will also include the postal and e-mail addresses of the owner.

Public Key Cryptography

It may seem like magic, but mathematicians have figured out how to use two prime numbers to digitally sign messages. The mathematicians who developed this are Ron Rivest, Adi Shamir, and Leonard Adleman. The system they developed is called RSA. The mathematics are complicated, but the end result is that the signer of a digital signature creates two keys—one which is kept private and is used to sign messages, and the second key which is made public and is used by others to verify that a message has been signed. Only the holder of the private key can create messages that the public key will verify. The public key will not work with a message signed by any other key, nor can it be used to create signatures.

Actually, there is another use for the public key—in addition to being used to verify public messages signed by the private key, it can be used to create secret messages that can only be decoded by the private key. This way anyone who has received a message that is digitally signed by the owner of the private key can send that owner a private message. (This is why you must first exchange digitally signed messages if you want to exchange encrypted messages in Outlook Express—by doing so, you are exchanging public keys.)

The trick to public key cryptography, and what makes it so useful for creating digital signatures, is the fact that it is difficult to find the two prime numbers that, when multiplied, result in any particular arbitrary number. Of course, if the numbers are small (between one and one thousand), a computer can just check all the possibilities within a hundredth of a second. If the number is larger (between one and one quadrillion), however, it can take much longer for a computer to check all the possibilities—so long, in fact, that it is impractical to use a computer to find the answer the hard way (by checking all the possible numbers). Public key cryptography uses these larger numbers.

You can learn more about the mathematics and algorithms behind public key cryptography in the excellent book, *Applied Cryptography*, by Bruce Scheier.

Authenticode

Authenticode is Microsoft's use of public key cryptography to provide authentication and secure communications with Internet Explorer 4. Authenticode uses digital certificates and certificate authorities (issuers of certificates) to make Internet computing safer. Digital certificates are used for:

- Establishing encrypted communications channels between two computers

- Encrypting and decrypting mail sent between e-mail clients

- Verifying the identity of client Web browsers to Web servers and Web servers to client Web browsers

- Signing and verifying who created an e-mail message

- Signing and verifying who created a software package

Three central concepts in Authenticode technology are as follows:

- Trusted Publishers

- Client Certificates

- Certificate Authorities

- Root Certificates

Trusted Publishers

Internet Explorer 4 contains a list of the certificates it has received. Some of those certificates are *publisher certificates* which are certificates from software publishers or other content providers. When IE 4 downloads a CAB file or other software (such as a Java-class file) that has been digitally signed, it checks its list of trusted publishers for one that matches the signer of the CAB file. If it finds a match, it uses the public key in the certificate to verify that the file has not been altered since it was signed. If the file has not been altered and that certificate is one that IE 4 has been configured to trust, then IE 4 may open the file and use it.

If you download a package that has been digitally signed but Internet Explorer 4 doesn't have that certificate in its list of certificates, you are given the choice of trusting packages from that publisher and placing the certificate as a trusted publisher certificate in the IE 4 list (see Figure 8.6). You can then use the IEAK Wizard to import certificate settings into your custom IE 4 package.

FIGURE 8.6

When you download a package that has been digitally signed by a publisher not in IE 4's list of trusted publishers, you can instruct IE 4 to place that publisher in IE 4's list of trusted publishers.

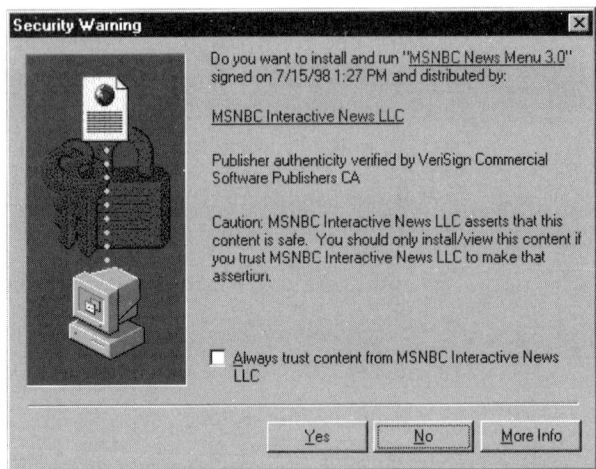

You receive a publisher certificate from a certificate authority to sign your code. Software developer certificates signed by a certificate authority are usually not free—the certificate authority must validate the information you provided for the creation of the certificate. You can, however, create your own test root certificate using the tools that came with the IEAK (see "Signing the CAB Files" in Chapter 6). That kind of certificate, of course, doesn't guarantee anything because anyone can create those certificates—it is not endorsed by a recognized certificate authority. When you sign your own CAB, EXE, or Java-class files for distribution over the Internet, you will want to get a real root certificate that others can trust, one that is endorsed by a certificate authority.

Client Certificates

You should recall from Chapter 4 that publisher certificates aren't the only kind of certificates that Internet Explorer 4 and associated components use. Outlook Express uses client certificates to exchange digitally-signed mail and to send and receive encrypted mail. See "Setting Security in the Microsoft Outlook Express" section of Chapter 4 for how client certificates are obtained and used.

Certificate Authorities

Just as you don't sign your own marriage certificate, the owner of a digital certificate doesn't sign it. Instead the certificate is signed digitally by a certificate authority. Microsoft lists a number of certificate authorities that support the Authenticode technology at `http://www.microsoft.com/security`. One such authority is VeriSign (`www.verisign.com`). Certificate authorities perform the following functions:

- Create digital certificates with owner-supplied information (public keys, organizational information, and contact information)

- Verify the information supplied by customers (certificate recipients)

- Verify authenticity of the certificates that the certificate authority has created

- Maintain a list of revoked certificates

In addition to owner information, certificates identify the certificate authority that created the certificate. When others want to check the validity of a certificate, they can contact the certificate authority directly to determine if the certificate is valid.

Root Certificates

Certificate authorities, of course, have their own certificates, called *root certificates*. The certificates created for customers by a certificate authority refer to the root certificate for that certificate authority. Internet Explorer 4 comes preloaded with several root certificates, including ones for Microsoft and for VeriSign. These root certificates are useful because you can configure IE 4 to automatically trust digitally signed items that were signed with digital certificates that originated from these root certificates. A certificate authority can create the following four kinds of certificates (beyond root certificates):

Server user Authentication   Provides assurance to client computers that a server is valid.

Client user authentication   Provides assurance to server computers that a client computer is valid.

E-mail encryption and authentication   Sends and receives private and validated e-mail.

Software publisher   Digitally signs distribution files.

Exercise 8.6 shows you how to configure Internet Explorer 4 to accept all digital certificates issued using a particular root certificate.

EXERCISE 8.6

Configuring Root Certificates

1. Launch Internet Explorer 4.

2. Select View ➤ Internet Options ➤ Content.

3. Click the Authorities button.

4. Scroll to VeriSign Class 1 Primary CA.

5. Select the VeriSign Class 1 Primary CA check box.

6. Click Close in the Certificate Authorities window.

7. Select OK in the Internet Options window.

Content Advisor

An internally-focused security issue with Internet Explorer 4 is that in some situations it is as important to restrict what the user of the browser can access as it is to keep external users (hackers) from accessing the browser. Many parents want to be sure that their children, for example, won't be able to access inappropriate Web sites, and some business owners may want to be sure that their employees are not spending time at Web sites that do not contribute to the "bottom line" of the company. The Content Advisor portion of IE 4 can help restrict the sites that users can browse by not displaying information that exceeds a content rating in one of the following four areas:

- Violence

- Nudity

- Sex

- Language

RSACi and PICS

Web pages may have ratings contained in HTML *meta tags* (tags that do not show up in the displayed Web page) that indicate the level of violence, nudity, sex, and language. Web page rating is voluntary. The most common format for ratings is called the *Platform for Internet Content Selection*, or PICS. Internet Explorer 4 supports RASCi (developed by the Recreational Software Advisory Council), which is based on PICS, and which provides the violence, nudity, sex, and language definitions in the PICS format for ratings meta tags.

RASCi defines levels 0 through 4 for each of four types of content. The RASCi definitions for the PICS tags are defined in Table 8.5.

T A B L E 8.5: RASCi Definitions for PICS Tags

Level	Violence	Nudity	Sex	Language
4	Rape or wanton, gratuitous violence	Frontal nudity qualifying as provocative display	Explicit sexual acts or sex crimes	Crude, vulgar language or extreme hate speech
3	Aggressive violence or death to humans	Frontal nudity	Non-explicit sexual acts	Strong language or hate speech
2	Destruction of realistic objects	Partial nudity	Clothed sexual touching	Moderate expletives or profanity
1	Injury to a human being	Revealing attire	Passionate kissing	Mild expletives
0	None of the above, or sports related	None of the above	None of the above, or innocent kissing; romance	None of the above

Configuring Content Advisor

You can configure Content Advisor in Internet Explorer 4 to restrict viewing of Web pages with content ratings in excess of fixed values in any of the four categories (see Figure 8.7). You can also configure IE 4 to restrict or allow viewing of Web pages without content ratings. You can always override the Content Advisor settings by supplying a supervisor password. Exercise 8.7 shows you how to configure content ratings.

EXERCISE 8.7

Configuring Content Ratings

1. Launch Internet Explorer 4.

2. Select View ➤ Internet Options ➤ Content.

3. Click the Enable button in the Content Advisor section.

4. Enter a supervisor password into the Password text field.

5. Type the password again in the Confirm Password text field. Click OK.

6. Click the General tab.

7. Select the Users Can See Sites That Have No Rating option, then click the OK button.

8. Select OK in the Internet Options window.

FIGURE 8.7

RASCi lets you set the permissible levels of violence, nudity, sex, and language for the Web browser.

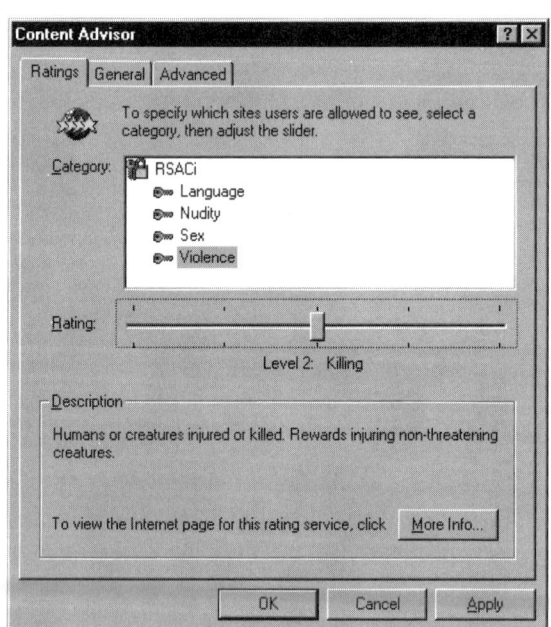

Secure Communications

The Internet is a new medium, and with every new medium people will figure out how to use it to do business. Security and convenience are two very important issues for doing business over any medium—people want to be assured that their purchase is safe and that they won't be taken advantage of, but they don't want to go to too much trouble. Microsoft Wallet, Cookies, and Secure Socket Layer (SSL) communications on Internet Explorer 4 help make Internet commerce easy and secure.

Microsoft Wallet

Ordering products online usually involves providing a name, delivery address, and credit card number so that a merchant can charge the items to a credit card and then send the purchase to the buyer. Making a few purchases online is easy. Making a lot of purchases online can be time consuming because of all the information that has to be entered (name, address, numbers, etc.) for each transaction. Microsoft Wallet makes online purchasing easier.

Microsoft Wallet (like a regular wallet) can contain identification information about you (your name and address), as well as payment methods (credit card numbers) that can be automatically transmitted to a merchant Web site so that you can order products over the Web and have them delivered (if appropriate) to your home or office. Naturally, you won't want the information contained in this wallet to get into the wrong hands, so Microsoft Wallet uses Secure Socket Layer encryption to make sure that only your computer and the merchant Web server are privy to the credit card numbers and personal information used to make the purchase. You have full control over what information in the wallet (if any) is sent to the merchant Web server when you make an online transaction.

Cookies and Profile Assistant

Credit card information and addresses aren't the only items that Internet Explorer 4 can remember for you so you don't have to keep typing them in. IE 4 supports cookies, which are given to IE 4 by a Web site to keep until the next time IE 4 accesses that Web site. A cookie can contain any sort of Web site data, including the last item you browsed on that site, the state of your electronic shopping cart (if it is an online merchant site), or your Web site preferences if it is the sort of Web site that you can customize. Cookies are stored on your hard drive, and IE 4 doesn't do anything with them other than keep them and later give them back to the Web server.

Cookies do not pose a security threat to your computer, although some people are uncomfortable with Web sites storing information on their computers. You, therefore, have three options on how Internet Explorer 4 will handle cookies:

- Do not accept cookies

- Prompt the user as to whether or not to accept a cookie

- Accept and store cookies

A related feature is the information stored by the Profile Assistant and transferred at the user's discretion to requesting Web sites. Some Web sites keep track of accesses to the site to build demographic information (what professions, gender, age group, and so on) of those who tend to visit the site. Other Web sites require more personal information before allowing the person browsing the site to venture further. The Profile Assistant keeps personal information (such as the name, e-mail address, phone numbers, etc.) of the Internet Explorer 4 user. A Web site that supports the Platform for Privacy Preferences (P3) standard can query this information so that the user doesn't have to type it into a Web site form. The information is not released automatically—the user must acknowledge the request and allow IE 4 to transfer the information to the Web site.

In Exercise 8.8, you will enter your contact information into the Profile Assistant and instruct Internet Explorer 4 to warn you when Web servers present cookies for your computer to store.

EXERCISE 8.8

Configuring Cookies and the Profile Assistant

1. Launch Internet Explorer 4.

2. Select View ➢ Internet Options ➢ Content.

3. Click the Edit Profile button.

4. Enter your name into the First, Middle, and Last text fields.

5. Enter your e-mail address into the Add New field, and then click the Add button.

6. Click the Home tab, and then enter your contact information into the fields in the window.

7. Click the OK button at the bottom of the window.

8. Click the Advanced tab in the Internet Options window.

9. Select the Prompt Before Accepting Cookies option.

10. Select OK in the Internet Options window.

SSL and PCT

In order to provide a secure link between Internet Explorer 4 and a Web server for electronic transactions (such as the transfer of a credit card number), IE 4 can encrypt the HTTP session using a Secure Socket Layer (or SSL). IE 4 also supports a related and more flexible secure communications method called PCT (for Private Communications Technology). Unlike encrypted e-mail between two Outlook Express users, you don't have to have a certificate from a Web server to establish SSL communications with that Web server. IE 4 and the Web server will do the equivalent of exchanging certificates (actually, just exchanging public keys) as a part of establishing the SSL or PCT connection. The only configuration decision you have to make regarding SSL and PCT is whether to allow them.

Network Administration and Security Considerations

All of the security features of Internet Explorer 4 discussed earlier in this chapter have been described from the perspective of the user of the Web browser. In a network environment there is another perspective, the network administrator perspective, on how IE 4 should be configured and used, and sometimes it is at odds with the browser-user perspective. The browser user usually wants the maximum of flexibility, for example, while a corporate administrator may want to restrict some flexibility in order to have a more easily-administered network of browsers. Some topics of interest to a network administrator include:

- Locking-down security zones
- Managing and locking-down certificates for deployed browsers
- Centrally managing Java security
- Centrally managing Content Advisor

Locking-Down Zones

You may not want the network users to change the zone settings you have established for the Trusted Sites, Local Intranet, Internet, and Restricted Sites zones, especially after you have enumerated the computers that should be trusted, restricted, or considered part of the Intranet. It is easy enough to lock-down those settings so that Internet Explorer 4 users can't change them.

You have two tools that you can use to lock-down zones: the IEAK (which you use to build a custom Internet Explorer 4 package with the zones already locked-down) and the IEAK Profile Manager. If you choose to use the Profile Manager, you must digitally sign the resulting CAB files and place the INS file in a location where the IE 4 browsers' autoconfiguration mechanisms will find it and apply the changes.

Managing and Locking-Down Certificates for Deployed Browsers

Another feature you may want to preconfigure and restrict is which certificates are trusted by Internet Explorer 4 in the deployed browsers. As you learned in Chapters 6 and 7, you must first configure IE 4 with the certificate settings you want before you can import the settings into either your IEAK custom package of IE 4 or the IEAK Profile Manager INS file.

Just as when you lock-down zones, if you use the IEAK Profile Manager, you must make the signed CAB files and the INS file available to the Internet Explorer 4 browsers.

Centrally Managing ActiveX and Java Security

A network is more sensitive to intrusion from the Internet than a single computer. Because computers in a network usually trust one another, a hacker that compromises one computer in the network has a much greater chance of compromising the other computers in the network. The greatest security weakness that Internet Explorer 4 introduces into a computer on the network is also IE 4's most useful feature—its expandability through ActiveX controls and through Java programs.

In a network environment, especially one that contains sensitive data, a network administrator might find it prudent to curtail or eliminate the plug-in and Java functionality in network Web browsers. Network administrators who implement an Intranet behind a firewall and use Java and ActiveX to create a flexible interface to enterprise data, might want to relax Java and ActiveX security for the Local Intranet zone in order to make it easier for the computing staff to develop the custom applications. Exactly how you configure Internet Explorer 4 Java and ActiveX security will depend on what your network contains and how it is used.

Centrally Managing Content Advisor

A parent that has a personal computer at home for the children to use might need to set the allowed content for a single Web browser. A corporate administrator may have to manage the Content Advisor settings for hundreds of computers. Fortunately, the IEAK Profile Manager and the IEAK make it easy to configure and lock-down Content Advisor settings.

Summary

The Internet is a wild and woolly place. There are people out there that would attack your computer or your communications for fun, to gather information, to use the computer as a temporary dumping ground, or just to do random damage. You need to protect your computer when you are browsing the Internet by configuring the security settings of Internet Explorer 4 appropriately.

Security in Internet Explorer 4 starts by making lists of computers you trust and computers you don't trust. The computers are divided into zones, and Web content from untrusted zones aren't given the same permissions as trusted zones. Digital certificates help matters by assuring you that the downloadable software (ActiveX controls and Java applets) are safe, but you can only trust the digital signature as much as you trust the person who applied the signature.

Since Java is a more complex environment than JScript or VBScript, Java has more security settings that you can modify. The common settings, however, are divided into High Safety, Medium Safety, and Low Safety (the safest route, of course, is to disable Java).

Content ratings provide a different protection for your network users. The RASCi system helps protect kids from offensive material and helps keep employees on task. Microsoft Wallet, cookies, and SSL/PCT help make Internet commerce safe and easy.

A network administrator sometimes has different objectives for Internet Explorer 4 configuration than the IE 4 users. The administrator may want to use the IEAK Wizard or IEAK Profile Editor to lock-down settings so that users can't create security weaknesses by opening up their computers to network intrusion. An administrator may also feel compelled to restrict the content that users (especially underage users) may view. The IEAK and IEAK Profile Manager can help the administrator make content ratings changes from a central location, saving time and effort.

Review Questions

1. You have a Web site inside your firewall that uses ActiveX to provide users a Web-based interface to your inventory and shipping database. Since the control will only be used internally, you don't want to go to the trouble of digitally signing it. You have used the IEAK Profile Manager to enter the DNS name into the Trusted Sites zone, and to update the Trusted Sites Download Unsigned ActiveX Controls Security option for the Trusted Sites zone to enable. Some users' Web browsers automatically download the ActiveX control when they access the site, other users' browsers prompt before downloading. What is wrong?

A. The Trusted Sites security level must be set to High before the ActiveX controls can be downloaded without prompting.

B. The IP address of the trusted site must also be added to the Trusted Sites zone.

C. The Web site must be added to the Local Intranet zone instead of the Trusted Sites zone.

D. The ActiveX control has a bug and must be recompiled.

2. Your IE 4 Web browser has accessed a Web page in the Local Intranet site, but the page refers to an unsigned ActiveX control located on a computer that is listed in the Restricted Sites zone. What happens?

A. The ActiveX control runs without the user being prompted.

B. The user is prompted whether or not to run the control.

C. The control does not run.

D. The computer crashes.

3. You don't want users' usernames and passwords to go out over the Internet when a Web server requests a username and password. What do you do?

A. Select automatic logon with current username and password.

B. Select automatic logon only in Intranet zone.

C. Prompt for username and password.

D. Configure Anonymous Logon.

4. You want Java programs to run in their own safe sandbox, but you also want them to have access to safe scratch-pad space on the hard disk so they can store information. Which Java safety level should you choose?

A. High safety

B. Medium safety

C. Low safety

D. Disable Java

5. Which of the following is not a Java security feature?

 A. Digitally-signed CAB files

 B. Security zones

 C. Security levels

 D. Content ratings

6. You want your Java programs to be able to connect via TCP sockets to an SQL server in addition to the Web server on which the applet was stored. Which safety level should you configure the Web server to be in?

 A. High safety

 B. Medium safety

 C. Low safety

 D. Disable Java

7. You can't find the Java Custom Settings button in IE 4. What must you do to make it appear?

 A. Select View ➤ Internet Options ➤ Security ➤ Custom ➤ Settings ➤ Custom (in Java Permissions).

 B. Select View ➤ Internet Options ➤ Programs ➤ Java ➤ Custom.

 C. There is no Java Custom Settings button in IE 4. You must use the IEAK Wizard to customize Java settings.

 D. There is no Java Custom Settings button in IE 4. You must use the IEAK Profile Editor to customize Java settings.

8. What does IE 4 use Authenticode technology for? Choose all that apply.

 A. Signing and verifying software packages

 B. Sending and receiving e-mail

 C. Establishing a secure connection between the Web browser and Web server

 D. Verifying the identity of the user of the Web browser to the Web server

9. You need a certificate to digitally sign the software packages you have created. What kind of certificate do you need?

   A. A root certificate

   B. A trusted publisher certificate

   C. A client certificate

   D. A client access license certificate

10. You need to restrict the kinds of Internet content the Web browsers in the grade-school computer lab can access. What should you do?

   A. Place the computers in the Restricted Sites zone.

   B. Establish RASCi limitations for the Web browsers.

   C. Install a firewall and filter out GIF files.

   D. Install client certificates on the computers.

11. You have received a software publisher digital certificate from Veri-Sign, and you want to use it in the IEAK. How do you get the certificate into the IEAK?

   A. Proceed through the IEAK Wizard until you reach the Content Ratings page in Stage 4. Select the Customize Content Ratings radio button, and click the Customize button. Locate the digital certificate file, and click Open.

   B. Import the certificate into IE 4. Proceed through the IEAK Wizard until you reach the Site Certificate and Authenticode Settings page in Stage 4. Select the Import radio button, and click the Modify Settings button.

   C. Open a command prompt. Go to the IEAK/tools/authenticode/ directory. Type **addcert /s <certificate file>**.

   D. Select File ➤ Open Certificate in the IEAK Wizard main window. Locate the certificate file, and then click the Import button.

12. You want to digitally sign your Java CAB files to test your program, but you don't want to get a digital certificate from a certificate authority just yet. What kind of certificate can you generate with the IEAK tools?

A. A test root certificate

B. A client certificate

C. A root certificate

D. You must acquire a certificate from VeriSign

13. What kind of certificate would you preload IE 4 and Outlook Express with so that the user can send and receive encrypted mail?

A. A root certificate

B. A publisher certificate

C. A client certificate

D. A test root certificate

14. Which of the following is not included in a certificate?

A. The owner's name

B. The owner's private key

C. The owner's public key

D. The certificate authority's digital signature

15. Which Java safety levels allows the applet to contact (via network I/O) only the Web site that the applet was downloaded from? Choose all that apply.

A. High safety

B. Medium safety

C. Low safety

D. Java Disabled

16. You manage an Intranet for your company. You have developed a Java applet that resides on your Intranet Web server and uses a corporate database (hosted on a computer that just responds to SQL requests over TCP/IP) to display and update product orders and delivery information. Most of the users of the applet are on the local Intranet zone, but some employees need to be able to run the Java program from outside your corporate firewall. You would like the program's communications to be encrypted, and you want to limit who may access the Web page that contains the program.

Required Result: Allow Intranet as well as Internet users to run the Java applet.

Optional Result 1: Encrypt the communications of the Java applet.

Optional Result 2: Limit who may access the Web page that contains the program.

Suggested Solution: Configure the IE 4 Web browsers used by employees to prompt for a username and password when accessing Web sites that require passwords (and configure your Web site to require passwords). Install client certificates in employees' Web browsers. Open up a port in the firewall corresponding to the port used by the applet to connect to the SQL server. Place the Intranet server and the SQL server in the Trusted Sites security zone for the Web browsers.

Which of the following is correct?

A. The suggested solution accomplishes the required result and both optional results.

B. The suggested solution accomplishes the required result and just one optional result.

C. The suggested solution accomplishes the required result only.

D. The suggested solution does not accomplish the required result.

17. You manage a network of 150 Windows 95 and Windows NT Work-station computers. Each department in your company maintains an Intranet Web site, and several use unsigned ActiveX controls. You are creating a custom IE 4 package to be deployed on the computers in your network. You must establish security zones settings for these browsers, allowing them to download the ActiveX controls from the Intranet servers. You don't want to allow users to change the settings you establish, but you want to be able to change the settings later without reinstalling IE 4 on all those computers.

Required Result: Configure IE 4 zone settings.

Optional Result 1: Lock-down zone settings.

Optional Result 2: Allow for the later changing of zone settings.

Suggested Solution: Create a custom IE 4 package using the IEAK Profile Manager with autoconfiguration enabled. Use the IEAK Profile Manager to create a profile that locks-down settings and that allows downloading of ActiveX controls in the Local Intranet zone.

Which of the following is correct?

A. The suggested solution accomplishes the required result and both optional results.

B. The suggested solution accomplishes the required result and just one optional result.

C. The suggested solution accomplishes the required result only.

D. The suggested solution does not accomplish the required result.

CHAPTER

9

Optimizing and Troubleshooting
Internet Explorer

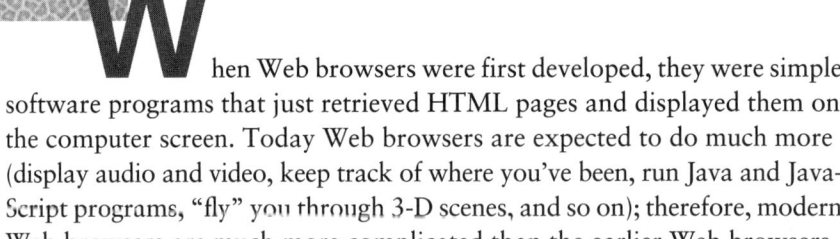

When Web browsers were first developed, they were simple software programs that just retrieved HTML pages and displayed them on the computer screen. Today Web browsers are expected to do much more (display audio and video, keep track of where you've been, run Java and Java-Script programs, "fly" you through 3-D scenes, and so on); therefore, modern Web browsers are much more complicated than the earlier Web browsers.

Internet Explorer 4 is one of the most feature-rich Web browsers you can get, and because of its power and flexibility it can make heavy use of your computer's resources (memory, hard drive space, network bandwidth, and processor power). Also, with complexity comes more things to go wrong. This chapter helps you optimize how IE 4 uses your PC and your network, and helps you troubleshoot IE 4.

Optimizing IE 4

When you optimize Internet Explorer 4, you must take into account where the IE 4 computer is situated—by itself, connected directly to an ISP (usually via a modem), or on a LAN sharing that LAN's connection to the Internet with many other computers that have Web browsers. In any case, you should optimize how IE 4 performs on the PC so that you can make the best use of processing power, memory, and disk space. If the computer resides on a LAN, however, you may want to take some additional measures to ensure that the IE 4 browsers cooperate to make the best use of the shared network bandwidth.

Optimizing IE 4 on the PC

There is no quick explanation for how to optimize Internet Explorer 4 on a PC because there are so many ways a PC can be configured. Some PCs have 486 processors, 8MB of memory, and are connected to the Internet by a 14.4 Kbps modem—others have Pentium II processors, 256MB of memory, and are connected to the Internet via a cable modem. Optimizations that you would make for the second PC would not be appropriate for the first PC.

The default Internet Explorer 4 configuration is optimistic—it assumes that your PC has plenty of disk space, memory, CPU power, and network bandwidth. If your PC is limited in one or more of these areas, you can configure IE 4 to be more conservative in how it uses that resource.

Evaluating PC Resources

First you need to determine if your PC is resource limited. To do so you must understand what *bottlenecks* are, because optimizing Internet Explorer 4 (or any other complex system) is a matter of finding the bottlenecks.

The bottleneck in a system is that part that is slowing everything else down. If you have a fast computer and a 14.4 modem, for example, no matter how much more memory or processing power you add to the PC, the Web pages won't be displayed any faster because the Web pages must go through the slow modem connection before they are displayed. The modem in this case is the bottleneck, and to speed up Web access you must either arrange for a faster connection or reduce the network bandwidth required by Internet Explorer 4.

If, on the other hand, you are using a 486 computer with a cable modem, plenty of RAM, and lots of hard drive space, it may be the case that an even faster network connection wouldn't do you any good—the 486 processor is being taxed to its limits interpreting the HTML and displaying the Web pages. The processor is the bottleneck in this case, and upgrading to a faster processor will yield significant improvements in the speed of your browser.

Any resource required by Internet Explorer 4 is a potential bottleneck, but the most common bottlenecks are CPU power, memory, hard drive space, and the network connection. To determine the bottleneck in your system, all you need is a little common sense, some experience, and a few tools. A helpful tool in Windows 95 and 98 is the System Monitor. In Windows NT, you can use the Performance Monitor to find the bottlenecks in your computer.

Using the System Monitor   You can find the System Monitor tools in the Start menu (Start ≻ Programs ≻ Accessories ≻ System Tools ≻ System Monitor). The System Monitor shows you a graph of how some of the resources in your computer are being used. See Figure 9.1 for a view of the System Monitor.

FIGURE 9.1

The System Monitor shows you how resources are being used in your Windows 95 or 98 computer.

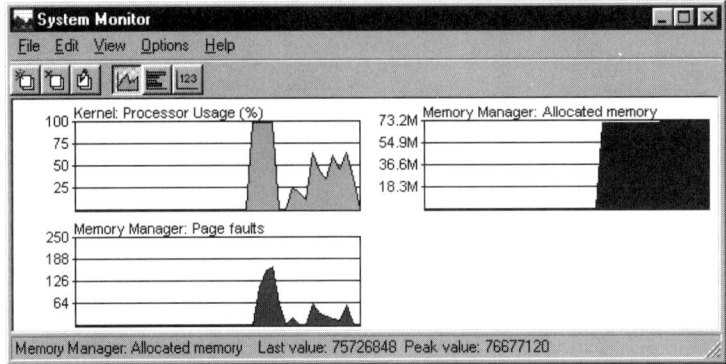

 If the System Monitor is not installed in your Start menu (because you did not choose to install all of the accessories when you installed the operating system), you can install it now from the Add/Remove Programs in the Control Panel. You must have your Windows 95 or 98 installation media (probably on CD-ROM) for Windows 95 or 98 to install it.

The System Monitor creates line charts, bar charts, and numeric displays of the File System, Kernel, Memory Manager, and Networking Client resource use. You can use it to see if, for example, the processor is always busy or if the operating system is always swapping data out to disk (indicating that the computer doesn't have enough memory to do what you're asking it to do). However, it doesn't display all this information at once—you must select what you want it to display from the many items (metrics or performance numbers) of which it keeps track.

Some of the items the System Monitor will graph are less important than others when you are trying to optimize Internet Explorer 4. Some pertinent items in the four general monitoring areas are as follows:

File System   Includes items that measure the amount of data that the hard disk (local to the PC) reads and writes. IE 4 uses the local hard disk drives to store its history and favorites links, as well as cached pages. If you think that your disk subsystem may be the limiting factor in your PC, you can watch the following:

- **Bytes Read/Second**   If this value is consistently high, and the bytes read/second are near the limit of your SCSI or IDE drives, then accessing cached information may be the limiting factor for IE 4. Due to virtual memory, insufficient RAM may cause inordinate reading and writing of data. Make sure you have enough memory before upgrading your disk subsystem.

- **Bytes Written/Second**   This value should follow Bytes Read/ Second, and if it is consistently high, then writing information to the disk may be the limiting factor in the computer (Web pages are written to the hard disk before they are displayed on the screen).

Kernel   Tracks the computing power used by running programs. All the running programs in your computer share the processor. To get a meaningful indication of how IE 4 uses your CPU, you should quit all other programs. You should watch the following item in the Kernel:

- **Processor Usage (%)**   A consistently high value (above 90 percent) indicates that the CPU is the bottleneck in the system.

Memory Manager   Shows how Windows 95 is using memory. The following items can tell you if memory is the limiting factor in your computer:

- **Allocated Memory**   The operating system can allocate more memory for programs than actually exists as RAM in the computer (this is called virtual memory, and it uses hard drive space to make up for non-existent memory). It is generally OK to have up to twice as much allocated memory as RAM (inactive programs don't use their memory), but a single program (such as IE4) that allocates excessive amounts of virtual memory will not run quickly.

- **Pageouts** This is the item that best indicates when a computer is low on memory. In order to use virtual memory when a program requests more memory than the computer actually has, the operating system has to page out something already in memory. A low level of pageouts is normal, but excessive pageouts indicates a program that requires more real memory.

Microsoft Networking Client Since IE 4 is an Internet tool rather than a Microsoft Networking (i.e. NetBIOS) tool, the items in this section aren't all that helpful in optimizing IE4. (Though they are very useful for optimizing network share performance.)

The System Monitor is a simple tool, and it is instructive to place it in a corner of your screen to watch while you do other work. Exercise 9.1 shows you how to use the System Monitor.

EXERCISE 9.1

Using the System Monitor

1. Open the System Monitor by selecting Start ➤ Programs ➤ Accessories ➤ System Tools ➤ System Monitor.

2. Select Edit ➤ Add Item, and then choose Kernel in the Category list.

3. Select Processor Usage (%) in the Item list, then click OK.

4. Select Edit ➤ Add Item, and then choose Memory Manager in the Category list.

5. Select Page Faults in the Item list, then click OK.

6. Track the behavior of the graphs as you open and close windows, launch programs, and browse the Web.

Using the Performance Monitor Windows NT has a tool similar to the System Monitor, but it is much more powerful. It is the Performance Monitor (see Figure 9.2), which can be found in the Administrative Tools section of the Start menu (select Start ➤ Programs ➤ Administrative Tools ➤ Performance Monitor).

The Performance
Monitor in NT allows
you to monitor almost
any aspect of the NT
operating system's
performance.

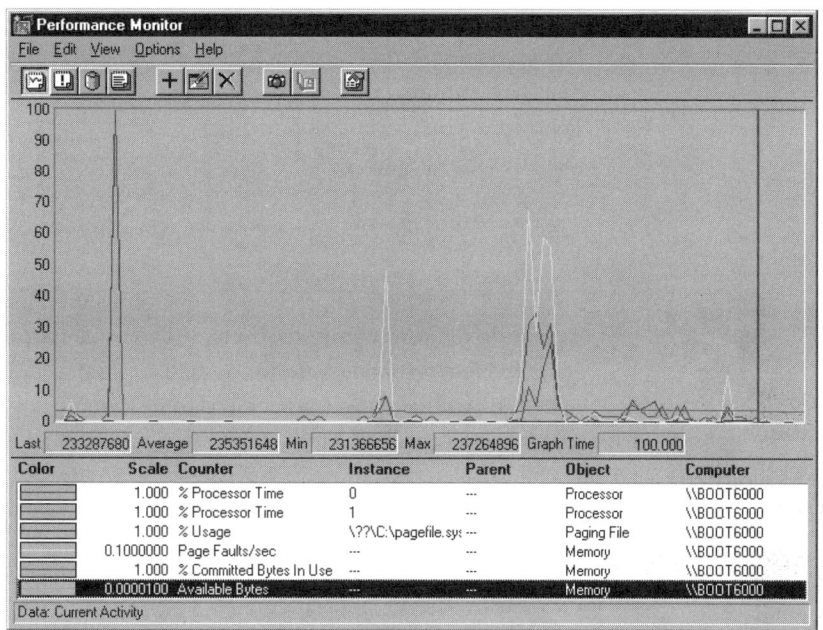

With the Performance Monitor you can graph many more operating
system items than you can with the System Monitor. In the Performance
Monitor, the general categories of items that you can watch are called
objects (such as the Processor object and the Disk object). Specific items you
can watch are called counters. You will want to watch counters that are
related to microprocessor performance and disk performance (described
later in this section) to see how IE 4 uses the resources of your computer. To
see how IE 4 uses the network, you will have to use the Network Monitor,
described later in its own section.

You cannot harm your system by experimenting with the Performance
Monitor, so feel free to view the effect of the different operating system
indicators.

Heisenberg's uncertainty principle states that to measure quantum phenomena is to change it. This principle is also true of performance monitoring. Running the Performance Monitor takes a small amount of CPU time, and enabling disk monitoring also slows input/output requests slightly. Therefore, you cannot measure system performance without causing the performance to change slightly. In almost every case, this change in performance is slight and will have no real effect on your measurements or the validity of your conclusions, but you should be aware that it is happening.

Be sure to let your computer finish the various logon processes before using the Performance Monitor to measure performance. A number of services are started in the background after logging on, and that will affect performance measurements taken right after booting.

Exercise 9.2 shows how to start the Performance Monitor. The remaining exercises in this chapter assume that the Performance Monitor is already loaded.

EXERCISE 9.2

Starting the Performance Monitor

1. Select Start ➤ Programs ➤ Administrative Tools ➤ Performance Monitor.

2. Size the Performance Monitor window so that it takes up about one-quarter of your screen.

3. Select Add to Chart in the Edit menu.

4. Click Add when the drop-down box opens with % Processor Time selected. This value is the measurement of the use of the microprocessor. Leave this measurement running throughout the remaining exercises.

Each Windows NT software object is associated with counters that are incremented each time that object performs a function. For instance, each time a network device driver reads a packet, the device driver increments the packet's read counter by one and the byte's read counter by the size of the packet. Or each time the processor switches threads, it updates the time spent in that thread in a counter used for that purpose.

Counters permeate all Windows NT objects, and they allow meaningful measurement to occur by accounting for everything that happens. Windows NT uses many of these counters to measure performance for its own automatic optimizations and is the first PC operating system to include this level of support for performance monitoring. Table 9.1 shows the objects that you can monitor with the Performance Monitor.

T A B L E 9.1 Windows NT Object Counters	Object	Purpose
	Cache	Microprocessor level 2 cache performance
	Logical disk	Mass storage performance, including network storage
	Memory	Memory performance and usage
	Objects	Process and thread counts
	Paging file	Virtual memory usage
	Physical disk	Hard disk drive performance
	Process	Executing process performance
	Processor	Microprocessor performance
	System	Windows NT performance
	Thread	Individual thread performance

You will also see objects for each network service you have installed. Actually, any software can be written to register performance monitoring counters with the system, so you may see even more counters than are shown here.

Microprocessor Performance   As with all performance objects, a few measurements will give you a good idea of whether the processor is a bottleneck in your system. The following are important processor-related counters:

- Processor: % Processor Time

- Processor: Interrupts/sec

- System: Processor Queue Length

Disk Performance   In Table 9.1, you'll notice two disk-related objects: logical disk and physical disk. Logical disk is used to measure performance at a higher level than physical disk.

The logical disk object can measure the performance of network connections that are mapped as drives and the performance of volume sets and stripe sets that cross physical disks. You will use the logical disk object to uncover bottlenecks initially and then move to the physical disk object to uncover the reasons why that bottleneck is occurring.

Physical disk measures only real transfers to and from actual hard disk drives. These measures isolate performance differences between disks in your system and provide detailed information about the specific performance of a certain disk.

Disk counters cause a measurable performance degradation by distracting the processor at critical input/output periods. These counters are disabled by default. If you attempt to monitor physical or logical disk performance without enabling these counters, you will not see any disk data.

On Intel-based computers, the disk counters cause about a two percent degradation in overall performance. You should enable them only when you need to monitor disk performance (and disable them when you are finished). Enabling the disk counters is shown in Exercise 9.3.

EXERCISE 9.3

Enabling the Disk Performance Counters

1. Select Start ➤ Programs ➤ Command Prompt.

2. Type **diskperf -y** in the input line and press Enter. A message indicates that disk performance counters on the system are set to start at boot time.

3. Restart your system.

When you have finished monitoring disk performance, remember to disable the disk performance monitors. Leaving them enabled serves no purpose and slows your machine down. Exercise 9.4 shows how to disable them.

EXERCISE 9.4

Disabling the Disk Performance Counters

1. Select Start ➤ Programs ➤ Command Prompt.

2. Type **diskperf -n** in the input line, and press Enter. A message will confirm the change.

3. Restart the system.

Once you've enabled the disk performance counters, as shown in Exercise 9.3, you'll be able to make meaningful disk throughput measurements. Important counters you'll want to watch are

- Memory: Pages/sec

- % Disk Time

- Disk Bytes/sec

- Disk Bytes/Transfer

- Current Disk Queue Length

 One thing that you should know—in order to monitor the processor queue length, you must also monitor a thread-specific counter. This is a limitation of how NT and the Performance Monitor were designed. Context Switches/sec shows how many thread switches occur each second, and is a good thread-specific counter to watch.

EXERCISE 9.5

Monitoring NT System Performance

Adding Processor: % Processor Time to the Performance Monitor

1. Click + in the Performance Monitor toolbar.

2. Select Processor in the Object drop-down list.

3. Select % Processor Time in the Counter drop-down box.

4. Click Add.

5. Close the Add to Chart window.

After adding this counter, let the computer idle for a moment, then move your mouse around on the screen and notice the effect on the Processor: % Processor Time measure. Dramatic, isn't it?

Adding Processor: Interrupts/sec to the Performance Monitor

6. Click + in the Performance Monitor toolbar.

7. Select Processor in the Object drop-down list.

8. Select Interrupts/sec in the Counter drop-down box.

9. Select 0.1 in the Scale drop-down list.

10. Click Add.

11. Close the Add to Chart window.

Adding System: Processor Queue Length to the Performance Monitor

12. Click + in the Performance Monitor toolbar.

13. Select System in the Object drop-down list.

14. Select Processor Queue Length in the Counter drop-down box.

15. Click Add.

16. Select Thread in the Object drop-down list.

17. Select Context Switches/sec in the Counter drop-down box.

18. Leave Total selected in the Instance drop-down box.

19. Close the Add to Chart window.

Adding Memory: Pages / sec to the Performance Monitor

20. Click + in the Performance Monitor toolbar.

21. Select Memory in the Object drop-down list.

22. Select Pages/sec in the Counter drop-down box.

23. Click Add.

24. Close the Add to Chart window.

Adding Logical Disk: % Disk Time to the Performance Monitor

25. Click + in the Performance Monitor toolbar.

26. Select Logical Disk in the Object drop-down list.

27. Select % Disk Time in the Counter drop-down box.

28. Click Add.

29. Close the Add to Chart window.

Adding Logical Disk: Disk Bytes / sec to the Performance Monitor

30. Click + in the Performance Monitor toolbar.

31. Select Logical Disk in the Object drop-down list.

32. Select Disk Bytes/sec in the Counter drop-down box.

33. Click Add.

34. Close the Add to Chart window.

Adding Logical Disk: Average Disk Bytes/Transfer to the Performance Monitor

35. Click + in the Performance Monitor toolbar.

36. Select Logical Disk in the Object drop-down list.

37. Select Average Disk Bytes/Transfer in the Counter drop-down box.

38. Click Add.

39. Close the Add to Chart window.

Adding Logical Disk: Current Disk Queue Length to the Performance Monitor

40. Click + in the Performance Monitor toolbar.

41. Select Logical Disk in the Object drop-down list.

42. Select Current Disk Queue Length in the Counter drop-down box.

43. Click Add.

44. Close the Add to Chart window.

Using Desktop Explorer, Disk Defragmenter, and ScanDisk The System Monitor in Windows 95 and 98 and Performance Monitor in NT show you memory and microprocessor bottlenecks, and let you know (unlikely though it may be) if the hard disk controller or hard drive data transfer speed is the limiting factor in your computer. More often, however, Internet Explorer 4 just runs out of disk space.

The easiest way to check free disk space is to view the properties of your C drive (or other drive letter that contains Internet Explorer 4) in the My Computer window (see Figure 9.3). Exercise 9.6 shows you how to use this method to check the free disk space. The pie chart and the statistics next to the chart will show you how much disk space you have used and how much free disk space you have remaining.

FIGURE 9.3

The Drive Properties window shows you graphically how much disk space you have.

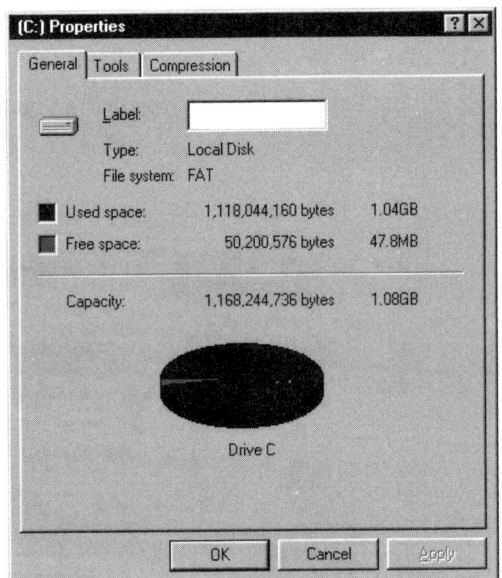

EXERCISE 9.6

Checking the Free Disk Space

1. Double-click the My Computer icon on the desktop.

2. Highlight the C drive (click once on it), then select Properties from the File menu to observe the amount of used and free disk space.

You can learn more about how a DOS FAT file system is being used, and you can run the ScanDisk program, which will tell you how many directories, files, sectors, and control blocks are being used on your hard disk. In addition, the ScanDisk program checks for file system damage which, if you find any, can explain strange Internet Explorer 4 behavior.

Another disk-based performance limiting factor for Internet Explorer 4 is the fragmentation level of your hard drive (Windows NT doesn't have this problem when you use the NTFS file system, but all Microsoft operating systems do when you use the FAT file system). You can defragment your hard drive (move file fragments around so that the operating system doesn't have to search all over the hard disk to retrieve all the parts of a file) using a program called Disk Defragmenter. See Exercise 9.7 for instructions on using ScanDisk to defragment your FAT file system.

EXERCISE 9.7

Running ScanDisk and Disk Defragmenter

1. Select Start ➤ Programs ➤ Accessories ➤ System Tools ➤ ScanDisk.

2. Select the C drive, select Standard, and then click Start.

3. Click OK when the Scan is completed.

4. Click Close.

5. Select Start ➤ Programs ➤ Accessories ➤ System Tools ➤ Disk Defragmenter.

6. Select the C drive, and then click OK.

7. Click OK when defragmentation is complete.

Reducing Processor and Memory Load

There are two ways to speed up Internet Explorer 4 when the computer is CPU or memory limited—one way is to increase the processing power and memory of the computer, and the other way is to reduce the demand that IE 4 makes on the computer. For people on a limited budget or organizations with many older computers, the second option is preferable.

The single feature of Internet Explorer 4 that takes the most processing power and memory is the Windows Desktop Update. It almost doubles the required memory in Windows 95 or NT. It inserts itself all throughout the user interface, allowing you to have Web content (including scripting and ActiveX controls) in otherwise static (hence not CPU-intensive) areas, such as the screen background.

If your computer is low on memory or computing power, do not install the Windows Desktop Update. You should remove Windows Desktop Update if it is already installed. You will also find that running the computer without WDU slightly reduces the disk space requirements of Internet Explorer 4.

Another feature that can slow a burdened Internet Explorer 4 computer is Active Scripting (VBScript or JScript) programs as well as Java programs. These Web programs require computing power to execute. Be careful when you disable these options, however, because some Web sites rely on Active Scripting or Java in order to be displayed properly.

There are other Internet Explorer 4 settings that are nice when you have a fast processor but can get in the way when your CPU is slow. If you find your computer's CPU is the bottleneck, you might want to do the following in the Advanced tab of the Internet Options window of IE 4, or in the IEAK Policy Editor:

- Disable Smooth Scrolling

- Disable Page Transitions

- Disable Page Hit Counting

- Disable Sounds

- Disable Animations

- Disable Smart Image Dithering

Reducing Hard Drive Space Requirements

As with CPU and memory bottlenecks, there are two ways to remove hard drive space limitations: improve the hardware or relax the requirements. Sometimes increasing the size of the hard drive is not an option.

The easiest way to reduce Internet Explorer 4's consumption of hard drive space is to install less software on the hard drive. Rather than a full installation, perhaps a Standard or Browser Only installation will suffice. You can create a custom IE 4 package containing only the software components that users need in your network.

You can reduce the disk space used by a previously-installed Internet Explorer 4 package by changing the caching settings of IE 4. You should be familiar with the Temporary Internet Files settings and the History settings. You can change these settings in the General tab of the Internet Options window or by using the IEAK Profile Manager. You can configure the Temporary Internet Files directory to use (at maximum) a smaller set percentage of your hard drive space, and you can move it to a different drive (if you have more free space elsewhere). You can configure the IE 4 History to keep track of where you've been (in IE 4) for fewer than the default 20 days. Exercise 9.8 shows you how.

Microsoft Exam Objective

Optimize caching and performance.

EXERCISE 9.8

Reduce the Caching in IE 4

1. Launch Internet Explorer 4.

2. Select View ➢ Internet Options.

3. Click the Settings tab in the Temporary Internet Files section of the General tab.

4. Move the Amount of Disk Space to Use slider to the left to reduce the disk space used for caching in IE 4. Click OK.

5. Reduce the Days to Keep Pages in History value to 5, then click OK.

Reducing Network Bandwidth

In some cases, the microprocessor, memory, and hard drive space of a PC are more than sufficient in speed and capacity. Instead the network bandwidth is the bottleneck—you can only get so much data through even the fastest analog modem.

One quick (although drastic) way to reduce the bandwidth used by Internet Explorer 4 is to turn off image downloading. Images take up a lot of bandwidth, and you will find that the HTML pages download much faster without the images. Unfortunately, turning off images disables the most useful feature of the Web—its graphical nature.

Another way to reduce network bandwidth (not a lot, just a little for sites you frequently visit) is to increase Internet Explorer 4's cache (the amount of space Temporary Internet Files is allowed to occupy on the hard drive). This, of course, increases the disk space used by IE 4, but any file that already resides in the cache (especially small graphic files that are used throughout a Web site) won't have to be downloaded again from the Internet.

You might also want to change how often Internet Explorer 4 checks to see if the cached content is current. When checking to see if the content is current, IE 4 has to communicate with the Web site over the Internet connection. From the General tab of the Internet Options window, you can select the frequency that you would like IE 4 to check the cached content. The frequency options are the following:

- Every time IE 4 is started (default setting)

- Every time the page is accessed

- Never

If you decide not to have IE 4 check to see if cached content is current, you will have to click the Refresh button to get the latest version of a Web page that is already stored in your cache.

Optimizing IE 4 in the Network

An individual user of Internet Explorer 4 wants to be able to make maximum use of the connection to the Internet. If that user's computer resides on a LAN, that inclination may run counter to the goals of the corporate network administrator, because the administrator must balance the network needs of the whole organization against the needs of individual users. One user watching real-time video over the Internet connection can slow down the Web browsing and e-mail use of many other network users, for example.

Smart use of proxy servers and careful management of site subscriptions (when creating your own Active Channels and by limiting Internet Explorer 4 subscriptions with the Profile Manager) can help you tame the wild browsers in your network.

Using Proxy Servers

Most corporate LANs that connect to the Internet do so through a single leased line, whether it is ISDN, Frame Relay, T1, or T3, and all of the network users must share that Internet connection. The Internet connection is usually much slower than the LAN. This makes the Internet connection a bottleneck. One way to alleviate pressure on this bottleneck is to install a proxy server on your network for all of the Web browsers to go through.

Proxy servers serve the same purpose for all the computers in your network as the Internet Explorer 4 Temporary Internet Files directory. A proxy server resides on your LAN, and local browsers connect to it rather than directly to remote Web sites when users browse the Web. If somebody else has already accessed a Web location, the proxy server does not go out to the Internet to get the Web pages—instead it gives the Web browser the pages it kept in its cache after the previous user accessed that external Web location.

You can use the IEAK to create a custom Internet Explorer 4 package that uses your proxy server by default, and you can use the IEAK Policy Manager to create autoconfiguration files that direct the Web browsers in your network to use your proxy server. If you want more dynamic control over how IE 4 uses proxy services, you can create autoproxy files. See Chapter 7 for further discussion on how to configure PCs in your LAN to use proxy services.

Managing Subscription Schedules

Internet Explorer 4 includes a new feature called Automatic Updates. It helps users keep up-to-date on information and software. Automatic Updates instructs Internet Explorer 4 as to where and how often to check for new or updated Web pages, Active Channel information, Active Desktop items, and software. While this feature frees IE 4 users from repetitively checking for updates themselves, it can cause IE 4 to use much more Internet bandwidth than it would otherwise.

Microsoft ✓ ***Exam Objective***

Set up schedules for automatic updates. Locations include:

- Site subscriptions
- Channels
- The Active Desktop

Microsoft **Use the IEAK Profile Manager to optimize network resources**
✓ ***Exam*** **and components.**
Objective

The problem with updates is that they take up bandwidth to retrieve information that the user may not even want to see immediately. When you create Active Channels and Software Update channels for users in your network, you should choose update schedules that won't interfere with regular LAN or Internet use—for example, you could configure a channel that downloads the company's Announcements Web page every night at 3 a.m.

Establishing reasonable default subscription times and frequencies is a good start to optimizing Internet Explorer 4, but the subscription schedule established in the Active Channels are just suggestions, and the user has the option of changing them for individual Web browsers, even to inconvenient times such as 8:35 in the morning, when everyone is trying to use the Internet to check their e-mail. Also, an IE 4 user is free to subscribe to channels that you don't control, with times and frequencies that can wreak havoc on your network. You need a way to lock-down IE 4 subscription times and frequencies without restricting user subscriptions.

Internet Explorer 4 gives you this feature, and the IEAK Profile Manager (or the IEAK itself when you build a custom Internet Explorer 4 package) is what you use to lock-down the settings. You can select the settings for the following options:

- Maximum KB of site subscriptions

- Maximum KB of channel subscriptions

- Maximum number of site subscriptions that can be installed

- Beginning of range in which to exclude Scheduled Subscription Updates (minutes from midnight)

- End of range in which to exclude Scheduled Subscription Updates (minutes from midnight)

- Maximum sites subscription crawl depth

In the preceding options (except for maximum sites subscription crawl depth), you can enter zero to disable the restriction.

By setting the maximum KB of site and channel restrictions you keep users from automatically (and frequently) downloading huge files that can swamp the network connection. Limiting the number of site subscriptions keeps users from subscribing to everything under the sun, also swamping your network. Subscription Exclusion Range settings are a more useful setting for when subscriptions are consuming network bandwidth that would be better used for other purposes. You can establish a "subscription-free time" in which users can have exclusive use of the network for other, more interactive purposes. A good time to set for the exclusion range is the working day— from 8 a.m. through 6 p.m. (depending, of course, on the hours that people generally work in your company).

While the previous settings govern site subscriptions and Active Channels in general, Internet Explorer 4 has some specific settings for Software Distribution Channel updates and Active Desktop autoconfiguration updates. You can lock-down these settings as well. Exercise 9.9 shows you how.

EXERCISE 9.9

Establishing Update Restrictions Using the IEAK Profile Manager

1. Start the IEAK Profile Manger.

2. Select File ➣ Open.

3. Browse to the INS autoconfiguration file for which you want to lock-down update restrictions. Click the Open button.

4. Open the System Policies and Restrictions branch in the left pane of the window.

5. Open the Subscriptions folder and select the Subscriptions item within that folder.

6. In the right pane of the window, type **1024** in the Maximum KB of Site Subscriptions field.

EXERCISE 9.9 (CONTINUED)

7. Type **1024** in the Maximum KB of Channel Subscriptions field.

8. Type **20** in the Maximum Number of Site Subscriptions field.

9. Type **5** in the Minimum Number of Minutes between Scheduled Subscription Updates field.

10. Type **480** in the Beginning of Range field.

11. Type **1020** in the End of Range field.

12. Open the Wizard Settings branch in the left pane.

13. Select the Automatic Browser Configuration item.

14. Type **0** in the Autoconfigure Every ___ Minutes field.

15. Select File ➢ Save.

Troubleshooting IE 4

Sometimes your problem is not that you want Internet Explorer 4 to run faster or stop interfering with other network users—sometimes you just want IE 4 to run correctly. Problems can crop up when you create a custom IE 4 package, when you install it, and when you try to use it to access Web content. Sometimes the problem exists in how you configured or installed IE 4, sometimes its source can be found in the operating system that is running IE 4, and sometimes the problem is in the LAN or on the Internet. Your job is to find where the problem is and, if possible, fix it.

Problems Working with IEAK Wizard

You should not have problems with the IEAK Wizard itself, because it is a simple program that just downloads files and puts them together according to your instructions. Any problems you experience are more likely to result from misconfiguration or inadequate resources needed by the IEAK (such as hard disk space or RAM). You may have problems with the resulting package, however, if you give the IEAK invalid or inappropriate settings.

Microsoft ✓ *Exam Objective*

Diagnose and resolve problems related to the IEAK wizard.

Synchronization

The first time you run the IEAK, all of the standard Internet Explorer 4 components will have a red X icon next to them indicating that you do not have the components. This is not a problem, because Microsoft expects you to synchronize the IEAK with their Web site in order to get the latest components. If you do not have a reliable Internet connection, however, this could be a problem. If you have trouble synchronizing the IE 4 packages, see "Network Connection Troubleshooting" later in this chapter to find out why.

Disk Space

The IEAK Wizard will alert you if you run out of disk space while creating a custom IEAK package. At that point you must either free existing disk space on your hard drive (by deleting or compressing other files) or abandon your custom IEAK package and install new disk space. Installing new disk space usually involves turning off your computer and installing hardware components, which is always something to be nervous about.

IE 4 Configuration

The IEAK relies on information maintained by Internet Explorer 4 to operate, including certificates, favorites, channels, and Windows Desktop Update settings. If you want to import WDU settings into your custom IE 4 package, you should install IE 4 with the Windows Desktop Update on the computer that is running the IEAK Wizard.

Using IEAK 3 *INS* Files

Version 4 of the IEAK uses the same format for INS files as version 3, so you can use IEAK 3 INS files to configure your custom Internet Explorer 4 package. The IEAK 3 INS files do not include all the settings for IE 4, however, so some options may not be available. Rather than using an older version of INS file, it is usually a better idea to create a new INS file with the IEAK that contains the information that the old file contained.

Can't Edit System Policies and Restrictions

If the folder containing the IEAK ADM files is compressed, the IEAK may not be able to read the ADM files, which means you won't be able to edit the System Policies for that custom IEAK package. This is a bug in the current version of the IEAK. You should install the IEAK to a different directory or uncompress that directory.

Custom Welcome Message Can't Contain Graphics

This is a bug in version 4 of the IEAK that will be fixed in the next version. You can configure your custom Internet Explorer 4 package to refer to a custom Welcome message, but that Welcome message HTML file cannot successfully refer to any other items such as graphic images, Java programs, or sounds.

Channel Description HTML Page Can't Contain Graphics

This is a bug in version 4 of the IEAK that will be fixed in the next version. You can configure your custom Internet Explorer 4 package to include custom channels and to include an HTML page describing that channel, but that channel description HTML file cannot successfully refer to any other items such as graphic images, Java programs, or sounds.

Can't See the Toolbar Buttons When You Include a Custom Toolbar Bitmap

The bitmap you supply must be a 256-color bitmap of any dimension (if it is too small, Internet Explorer 4 will tile the bitmap, and if it is too big, IE 4 will crop it). The colors used in the bitmap should be light so that the IE 4 buttons can be seen when drawn on top of the bitmap. If your bitmap is too "busy," users may not be able to see the buttons.

Your Custom Active Setup Bitmap Doesn't Appear

The Active Setup bitmap must be a 256-color BMP file that is 120 pixels wide by 239 pixels high. Any other kind of image will not work properly.

IE 4 Displays the Default Active Setup Bitmap Even Though You Supplied a Correct Bitmap to the IEAK

When you run Active Setup on a computer that has less than a 256-color display (such as a PC with only 16-color VGA), the default bitmap is displayed instead. You cannot supply a 16-color bitmap, and the 256-color bitmap is not interpolated down to 16 colors.

Importing Favorites Doesn't Import the Folder Containing the Favorites

When you import favorites folders into the custom Favorites created by the IEAK, the folder containing the favorites is not also imported. If you want to import the folder structure, you must create a higher-level folder in Internet Explorer 4 and place the folder of favorites in it. You can then import the new folder and its contents (containing favorites) into your custom IEAK package.

Installation Problems

If you are lucky and plan your deployment well, you will simply create your custom Internet Explorer 4 package with the IEAK and then roll it out onto the desktop computers. Sometimes, however, things don't go quite that smoothly, and you have to figure out why IE 4 won't install or run properly on a particular PC. The following may help you diagnose common IE 4 installation problems.

Microsoft ✓ *Exam* *Objective*   **Diagnose and resolve the deployment failure of a preconfigured version of Internet Explorer 4.0.**

Version Mismatch

You can download a perfectly fine custom Internet Explorer 4 package that won't run on your computer. This can happen because you can use the IEAK to create IE 4 packages for different platforms, and the one you download must be appropriate for that computer. You may receive the following message:

```
The Internet Explorer files on your computer are not the
correct files for your operating system. To continue, you
must download the correct files from the Internet. Do you
want to continue?
```

You can select Yes to download the appropriate files.

Language Mismatch

Windows operating systems come in language specific versions (such as English, French, Russian, Japanese, and so on). Internet Explorer 4 also comes in multiple language versions. The standard IE 4 browser will still operate if there is a language mismatch (such as a Russian browser on an English Windows operating system), but the Windows Desktop Update, which is closely tied to the operating system, will not be enabled when the language version of the browser is different from the language version of the operating system. If you have a language mismatch problem and you want to use Windows Desktop Update, you must download the version of the browser that matches your operating system.

Kernel Fault

If you are low on hard disk space when you try to install additional IE 4 components from a components download Web site (either Microsoft's additional components site or your own custom site), the `Kernel32.dll` file may cause Windows to have an invalid page fault. This can cause Windows to lock up and you may not be able to restart Windows without turning the power off. To avoid this problem have plenty of hard drive space before you install additional components.

IE 4 and NT Service Pack 3

IE 4 requires NT Service Pack 3. If, for some reason, you feel the need to reapply or uninstall Service Pack 3 after you have already installed IE 4, you may see the following message the next time you run IE 4:

```
Update.exe:
This program may not run correctly because of the new
features in Internet Explorer 4. You may need to obtain an
updated version of this program. For information about
obtaining an updated version, click Details. If you want to
try running this program, click Details to determine whether
it will cause other problems. Then, if running this program
will not cause other problems, click Run Program.
```

Uninstalling or reinstalling Service Pack 3 overwrites certain files that IE 4 needs to operate. In order to run IE 4, you need to reinstall Service Pack 3 (if you have removed it) and reinstall IE 4. If you really want to uninstall Service Pack 3, remove IE 4 first to avoid any other complications.

Slow Connections

One possible cause of slow connections is using the Novell NetWare 32-bit networking client and connecting through a proxy server. You can configure Internet Explorer 4 to work correctly in this configuration by adding a binary value setting to the Registry, as follows:

`DontUseDNSLoadBalancing` with the value of 01 00 00 00 under the Registry key

`HKEY_CURRENT_USER\Software\Microsoft\Windows\CurrentVersion\Internet Settings`

You must restart your computer after making this change.

Webcasting Problems

As with any new feature, the webcasting capabilities of Internet Explorer 4 (Active Channels, Software Updates, etc.) can sometimes give you problems.

Microsoft ✓ *Exam Objective*

Diagnose and resolve failures of webcasting. Types of webcasting include:

- Site subscriptions
- Channels
- Active Desktop items

Unattended Dial-Up and NetWare Servers

If you use your Windows 95 computer on a NetWare network but you use a modem to connect to your Internet service provider, the dial-up adapter may still be bound to the NWLink (IPX/SPX) protocol. When this is the case and you configure an unattended dial-up connection to the Internet (for example, to get your mail or to automatically download Active Channel content), the dial-up will pause and present you with the following dialog box:

```
You are currently using NetWare servers, which will be
inaccessible if you establish this connection.
Click OK to continue dialing. Click Cancel if you do not
want to dial at this time.
```

This message halts the connection process. To allow automatic dial-up to the ISP to continue unimpeded, you should disable the NWLink protocol for the dial-up adapter.

E-Mail Notification Failure

When a user subscribes to an Active Channel, the user has the option of being notified by e-mail when there is an update to that channel. Three criteria must be met before the user will receive e-mail notification of a change:

- The <USAGE VALUE= "Email" /> tag must be specified in the CDF file for the channel.

- The user must choose to receive e-mail in the Channel Subscription window when the user subscribes to the channel.

- The user must click the Change Address button when prompted and supply the correct SMTP server name for mail to be sent.

No Visual Indication of Updates

Internet Explorer 4 Web browsers inform users when Active Channel content has changed by placing a red gleam in the corner of the Active Channel icon. Sometimes, however, the Web pages that the channels define change, but the gleam does not appear.

Internet Explorer 4 will only place a gleam on the icon of a channel when the Channel Definition file is updated, not when Web content changes. It is the job of the Channel Maintainer to update the CDF file when the Web content changes so that Web browsers can be updated. This is not a bug in IE 4 or caused by improper installation or use of IE 4—it is an indication of lax Web site administration.

Subscription Image Downloading

Image downloading of Active Desktop items is due to the implementation of Internet Explorer 4. You will not see images if you configured Active Desktop so that it will not download images. The images are still downloaded, however, unless you also disable image downloading in regular Internet Explorer 4 Web pages.

Caching Problems

Caching (using data stored in the Temporary Internet Files directory or data stored in a proxy server) can sometimes cause problems for users who want up-to-the-minute information about real-time events (such as stock quotes, traffic conditions, or the weather).The problem occurs because Internet Explorer 4 will not check to see if there is new data on the Web site unless the file in the cache has expired. You can configure the length of time files can remain in the cache before they expire in the Temporary Internet Files Settings window.

There are three options for checking for new content when something is in the cache: IE4 checks for new content with every visit to the page, every time you start Internet Explorer, or never. This feature is only useful for Web pages that do not already have expiration dates encoded directly in the page as it is transferred from the Web server to the Web browser. Most Web sites with time-sensitive information use these new methods of informing the Web browser which pages must not be cached and which it is OK to cache. You only need to worry about cache problems when you access older sites that do not encode this information in their Web sites.

If Internet Explorer 4 users commonly access Web sites with data that must be up-to-the-minute, you can set the caching status to update with every visit to the page. Recognize that this setting essentially disables the usefulness of the caching feature.

Proxy servers introduce a similar caching problem, except the cache files are stored on the proxy server instead of the Web browser. If the cache problems are due to the proxy server returning cached files, you may have to configure your Web browser to bypass the proxy server for certain Web sites or train users to click the Refresh button every time they visit the site.

Microsoft ✓ *Exam* *Objective*   **Diagnose and resolve failures of caching.**

Network Connection Troubleshooting

Sometimes the problems that arise are not with Internet Explorer 4—instead there is a misconfiguration in the operating system, failure in the network, the Internet is simply congested, the Domain Name Service is not up to date, or the destination computer simply isn't responding to Web browser requests. There are several tools you can use to help you diagnose problems with the network when IE 4 is working perfectly fine but you still can't reach a Web site.

Microsoft ✓ *Exam Objective*

Choose the appropriate tools for troubleshooting network connection failures. Tools for troubleshooting include:

- IP configuration
- PING
- Trace route
- Network Monitor
- Nslookup

There are a number of tools you can use to help you diagnose a network fault. Useful tools may include the following:

- Winipcfg (for Windows 95 and 98) or Ipconfig (for Windows 98 and NT)
- PING (95, 98 and NT)
- Trace route (95, 98, and NT)
- Nslookup (NT only)
- Network Monitor (NT only)

IP Configuration

The first thing you should check when the network doesn't seem to work is that the computer is configured properly to talk to the network. A computer connected to the Internet needs at least an IP address and subnet mask in order to send and receive information. In addition, the computer should have a default gateway, know where to find one or more DNS servers, and have a host name. Some computers get this information automatically from a Dynamic Host Configuration Protocol (DHCP) server, others must have these settings supplied to them in the Network Control Panel.

There are two programs that make verifying the IP configuration settings easy. They are the Winipcfg and Ipconfig programs, and they come with Windows 95 and Windows NT respectively. Winipcfg is a graphical program that you can use in Windows 95 to view network settings as well as release and renew DHCP leases on IP addresses (see Figure 9.4). Ipconfig is a command-line program that you can use in Windows NT to view and configure network and DHCP settings for an NT workstation or server (see Figure 9.5).

F I G U R E   9.4

Winipcfg displays the IP configuration of Windows 95 and 98 computers.

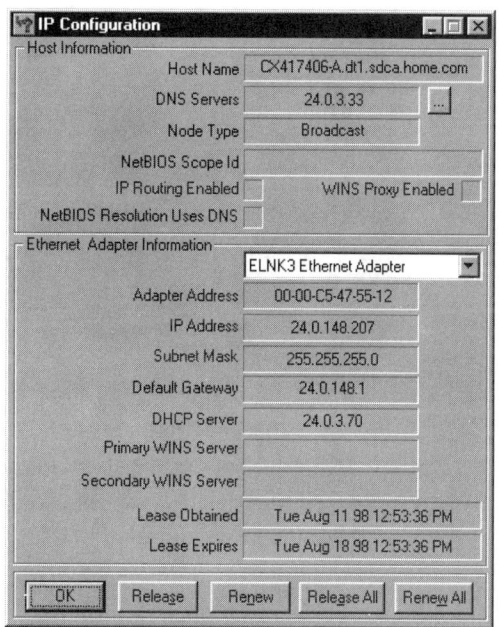

If your computer uses DHCP, you can tell right away if the network settings are wrong by attempting to renew the leases for a network adapter. If the values go to zero or a new lease cannot be obtained, you can be sure that the networking problem is somewhere between your computer and the DHCP server.

FIGURE 9.5

Ipconfig displays the
IP configuration of
Windows NT
computers.

```
Command Prompt                                              _ □ ✕

        Host Name . . . . . . . . . . : lucretius
        DNS Servers . . . . . . . . . :
        Node Type . . . . . . . . . . : Hybrid
        NetBIOS Scope ID. . . . . . . :
        IP Routing Enabled. . . . . . : Yes
        WINS Proxy Enabled. . . . . . : No
        NetBIOS Resolution Uses DNS : No

Ethernet adapter Elnk31:

        Description . . . . . . . . . : ELNK3 Ethernet Adapter.
        Physical Address. . . . . . . : 00-20-AF-9F-BF-BB
        DHCP Enabled. . . . . . . . . : Yes
        IP Address. . . . . . . . . . : 0.0.0.0
        Subnet Mask . . . . . . . . . : 0.0.0.0
        Default Gateway . . . . . . . :
        DHCP Server . . . . . . . . . : 255.255.255.255

Ethernet adapter NE20002:

        Description . . . . . . . . . : Novell 2000 Adapter.
        Physical Address. . . . . . . : 00-00-E8-2C-47-BA
        DHCP Enabled. . . . . . . . . : Yes
        IP Address. . . . . . . . . . : 10.1.1.2
        Subnet Mask . . . . . . . . . : 255.255.255.0
        Default Gateway . . . . . . . :
        DHCP Server . . . . . . . . . : 10.1.1.1
        Lease Obtained. . . . . . . . : Thursday, October 30, 1997 8:54:15 AM
        Lease Expires . . . . . . . . : Monday, January 18, 2038 7:14:07 PM

Ethernet adapter NdisWan6:

        Description . . . . . . . . . : NdisWan Adapter
        Physical Address. . . . . . . : 00-00-00-00-00-00
        DHCP Enabled. . . . . . . . . : No
        IP Address. . . . . . . . . . : 0.0.0.0
        Subnet Mask . . . . . . . . . : 0.0.0.0
        Default Gateway . . . . . . . :

Ethernet adapter NdisWan5:

        Description . . . . . . . . . : NdisWan Adapter
        Physical Address. . . . . . . : 00-00-00-00-00-00
        DHCP Enabled. . . . . . . . . : No
        IP Address. . . . . . . . . . : 0.0.0.0
        Subnet Mask . . . . . . . . . : 0.0.0.0
        Default Gateway . . . . . . . :

C:\>
```

If your computer does not use DHCP, you must determine (by asking the individual who assigns the numbers in your network) what the IP settings should be and then compare that to the settings Winipcfg or Ipconfig shows you (the settings should match).

PING

If your network settings are OK but you still can't access a particular Web site or other network host using the Web browser, you need to check to see if the host is actually responding. The PING command was designed for just this purpose. It will attempt to connect to an IP number or DNS name you supply to it, and if it can connect, it will tell you how long (in microseconds) it took for the message to get to the other computer and back.

You can use PING to see if DNS is working correctly. Since you can query the host by both the IP number and DNS name, if the IP address works but the name doesn't, you can be fairly confident that the DNS system is at fault.

Trace Route

Sometimes a network host will respond to your PING command, but the response will be consistently slow. When that happens, you want to know just where in the network the delay is happening. You can check the path that the message is taking to get to the host using the tracert command.

Tracert discovers and tells you the host name of each intermediary computer between your Web browser and the destination host (see Figure 9.6) by sending special IP packets that expire after being passed through a certain number of computers. When a packet expires, the computer that sent it is informed. The tracert program asks the computer that sent the "your packet has expired" message who it is, then sends out a special IP packet with an expiration counter one greater than the last one. Eventually the intended recipient responds, and tracert has discovered the number of computers between your computer and the destination, how long it takes to talk to them, their names, and their addresses.

FIGURE 9.6

Trace route shows you the network path used to connect your computer to another over the Internet.

```
MS-DOS Prompt                                    _ □ X
7 x 12

Tracing route to www6.yahoo.com [204.71.177.71]
over a maximum of 30 hops:

  1    15 ms    16 ms    17 ms  cr2-hfc4.dt1.sdca.home.net [24.0.148.1]
  2    13 ms    12 ms    10 ms  24.0.128.1
  3     7 ms    12 ms    12 ms  bb1-at2-0-0-t3.rdc1.sdca.home.net [10.0.216.11]

  4    24 ms    26 ms    23 ms  172.16.3.189
  5    48 ms    25 ms    23 ms  w1-fe0-0-0-100bt.rdc1.sfba.home.net [24.0.0.12]

  6    29 ms    42 ms    26 ms  hssi1-1.br3.SNV.globalcenter.net [206.251.7.201]

  7    27 ms    28 ms    28 ms  fe1-0.cr1.SNV.globalcenter.net [206.251.5.12]
  8    27 ms    30 ms    28 ms  pos0-0.wr1.SNV.globalcenter.net [206.251.0.106]

  9    32 ms    34 ms    31 ms  pos1-0-OC12.wr1.NUQ.globalcenter.net [206.251.0.
73]
 10    50 ms    33 ms    35 ms  pos5-0.cr1.NUQ.globalcenter.net [206.251.0.121]

 11    32 ms    26 ms    43 ms  www6.yahoo.com [204.71.177.71]

Trace complete.

C:\WINDOWS>
```

Nslookup

Another tool that comes with Windows NT (but not Windows 95) that you can use to diagnose network problems is the Nslookup program. Nslookup is a command-line program that queries Domain Name servers to determine the IP Address corresponding to the DNS name of a computer on the Internet. It can also help you discover which DNS server has registered (or mis-registered) its name and address information.

If you find that one computer correctly finds the IP address of an Internet host but another cannot, you can use nslookup to figure out why there is a discrepancy. Typing nslookup and then the Internet name on each computer tells you what IP address the DNS server thinks that the computer uses. If the two numbers differ, you can type just nslookup on each computer to see which DNS servers they are communicating with. Often a service (such as a company Web site) moves from one Internet service provider to another, and while the new ISP may have updated its DNS servers with the correct information, ISPs are notorious for being tardy in removing old information. A little prodding from customers (especially with high-voltage electricity) can sometimes motivate them to keep their DNS information up-to-date.

The Network Monitor

All of the tools that we've discussed are useful for diagnosing network problems. They are hammers and chisels for chipping away at network problems, and precision tools for when you need to know how your network is configured or why it is behaving the way it is in a particular instance. However, there is another tool that comes with Windows NT that you can turn to when faced with particularly thorny network problems—the Windows NT Network Monitor. The Windows NT Network Monitor is both a jack-hammer and a chain saw.

The Network Monitor monitors data sent over the network. Data is sent through the network in frames or packets, each containing header information that identifies the protocols being used to send the frame, a destination address, a source address, and the data.

In TCP/IP (the transport protocol for the Internet), long messages are broken up into short pieces called *packets*, much like a continuing correspondence between two people can be broken up into individual letters. Like letters, each packet must contain a source address and a destination address to be delivered correctly.

Most people don't open mail that is not addressed to them. The network is the same way. By default, a network card will ignore any packet that is not addressed to its computer. On the other hand, network monitors really don't care who a packet is sent to. They are able to watch and record all packets on the network. Unlike letters, the sender and recipient have no way of knowing that their mail has been read.

Network monitors use a special mode that is supported by most modern network cards called *promiscuous mode*. Promiscuous mode allows the network adapter to capture all the data packets on the network. Special promiscuous-mode drivers work by capturing the data of every packet, as opposed to capturing only packets that are addressed to the computer network card.

The Network Monitor that ships with NT Server 4 is not a fully-functional network monitor. It is a limited version of the Network Monitor that ships with SMS (a Microsoft BackOffice application that can be purchased separately). Instead of being able to capture all of the networks packets, this version of Network Monitor can capture only the following:

- Frames sent from the server

- Frames sent to the server

- Broadcast frames

- Multicast frames

Because the Network Monitor that ships with NT Server 4 is not fully functional and does not capture every network packet, the server's network card driver does not have to run in promiscuous mode. Network Monitor is able to use the network driver interface specification (NDIS) that your network card uses. The frames that are detected are then copied to the servers memory in a capture buffer. Using the NDIS 4 standard instead of using promiscuous mode reduces the CPU load up to 30 percent.

In contrast, the Network Monitor that ships with the SMS product is able to capture all packets on the network, regardless of the source or destination computer address. The SMS Server must use a promiscuous mode network driver.

The limited version of the Network Monitor that ships with Windows NT Server 4 does not support promiscuous mode. Therefore, it can capture only packets sent to the server or to all stations.

Installing Network Monitor

Installing the Network Monitor is similar to installing any service in Windows NT Server 4. Exercise 9.10 shows how to install the Network Monitor.

EXERCISE 9.10

Installing Network Monitor

1. Right-click the Network Neighborhood icon.

2. Select Properties.

3. Click the Services tab.

4. Click the Add button, and choose Network Monitor Tools and Agent.

5. Click OK.

6. Enter the path for NT Server CD, and click OK.

7. Click Close on the Network dialog box.

8. Click Yes when the Network Settings dialog box prompts you to restart your computer so that the changes can take effect.

Once the Network Monitor has been installed, you will notice a new control panel for the Monitoring Agent, and the Network Monitor Tool menu item will appear in the Administrative Tools menu.

Using the Network Monitor

In this section you will learn how to manually initiate a data capture with the Network Monitor (see Figure 9.7), view information generated by a data capture, and save captured data.

Using Network Monitor, you can capture only as much data as will fit into system memory.

You can manually capture data at any time by running the Network Monitor and choosing to start a capture. When you are done capturing data, you can simply stop the capture and view the data at a later time. You can also stop the capture and view the data within a single menu choice.

FIGURE 9.7

The Network Monitor

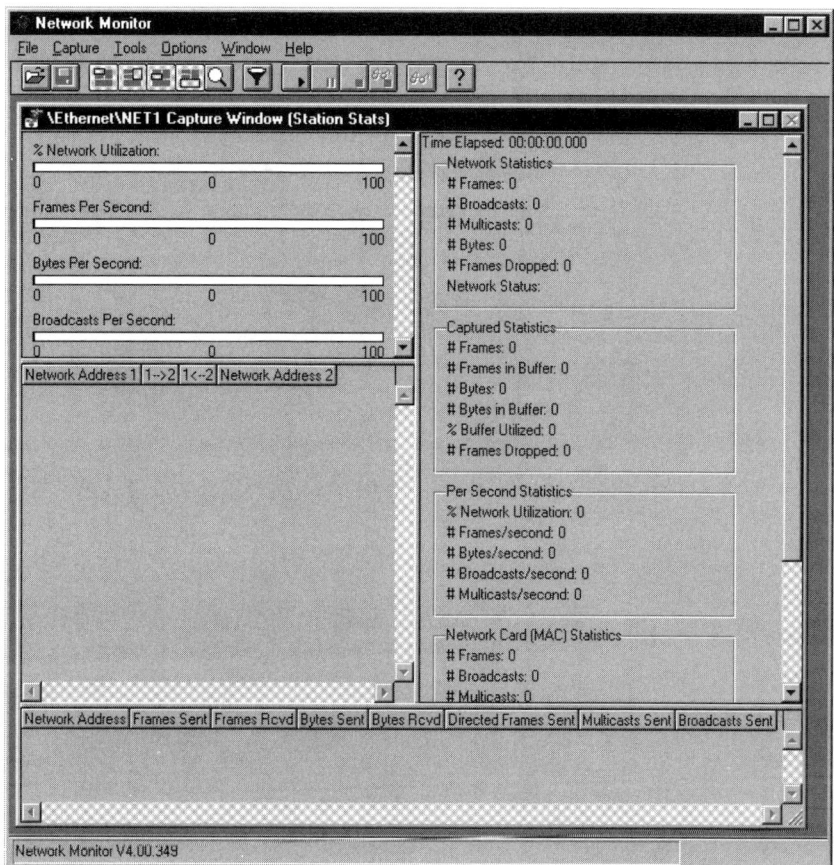

Information Captured by the Network Monitor   The Network Monitor can provide both real-time information and cumulative, saved data. In Figure 9.7, notice that the Network Monitor user interface has four main sections:

> **Bar graphs**   Provide information on real-time network activity. The bar graphs show network utilization, frames per second, bytes per second, broadcasts per second, and multicasts per second. The utilization statistic shows you how much traffic (both to and from the server) is affecting segment performance.

Session statistics   Show the conversations that are taking place on the network. This information is real-time and cumulative for the capture session. Because of the limitations placed on this utility, you will only see sessions that include the NT Server.

Station statistics   Provide information on the network conversations. You can see the network address, frames sent, frames received, bytes sent, bytes received, directed frames sent, multicasts sent, and broadcasts sent.

Summary statistics   Include network statistics, captured statistics, per second statistics, network card media access control statistics, and network card physical layer error statistics.

During the network capture, all packets that the server sends or receives are saved in the server's memory buffer. To see the frames that have been captured, from the Network Monitor dialog box select Capture ➤ Display Captured Data. Double-click a packet name to see its specific information (see Figure 9.8).

F I G U R E   9.8

Network Monitor
information for a
packet

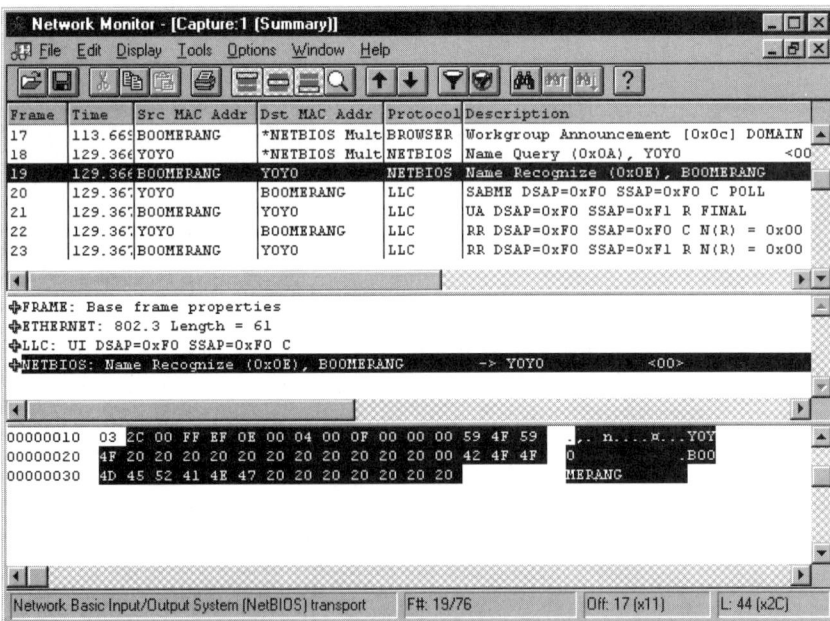

Notice in Figure 9.8 that each frame's detail screen consists of three sections:

- Top section: Summary pane

- Middle section: Detail pane

- Bottom section: Hex pane

The Summary pane lists all the frames in the current capture. By highlighting specific frames, the information about that frame appears in the Detail pane and Hex pane. The Summary pane lists columns for the frame number, the time (relative to the capture process), the source MAC address, the destination MAC address, the protocol used to transmit the frame, and a description that summarizes the frame's contents.

The Detail pane shows all the protocol information associated with the specific frame. If a + sign appears to the left of the protocol, you can click the protocol for more detailed information.

The Hex pane shows the hexadecimal information associated with the selected frame. The hex values appear to the left of this pane, and the corresponding ASCII characters appear to the right.

Saving Captured Data   You can save captured data to a file for archiving purposes or to be analyzed by another source. By default, captured data is saved in the root directory in which Windows NT has been installed under \SYSTEM32\NETMON\CAPTURES, and the file is saved with a CAP extension. Exercise 9.11 shows you how to capture, view, and save data with the Network Monitor.

EXERCISE 9.11

Manually Initiating a Data Capture

1. Select Start ➤ Programs ➤ Administrative Tools ➤ Network Monitor.

2. Select Start from the Capture menu.

3. Allow the capture to run for one or two minutes.

4. Select Capture ➤ Stop.

5. Select Capture ➤ Display Captured Data.

6. Select a frame from the Capture dialog box, and double-click anywhere on the frame. You should see something similar to Figure 9.8.

7. Select File ➢ Save As.

8. Type **TESTCAPT** in the Save Data as text box, and click OK. Your captured data has now been saved.

If you save captured data on a regular basis, you may want to use the date as your file name, so that you can easily identify the files.

Filtering Captured Data You can very easily accumulate a large amount of data in a very short time during data captures. Capturing data on a heavily-loaded server over an extended period of time tends to produce copious amounts of data that can be difficult to store and wade through. Looking for specific information can be as challenging as looking for a needle in a haystack. Luckily, the Network Monitor enables you to filter frames based on transport protocol, computer address, and protocol properties.

By default, the filter is not set and displays all protocols, all computer addresses, and all protocol properties. To filter network data, choose Display ➢ Filter (see Figure 9.9). Then configure the filter to display frames that match the values that you specify in the Expression Input box.

FIGURE 9.9

Network Monitor
Display Filter
dialog box

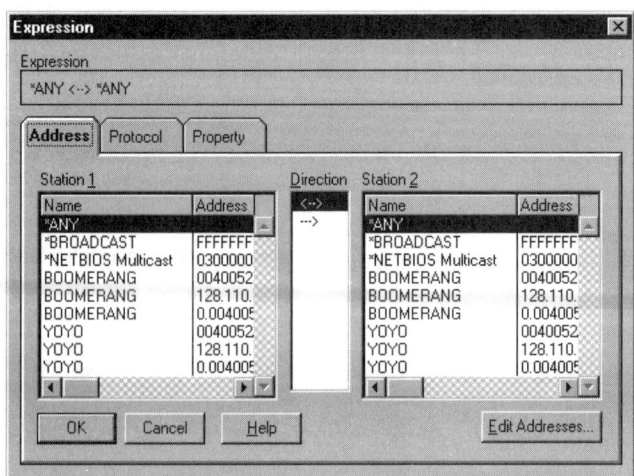

The following examples illustrate why you would filter data. Assume that you suspect that the network card in Pam's machine is failing and is causing excessive network traffic to the server even though Pam is not currently using her machine. You can filter and view all the packets that are being sent from Pam's network card by selecting her network address to filter by.

Some documentation recommends that you install all protocols if you're not sure which protocol to use (TCP/IP, NWLink IPX/SPX, or NetBEUI)—not that this is such a great idea, because using more protocols than you need places a greater load on the file server and on the network. However, if you do install multiple protocols and want to see the impact of each protocol on server traffic, you could create a filter for each specific protocol and see how many packets each protocol generates.

Network Monitor Security

As previously noted, the Network Monitor allows you to view network packets that are transmitted or received by the Windows NT. These packets could potentially contain sensitive data that you want to protect. The Network Monitor provides two security features to help protect against unauthorized use of Network Monitor: password protection and detection of other Network Monitor installations.

Password Protection   In order for the Network Monitor to capture packets, the Network Monitoring Agent must be running. The Network Monitoring Agent is capable of using dual-level passwords to control who can view captured data and who can capture and view captured data files. Exercise 9.12 shows how to set network monitoring passwords.

EXERCISE 9.12

Setting Network Monitor Passwords

1. Select Start ➤ Settings ➤ Control Panels.

2. Double click Monitoring Agent.

3. Click Change Password.

4. Enter passwords in the Change password text box.

WARNING The Network Monitor and Monitoring Agent do not have a default password. Therefore, anybody running Network Monitor can connect to your server and capture and view your frames.

Detection of Other Network Monitor Installations Network Monitor enables you to detect whether other instances of Network Monitor are running (through SMS or Windows NT Network Monitor). If other instances of Network Monitor are running, you will see:

- The computer name from which Network Monitor is being run
- The user who is currently logged on to the computer running Network Monitor
- The MAC address of the computer running Network Monitor
- The state of Network Monitor (running, capturing, or transmitting)
- The version of Network Monitor

To learn whether other instances of Network Monitor are currently running, access Network Monitor from the Administrative Tools group and select Tools ➢ Identify Network Monitor Users.

Summary

Optimizing a computer with Internet Explorer 4 is a matter of finding the bottlenecks in the computer and then either increasing the capacity of the computer or decreasing the demands IE 4 places on that resource. In a memory-limited computer, for example, you can add more memory or you can decide not to install Windows Desktop Update. You have similar choices when it comes to microprocessor power, disk space, and Internet connection bandwidth.

Optimizing Internet Explorer 4 for a network is a little different—a fully optimized IE 4 browser can use too much Internet bandwidth and limit what other network users can do. A corporate administrator may want to limit some of the functionality of IE 4 so that the limited bandwidth available can be used for the most important tasks.

A custom Internet Explorer 4 package can have problems at several stages in its existence—as you use the IEAK to create it, when you deploy it on end-user PCs, and as the browser is used on the network. You must be familiar with common browser problems in each stage, and you should be very familiar with the tools you use to diagnose network problems.

Review Questions

1. You have a Windows 95 computer that is browsing the Web slowly. You want to find out if the bottleneck is the processor or the memory. What tool should you use to find the bottleneck?

   A. Performance Monitor

   B. System Monitor

   C. ScanDisk

   D. Microsoft Diagnostics (MSD)

2. You have a Windows NT Workstation computer that is browsing the Web slowly. You think that the bottleneck is either the processor or the memory. What tool can you use to determine where the bottleneck is?

   A. Performance Monitor

   B. System Monitor

   C. Disk Administrator

   D. Microsoft Diagnostics (MSD)

3. Using the System Monitor you discover that the bytes being written to and read from the hard disk are very high for your Windows 95 PC, and that the Pageouts count is also high. What is most likely the bottleneck in the system?

   A. Your processor is too slow.

   B. You have too little RAM.

   C. You have too little hard drive space.

   D. Your modem is too slow.

4. You want to speed up disk access in your Windows 95 computer. What tool can you use to optimize hard disk performance?

   A. Disk Administrator

   B. ScanDisk

   C. Disk Defragmenter

   D. Desktop Explorer

5. You want to reduce the bandwidth used by IE 4 so that HTML pages load faster over your 28.8 Kbps modem. Which of the following will not reduce bandwidth?

   A. Disable smooth scrolling

   B. Disable graphics

   C. Disable Active Channels

   D. Set Check for Newer Versions of Stored Pages option to Never

6. Which of the following can help you reduce the combined Internet bandwidth used by browsers on your network that is connected to the Internet through a T1 leased line? Choose all that apply.

   A. Installing a proxy server

   B. Disabling Windows Desktop Update

   C. Limiting Active Channels

   D. Upgrading the Internet connection to a T3

7. How many ranges during the day may IE 4 be prohibited from performing Active Channel updates?

   A. Zero

   B. One

   C. Ten

   D. No Limit

8. You currently have a maximum bandwidth of site subscriptions limited to 1024 KB. You want to disable this restriction. What should you enter in the Maximum KB of Site Subscriptions field?

   A. None

   B. Zero

   C. Unlimited

   D. Disabled

9. What tools can you use to limit the bandwidth and times used by site subscriptions in your network? Choose all that apply.

   A. The IEAK Wizard

   B. The IEAK Profile Manager

   C. The User Manager for Domains

   D. The Profile Control Panel

10. You have a red X next to all of the components you want to include in your custom IE 4 package. What should you do?

   A. Download the IEAK again.

   B. Order the IEAK on CD-ROM.

   C. Synchronize the components.

   D. Proceed. The red X icons will turn to green icons as each component is configured.

11. You can't edit the System Policies and Restrictions in the IEAK Wizard. What might be wrong?

   A. You have not synchronized all of the IE 4 components.

   B. One of the IEAK folders is compressed.

   C. You have not logged on as administrator.

   D. You have an older version of the IEAK.

12. You have created an Active Setup bitmap and included it in your custom IE 4 package, but the default bitmap appears instead. What might be the problem? Choose all that apply.

   A. The bitmap is in the wrong format.

   B. The computer is in 16-color mode.

   C. You didn't digitally sign the image.

   D. You have used the wrong colors. You must choose colors that the Active Setup buttons will be visible over.

13. You want to include a folder in the Favorites menu called Local, and in the Local folder you want to have links to Intranet Web sites. What must you do?

   A. In Stage 4 of the IEAK, click Create Folder. Enter Local as the folder name, then add URLs to the favorites that you want to be included in that folder.

   B. In IE 4, create a folder called Local. Browse each Intranet site and add that site to the Local folder in Favorites. Import the Local folder into your custom IE 4 package using the IEAK.

   C. In IE 4, create a folder called Temp, and another folder called Local within Temp. Browse each Intranet site and add that site to the Local folder in Favorites. Import the Temp folder into your custom IE 4 package using the IEAK.

   D. You cannot import folders into the IE 4 Favorites directory.

14. You cannot get Windows Desktop Update to work in your Spanish version of Windows 95. What might be the problem?

   A. Microsoft does not distribute a Spanish version of IE 4.

   B. You have installed an English version of IE 4 on the Spanish version of Windows.

   C. Windows Desktop Update requires Service Pack 3 on Windows 95, and there is no Spanish version of Service Pack 3.

   D. The Spanish version of Windows requires more disk space.

15. What network diagnostic tool should you use to display the IP configuration settings of your Windows 95 computer?

A. Winipcfg

B. Ipconfig

C. PING

D. Nslookup

16. Your network has only a 56 Kbps frame relay connection to the Internet. You want to give network bandwidth priority to electronic mail and Web browsing by users rather than to automatic Active Channel updates. Since many users access the same sites every morning, you would prefer that those Web pages are only retrieved over the 56K link once each morning, rather than once per user. In addition, some users access financial information pages that are updated frequently but do not include time-stamping information, and you don't want these users to retrieve stale Web pages. You would also like to keep users from downloading large graphic files during office hours.

Required Result: Limit Active Channel bandwidth use during working hours.

Optional Result 1: Reduce duplicate page retrievals.

Optional Result 2: Protect users from retrieving stale Web pages.

Suggested Solution: Use the IEAK Profile Manager to disallow Active Channel updates between 8 a.m. and 5 p.m. Establish a Proxy Server on your network to cache Internet Web pages.

Which of the following is correct?

A. The suggested solution accomplishes the required result and both optional results.

B. The suggested solution accomplishes the required result and just one optional result.

C. The suggested solution accomplishes the required result only.

D. The suggested solution does not accomplish the required result.

17. Your Windows NT Workstation computer is running very sluggishly. You use the Performance Monitor to try to find the bottleneck in your computer. The user of this computer keeps many programs open at once—a spread sheet, a word processor, a CAD package, Outlook Express, IE 4, and a desktop publishing package. You discover that the number of pages per second is excessive when compared with the same counter on another computer that is operating normally. You need to speed up this computer. You don't want to change the hardware configuration of the computer, but you also prefer not to restrict how the user works with the computer.

Required Result: Increase the performance of the computer

Optional Result 1: Leave the hardware configuration alone.

Optional Result 2: Leave the user's habits alone.

Suggested Solution: Add memory to the computer.

Which of the following is correct?

A. The suggested solution accomplishes the required result and both optional results.

B. The suggested solution accomplishes the required result and just one optional result.

C. The suggested solution accomplishes the required result only.

D. The suggested solution does not accomplish the required result.

CHAPTER

10

Optimizing and Troubleshooting
Outlook Express and NetMeeting

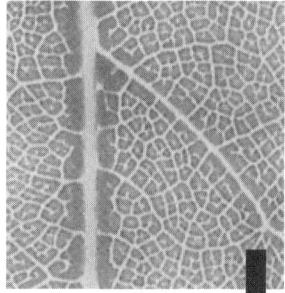

In the last chapter, you learned how to optimize and troubleshoot Internet Explorer 4, which is a program that primarily uses one protocol (HTTP) and does one thing (display Web pages). In this chapter, you will learn how to optimize and troubleshoot Outlook Express and NetMeeting, which use many protocols and perform a wide variety of functions for the user. These more complex systems provide more opportunity for problems to arise, so with these two programs there is a lot to optimize and troubleshoot.

You optimize and troubleshoot Outlook Express and NetMeeting the same way you do Internet Explorer 4 itself—you identify individual PC performance issues, LAN performance issues, and hardware, software, or network failure issues. When you find an issue, you determine what is causing it and then fix it.

Troubleshooting Outlook Express

As you saw in Chapter 4, Outlook Express is a natural complement to Internet Explorer 4 because (after the Web) it provides the other two core communications features needed by Internet users—Internet mail and Internet news. These two features are not bandwidth intensive, because they are both primarily textual. Although Outlook Express can easily display HTML formatted mail and news articles with embedded pictures, graphics, programs, and sound, few people use these features in their private e-mail or public news postings.

Because Outlook Express can connect to so many different information sources using different protocols (IMAP, POP, SMTP, and NNTP), Outlook Express is more vulnerable to network problems or misconfiguration than is Internet Explorer 4. The two main problem areas in Outlook Express that you will have to troubleshoot are installation problems and connection failures.

| ***Microsoft*** *Exam* *Objective* | **Diagnose and resolve connection failures of Outlook Express.** |

Solving Installation Problems

Outlook Express is not an complex program—it doesn't require an extremely fast processor, specialized hardware (such as a video camera), lots of memory, or lots of hard drive space. It does require that you have some disk space free for storage of e-mail messages, and Outlook Express tries to make things easier for you by importing data from the Windows Address Book. Also, if Outlook Express is your default mail client, you can click a Mail To link in Internet Explorer 4 and use Outlook Express to send mail to the individual. Three common installation problems are as follows.

Outlook Express Is Not the Default Mail Client

Windows makes it easier for the user to perform certain tasks by associating default programs with those tasks. The default bitmap file (BMP) editor, for example, is Microsoft Paint, and the default editor of files with the DOC extension is Microsoft Word. Windows comes with some associations preset, but as you install new programs on your Windows computer, the install process usually makes associations for those new programs. So, for example, when you double-click a PDF file, Adobe Acrobat opens and displays the file for you.

When you install Outlook Express, you can make it the default mail and news client for your computer. This means that when another program (that does not include e-mail functionality) needs that functionality (for example, when you click a Mail To link in Internet Explorer 4), Outlook Express will be launched for you to compose mail.

When you install another e-mail program, such as Eudora, Netscape Communicator, or the full Microsoft Outlook product, that e-mail program may set itself to be the default mail client. That is OK if you actually want to use that other program as the default mail client, but if you prefer Outlook Express (perhaps because it handles multiple external e-mail accounts so well), you will want to make Outlook Express the default mail client again.

Internet Explorer 4 uses the default file types defined in Windows. Changing the default mail client for IE 4 also changes the default mail client used by any other programs that refer to the Windows file types. Exercise 10.1 shows you how to make Outlook Express the default e-mail client from the My Computer icon (see Figure 10.1). You can also set the default mail client from within IE 4 in the Programs tab of the Internet Settings window.

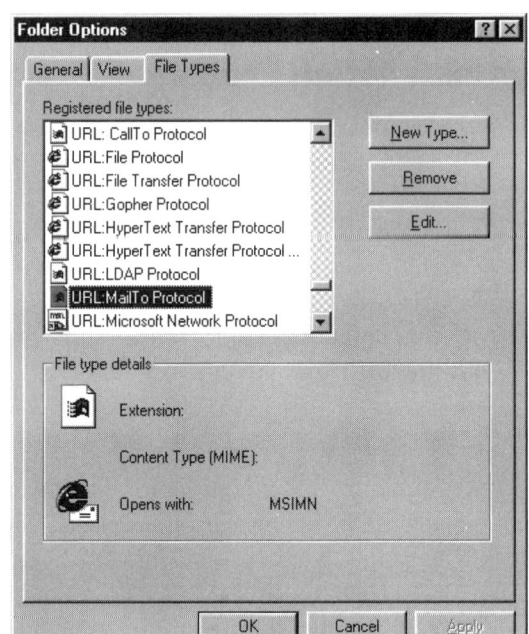

F I G U R E   10.1

IE 4 defers to the operating system settings for which program to use to send mail when the user clicks on a URL with the Send To HTML tag.

EXERCISE 10.1

Setting Outlook Express to Be the Default Mail Client

1. Open the My Computer icon on the desktop.

2. In the My Computer window, select View ➤ Folder Options.

3. Click the File Types tab.

4. Scroll down to URL:MailTo Protocol.

5. Click the Edit button.

6. Select the Open item in the Actions list, then click the Edit button.

7. In the Application Used to Perform Action text box, enter **C:\Program Files\Outlook Express\Msimm.exe /mailurl:%1**.

8. Click OK, click Close, and then click Close again.

Problems Importing Address Book

Outlook Express can import contact data (including e-mail addresses) from the Address Book used by Windows. If the Wabmig.exe file is missing or damaged, however, the import process will fail. If the file is missing, you can fix it by reinstalling Outlook Express. If the file is damaged, you may have to rename the file (find it by using the Find ➢ Files or Folders option in the Start menu) before you reinstall Outlook Express.

Disk Space Problems

Outlook Express, like most other Windows programs, requires disk space to run. It needs space to store the e-mail, and Windows needs space for virtual memory to run Outlook Express (you may be surprised to find that even when you have lots of real RAM, Windows uses virtual memory anyway). Pull up the System Monitor and watch it while you use your programs. The following two error messages often show up when your computer is low on disk space:

- There was an error opening this message. You may see this message after pressing the space bar in response to the Press <Space> to display the selected message…prompt.

- The command failed to execute. You may see this message when you attempt to save a mail attachment and there is not enough space on the hard drive.

If you see either error message, your only option to fix the problem is to create more disk space on the hard drive. You can remove files you don't need from the hard drive, empty the Recycle Bin, or (if your operating system supports it) compress some files. As a last resort, you can delete the Internet Explorer 4 Setup folder, but doing so removes some files that you will need if you have to uninstall IE 4 later.

Solving Connection Failures

Internet Explorer 4 should be able to connect to any computer on the Internet because you never know where a hypertext link will point. If IE 4 can't connect to a handful of links, that's OK because Internet sites are always coming and going anyway. Outlook Express, on the other hand, only has to connect to a handful of computers to perform its function, and if it can't contact them then it may not be able to work at all.

IMAP, POP, and SMTP

Outlook Express gets the user's mail from (at least one) mail server and its news from (at least one) news server. In order to exchange mail and news, these servers must, of course, be reachable using TCP/IP (the last section of Chapter 9 shows you how to check TCP/IP connectivity). Like Internet Explorer, Outlook Express uses protocols to make the connection between itself and the mail or news server.

Outlook Express can use either IMAP or SMTP and POP to connect to any particular mail server, depending on what protocols that server supports. You can use IMAP to connect to one server and use SMTP and POP to connect to another, if you want. Each protocol uses a different TCP port number—that's how a server that supports many services, such as Windows NT or UNIX, can tell which service is being requested. Not only must the server computer be operating, the services must be responding to mail or news requests on those ports.

If you suspect that the server is not responding correctly or that you have been given incorrect or out-of-date mail and news server addresses, you can check them using the Telnet program (see Table 10.1 and Figure 10.2).

T A B L E 10.1	**Protocol**	**Port**
Ports used by Outlook Express	IMAP	port 143
	SMTP	port 25
	POP	port 110
	NNTP	port 119

F I G U R E 10.2

If you can PING a computer but Telnet reports that it cannot connect to port 110 on that computer, then the POP server on that computer is not responding to mail requests.

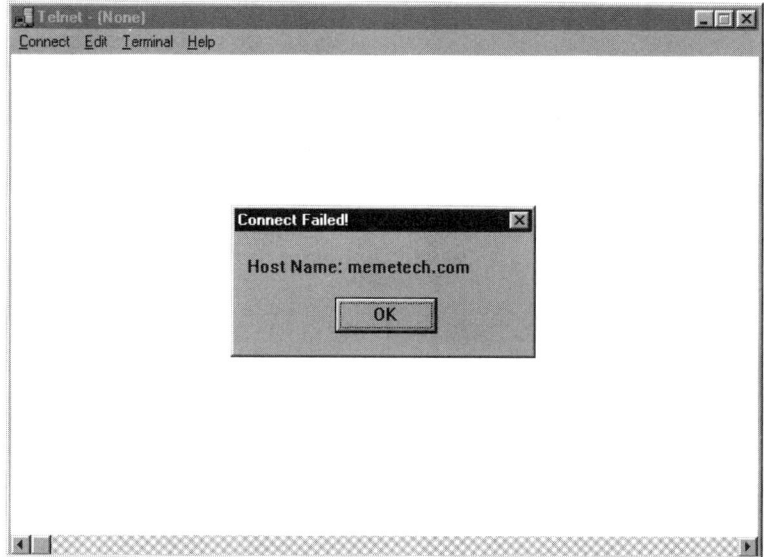

EXERCISE 10.2

Using Telnet to Troubleshoot Outlook Express

1. Connect to your ISP, if necessary.

2. Select Start ➢ Run, then type **Telnet** in the Open text field. Click OK.

3. Select Connect ➢ Remote System.

4. Enter the Internet name or IP address of the IMAP server in the Host Name field.

5. Type **143** in the Port field.

6. Click the Connect button.

If a connection is established, then the server you identified in the Host Name field is responding to IMAP requests. If the connection is refused or times out, then the IMAP service on that computer is not responding.

7. If you get the Connect Failed! message box, click OK; otherwise, select Connect ➢ Cancel.

8. Select Connect ≻ Remote System.

9. Enter the Internet name or IP address of the SMTP server in the Host Name field.

10. Type **25** in the Port field.

11. Click the Connect button.

If a connection is established, then the server you identified in the Host Name field is responding to SMTP requests. If the connection is refused or times out, then the SMTP service on that computer is not responding.

12. If you get the Connect Failed! message box, click OK; otherwise select Connect ≻ Cancel.

13. Select Connect ≻ Remote System.

14. Enter the Internet name or IP address of the POP server in the Host Name field.

15. Type **110** in the Port field.

16. Click the Connect button.

If a connection is established, then the server you identified in the Host Name field is responding to POP requests. If the connection is refused or times out, then the POP service on that computer is not responding.

17. If you get the Connect Failed! message box, click OK; otherwise, select Connect ≻ Cancel.

POP and NNTP Passwords

A setting that is usually required for mail but usually not required for news is a password for each user to access the server. When one user experiences a problem connecting to a mail or news server but access by other users works just fine, you should check the account name and password information for that user's mail and news connections to see if the wrong account information (or no information) has been entered for that user.

Multiple Accounts

In Outlook Express, a user can have more than one Internet mail account, and each Internet mail account must be set up separately, complete with a POP or IMAP username and password for that account, as well as an Internet address for that server (just one for IMAP or one each for SMTP and POP). A user can have more than one mail account on the same mail server, each with a different account name and password (for example, one user might have their own personal mail account but also be responsible for the user_ support mail and administrator accounts as well). The same user might also check mail that is being sent to more than one mail server but with the same account name (and password, but lets hope not) on each server (Henry J Tillman might be `hjtillman@home.com`, `hjtillman@aol.com`, and `hjtillman@tillmanworldenterprises.com`, for example). The user must be careful not to mix up the usernames, server locations, and passwords for each account.

Sometimes users will check their mail from more than one computer. This can cause problems, especially when the users like to keep already-read mail. When Outlook Express retrieves mail, its default behavior is to delete the mail from the server after it has been downloaded. This can cause problems when the user reads the message at home (for example) but later looks for that message at work. Users should be aware of how Outlook Express handles mail, and users that check mail from more than one location should configure Outlook Express on all computers but one to leave the mail on the server. That way the user can expect to find read mail in one place.

A related potential for trouble arises when several users check the same mail account for new mail. For example, problems can occur when several people in the Tech Support department check the mail for users' problems— one technician may read a bug fix bulletin and not pass on the information to the other technicians. The resolution is to have just one user's configuration delete the mail from the server (presumably on the computer of a supervisor who can be relied upon to make sure that the mail gets its proper attention).

Firewalls and Proxy Servers

A potential connection problem with Outlook Express arises when the mail or news servers reside outside a corporate firewall. The protocols (IMAP, POP, SMTP, and NNTP) require that certain ports be open so that Outlook Express can connect to the mail or news services on the remote computer (the ports required are those you checked with Telnet in the preceding sections). If you have a firewall between your network and the Internet and you can PING a mail or news server but POP and SMTP don't reach the site, you should check your firewall configuration to make sure that those ports are open (but only, of course, if company policy allows those ports to be open).

Optimizing and Troubleshooting NetMeeting

Unlike Outlook Express, NetMeeting supports the kinds of communications that can easily swamp an Internet connection (real-time audio and full-motion video). In addition to developing NetMeeting connection troubleshooting skills, you will want to know how to optimize NetMeeting so that a few Internet users don't monopolize the bandwidth of your connection.

Microsoft ✓ *Exam Objective*
Diagnose and resolve connection failures of NetMeeting.

Limiting the Bandwidth Used by NetMeeting

The impact of using NetMeeting on a shared Internet connection can be considerable. A real-time audio stream can saturate a 14.4 Kbps modem and a video stream can take anywhere from all of the bandwidth of a 56K frame relay connection to all the bandwidth of a cable modem or multiple T1 lines, depending on the resolution, compression, and frame rate of the video. People browsing the Web or checking their mail are understandably annoyed when things slow to a crawl because a user is checking out the latest Rolling Stones video or chatting with his mother.

You can disable or limit the bandwidth used for audio and video with either the IEAK Wizard or the IEAK Profile Manager. Using the IEAK Profile Manager to create an autoconfiguration file gives you the most flexibility because you can change the INS file later. It would take a good deal more effort to create another custom Internet Explorer 4 package later with the IEAK Wizard if your initial NetMeeting settings were too restrictive or too lenient for your network users. Exercise 10.3 shows you how to limit Net-Meeting bandwidth (see Figure 10.3).

FIGURE 10.3

You can limit the bandwidth used by NetMeeting using the IEAK Profile Manager.

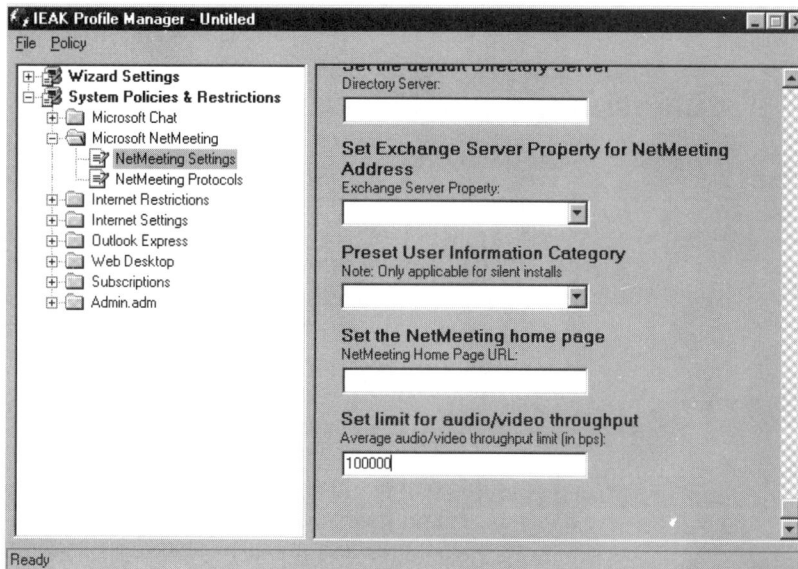

EXERCISE 10.3

Limiting the Bandwidth Used by NetMeeting

1. Open the IEAK Profile Manager by selecting Start ➢ Programs ➢ Microsoft IEAK ➢ IEAK Profile Manager.

2. Open the INS autoconfiguration file for your network (for example, select File ➢ Open, browse to C:\IEAKCustom\en and double-click custom.INS).

3. Open the System Policies and Restrictions branch in the left-hand pane of the IEAK Profile Editor window.

4. Open the Microsoft NetMeeting item, and then select the NetMeeting Settings item in the left-hand pane.

EXERCISE 10.3 (CONTINUED)

5. Scroll down to the bottom of the right-hand pane, and type **50000** in the Set Limit for Audio/Video Throughput text field.

6. Select Save in the File menu.

Troubleshooting NetMeeting Configuration

NetMeeting, more so than Internet Explorer 4 or Outlook Express, is sensitive to how your computer is configured. The audio and video features of NetMeeting require that you have additional hardware in your PC. Sound cards, video capture cards, microphones, and cameras all have to be installed and configured correctly before you can use NetMeeting to its fullest extent. If you have trouble with NetMeeting, you should first check to see that these components are functioning correctly.

Hardware Setup

There are too many kinds of sound cards and video capture cards for this book to explain how to diagnose and troubleshoot every hardware combination. Most adapters, however, come with clear instructions and diagnostic software to help you install and configure the adapters in your computer. Once the hardware and software drivers are installed, however, you still have to configure NetMeeting to use the devices. Sometimes there are problems with the audio or video, as the following describes.

Audio   Problems with NetMeeting audio can be summarized in four cases: you can't hear anything, you can't hear much, sometimes you can hear the audio and sometimes you can't, or you can hear the audio but the person on the other end can't hear you.

If you are having audio problems, you should use the Audio Tuning utility of NetMeeting to try to resolve the problem. If that doesn't work, check to see if any of the following conditions exist:

- Your microphone or the microphone of the person you are talking to is not plugged in.

- The volume is set low on the sound card, in the volume control utility, or in the speakers.

- The speakers are not connected.

- You are using a slirp dial-up connection to the Internet (NetMeeting cannot transmit audio over a slirp connection).

- You or the person you are talking to are not using full-duplex sound.

- A firewall is blocking ports 1720 and 1731.

- The network administrator has disabled NetMeeting audio as a system policy.

- You are using a 16-bit Winsock DLL to connect to the Internet.

- You are using a 16-bit sound card driver to drive the sound card.

Generally, if you can use the Sound Recorder that comes with Windows to record and play back sounds on your computer, you should be able to use NetMeeting for audio teleconferencing—unless external factors (such as a firewall or the type of dial-up connection) interfere. There is a more extensive discussion of firewalls in the section "NetMeeting and Firewalls" later in this chapter.

Since Creative Labs sound cards are popular, you should know that for Windows NT 4 the SoundBlaster drivers posted on their Web site on January 15, 1997 will not work with NetMeeting. You can use the drivers that come on the NT installation CD-ROM, or later drivers supplied by Creative Labs. Another NT-specific problem applies to computers that use older Pentium chips and have the floating-point bugfix installed. This bugfix can cause audio to drop drastically in quality or not to work at all.

Video Capture When you say "teleconferencing" most people think of person-to-person video. If you have verified that the video capture hardware works (by reading and following the instructions that came with your video capture unit) but you still see a boring little black square where the image of a loved one or co-worker should be, you should check to see if any of the following are interfering:

- You are connected to the Internet through a slirp or other SLIP connection that uses header compression.

- The video capture card is not configured to use one of the following video formats: RGB4, RGB8, RGB16, RGB24, or YVU9.

- The video capture card is using video overlay mode.

- The video capture card does not support Microsoft Video 1 for Windows.

NetMeeting can't use video capture cards that use overlay mode because that video mode places the captured images directly in the video adapter's memory. NetMeeting needs the video images to be placed in the PC's main memory first, so it can send the images to the other person in the video conference (you aren't using NetMeeting to watch yourself, after all).

If you are using Windows NT, you have to have Service Pack 3 installed (which you installed to run Internet Explorer 4). On NT you may also need to upgrade to DirectDraw 3 if you have trouble seeing an image in the display window.

Software Setup

Aside from audio and video configuration there are a few software issues that can cause problems with NetMeeting. One particularly difficult-to-diagnose problem with NetMeeting can occur if you have upgraded a computer to Windows 95 that previously had any Hewlett-Packard fonts installed on it. The fonts that Microsoft and Hewlett-Packard have identified that cause NetMeeting to freeze up (and similar problems to occur with other Windows 95 programs) are as follows:

- Artistik
- Ashley Inline
- Boxed In
- Broadway
- Creepy
- Challenge Extrabold
- Eclipse
- Gallia
- Stencil Sans
- Harlow
- Holidays
- Kidprint
- Old English
- Party

- ITC Pioneer

- Snowdrift

- Thunderbird

- Torino Outline

- Traffic

- Yearbook Outline

If you are using a laptop or desktop computer that can be suspended, you may have to restart NetMeeting after suspending and resuming the computer. All network connections will be lost, but NetMeeting itself gets confused as to the state of networking before and after the suspension. Restarting the computer will require the operating system to start the networking protocols from scratch, and thereby clear out any stale network connections.

If you are using NetMeeting on a computer with Windows NT Workstation or Windows NT Server, you should know that application sharing in NetMeeting can slow down display performance.

Troubleshooting NetMeeting Connections

You can have the hardware and software in your computer set up correctly but still have problems with NetMeeting. You need to be able to diagnose and solve connection problems (when the solution to the problem is something that you can fix, of course). This section will help you determine if the NetMeeting problem lies in the network or if the destination simply isn't responding to NetMeeting connections.

The first step, of course, is to determine if the destination computers can be reached. Since NetMeeting uses an ILS (Internet Locator Service) to establish connections, you will want to make sure that you can reach that computer from your NetMeeting computer. You can use PING and the other network connection tools described in Chapter 9 to verify the connection to this computer.

The ILS computer isn't the only computer you need to be able to communicate with, however—the whole point of NetMeeting is to let you establish audio and video connections directly with other people's computers on the Internet. If you are having difficulty connecting to a specific computer, you should verify that you have network connectivity to that computer as well, using the tools described at the end of Chapter 9. Exercise 10.4 shows you how to use Telnet to test NetMeeting connections.

EXERCISE 10.4

Using Telnet to Test NetMeeting Connectivity

1. Connect to your ISP, if necessary.

2. Select Start ➢ Run, then type **Telnet** in the Open text field. Click OK.

3. Select Connect ➢ Remote System.

4. Enter the Internet name or IP address of the directory server in the Host Name field.

5. Type **389** in the Port field.

6. Click the Connect button.

If a connection is established, then the server you identified in the Host Name field is responding to ILS requests. If the connection is refused or times out, then the ILS service on that computer is not responding.

7. If you get the Connect Failed! message box, click OK; otherwise, select Connect ➢ Cancel.

8. Select Connect ➢ Remote System.

9. Enter the Internet name or IP address of the directory server in the Host Name field.

10. Type **522** in the Port field.

11. Click the Connect button.

If a connection is established, then the server you identified in the Host Name field is responding to ULS requests. If the connection is refused or times out, then the ULS service on that computer is not responding.

12. If you get the Connect Failed! message box, click OK; otherwise select Connect ➢ Cancel.

13. Select Connect ➢ Remote System.

14. Enter the Internet name or IP address of the other NetMeeting client computer that you want to teleconference with in the Host Name field.

15. Type **1503** in the Port field. (You can alternatively type **1720** or **1731**— Outlook Express should respond to all three ports.)

16. Click the Connect button.

If a connection is established, then the computer you identified in the Host Name field is responding to NetMeeting connection requests. If the connection is refused or times out, then the NetMeeting on that computer is not responding.

17. If you get the Connect Failed! message box, click OK; otherwise select Connect ≻ Cancel.

There are some additional connectivity issues with NetMeeting, beyond simple IP connectivity and checking to make sure that the services are actually responding on the destination computers. Watch out for the following:

- In Windows 95 Version 4.00.950B, you can experience a delay of up to 2 minutes if you cancel the Dial-Up Networking dialog box that appears when you start NetMeeting. You also will have to connect to your ISP manually and log on to the directory server from the Call menu of NetMeeting.

- If you have a 28.8 Kbps modem connection, you may actually get better audio and video quality using the ISDN or LAN choice for the Network Bandwidth setting in NetMeeting.

- In Windows NT, you may need to uninstall Dial-Up Networking if you use a LAN connection and a proxy to connect to a directory server.

- If your ISP, or any other network entity between your computer and the ILS server, has disabled ICMP, then NetMeeting may disconnect from an ILS server after two minutes. This happens when the Auto-Dial feature in Dial-Up Networking is enabled. To work around this problem, you should disable the AutoDial feature in Internet Explorer.

NetMeeting and Firewalls

NetMeeting, like Outlook Express, sometimes has trouble with firewalls. The difficulty for NetMeeting is a little more severe, however, because (for video, at least) the ports required can't always be determined in advance. If you are having trouble getting video and audio through your firewall, or you are simply having trouble connecting to the LDAP (ILS) server, you might want to open the ports listed in Table 10.2.

T A B L E 10.2 Ports used by Microsoft NetMeeting	Port	What It Is
	389	Internet Locator Server
	522	User Location Service
	1503	T.120 Conferencing
	1720	H.323 Call Setup
	1731	Audio Call Control
	Dynamic	H.323 Call Control
	Dynamic	H.323 Streaming (RTP over UDP)

It is these last two ports (H.323 Call Control and Streaming) required by NetMeeting audio and video that are the most troublesome when a network administrator is trying to configure a firewall. In the H.323 protocol, the ports actually used for the conference are not fixed, instead each of the two computers are allowed to select ports to use when the call is set up. Unfortunately, the next available port in the computer is usually the one selected. This means that to support audio and videoconferencing through a firewall, a network administrator must abandon port-level control of network traffic in and out of the network.

The T.120 conferencing features of NetMeeting (used for application sharing, shared clipboard, file transfer, whiteboard, and chat) do not require dynamic port assignment. Therefore, they allow a more stringent firewall configuration.

Summary

Troubleshooting Outlook Express is relatively simple—just make sure that the mail servers specified for each mail account are correct for that user, verify that the client computer can connect to the host (using the tools described in Chapter 9), and test the ports of the mail servers to make sure they are responding to mail requests. These three steps should narrow down an Outlook Express problem to Outlook Express settings, network problems, or mail host problems—and once you know where the problem is, you can fix it (or apply pressure to get it fixed, if the mail host or network segment with a problem is out of your direct control).

NetMeeting can be more difficult to troubleshoot than Internet Explorer 4 or Outlook Express because of the greater demands it places both on PC hardware and on network connectivity. NetMeeting requires sound cards and video capture cards that have not been standardized across all PC platforms, so you never know what sound card or capture card you'll find in a computer. Therefore, you never know just what software drivers to install, settings to configure, and steps to take when troubleshooting the hardware.

Fortunately, most hardware makers include drivers for Windows 95 (fewer do so for Windows NT) and include instructions for installation and configuration of the hardware. NetMeeting will work with just about any correctly configured sound card, and will work with most video cards that provide non-overlay video capture. If you can record and play back sound with the Audio Recorder, NetMeeting can probably use your sound setup (although the Audio Tuner will tell you for sure).

The biggest difficulty of NetMeeting as far as network troubleshooting is concerned is the large number of ports it uses and that the H.323 standard uses the next available port rather than a specific port for the streaming data. While this feature allows one computer to participate in multiple conferences (the computer can open several ports), it does weaken network security by requiring that a wide range of ports be open on a firewall.

Review Questions

1. You want users on your network to be able to check mail on mail servers external to your network using the POP protocol. What port do you need to open up in your firewall for outgoing connections?

   A. 21

   B. 25

   C. 110

   D. 143

2. You have set up an Exchange Server mail server package with the Internet conduit so that other computers on the Internet can deliver mail to your Exchange host using SMTP. The computers on your network use IMAP to check the mail server for new mail and to deposit mail for delivery. The mail server resides inside your corporate firewall. What port do you need to open on the firewall so that your mail server can send and receive mail with other Internet mail hosts?

   A. 21

   B. 25

   C. 110

   D. 143

3. When you click a Mail To link in IE 4, Eudora Lite appears instead of Outlook Express. You want to use Outlook Express to send mail from IE 4. Where do you reset the default mail client to be Outlook Express? Choose all that apply.

   A. Start ➢ Programs ➢ Internet Explorer ➢ Internet Explorer ➢ View ➢ Internet Options ➢ Programs.

   B. My Computer ➢ View ➢ Folder Options ➢ File Types.

   C. Start ➢ Settings ➢ Control Panel ➢ System ➢ MIME Map.

   D. Start ➢ Settings ➢ Control Panel ➢ Mail.

4. If you see `The command failed to execute.` message in Outlook Express, what most likely is the problem?

   A. You have not installed Service Pack 3 on your Windows NT computer.

   B. Your computer is low on disk space.

   C. Your computer has insufficient RAM.

   D. You attempted to download a CAB file that has not been digitally signed.

5. You are unable to send mail via SMTP using Outlook Express. You want to make sure that there is no network problem between your computer and the mail server. What tools can you use to check the network path between your computer and the mail server? Choose all that apply.

   A. NSLOOKUP

   B. Tracert

   C. Network Monitor

   D. PING

6. You are unable to send mail via SMTP using Outlook Express. You want to make sure that the mail server is responding to mail requests on port 25. What tool can you use to see if the mail host is accepting connections on that port?

   A. Tracert

   B. PING

   C. Telnet

   D. NSLOOKUP

7. You want your network users to be able to check their e-mail using the POP protocol. What other protocol must also be enabled if you are using the POP protocol to receive mail?

   A. NNTP

   B. IMAP

   C. ISAPI

   D. SMTP

8. You use an older directory service outside your firewall for Net-Meeting that uses the ULS protocol rather than the ILS protocol to connect to the directory service. What port must you open in your firewall to allow ULS connections?

   A. 389

   B. 522

   C. 110

   D. Dynamic

9. Your directory service uses ULS to provide LDAP support for Net-Meeting users. The directory service resides outside your firewall, but you want users inside your firewall to be able to connect to it. What port should you open in your firewall?

   A. 389

   B. 522

   C. 110

   D. Dynamic

10. NetMeeting users are able to connect to an LDAP server and establish audio and video conferences with other users, but after two minutes the users are consistently detached from the directory service. What is wrong?

A. The users are attaching to the network over a link that uses SLIP with header compression.

B. The network path to the directory service passes through a segment that blocks ICMP traffic.

C. The users' computers do not have Service Pack 3 installed.

D. The users' computers have HP fonts installed.

11. If you are willing to open specific TCP ports in your firewall but are unwilling to open a wide range of ports, what NetMeeting features will not function?

A. Chat

B. Application Sharing

C. Videoconferencing

D. Whiteboard

12. You can perform whiteboard teleconferencing between computers in your LAN but you cannot perform whiteboard teleconferencing with computers outside your LAN. You think that your firewall is blocking the port used for T.120 collaboration. How can you check?

A. Ping the destination computer.

B. Telnet to port 1503 on the destination computer.

C. Telnet to a dynamic port on the destination computer.

D. Use Tracert to find the path from your computer to the destination computer.

13. You are trying to establish a videoconference between your computer and another computer on the Internet. The person on the other end can hear you but cannot see you. You can see the other person just fine. Which of the following might be the culprit? Choose all that apply.

    A. Either you or the destination computer is using SLIP with header compression to connect to an ISP.

    B. Your video card uses video overlay to capture the images.

    C. Your video card does not support Microsoft Video for Windows 1.0.

    D. You have a firewall between your computer and the destination computer that is not passing the required ports for H.323 videoconferencing.

14. You want to share applications using NetMeeting, but you have a firewall between your network and the Internet. What ports must you open on the firewall to connect to an ILS server and to collaborate in this manner with another computer over the Internet? Choose all that apply.

    A. 389

    B. 522

    C. 1503

    D. 1720

15. What tools can you use to restrict the bandwidth used by Microsoft NetMeeting on client computers in your network after you have distributed IE 4? Choose all that apply.

    A. The IEAK Wizard

    B. The IEAK Profile Manager

    C. User Manager for Domains

    D. The Policies Control Panel

16. Your users can connect to an LDAP server, can use the whiteboard, and can chat using Microsoft NetMeeting, but they cannot establish a videoconference beyond your LAN. You have a firewall, and you suspect that it is blocking the ports required for videoconferencing.

Required Result: Determine if the firewall is blocking the NetMeeting ports required by videoconferencing.

Optional Result 1: Determine if the remote computer is responding to the NetMeeting videoconferencing ports.

Optional Result 2: Determine if there is a network failure between your computer and the destination computer.

Suggested Solution: PING the remote computer.

Which of the following is correct?

A. The suggested solution accomplishes the required result and both optional results.

B. The suggested solution accomplishes the required result and just one optional result.

C. The suggested solution accomplishes the required result only.

D. The suggested solution does not accomplish the required result.

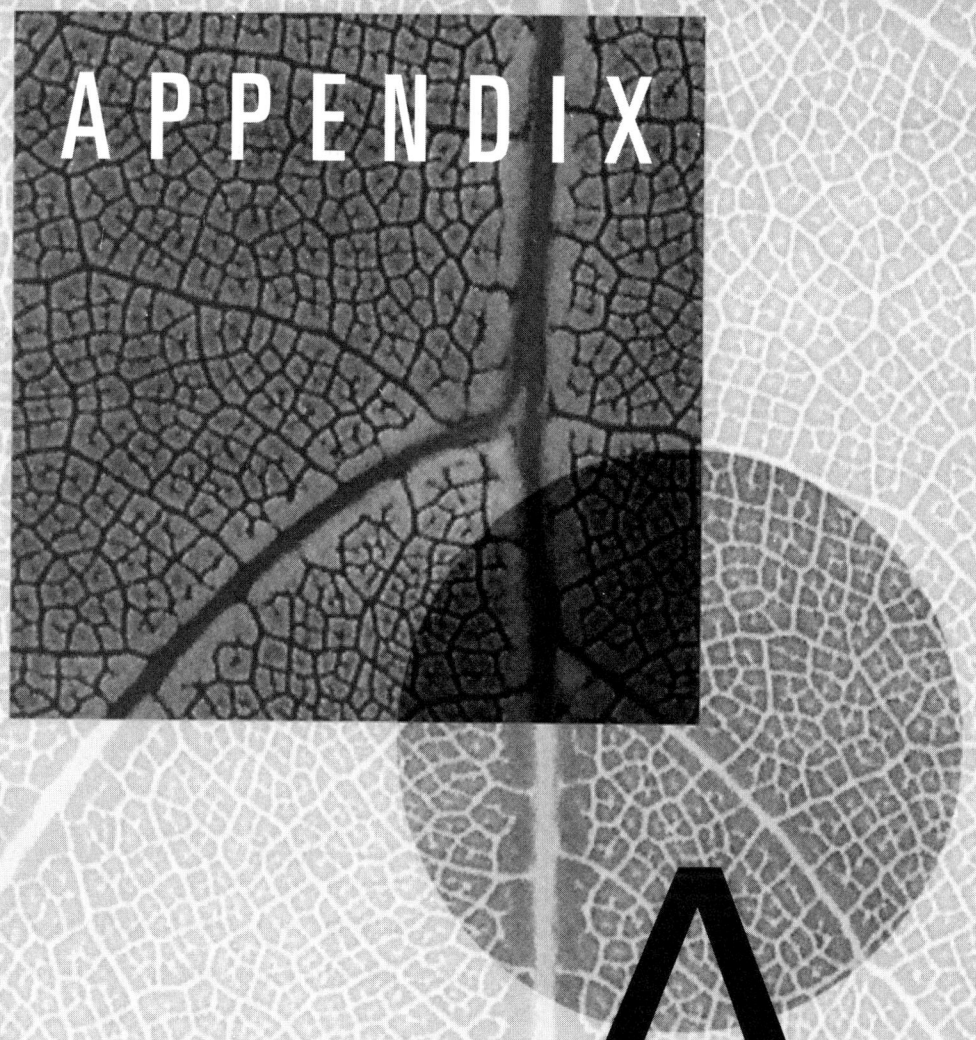

APPENDIX

A

Review Questions and Answers

Chapter 1

1. You want to enable Internet traffic on your LAN. What protocol must the router that links your LAN to the Internet support?

   A. NetBEUI

   B. TCP/IP

   C. Ethernet

   D. IPX/SPX

   Answer: B

2. What protocol does the Web browser and Web server use to exchange hypertext files?

   A. IPX/SPX

   B. HTML

   C. HTTP

   D. Java

   Answer: C

3. You have performed a full installation of Internet Explorer 4, and you want to chat with other users on the Internet. What else do you need to add to your Windows 95 computer in order to use Microsoft Chat?

   A. The Microsoft Chat package from the Add/Remove Components section of Active Setup

   B. Windows 95 OSR2

   C. The Windows NT Option Pack

   D. Nothing, Microsoft Chat is included with a full install of IE 4

   Answer: D

4. You want to use an electronic whiteboard to collaborate with coworkers over the Internet. What package should you use?

A. Microsoft Chat

B. Microsoft NetShow

C. Microsoft NetMeeting

D. Microsoft Outlook Express

Answer: C

5. Which of the following platforms does Internet Explorer not run on?

A. Windows 95

B. Windows 3.11

C. MacOS

D. OS/2

Answer: D

6. Which Web technology does not work in non-Microsoft Web browsers?

A. JavaScript

B. HTML

C. Java

D. ActiveX

Answer: D

7. Which of the following is a complete and correctly formed URL?

A. www.microsoft.com

B. \\www.memetech.com\default.htm

C. ftp://www.starlingtech.com/pub/archive.z

D. http/www.niftyvideo.com/products.asp

Answer: C

8. You have performed a full installation of Internet Explorer 4. You want to view and manipulate three-dimensional figures in your IE 4 Web browser. What else do you need to add to your Windows 95 computer in order to add this capability to IE 4?

   A. The VRML 2 Viewer package from the Add/Remove Components section of Active Setup

   B. Windows 95 OSR2

   C. The Windows NT Option Pack

   D. Nothing, the VRML 2 Viewer is installed with a full install of IE 4

   Answer: A

9. You want to send and receive encrypted e-mail over the Internet. Which tool should you launch?

   A. Outlook Express

   B. NetMeeting

   C. Chat

   D. Macromedia Shockwave Flash

   Answer: A

10. You want to run a Web server on your Windows 95 computer. What Microsoft Web server provides this capability?

    A. Peer Web Services

    B. Internet Information Server

    C. Personal Web Server

    D. Windows Web Server

    Answer: C

11. You use a Windows NT Workstation computer with a standard installation of IE 4 to browse a Web page that has a JScript program embedded in it. The JScript program has an error but you are not given the option of running the Microsoft Script Debugger to determine what the problem is. Why is this?

    A. The Microsoft Script Debugger only runs under Windows 95, not Windows NT.

    B. The Full installation of IE 4 does not include the Microsoft Script Debugger.

    C. You must enable debugging in the User Manager or User Manager for Domains program.

    D. You must install the Microsoft J++ software development environment to debug JScript programs.

    Answer: B

12. Which two browser extension technologies are only supported by Internet Explorer?

    A. JavaScript

    B. VBScript

    C. ActiveX

    D. Java

    Answer: B, C

13. Which of the following tools are not distributed with IE 4?

    A. NetMeeting

    B. Outlook Express

    C. J++

    D. NetShow Live

    Answer: C

14. You want to write a simple program that will run on the majority of Web browsers, including non-Microsoft Web browsers. Which technology should you choose?

   A. ActiveX

   B. JavaScript

   C. VBScript

   D. C++

   Answer: B

15. Who controls the Internet?

   A. The International Standards Organization

   B. The National Security Agency

   C. The Department of Defense

   D. No single person or group

   Answer: D

16. You want to reduce the Internet support burden for your network by standardizing on one suite of Internet tools.

   Required Result: Provide basic Web browsing and e-mail functionality.

   Optional Result 1: Allow users to participate in newsgroups and Internet chat forums.

   Optional Result 2: Allow users to host their own Web pages on their Windows 95 computers.

   Suggested Solution: Distribute IE 4 and associated components to the computers on your network.

   Which of the following is correct?

A. The suggested solution accomplishes the required result and both optional results.

B. The suggested solution accomplishes the required result and just one optional result.

C. The suggested solution accomplishes the required result only.

D. The suggested solution does not accomplish the required result.

Answer: B

17. You manage a heterogeneous network containing Windows 95, Windows NT, MacOS, and Linux computers. You want to use the same Web browser on all the computers in your network. You would also like to use the same software on all of the computers for e-mail, videoconferencing, and newsgroup reading.

Required Result: Select a Web browser that will work on all computers in your network.

Optional Result 1: Select software packages for e-mail and news reading that will work on all the computers in your network.

Optional Result 2: Select software packages for videoconferencing that will work on all the computers in your network.

Suggested Solution: Choose Internet Explorer 4, Outlook Express, and Microsoft NetMeeting.

Which of the following is correct?

A. The suggested solution accomplishes the required result and both optional results.

B. The suggested solution accomplishes the required result and just one optional result.

C. The suggested solution accomplishes the required result only.

D. The suggested solution does not accomplish the required result.

Answer: D

Chapter 2

1. You want to change the versions of Internet Explorer 4 that you distribute with your Internet Stock Quote application so that they reflect your company's image. Which of the following items are you not allowed to change?

    A. The default Web page

    B. The Taskbar image

    C. The spinning "e"

    D. The Active Setup bitmap

    Answer: C

2. You want to distribute Internet Explorer 4 on a CD-ROM with your Internet-based multiplayer video game. Which licensing role should you choose?

    A. Corporate administrator

    B. ISP

    C. ICP

    D. ICQ

    Answer: C

3. You provide dial-up access to the Internet for people in your community. You want to make it easier for your customers, many of whom do not already have a Web browser, to get on the Web. You decide to include Internet Explorer 4 with your installation software. Which licensing role should you choose?

    A. Corporate administrator

    B. ISP

    C. ICP

    D. DNS

    Answer: B

4. Your company network is comprised of four LANs with mixed Windows 95 and Windows NT Workstation computers. You have two RAS servers allowing remote connection to your network. You want to ease your Internet support burden by crafting a custom version of Internet Explorer 4 that is pre-configured for your network and that uses the Autoupdate feature of IE 4. Which licensing role should you choose?

A. Corporate administrator

B. ISP

C. ICP

D. DSP

Answer: A

5. You manage an ISP service, and you make a custom version of Internet Explorer 4 available for download on your Web site. You also distribute it on CD-ROM to new customers. How should you report to Microsoft your distributions?

A. Monthly, combined CD-ROM and downloaded totals

B. Yearly, CD-ROM and downloaded totals separately

C. Quarterly, combined CD-ROM and downloaded totals

D. Quarterly, CD-ROM and downloaded totals separately

Answer: C

6. You provide information to clients over the Internet. You have a free service and a for-fee service. You want to structure the services as channels. How many channels can you add to the Channel bar with your ICP license?

A. One

B. Two

C. Three

D. Zero

Answer: A

7. You chair the Committee for Moral Profundity. You provide information over the Internet on good sites for children to visit. You want to make a "safe" version of Internet Explorer available for download from your Web site, but you don't like some of the channels that Microsoft has established in the Channel bar. How many of these channels can you remove?

    A. One

    B. Two

    C. Three

    D. Zero

Answer: D

8. You want to include several custom components for encrypted financial data exchange over the Internet with your custom version of Internet Explorer 4. How many custom components can you include?

    A. Zero

    B. One

    C. Three

    D. 10

Answer: D

9. You want to make installing your version of Internet Explorer 4 as flexible as possible. How many installation options (standard, custom, full, and so on) can you configure in the IEAK?

    A. Zero

    B. Three

    C. Five

    D. 10

Answer: D

10. You want to build your own custom Internet Explorer 4 package containing all of the general IE 4 components. How much space do you need to download the components, run the IEAK, and contain the resulting custom IE 4 package?

   A. 60MB

   B. 80MB

   C. 110MB

   D. 160MB

Answer: D

11. What are your options for getting the IEAK? Choose all that apply.

   A. Download it from Microsoft's Web site

   B. Purchase it on CD-ROM from Microsoft's Web site

   C. Purchase the Internet Explorer Resource Kit

   D. Load it from the Windows 95 installation CD-ROM

Answer: A, B, C

12. You used the INS Editor with the previous version of the IEAK. You find that it is not included in the new IEAK. What has replaced it?

   A. User Manager for Domains

   B. System Profile Editor

   C. Profile Editor

   D. Syscon

Answer: C

13. You have included the Microsoft add-on package Fluff version 1.04 in your custom installation of Internet Explorer 4. Microsoft came out with Fluff version 1.05 a month later. What are your obligations according to the IEAK license?

    A. You must make version 1.05 available to your customers.

    B. You must upgrade all of your customers to version 1.05.

    C. You don't have to do anything.

    D. You must renew your IEAK license with Microsoft.

Answer: C

14. You have included the Microsoft add-on package Fluff version 1.04 in your custom installation of Internet Explorer 4. Microsoft came out with Fluff version 1.10 a month later. What are your obligations according to the IEAK license?

    A. You must make version 1.10 available to your customers.

    B. You must upgrade all of your customers to version 1.10.

    C. You don't have to do anything.

    D. You must renew your IEAK license with Microsoft.

Answer: A

15. You need to provide graphic images to the printing department for the promotional packaging of your product containing IE 4. Where can you get the images?

    A. `http://www.microsoft.com/images/presskit`.

    B. You must order the images from Microsoft; they will be delivered in 2-5 working days by Federal Express.

    C. You can scan and use images from other Microsoft products such as Windows 95 or Windows NT.

    D. Get them from `Reskit\Graphics\Samples\Cpyr_art` in the IEAK directory.

Answer: D

16. Your company provides for automatic futures trading over the Internet. Customers can trade using any Web browser, but you have developed a custom IE 4 ActiveX control that makes trading much more intuitive. The ActiveX control requires your Web site to be in the Trusted Sites zone of the IE 4 Web browser. You want to distribute a custom IE 4 package that increases your company's product visibility (through the branding options of the IEAK), and you want to preconfigure the security zones settings of IE 4, as well as comply with Microsoft's license restrictions.

Required Result: Comply with Microsoft's license restrictions.

Optional Result 1: Brand IE 4 to increase company product visibility.

Optional Result 2: Customize IE 4 settings to allow proper operation of the ActiveX control.

Suggested Solution: Use the IEAK to create a custom IE 4 package. Supply a custom toolbar bitmap, custom Active Setup bitmap, custom logo to replace the spinning 'e', and a custom Outlook Express info-pane. In the Policies section of the IEAK, preconfigure the security zones of the custom package with your site listed in the Trusted Sites zone.

Which of the following is correct?

A. The suggested solution accomplishes the required result and both optional results.

B. The suggested solution accomplishes the required result and just one optional result.

C. The suggested solution accomplishes the required result only.

D. The suggested solution does not accomplish the required result.

Answer: D

17. Your company provides for automatic futures trading over the Internet. Customers can trade using any Web browser, but you have developed a custom IE 4 ActiveX control that makes trading much more intuitive. The ActiveX control requires your Web site to be in the Trusted Sites zone of the IE 4 Web browser. You want to distribute a custom IE 4 package that increases your company's product visibility (through the branding options of the IEAK) and preconfigure the security zones settings of IE 4, as well as comply with Microsoft's license restrictions.

Required Result: Comply with Microsoft's license restrictions.

Optional Result 1: Brand IE 4 to increase company product visibility.

Optional Result 2: Customize IE 4 settings to allow proper operation of the ActiveX control.

Suggested Solution: Use the IEAK to create a custom IEAK package. Supply a custom toolbar bitmap, custom Active Setup bitmap, and a custom Outlook Express infopane.

Which of the following is correct?

A. The suggested solution accomplishes the required result and both optional results.

B. The suggested solution accomplishes the required result and just one optional result.

C. The suggested solution accomplishes the required result only.

D. The suggested solution does not accomplish the required result.

Answer: B

Chapter 3

1. You have Internet Explorer 3 installed on your Windows 95 computer. You want to upgrade to IE 4. How can you get IE 4? Choose all that apply.

A. Purchase it on CD-ROM from your local computer software store.

B. Install it from the Windows 95 installation CD-ROM.

C. Download it from Microsoft's Web site (www.microsoft.com/ie/download) using IE3.

D. Download it from Microsoft's FTP site (ftp.microsoft.com/ie/download) using FTP.

Answer: A, C

2. You want to use Microsoft NetMeeting. Which form of installation should you use?

   A. None. It comes with Windows 95 and Windows NT.

   B. Minimal.

   C. Standard.

   D. Full.

   Answer: D

3. You want to use Outlook Express. Which form of installation should you use?

   A. None. It comes with Windows 95 and Windows NT.

   B. Minimal.

   C. Standard.

   D. Full.

   Answer: C

4. You want to use IE 4 on a laptop that has very little free disk space. Which form of installation should you use?

   A. None. It comes with Windows 95 and Windows NT.

   B. Minimal.

   C. Standard.

   D. Full.

   Answer: B

5. You want to have the Internet FTP protocol on your desktop as well as IE 4. Which form of installation should you use?

   A. None. It comes with Windows 95 and Windows NT.

   B. Minimal.

   C. Standard.

   D. Full.

   Answer: A

6. You want to remove Microsoft Chat from your Windows 95 computer. How should you do it? Choose all that apply.

   A. Locate the Microsoft Chat executable file and delete it using the Desktop Explorer.

   B. Launch Add/Remove Programs from the Control Panel and remove the check next to Microsoft Chat.

   C. Run IE4Setup.exe and remove the Microsoft Chat component.

   D. Type **IERemove.exe /app:Chat** at the command prompt.

   Answer: B, C

7. You have performed a full installation of IE 4 on your Windows 95 OSR2 computer. You want to reinstall Windows 95 OSR2. What must you do first?

   A. Remove IE 4 and Windows Desktop Update.

   B. Format your hard drive.

   C. Install Windows Desktop Update.

   D. Remove the Program Files/Internet Explorer folder.

   Answer: A

8. You want to change the appearance of a folder on your hard drive in Web View. Which file should you modify?

A. Mycomp.htt

B. Webview.htt

C. Folder.htt

D. Controlp.htt

Answer: C

9. You have configured Windows 95 to use Active Desktop. You have installed several Active Desktop components, and you want to disable one. How do you disable an Active Desktop component?

A. Disconnect from the Internet.

B. Open the Web tab of the Display Properties page and remove its check mark.

C. Left-click on that component and select Unsubscribe from the pop-up menu.

D. Remove Windows Desktop Update using the ACME maintenance mode.

Answer: B

10. How do you subscribe to an Active Channel? Choose all that apply.

A. Click on a link that refers to a CDF file.

B. Click on a link that refers to a HTT file.

C. Select Add to Favorites in the Favorites menu, then choose one of the two page subscription options.

D. Drag a link to the page into the Channel bar.

Answer: A, C

11. You want to install IE 4 with minimal prompting during the installation. You have downloaded the `IE4Setup.exe` program already. What command will achieve your goal?

A. `IE4Setup /quiet`

B. `Setup.exe /quiet`

C. `IF4wzd.exe /q /c:/x /m:1 /I:n /r:y`

D. `IE4Setup /q /c:"IE4wzd.exe /x /q1 /m:1 /I:n /r:y"`

Answer: D

12. You have downloaded the `IE4Setup.exe` program for your Windows 95 and NT computers. You also have an older computer running Windows 3.1 on which you want to install IE 4. What should you do?

A. Use the `IE4Setup.exe` program.

B. Download the `Setup.exe` program that will install IE 4 on Windows 3.*x* computers.

C. Download the `IE4Win3.exe` program that will install IE 4 on Windows 3.*x* computers.

D. Download IE3, because IE 4 only runs on Windows 95 and Windows NT.

Answer: B

13. How can you get Internet Explorer 4 for Macintosh?

A. IE 4 is not supported on the Macintosh platform.

B. `www.microsoft.com/ie/download`

C. `www.microsoft.com/apple/IE4`

D. `ftp.apple.com/microsoft/ie`

Answer: B

14. You want to enable passwords so that several people can use the same Windows 95 computer and each have their own set of favorites. How do you enable profiles?

   A. Select Start ➤ Settings ➤ Control Panel ➤ Passwords.

   B. Select Start ➤ Settings ➤ Control Panel ➤ User Manager.

   C. Select Start ➤ Programs ➤ Administrative Tools ➤ User Manager.

   D. Profiles are automatically enabled in Windows 95 when more than one unique password is used to log on.

Answer: A

15. What can't you do in ACME maintenance mode?

   A. Remove IE 4.

   B. Remove an IE 4 component.

   C. Customize IE 4 for distribution.

   D. Add an IE 4 component.

Answer: C

16. You have downloaded `IE4Setup.exe` to a network share to which the client computers on your network have a drive mapped. You want to install the software without many user interactions. You would like to install Windows Desktop Update and you want it to reboot automatically without prompting the user.

Required Result: Install IE 4.

Optional Result 1: Install without many user interactions.

Optional Result 2: Reboot automatically.

Suggested Solution: Issue the command `IE4Setup.exe /q / c:"ie4wzd.exe /x /qa /m:1 /I:y /r:s"`.

Which of the following is correct?

A. The suggested solution accomplishes the required result and both optional results.

B. The suggested solution accomplishes the required result and just one optional result.

C. The suggested solution accomplishes the required result only.

D. The suggested solution does not accomplish the required result.

Answer: A

17. Your Intranet Web site uses an ActiveX control that only runs in IE 3. You discover this after upgrading to IE 4. You want to revert back to IE 3 on the computer you use to access the Intranet Web site.

Required Result: Remove IE 4 from the computer.

Optional Result 1: Cleanly uninstall any DLLs installed by IE 4.

Optional Result 2: Restore the previously installed Web browser.

Suggested Solution: Run the IERemove.exe program on the computer.

Which of the following is correct?

A. The suggested solution accomplishes the required result and both optional results.

B. The suggested solution accomplishes the required result and just one optional result.

C. The suggested solution accomplishes the required result only.

D. The suggested solution does not accomplish the required result.

Answer: C

Chapter 4

1. You want to send encrypted mail over the Internet. What do you need in order to configure Outlook Express to encrypt and decrypt the mail for you?

   A. A hardware encryption dongle

   B. The Pretty Good Privacy encryption tool suite

   C. A digital ID from a Certificate Authority

   D. The Microsoft Encryption Client software package

   Answer: C

2. You have performed a full installation of IE 4. You want to watch ASF video streams over the Internet. What additional tool do you have to install?

   A. Microsoft NetMeeting

   B. Nothing, because Microsoft NetMeeting is already installed.

   C. Microsoft NetShow

   D. Nothing, because Microsoft NetShow is already installed.

   Answer: D

3. Which component does not come as a separate program, but is available as a part of Internet Explorer 4?

   A. Microsoft NetShow

   B. Microsoft Wallet

   C. Microsoft Chat

   D. Microsoft Outlook Express

   Answer: B

4. You routinely send identical status update e-mail messages to everyone in your department. You want to do this with minimal effort. What is the most efficient way to send the message to each of your coworkers?

   A. Type the message once, copy it to the clipboard, and paste it into a message for each recipient.

   B. Type the message once. Type the e-mail address of each recipient into the To field.

   C. Create a group in the Address Book. Add each coworker to the group. Send the message to the group.

   D. Send the message to the first person in the group with a note at the bottom requesting them to forward it to the next person in the group.

   Answer: C

5. You see a little ribbon next to an e-mail message you have received in Outlook Express. What does the ribbon mean?

   A. The message is important.

   B. The message is an award winner.

   C. The message is encrypted.

   D. The message is digitally signed.

   Answer: D

6. You don't want to see any Internet news messages from a particularly offensive newsgroup member. What can you do so that you never view messages from this person?

   A. E-mail the person, and ask them to stop being offensive.

   B. E-mail the person's Internet service provider and ask that their account be terminated.

   C. Create a filter that blocks posts from that user.

   D. Create a filter that removes posts from that user from Internet news servers.

   Answer: C

7. Which of the following is not a field that you can base a mail rule in Outlook Express?

  A. Subject

  B. To

  C. From

  D. Date Sent

  Answer: D

8. You have a video camera that you want to use for videoconferencing over the Net. What package should you use?

  A. Microsoft NetMeeting

  B. Microsoft NetShow

  C. Microsoft Exchange

  D. Microsoft Outlook Express

  Answer: A

9. Which of the following e-mail packages will Outlook Express import mail messages from? Choose all that apply.

  A. Outlook

  B. Netscape Communicator

  C. Eudora Light

  D. Microsoft Exchange

  Answer: A, B, C, D

10. Which credit cards is Microsoft Wallet configured to handle? Choose all that apply.

  A. Visa

  B. MasterCard

  C. American Express

  D. Discover

  Answer: A, B, C, D

11. What Microsoft tool helps you manage your personal Internet mail?

   A. Inbox Assistant

   B. Web Publishing Wizard

   C. Exchange Server

   D. Microsoft Bob

   Answer: A

12. You maintain a copy of your personal Web site on your computer. You make changes to your Web pages on your computer and then upload them to your Web space on your Internet service provider. You have been using FTP to copy the files one by one. What tools can help you manage and move the Web pages more efficiently?

   A. Inbox Assistant

   B. Web Publishing Wizard

   C. FrontPage Express

   D. Personal Web Server

   Answer: B, C

13. How do you configure Microsoft Wallet with your financial and Contact information?

   A. Select Start ➤ Programs ➤ Internet Explorer ➤ Microsoft Wallet, and enter the information in the Contacts and Payments tabs.

   B. Enter the information in the Addresses and Payments sections by selecting View ➤ Internet Options ➤ Content.

   C. Enter the information in the Addresses and Payments tabs by selecting View ➤ Microsoft Wallet.

   D. Enter the information by selecting File ➤ Security ➤ Financial.

   Answer: B

14. You want to edit your home page on your Internet service provider. What tool that comes with IE 4 can you use?

   A. Outlook Express

   B. FrontPage Express

   C. FrontPage

   D. Web Publishing Wizard

Answer: B

15. You want to talk with other people over the Internet using IRC. What program that comes with IE 4 can you use?

   A. Microsoft NetMeeting

   B. Microsoft Chat

   C. Microsoft IRC

   D. Outlook Express

Answer: B

16. You want to encrypt the communications between your sales people (who have laptops and use the Internet to communicate with the main office) and the office. You also want the sales force to be certain that e-mail messages they receive from the home office actually came from the home office and were not forged by a hacker. You would also like to provide for encrypted file transfers.

Required Result: Establish encrypted e-mail exchange.

Optional Result 1: Provide for e-mail authentication.

Optional Result 2: Encrypt FTP data transfers.

Suggested Solution: Install Outlook Express on all of the sales laptops and on the main office computers. Obtain digital certificates for each and install them. Send a digitally signed message from the main office to the sales force, and reply to the main office with a digitally signed message.

Which of the following is correct?

A. The suggested solution accomplishes the required result and both optional results.

B. The suggested solution accomplishes the required result and just one optional result.

C. The suggested solution accomplishes the required result only.

D. The suggested solution does not accomplish the required result.

Answer: B

17. As the network administrator, you have to deal with a tremendous amount of e-mail. You want to prioritize the e-mail so that you can deal with urgent messages first, routine e-mail later, and UFO-interest-L mailing list mail at your leisure. You also want to discard all mail that comes from the `spam.net` domain.

Required Result: Route urgent mail to the URGENT folder.

Optional Result 1: Delete mail originating from the `spam.net` domain.

Optional Result 2: Move mail from the mailing list to the LIST folder.

Suggested Solution: In Outlook Express create two new folders—URGENT and LIST. Create three rules: 1) move mail containing URGENT in the subject field to the URGENT folder; 2) move mail containing UFO-interest-L in the source field to the LIST folder; 3) delete mail containing `spam.net` in the source field. Inform network users that priority mail should contain URGENT in the subject field.

Which of the following is correct?

A. The suggested solution accomplishes the required result and both optional results.

B. The suggested solution accomplishes the required result and just one optional result.

C. The suggested solution accomplishes the required result only.

D. The suggested solution does not accomplish the required result.

Answer: A

Chapter 5

1. Which licensing mode allows you to create single floppy disk distributions?

   A. ISP

   B. ICP

   C. CORP

   D. MCP

   Answer: A

2. Which licensing modes allow you to create multiple floppy disk distributions?

   A. ISP

   B. ICP

   C. CORP

   D. MCP

   Answer: A, B, C

3. Which licensing modes allow you to create CD-ROM distributions?

   A. ISP

   B. ICP

   C. CORP

   D. MCP

   Answer: A, B, C

4. What kind of server does NetMeeting use to find other users of NetMeeting?

    A. LDAP

    B. ICQ

    C. Windows NT

    D. TCP/IP

Answer: A

5. You are replacing IE 3 browsers that use the JScript autoproxy feature. You want to have the same functionality in the new IE 4 browsers, and you want to exert the least amount of effort possible. What must you do?

    A. Create equivalent INS files for IE 4.

    B. Import the JC files into your custom IE 4 browser using the IEAK.

    C. Nothing, IE 4 will import the IE 3 autoproxy settings.

    D. IE 4 does not support autoproxy.

Answer: C

6. Which of the following will IE 4 import automatically from Netscape Navigator?

    A. Proxy Settings

    B. Bookmarks

    C. Plug-ins

    D. Helper applications

Answer: A, B

7. Your network users are accustomed to the helper applications (not plug-ins) set up in Netscape Navigator. What must you do to enable IE 4 to use these same helper applications?

   A. Nothing, IE 4 will import them automatically.

   B. Import equivalent helper applications from the Microsoft Web site.

   C. Configure the MIME types and file extensions for the helper applications in the Web browser.

   D. IE 4 will not use Netscape helper applications.

   Answer: C

8. You want to include a software package as a custom component in your version of IE 4. What form must the custom component take in order to be included by the IEAK and expanded by Active Setup? Choose all that apply.

   A. CAB files

   B. ZIP files

   C. A self-extracting EXE archive

   D. An ISAPI DLL

   Answer: A, C

9. You have created CAB files for custom component, digitally signed them, and included them in your distribution with the IEAK. However, Active Setup refuses to install them. What might be the problem?

   A. The software must be in the form of a self-extracting EXE archive.

   B. You must have Microsoft digitally sign the software for Active Setup to accept the signature.

   C. You must configure Active Setup to accept the digital signature that you used to sign the component.

   D. Only Internet content providers can provide custom components.

   Answer: C

10. You want to use IE 4 autoconfiguration to manage Windows 95 settings that are not in the IEAK. How can you lock-down the settings (such as Dial-Up Networking, Desktop icons, and Start menu items) for a group of users?

    A. You cannot use IE 4 autoconfiguration to modify Windows 95 User Profile or policy settings.

    B. Create an autoproxy JScript applet that manipulates the users' profile settings upon start-up of IE 4.

    C. Create a CAB archive of the users' mandatory `User Policy` directory and include it as a custom component in the IEAK.

    D. Create an ADM file of policy settings with `poledit`, and import the file into the IEAK.

    Answer: D

11. You want to brand the CD-ROM autorun screen. What options does the IEAK give you to custome the screen that appears when you put the CD-ROM in the drive? Choose all that apply.

    A. The background bitmap

    B. The CD-ROM button image

    C. The window title text

    D. The text and highlight colors

    Answer: A, B, C, D

12. You want your Web servers to be able to identify when users of your custom Web browser access your Web sites. What customization feature can you use to achieve this?

    A. The version number

    B. The Configuration Identifier

    C. The User Agent string

    D. The customization code

    Answer: C

13. Which IE 3 plug-ins will IE 4 import automatically? Choose all that apply.

   A. Shockwave

   B. RealAudio Player

   C. QuickTime Player

   D. None

Answer: D

14. You do not have an LDAP server on your network, and you want to use NetMeeting for collaboration over the Internet. You need an LDAP server so users can find each other and establish connections. What must you install in addition to installing IE 4 with NetMeeting on client computers?

   A. Install an LDAP server on a Windows NT computer in your network.

   B. Install Microsoft Exchange on a Windows NT computer in your network.

   C. Install an ICQ server on a Windows NT computer in your network.

   D. Nothing, you can use LDAP services provided by Microsoft.

Answer: D

15. You have installed IE 4 on a computer that previously had Netscape Navigator installed. You notice that Navigator is still present on the desktop and in the Start menu. Why is this?

   A. You must specify Remove Navigator in the IEAK to remove the software when IE 4 is installed.

   B. Your Microsoft license agreement restricts you from removing competing browser software.

   C. You must create a custom uninstall autoconfiguration (INS) file to remove Netscape.

   D. The IE 4 installation process will not automatically remove competing browsers.

Answer: D

16. You manage a large network that contains Windows 95 and 98 computers (browsing the Internet using IE 4), Windows 3.1 computers (browsing the Internet using IE 3), and Linux computers (browsing the Internet using Netscape). You want to automatically configure all of these Web browsers to find and use the proxy server. You would like the Web browsers to bypass the proxy server if the connection is made using the HTTPS protocol. You would like to use a single file for managing automatic proxy configuration.

Required Result: Establish automatic proxy configuration for all the browsers in the network.

Optional Result 1: Bypass the proxy server for HTTPS traffic.

Optional Result 2: Use a single automatic proxy configuration file.

Suggested Solution: Create a JS autoproxy file that checks to see if the access is via HTTPS. If so, it returns the location of the destination resource; otherwise, it returns the address of the proxy server.

Which of the following is correct?

A. The suggested solution accomplishes the required result and both optional results.

B. The suggested solution accomplishes the required result and just one optional result.

C. The suggested solution accomplishes the required result only.

D. The suggested solution does not accomplish the required result.

Answer: A

17. You manage a large network that contains Windows 95 and 98 computers (browsing the Internet using IE 4), Windows 3.1 computers (browsing the Internet using IE 3), and MacOS computers (browsing the Internet using Netscape). You want to automatically configure how all of these Web browsers find and use the proxy server. You don't want to do any programming and you want to lock-down browser security settings.

Required Result: Establish automatic proxy configuration for all the Web browsers in the network.

Optional Result 1: Avoid programming.

Optional Result 2: Lock-down security settings.

Suggested Solution: Install IE 4 on the Windows 3.1 and MacOS computers. Configure all IE 4 browsers to use autoconfiguration. Use the IEAK Profile Wizard to create an INS file, specifying the proxy server location and locking-down security settings.

Which of the following is correct?

A. The suggested solution accomplishes the required result and both optional results.

B. The suggested solution accomplishes the required result and just one optional result.

C. The suggested solution accomplishes the required result only.

D. The suggested solution does not accomplish the required result.

Answer: A

Chapter 6

1. You want to add an Active Channel to your custom IE 4 package. You are using the IEAK in corporate administrator mode. How do you add the channel?

A. You are not allowed to add channels to the IEAK in corporate administrator mode.

B. Select the Add Channel button on the Configure Channels screen of Stage 4 of the IEAK.

C. Configure Active Channels in your IE 4 Web browser, then import the channel configuration in the IEAK.

D. Configure the Active Channels using the Policy Editor, then import the channel configuration in the IEAK.

Answer: C

2. The first time you run the IEAK all of the components in the AVS screen show up with red X icons next to them. What is wrong?

  A. The IEAK cannot contact the Microsoft Web site.

  B. The components have not been digitally signed by Microsoft.

  C. You have not digitally signed the components.

  D. Nothing is wrong. The first time you run the IEAK you need to synchronize all the components.

Answer: D

3. You see yellow caution symbols next to several components in the AVS screen. What do these caution symbols mean?

  A. You have older components. You should synchronize those components to get the latest versions.

  B. The components have not been digitally signed. You should get a digital certificate and sign these components.

  C. The IEAK cannot find these components. You need to download them again.

  D. The components are present and up-to-date but have not yet been selected for inclusion in your custom IE 4 package.

Answer: A

4. What restrictions does selecting Silent Install place on your version of IE 4? Choose all that apply.

  A. You can specify only one download location.

  B. You can specify only one installation option.

  C. You can specify only one Active Channel.

  D. The installation process must not reboot the computer.

Answer: A, B

5. You want to make English, Spanish, German, and French custom versions of IE 4. How many times must you run the IEAK?

   A. One

   B. Two

   C. Three

   D. Four

   Answer: D

6. You installed your custom IE 4 package on an older computer. Instead of your custom bitmaps you see the default IE 4 bitmaps displayed at a lower resolution. What is the problem?

   A. You have included your bitmaps in the wrong format. They must be 256-color BMP images.

   B. You have not digitally signed the images. Active setup has rejected them and replaced them with 16-color standard bitmaps.

   C. The computer is only configured to support 16-color images (standard VGA), so your bitmaps can't be displayed. The default bitmaps are displayed instead.

   D. Windows 3.1 does not support 256-color images. You must upgrade to Windows 95 or Windows NT.

   Answer: C

7. You are creating your custom IE 4 package on a Laptop that is not currently connected to the Internet. (You previously ran the IEAK while connected to the Internet and synchronized all the components.) You run the IEAK again with AVS turned off. In the AVS screen all of the components show up with yellow caution icons. What is wrong?

   A. Microsoft has updated all of the components. You must synchronize components to get the latest versions.

B. You do not have any of the components necessary to build a custom IE 4 package. You must connect to the Internet and download the components.

C. You must digitally sign all of the components.

D. Nothing is wrong. The IEAK is indicating that it can't verify whether or not the components are the latest versions.

Answer: D

8. You need a certificate to digitally sign your custom components and the components that IEAK prepares for you. You just want a test certificate for in-house testing of your version of IE 4. Which tool will generate test certificates for you?

A. IExpress.exe

B. IEAK

C. Makecert.exe

D. Signcode.exe

Answer: C

9. You have received a certificate from Verisign, and now you want to sign the IE 4 CAB files. What tool can you use to sign the files using that certificate?

A. IExpress.exe

B. Signcabs.exe

C. Makecert.exe

D. Signcode.exe

Answer: D

10. You have auto-proxy files already created for the IE 3 computers in your network. You want the same functionality in IE 4, but want to expend a minimum of effort. What can you do?

    A. Translate the autoproxy JS file into an autoconfiguration INS file using the IExpress Wizard. Configure your custom IE 4 package to use the autoconfiguration file.

    B. Translate the autoproxy JS file into an autoconfiguration INS file using the IEAK Profile Manager. Configure your custom IE 4 package to use the autoconfiguration file.

    C. Configure your custom IE 4 package to use the autoproxy JS file.

    D. Create a new INS file that has the equivalent functionality of the autoproxy JS file.

Answer: C

11. How do you configure your custom version of IE 4 to trust specific software publishers when downloading ActiveX controls?

    A. Add the publisher's certificate to those trusted in the Content tab of IE 4. Import the settings into the IEAK.

    B. Add the publisher's Internet address to the trusted sites list in the Security tab of IE 4. Import the settings into the IEAK.

    C. Add the publisher's certificate to the list of certificates at the end of Stage 2 (Customizing Active Setup) of the IEAK.

    D. You cannot preload IE 4 with trusted certificates. The user must choose to accept the certificate the first time he or she downloads the ActiveX control.

Answer: A

12. The IEAK does not provide you with an option to change one bitmap for branding purposes. Which bitmap is it?

A. CD-ROM autorun bitmap

B. Toolbar background bitmap

C. Explorer spinning "e" bitmap

D. Active Setup bitmap

Answer: C

13. You want to provide a custom Active Channel for news about your company. You need to prepare bitmaps for the channel. What sizes should they be? Choose all that apply.

A. 32x32

B. 80x32

C. 64x64

D. 192x32

Answer: A, B, D

14. What formats can the large (192x32) bitmap image for a custom Active Channel be? Choose all that apply.

A. GIF

B. BMP

C. JPG

D. TIFF

Answer: A, B, C

15. You want to include your own custom component with your custom IE 4 package. Your component consists of several program files, a dozen or so data files, and a `setup.exe` program that installs the component. What archival formats can you put this component into so that Active Setup will download and install it? Choose all that apply.

A. ARC

B. CAB

C. ZIP

D. EXE

Answer: B, D

16. You are creating a custom IE 4 package to enable customers to easily connect to the ISP you manage. You want to include a custom software component that keeps track of the connection time that will be displayed and billed to the user. You want the user to be able to download and install the custom IE 4 package using the Active Setup program and the single floppy distribution process. You would like the user to be assured that the custom package was produced by a reputable firm, and that the software has not been tampered with.

Required Result: Create distribution files that Active Setup can download and install.

Optional Result 1: Assure the user that your company is reputable.

Optional Result 2: Assure the user that the files have not been tampered with.

Suggested Solution: Digitally sign the files with the test root certificate using the `makecert`, `cert2spc`, and `signcode` programs.

Which of the following is correct?

A. The suggested solution accomplishes the required result and both optional results.

B. The suggested solution accomplishes the required result and just one optional result.

C. The suggested solution accomplishes the required result only.

D. The suggested solution does not accomplish the required result.

Answer: C

17. You manage Windows NT Workstation computers and Windows 95 computers in a public access computer laboratory at your college. Guests use the GUEST_STUDENT account. You want to lock-down settings in IE 4 so that students have a consistent IE 4 configuration no matter what computer they use and no matter who has used the computer previously. In addition to locking-down IE 4 settings, you would also like to restrict the operating system options (including desktop settings) that the user is allowed to modify. You also want to create one custom IEAK package for both Windows 95 and Windows NT.

Required Result: Lock-down IE 4 settings.

Optional Result 1: Lock-down desktop settings for Windows 95 and Windows NT Workstation.

Optional Result 2: Create just one custom package for both Windows 95 and Windows NT.

Suggested Solution: Run the IEAK twice. Lock-down the IE 4 settings in both, but only import the Windows NT ADM file to one custom IE4 package and import the Windows 95 ADM file to the other custom IE4 package in order to lock-down operating system settings.

Which of the following is correct?

A. The suggested solution accomplishes the required result and both optional results.

B. The suggested solution accomplishes the required result and just one optional result.

C. The suggested solution accomplishes the required result only.

D. The suggested solution does not accomplish the required result.

Answer: B

Chapter 7

1. You want to modify your autoconfiguration (INS) file to reflect the latest proxy server settings for your network. What tool is most appropriate for this purpose?

    A. The IEAK Wizard

    B. The IEAK Profile Manager

    C. The IEAK INS Editor

    D. A text editor

    Answer: B

2. You want to modify your autoproxy (PAC) file to reflect the latest proxy server settings for your network. What tool is most appropriate for this purpose?

    A. The IEAK Wizard

    B. The IEAK Profile Manager

    C. The IEAK INS Editor

    D. A text editor

    Answer: D

3. You have created new INS and INF files using the IEAK Profile Manager, and you have placed them in the appropriate locations on your Web server. Your IE 4 users complain that their browsers are not being updated to reflect the changes you have made. What might be the problem? Choose all that apply.

    A. You have not digitally signed the new CAB files generated by the IEAK Profile Manager.

    B. You have not installed Windows Desktop Update.

    C. You have not enabled Roaming Profiles on the client computers.

    D. The Web browsers have not been configured to use autoconfiguration.

    Answer: A, D

4. You want to manage proxy settings for all of the Web browsers in your network. Some network users insist on using Netscape instead of IE 4 software. What automatic configuration mechanism is most appropriate in this situation?

A. Autoconfiguration INS files

B. Automatically downloaded batch files

C. PAC Autoproxy files

D. There is no common method for automatic configuration that works for both IE 4 and Netscape Navigator.

Answer: C

5. You want to import policy settings for the Windows 95 operating system into the IE 4 autoconfiguration files for your network. What file should you import into the IEAK Profile Manager?

A. Config.pol

B. Autoexec.bat

C. Admin.adm

D. Admin.ins

Answer: C

6. You import policy settings from Windows 95 into the IEAK Profile Editor, but the Editor informs you that there are duplicate keys. What have you done wrong?

A. You have not digitally signed the resulting INS file.

B. You have imported the wrong file.

C. You need to convert the file before importing it with the IE4Convert.exe program.

D. You have done nothing wrong. The IE 4 policy settings already contain some operating system Registry keys.

Answer: D

7. You manage Windows 95 computers on a Windows NT–based network domain. You already use system policies to control some aspects of Windows desktop behavior for network users. You use IE 4 auto-configuration to lock-down many browser, Active Desktop, and Shell settings. Users note inconsistent operating system behavior. What is the problem?

 A. System policies and IE 4 policies are conflicting, so users get different behavior when they log on to the network and when they start IE 4.

 B. Windows NT policy settings are being applied to Windows 95 computers, which has confused the Registry.

 C. You have imported Windows NT policy information into the IEAK Policy Editor, and the duplicate keys are causing problems.

 D. You have imported Windows 95 policy information into the IEAK Policy Editor, and the duplicate keys are causing problems.

Answer: A

8. What is the most efficient way to support different groups of users that have different IE 4 Active Desktop Update configuration settings needs?

 A. Create multiple custom IE 4 packages using the IEAK.

 B. Create multiple custom autoproxy files using a text editor.

 C. Create multiple custom autoconfiguration files using the IEAK Profile Manager.

 D. Create multiple custom system policy files using the System Policy Editor.

Answer: C

9. You need to establish autoconfiguration in an already installed Web browser. How do you do it?

A. Select View ➤ Internet Options ➤ Connection ➤ Configure.

B. Select File ➤ Internet Options ➤ Advanced ➤ Autoconfigure.

C. Select File ➤ Preferences ➤ Connection ➤ Configure.

D. Select View ➤ Internet Options ➤ Advanced ➤ Autoconfigure.

Answer: A

10. What is the easiest way to stop users from changing their Active Desktop settings in previously-installed IE 4 Web browsers?

A. Select Do Not Allow Changes to Active Desktop in the System Policy Editor, and save the policy to a `config.pol` file.

B. Select Do Not Allow Changes to Active Desktop in the IEAK Policy Editor, and save the policy to an `INS` file. Configure browsers to use the autoconfiguration file.

C. Select Do Not Allow Changes to Active Desktop in the Policies section of the IEAK Wizard.

D. Select Do Not Allow Changes to Active Desktop in the Advanced tab of the IE 4 Internet Options window.

Answer: B

11. How do you input restricted Web sites into IE 4 policy files?

A. Enter the restricted sites into the IE 4 Web browser, then import the settings into the Security Zones and Restrictions portion of the IEAK Profile Manager.

B. Enter the settings into the Security Zones and Content Ratings section of the IEAK Profile Manager.

C. Edit the `INF` files with a text editor.

D. You can't. Blocking Web sites is a function of a firewall not a Web browser.

Answer: B

12. You want to distribute software over the Web and use Active Channel technology to have updates to it automatically installed by IE 4. However, you want to distribute the software separately from your custom IE 4 package. What distribution method should you use?

A. Shrink-wrap

B. Active Setup

C. MSICD

D. FTP

Answer: C

13. What two packaging options do you have for distributing MSICD (and Active Setup) software?

A. .ZIP

B. .PKG

C. .EXE

D. .CAB

Answer: C, D

14. You must create an Active Channel that contains the scheduling information for browsers to check for software updates, the location of the software, and icons for the Channel bar, menu, and Explorer bar. What file do you need to create?

A. An HTML file

B. An OSD file

C. A CDF file

D. An INF file

Answer: C

15. You are using the CAB distribution format for your Software Distribution Channel. You have already created a Channel Distribution Format file. What additional file do you need to create ?

A. An OCD file

B. An SID file

C. An EXE file

D. A TXT file

Answer: A

16. You manage the computers used by children in a grade school. You are required to restrict the Web browsers on the computers from accessing Web sites that are rated to have explicit sexual, vulgar, violent, or pornographic content. In addition, you would like to keep the users from downloading files from specific computers or Internet domains that you know contain files with viruses, Trojan horses, and pirated software. You want teachers to be able to override these restrictions.

Required Result: Prevent browsing of sites with content ratings beyond what is acceptable to your school.

Optional Result 1: Block software downloading from known hacker sites and networks.

Optional Result 2: Provide a method for teachers to override the restrictions.

Suggested Solution: Configure browsers to use profiles. Use the IEAK Profile Manger to create an INS file that includes Content Ratings restrictions and lists known hacker sites and networks in the Restricted Sites zone. Assign a supervisor password for the Content Advisor and give that password to the teachers in the school.

Which of the following is correct?

A. The suggested solution accomplishes the required result and both optional results.

B. The suggested solution accomplishes the required result and just one optional result.

C. The suggested solution accomplishes the required result only.

D. The suggested solution does not accomplish the required result.

Answer: B

17. You manage the computers used by children in a grade school. You are required to restrict the Web browsers on the computers from accessing Web sites that are rated to have explicit sexual, vulgar, violent, or pornographic content. In addition you would like to keep the users from downloading files from specific computers or Internet domains that you know contain files with viruses, Trojan horses, and pirated software. You want teachers to be able to override these restrictions.

Required Result: Prevent browsing of sites with content ratings beyond what is acceptable to your school.

Optional Result 1: Block software downloading from known hacker sites and networks.

Optional Result 2: Provide a method for teachers to override the restrictions.

Suggested Solution: Configure browsers to use profiles. Use the IEAK Profile Manger to create an INS file that includes Content Ratings restrictions and lists known hacker sites and networks in the Restricted Sites zone. Modify the security settings to disable downloading software from the Restricted Sites zone.

Which of the following is correct?

A. The suggested solution accomplishes the required result and both optional results.

B. The suggested solution accomplishes the required result and just one optional result.

C. The suggested solution accomplishes the required result only.

D. The suggested solution does not accomplish the required result.

Answer: B

Chapter 8

1. You have a Web site inside your firewall that uses ActiveX to provide users a Web-based interface to your inventory and shipping database. Since the control will only be used internally, you don't want to go to the trouble of digitally signing it. You have used the IEAK Profile Manager to enter the DNS name into the Trusted Sites zone, and to update the Trusted Sites Download Unsigned ActiveX Controls Security option for the Trusted Sites zone to enable. Some users' Web browsers automatically download the ActiveX control when they access the site, other users' browsers prompt before downloading. What is wrong?

   A. The Trusted Sites security level must be set to High before the ActiveX controls can be downloaded without prompting.

   B. The IP address of the trusted site must also be added to the Trusted Sites zone.

   C. The Web site must be added to the Local Intranet zone instead of the Trusted Sites zone.

   D. The ActiveX control has a bug and must be recompiled.

   Answer: B

2. Your IE 4 Web browser has accessed a Web page in the Local Intranet site, but the page refers to an unsigned ActiveX control located on a computer that is listed in the Restricted Sites zone. What happens?

   A. The ActiveX control runs without the user being prompted.

   B. The user is prompted whether or not to run the control.

   C. The control does not run.

   D. The computer crashes.

   Answer: C

3. You don't want users' usernames and passwords to go out over the Internet when a Web server requests a username and password. What do you do?

   A. Select automatic logon with current username and password.

   B. Select automatic logon only in Intranet zone.

   C. Prompt for username and password.

   D. Configure Anonymous Logon.

   Answer: D

4. You want Java programs to run in their own safe sandbox, but you also want them to have access to safe scratch-pad space on the hard disk so they can store information. Which Java safety level should you choose?

   A. High safety

   B. Medium safety

   C. Low safety

   D. Disable Java

   Answer: B

5. Which of the following is not a Java security feature?

   A. Digitally-signed CAB files

   B. Security zones

   C. Security levels

   D. Content ratings

   Answer: D

6. You want your Java programs to be able to connect via TCP sockets to an SQL server in addition to the Web server on which the applet was stored. Which safety level should you configure the Web server to be in?

A. High safety

B. Medium safety

C. Low safety

D. Disable Java

Answer: C

7. You can't find the Java Custom Settings button in IE 4. What must you do to make it appear?

A. Select View ➤ Internet Options ➤ Security ➤ Custom ➤ Settings ➤ Custom (in Java Permissions).

B. Select View ➤ Internet Options ➤ Programs ➤ Java ➤ Custom.

C. There is no Java Custom Settings button in IE 4. You must use the IEAK Wizard to customize Java settings.

D. There is no Java Custom Settings button in IE 4. You must use the IEAK Profile Editor to customize Java settings.

Answer: A

8. What does IE 4 use Authenticode technology for? Choose all that apply.

A. Signing and verifying software packages

B. Sending and receiving e-mail

C. Establishing a secure connection between the Web browser and Web server

D. Verifying the identity of the user of the Web browser to the Web server

Answer: A, C, D

9. You need a certificate to digitally sign the software packages you have created. What kind of certificate do you need?

   A. A root certificate

   B. A trusted publisher certificate

   C. A client certificate

   D. A client access license certificate

   Answer: B

10. You need to restrict the kinds of Internet content the Web browsers in the grade-school computer lab can access. What should you do?

    A. Place the computers in the Restricted Sites zone.

    B. Establish RASCi limitations for the Web browsers.

    C. Install a firewall and filter out GIF files.

    D. Install client certificates on the computers.

    Answer: B

11. You have received a software publisher digital certificate from Veri-Sign, and you want to use it in the IEAK. How do you get the certificate into the IEAK?

    A. Proceed through the IEAK Wizard until you reach the Content Ratings page in Stage 4. Select the Customize Content Ratings radio button, and click the Customize button. Locate the digital certificate file, and click Open.

    B. Import the certificate into IE 4. Proceed through the IEAK Wizard until you reach the Site Certificate and Authenticode Settings page in Stage 4. Select the Import radio button, and click the Modify Settings button.

    C. Open a command prompt. Go to the IEAK/tools/authenticode/ directory. Type **addcert /s <certificate file>**.

    D. Select File ➤ Open Certificate in the IEAK Wizard main window. Locate the certificate file, and then click the Import button.

    Answer: B

12. You want to digitally sign your Java CAB files to test your program, but you don't want to get a digital certificate from a certificate authority just yet. What kind of certificate can you generate with the IEAK tools?

A. A test root certificate

B. A client certificate

C. A root certificate

D. You must acquire a certificate from VeriSign

Answer: A

13. What kind of certificate would you preload IE 4 and Outlook Express with so that the user can send and receive encrypted mail?

A. A root certificate

B. A publisher certificate

C. A client certificate

D. A test root certificate

Answer: C

14. Which of the following is not included in a certificate?

A. The owner's name

B. The owner's private key

C. The owner's public key

D. The certificate authority's digital signature

Answer: B

15. Which Java safety levels allows the applet to contact (via network I/O) only the Web site that the applet was downloaded from? Choose all that apply.

   A. High safety

   B. Medium safety

   C. Low safety

   D. Java Disabled

   Answer: A, B

16. You manage an Intranet for your company. You have developed a Java applet that resides on your Intranet Web server and uses a corporate database (hosted on a computer that just responds to SQL requests over TCP/IP) to display and update product orders and delivery information. Most of the users of the applet are on the local Intranet zone, but some employees need to be able to run the Java program from outside your corporate firewall. You would like the program's communications to be encrypted, and you want to limit who may access the Web page that contains the program.

   Required Result: Allow Intranet as well as Internet users to run the Java applet.

   Optional Result 1: Encrypt the communications of the Java applet.

   Optional Result 2: Limit who may access the Web page that contains the program.

   Suggested Solution: Configure the IE 4 Web browsers used by employees to prompt for a username and password when accessing Web sites that require passwords (and configure your Web site to require passwords). Install client certificates in employees' Web browsers. Open up a port in the firewall corresponding to the port used by the applet to connect to the SQL server. Place the Intranet server and the SQL server in the Trusted Sites security zone for the Web browsers.

   Which of the following is correct?

A. The suggested solution accomplishes the required result and both optional results.

B. The suggested solution accomplishes the required result and just one optional result.

C. The suggested solution accomplishes the required result only.

D. The suggested solution does not accomplish the required result.

Answer: B

17. You manage a network of 150 Windows 95 and Windows NT Workstation computers. Each department in your company maintains an Intranet Web site, and several use unsigned ActiveX controls. You are creating a custom IE 4 package to be deployed on the computers in your network. You must establish security zones settings for these browsers, allowing them to download the ActiveX controls from the Intranet servers. You don't want to allow users to change the settings you establish, but you want to be able to change the settings later without reinstalling IE 4 on all those computers.

Required Result: Configure IE 4 zone settings.

Optional Result 1: Lock-down zone settings.

Optional Result 2: Allow for the later changing of zone settings.

Suggested Solution: Create a custom IE 4 package using the IEAK Profile Manager with autoconfiguration enabled. Use the IEAK Profile Manager to create a profile that locks-down settings and that allows downloading of ActiveX controls in the Local Intranet zone.

Which of the following is correct?

A. The suggested solution accomplishes the required result and both optional results.

B. The suggested solution accomplishes the required result and just one optional result.

C. The suggested solution accomplishes the required result only.

D. The suggested solution does not accomplish the required result.

Answer: A

Chapter 9

1. You have a Windows 95 computer that is browsing the Web slowly. You want to find out if the bottleneck is the processor or the memory. What tool should you use to find the bottleneck?

   A. Performance Monitor

   B. System Monitor

   C. ScanDisk

   D. Microsoft Diagnostics (MSD)

   Answer: B

2. You have a Windows NT Workstation computer that is browsing the Web slowly. You think that the bottleneck is either the processor or the memory. What tool can you use to determine where the bottleneck is?

   A. Performance Monitor

   B. System Monitor

   C. Disk Administrator

   D. Microsoft Diagnostics (MSD)

   Answer: A

3. Using the System Monitor you discover that the bytes being written to and read from the hard disk are very high for your Windows 95 PC, and that the Pageouts count is also high. What is most likely the bottleneck in the system?

   A. Your processor is too slow.

   B. You have too little RAM.

   C. You have too little hard drive space.

   D. Your modem is too slow.

   Answer: B

4. You want to speed up disk access in your Windows 95 computer. What tool can you use to optimize hard disk performance?

   A. Disk Administrator

   B. ScanDisk

   C. Disk Defragmenter

   D. Desktop Explorer

Answer: C

5. You want to reduce the bandwidth used by IE 4 so that HTML pages load faster over your 28.8 Kbps modem. Which of the following will not reduce bandwidth?

   A. Disable smooth scrolling

   B. Disable graphics

   C. Disable Active Channels

   D. Set Check for Newer Versions of Stored Pages option to Never

Answer: A

6. Which of the following can help you reduce the combined Internet bandwidth used by browsers on your network that is connected to the Internet through a T1 leased line? Choose all that apply.

   A. Installing a proxy server

   B. Disabling Windows Desktop Update

   C. Limiting Active Channels

   D. Upgrading the Internet connection to a T3

Answer: A, C

7. How many ranges during the day may IE 4 be prohibited from performing Active Channel updates?

   A. Zero

   B. One

   C. Ten

   D. No Limit

Answer: B

8. You currently have a maximum bandwidth of site subscriptions limited to 1024 KB. You want to disable this restriction. What should you enter in the Maximum KB of Site Subscriptions field?

   A. None

   B. Zero

   C. Unlimited

   D. Disabled

Answer: B

9. What tools can you use to limit the bandwidth and times used by site subscriptions in your network? Choose all that apply.

   A. The IEAK Wizard

   B. The IEAK Profile Manager

   C. The User Manager for Domains

   D. The Profile Control Panel

Answer: A, B

10. You have a red X next to all of the components you want to include in your custom IE 4 package. What should you do?

A. Download the IEAK again.

B. Order the IEAK on CD-ROM.

C. Synchronize the components.

D. Proceed. The red X icons will turn to green icons as each component is configured.

Answer: C

11. You can't edit the System Policies and Restrictions in the IEAK Wizard. What might be wrong?

A. You have not synchronized all of the IE 4 components.

B. One of the IEAK folders is compressed.

C. You have not logged on as administrator.

D. You have an older version of the IEAK.

Answer: B

12. You have created an Active Setup bitmap and included it in your custom IE 4 package, but the default bitmap appears instead. What might be the problem? Choose all that apply.

A. The bitmap is in the wrong format.

B. The computer is in 16-color mode.

C. You didn't digitally sign the image.

D. You have used the wrong colors. You must choose colors that the Active Setup buttons will be visible over.

Answer: A, B

13. You want to include a folder in the Favorites menu called Local, and in the Local folder you want to have links to Intranet Web sites. What must you do?

  A. In Stage 4 of the IEAK, click Create Folder. Enter Local as the folder name, then add URLs to the favorites that you want to be included in that folder.

  B. In IE 4, create a folder called Local. Browse each Intranet site and add that site to the Local folder in Favorites. Import the Local folder into your custom IE 4 package using the IEAK.

  C. In IE 4, create a folder called Temp, and another folder called Local within Temp. Browse each Intranet site and add that site to the Local folder in Favorites. Import the Temp folder into your custom IE 4 package using the IEAK.

  D. You cannot import folders into the IE 4 Favorites directory.

Answer: C

14. You cannot get Windows Desktop Update to work in your Spanish version of Windows 95. What might be the problem?

  A. Microsoft does not distribute a Spanish version of IE 4.

  B. You have installed an English version of IE 4 on the Spanish version of Windows.

  C. Windows Desktop Update requires Service Pack 3 on Windows 95, and there is no Spanish version of Service Pack 3.

  D. The Spanish version of Windows requires more disk space.

Answer: B

15. What network diagnostic tool should you use to display the IP configuration settings of your Windows 95 computer?

  A. Winipcfg

  B. Ipconfig

  C. PING

  D. Nslookup

Answer: A

16. Your network has only a 56 Kbps frame relay connection to the Internet. You want to give network bandwidth priority to electronic mail and Web browsing by users rather than to automatic Active Channel updates. Since many users access the same sites every morning, you would prefer that those Web pages are only retrieved over the 56K link once each morning, rather than once per user. In addition, some users access financial information pages that are updated frequently but do not include time-stamping information, and you don't want these users to retrieve stale Web pages. You would also like to keep users from downloading large graphic files during office hours.

Required Result: Limit Active Channel bandwidth use during working hours.

Optional Result 1: Reduce duplicate page retrievals.

Optional Result 2: Protect users from retrieving stale Web pages.

Suggested Solution: Use the IEAK Profile Manager to disallow Active Channel updates between 8 a.m. and 5 p.m. Establish a Proxy Server on your network to cache Internet Web pages.

Which of the following is correct?

A. The suggested solution accomplishes the required result and both optional results.

B. The suggested solution accomplishes the required result and just one optional result.

C. The suggested solution accomplishes the required result only.

D. The suggested solution does not accomplish the required result.

Answer: B

17. Your Windows NT Workstation computer is running very sluggishly. You use the Performance Monitor to try to find the bottleneck in your computer. The user of this computer keeps many programs open at once—a spread sheet, a word processor, a CAD package, Outlook Express, IE 4, and a desktop publishing package. You discover that the number of pages per second is excessive when compared with the same counter on another computer that is operating normally. You need to speed up this computer. You don't want to change the hardware configuration of the computer, but you also prefer not to restrict how the user works with the computer.

Required Result: Increase the performance of the computer.

Optional Result 1: Leave the hardware configuration alone.

Optional Result 2: Leave the user's habits alone.

Suggested Solution: Add memory to the computer.

Which of the following is correct?

A. The suggested solution accomplishes the required result and both optional results.

B. The suggested solution accomplishes the required result and just one optional result.

C. The suggested solution accomplishes the required result only.

D. The suggested solution does not accomplish the required result.

Answer: B

Chapter 10

1. You want users on your network to be able to check mail on mail servers external to your network using the POP protocol. What port do you need to open up in your firewall for outgoing connections?

A. 21

B. 25

C. 110

D. 143

Answer: C

2. You have set up an Exchange Server mail server package with the Internet conduit so that other computers on the Internet can deliver mail to your Exchange host using SMTP. The computers on your network use IMAP to check the mail server for new mail and to deposit mail for delivery. The mail server resides inside your corporate firewall. What port do you need to open on the firewall so that your mail server can send and receive mail with other Internet mail hosts?

   A. 21

   B. 25

   C. 110

   D. 143

   Answer: B

3. When you click a Mail To link in IE 4, Eudora Lite appears instead of Outlook Express. You want to use Outlook Express to send mail from IE 4. Where do you reset the default mail client to be Outlook Express? Choose all that apply.

   A. Start ➢ Programs ➢ Internet Explorer ➢ Internet Explorer ➢ View ➢ Internet Options ➢ Programs.

   B. My Computer ➢ View ➢ Folder Options ➢ File Types.

   C. Start ➢ Settings ➢ Control Panel ➢ System ➢ MIME Map.

   D. Start ➢ Settings ➢ Control Panel ➢ Mail.

   Answer: A, B

4. If you see `The command failed to execute.` message in Outlook Express, what most likely is the problem?

   A. You have not installed Service Pack 3 on your Windows NT computer.

   B. Your computer is low on disk space.

   C. Your computer has insufficient RAM.

   D. You attempted to download a `CAB` file that has not been digitally signed.

   Answer: B

5. You are unable to send mail via SMTP using Outlook Express. You want to make sure that there is no network problem between your computer and the mail server. What tools can you use to check the network path between your computer and the mail server? Choose all that apply.

   A. NSLOOKUP

   B. Tracert

   C. Network Monitor

   D. PING

Answer: B, D

6. You are unable to send mail via SMTP using Outlook Express. You want to make sure that the mail server is responding to mail requests on port 25. What tool can you use to see if the mail host is accepting connections on that port?

   A. Tracert

   B. PING

   C. Telnet

   D. NSLOOKUP

Answer: C

7. You want your network users to be able to check their e-mail using the POP protocol. What other protocol must also be enabled if you are using the POP protocol to receive mail?

   A. NNTP

   B. IMAP

   C. ISAPI

   D. SMTP

Answer: D

8. You use an older directory service outside your firewall for Net-Meeting that uses the ULS protocol rather than the ILS protocol to connect to the directory service. What port must you open in your firewall to allow ULS connections?

A. 389

B. 522

C. 110

D. Dynamic

Answer: B

9. Your directory service uses ULS to provide LDAP support for Net-Meeting users. The directory service resides outside your firewall, but you want users inside your firewall to be able to connect to it. What port should you open in your firewall?

A. 389

B. 522

C. 110

D. Dynamic

Answer: A

10. NetMeeting users are able to connect to an LDAP server and establish audio and video conferences with other users, but after two minutes the users are consistently detached from the directory service. What is wrong?

A. The users are attaching to the network over a link that uses SLIP with header compression.

B. The network path to the directory service passes through a segment that blocks ICMP traffic.

C. The users' computers do not have Service Pack 3 installed.

D. The users' computers have HP fonts installed.

Answer: B

11. If you are willing to open specific TCP ports in your firewall but are unwilling to open a wide range of ports, what NetMeeting features will not function?

A. Chat

B. Application Sharing

C. Videoconferencing

D. Whiteboard

Answer: C

12. You can perform whiteboard teleconferencing between computers in your LAN but you cannot perform whiteboard teleconferencing with computers outside your LAN. You think that your firewall is blocking the port used for T.120 collaboration. How can you check?

A. Ping the destination computer.

B. Telnet to port 1503 on the destination computer.

C. Telnet to a dynamic port on the destination computer.

D. Use Tracert to find the path from your computer to the destination computer.

Answer: B

13. You are trying to establish a videoconference between your computer and another computer on the Internet. The person on the other end can hear you but cannot see you. You can see the other person just fine. Which of the following might be the culprit? Choose all that apply.

A. Either you or the destination computer is using SLIP with header compression to connect to an ISP.

B. Your video card uses video overlay to capture the images.

C. Your video card does not support Microsoft Video for Windows 1.0.

D. You have a firewall between your computer and the destination computer that is not passing the required ports for H.323 videoconferencing.

Answer: B, C

14. You want to share applications using NetMeeting, but you have a firewall between your network and the Internet. What ports must you open on the firewall to connect to an ILS server and to collaborate in this manner with another computer over the Internet? Choose all that apply.

A. 389

B. 522

C. 1503

D. 1720

Answer: A, C

15. What tools can you use to restrict the bandwidth used by Microsoft NetMeeting on client computers in your network after you have distributed IE 4? Choose all that apply.

A. The IEAK Wizard

B. The IEAK Profile Manager

C. User Manager for Domains

D. The Policies Control Panel

Answer: B

16. Your users can connect to an LDAP server, can use the whiteboard, and can chat using Microsoft NetMeeting, but they cannot establish a videoconference beyond your LAN. You have a firewall, and you suspect that it is blocking the ports required for videoconferencing.

Required Result: Determine if the firewall is blocking the NetMeeting ports required by videoconferencing.

Optional Result 1: Determine if the remote computer is responding to the NetMeeting videoconferencing ports.

Optional Result 2: Determine if there is a network failure between your computer and the destination computer.

Suggested Solution: PING the remote computer.

Which of the following is correct?

A. The suggested solution accomplishes the required result and both optional results.

B. The suggested solution accomplishes the required result and just one optional result.

C. The suggested solution accomplishes the required result only.

D. The suggested solution does not accomplish the required result.

Answer: D

APPENDIX

B

Glossary

Account policies Account policies are used to determine password and logon requirements. Account policies are set through User Manager for Domains. See *User Manager for Domains*.

accounts Containers for security identifiers, passwords, permissions, group associations, and preferences for each user of a system. A user name and password you create to give a user access to the network (or to a single machine). Along with the name and password, an account includes other information about the user, such as groups the user belongs to and directories and files the user can access. The User Manager for Domains utility is used to administer accounts. See *password, preferences*.

Acme Setup The portion of the IE 4 setup process that retrieves files from the IE 4 CAB files and installs them in their proper places in your operating system.

Active Channel A Web site that includes version information and download frequency suggestions as well as Channel bar graphics. IE 4 can subscribe to Active Channels, which causes the browser to check the Web site regularly for updated Web pages. It either notifies the user of changes to the Web site or automatically downloads the changed Web site information. See *CDF files*.

Active Desktop An extension of the Windows Desktop Explorer to include Web data (such as HTML text, graphics, JScript, Java applets, video, and audio) in the Start menu, on the Taskbar, in the screen background, and in directory windows.

Active Setup The portion of the IE 4 setup process that downloads the appropriate IE 4 CAB files from the Internet and checks their digital signatures to make sure they have not been altered.

Active Streaming Format (ASF) The format used by NetShow for viewing video and listening to audio streamed over the Internet.

ActiveX Microsoft's control plug-in technology for Web browsers that allows compiled controls to be referenced from HTML documents and automatically downloads and installs the controls if they are not already plugged into the Web browser.

Address Resolution Protocol (ARP)   An Internet protocol for resolving an IP address into a physical layer address (such as an Ethernet media access controller address). See *Internet Protocol*.

ADM files   Files of this type contain possible System Policies and Restrictions. ADM files are used by the System Policy Editor of Windows NT, the `Poledit.exe` program of Windows 95, and the IEAK Policy Editor.

Administrator account   A special account in Windows NT that contains the ultimate set of security permissions. The Administrator account is used to correct security problems and assign permissions to any user or group.

Administrator   Any user who is able to perform administrative tasks, such as creating or modifying user accounts. By default, Windows NT includes an account called Administrator with these privileges.

Administrators   Users who are part of the Administrators group. Members of this group have the same permissions as the Administrator account. See *Administrator account*.

Advanced Research Projects Agency Network (ARPANET)   Predecessor to the Internet that was developed by the Department of Defense in the late 1960s.

applet   A small application (typically written in Java) that runs inside another application, such as a Web browser. See *Java*.

Application Programming Interface (API)   A set of related procedures built into Windows NT that are called by applications to perform a specific function.

applications   Large software packages that perform specific functions, such as word processing, Web browsing, or database management. Applications typically consist of more than one program. See *Program*.

ARP   See *Address Resolution Protocol*.

ARPANET   See *Advanced Research Projects Agency Network*.

ASF   See *Active Streaming Format*.

authentication   The process used to recognize a user and grant privileges based on user account name and password. The authentication process is designed to avoid storing passwords as text or sending them over the network.

Authenticode   The public key encryption technology and trust-based security structure promoted by Microsoft to provide safe downloading of programs and plug-ins over the Internet. See *certificate authority, signing code, digital certificates.*

autoconfiguration   IE 4 can check for new configuration settings when it launches (or at fixed intervals while it is running). These settings are stored in a file with the INS file name extension at a URL specified in the Autoconfiguration Settings window of the Web browser.

auto proxy   Automatic configuration of a Web browser to find and use a proxy server. Auto proxy uses JScript/JavaScript programs to determine where to direct Web requests. IE 3 and Netscape also support auto proxy.

BIOS (Basic Input/Output System)   When the computer is first powered on, the microprocessor needs instructions for locating and using the computer hardware (hard disk drive, keyboard, memory, etc.) to find and load the operating system. The BIOS is a simple program stored in ROM or flash RAM that contains these instructions.

bit   A binary digit. A numeral having only two possible values, zero or one. Computers represent these two values as a high (voltage present) or low (no voltage present) state on a control line. Bits are accumulated in sets of certain sizes to represent higher values.

Bootstrap Protocol (BOOTP)   Predecessor to the DHCP protocol. BOOTP was used to assign IP addresses to diskless workstations. See *Dynamic Host Configuration Protocol.*

border gateways   Routers that attach a private network to the Internet. They are usually used in a system as security checkpoints that force all traffic into and out of a secured system through a single point of access control. Traffic passing through the border gateways is security tested before being passed through to the secure system. Firewalls are an example of border gateways. See *firewall.*

border A security perimeter formed by natural or logical boundaries that can only be passed at defined locations called border gateways.

bottlenecks Components operating at their peak capacity that restrict the flow of information through a system. Used singularly, the term indicates the single most restrictive component in a system.

branding Replacing some of the graphics and text (in IE 4, Active Setup, and the CD-ROM Autorun program) with your own graphics and text that advertise your product or service.

breach A loss of security due to a successful attack.

browser See *Web browser*.

CA See *corporate administrator mode*.

CAB files See *Cabinet files*.

Cabinet files The standard Microsoft software distribution format uses Cabinet files (files with the CAB filename extension) to collect the various files a software package needs. CAB files can be digitally signed for safe distribution over the Internet. Active Setup retrieves CAB files, and ACME Setup expands and installs them.

caching A speed optimization technique that keeps a copy of the most recently used data in a fast, high-cost, low-capacity storage device rather than in the device upon which the actual data resides. Caching assumes that recently used data is likely to be used again. Fetching data from the cache is faster than fetching data from the slower, larger storage device. Most caching algorithms also copy the data that is most likely to be used next and perform write caching to further increase speed gains.

CDF files Files that use the CDF extension and describe Active Channels for Web sites. The files contain suggested frequency for checking updates, version information, and references to the HTML pages that comprise the Active Channel.

CD-ROM See *compact disk-read only memory*.

central processing unit (CPU)   The central processing unit of a computer. In microcomputers such as IBM/PC compatible machines, the CPU is the microprocessor. See *microprocessor*.

certificate authority   An individual or organization that issues digital certificates. The role of the certificate authority is to assure that the information contained in the digital certificate is correct. A certificate authority providing a digital certificate to a company, for example, should make sure that the company is a valid company and the contact information is correct. The trustworthiness of a certificate is only as good as the trustworthiness and diligence of the certificate authority. See *Authenticode*.

certificates   Encrypted electronic documents that attest to the authenticity of a service, provider, or vendor of a product. Forgery of certificates is infeasible, so the information they contain may be trusted (as long as the certificate authority issuing the certificate can be trusted). To require connection using secure socket layer, a key with a valid certificate must be installed. See *key, Secure Socket Layer*.

CGI   See *Common Gateway Interface*.

CIF file   This file uses the CIF extension and it lists which CAB files the IE4Wzd.exe must download from the download server.

cipher   Protects a message by permuting its text (by rearranging it or performing modifications to the encoding, rather than the meaning, of the message).

ciphertext   An encrypted message that requires a cipher and a key to decrypt.

Class A domain   Large networks on which the first byte specifies the network number and the last three bytes specify the local addresses.

Class B domain   Medium networks on which the first two bytes specify the network number and the last two bytes specify the local addresses.

Class C domain   Small networks on which the first three bytes specify the network number and the last byte specifies the local address.

classless addressing   A subnet mask that splits the network number and the host number without regard for byte boundaries.

cleartext   The message or data in an encryption system to be sent from the sender to the receiver. This is what must be protected from being intercepted and understood. See *plaintext*.

client   A computer on a network that subscribes to the services provided by a server. See *server*.

client/server   A network architecture that dedicates certain computers, called *servers,* to act as service providers to computers, called *clients*, that users operate to perform work. Servers can be dedicated to providing one or more network services such as file storage, shared printing, communications, e-mail service, and Web response. See *peer, share*.

client/server applications   Applications that split large applications into two components: compute-intensive processes that run on application servers and user interfaces that run on client computers. Client/server applications communicate over the network through interprocess communication mechanisms. See *client, server*.

Commercial Internet Exchange (CIX)   Locations where top-tier ISPs maintain routers to route IP packets between their respective networks. CIX locations connect ISPs together from discrete TCP/IP wide area networks to form the Internet. See *Internet*.

Common Gateway Interface (CGI)   A standard for starting programs that return dynamically created HTML documents to the HTTP service for transmission to the remote client. A new instance of the CGI application is started each time a connection is made, which can put excessive load on an Internet server.

compact disk-read only memory (CD-ROM)   A media for storing extremely large software packages on optical read-only discs. CD-ROM is an adaptation of the CD medium used for distributing digitized music. CD-ROM discs can hold up to 650MB of information and cost very little to produce in large quantities.

components   Software packages or resource files distributed with IE 4.

Content Advisor   An IE 4 tool that allows administrators (and parents) to block out rated content that the administrator (or parent) deems inappropriate.

cookie A small amount of information presented to the Web browser from a Web server that the Web server may ask for the next time the browser visits the server. Cookies allow the Web browser to keep track of where you are in a Web site and allow the browser to "pick up where it left off" at the last visit.

corporate administrator (CA) mode The mode of using the IEAK if you are preparing a custom IE 4 package for exclusive use in your own LAN.

Desktop The Desktop is the user interface behind application windows and the Start menu. The Desktop contains icons and a background color, patterns, and bitmaps. With Windows Desktop Update the Desktop can also contain HTML text, graphics, animations, and programs. Items on the Desktop are contained in a directory in the Windows or Winnt/Profiles folder. See *Desktop Explorer, shell.*

Desktop Explorer The default shell for Windows 95 and Windows NT 4. Explorer implements the more flexible Desktop objects paradigm rather than the Program Manager paradigm used in earlier versions of Windows. See *Desktop.*

DHCP See *Dynamic Host Configuration Protocol.*

dial-up connections Data link layer digital connections made via modems over regular telephone lines, thus providing network connections (analog or digital) that can be made to any receiving station in the world by specifying (dialing) the receiver's unique address. The term *dial-up* refers to temporary digital connections, as opposed to leased telephone lines that provide permanent connections. See *modem, Public Switched Telephone Network.*

digital certificates Special files that use public key encryption to certify the identity of the bearer of the digital certificate and to enable encrypted communication with the bearer of the digital certificate. Digital certificates are also used to digitally sign software packages for distribution. See *Authenticode, certificate authority.*

directories In a file system, directories are containers that store files or other directories. Mass storage devices have a root directory that contains all other directories, thus creating a hierarchy of directories sometimes referred to as a *directory tree.* See *file, file system.*

DNS   See *Domain Name Service.*

domain   In Microsoft networks, a domain is an arrangement of client and server computers referenced by a specific name that share a single security permissions database. On the Internet, a domain is a named collection of hosts and sub-domains, registered with a unique name by the InterNIC. See *InterNIC.*

domain name   The textual identifier of a specific Internet host. Domain names are in the form of *server.organization.type* (as in `www.microsoft.com`) and are translated to Internet addresses by domain name servers. See *domain name server.*

domain name server   An Internet host dedicated to the function of translating fully qualified domain names into IP addresses. See *domain name.*

Domain Name Service (DNS)   The TCP/IP network service that translates textual Internet network addresses into numerical Internet network addresses. See *domain name, Internet, TCP/IP.*

driver   A program that provides a software interface to a hardware device. Drivers are written for the specific device they control, but they present a common software interface to the computer's operating system, allowing all devices (of a similar type) to be controlled as if they were the same. See *operating system.*

Dynamic Host Configuration Protocol (DHCP)   A method of automatically assigning IP addresses to client computers on a network.

eavesdropping   Gathering information about a target network or computer by listening in on transmitted data.

electronic mail (e-mail)   A type of client/server application that provides a routed, stored-message service between any two user e-mail accounts. E-mail accounts are not the same as user accounts, but a one-to-one relationship usually exists between them. Because all modern computers can attach to the Internet, users can send e-mail over the Internet to any location that has telephone or wireless digital service. See *Internet.*

encryption   The process of obscuring information by modifying it according to a mathematical function known only to the intended recipient. Encryption secures information being transmitted over non-secure or untrusted media. See *security.*

Ethernet   The most popular data link layer standard for local area networking. Ethernet implements the carrier sense multiple access with collision detection (CSMA/CD) method of arbitrating multiple computer access to the same network. This standard supports the use of Ethernet over any type of media including wireless broadcast. Standard Ethernet operates at 10 megabits per second. Fast Ethernet operates at 100 megabits per second.

Exchange   Microsoft's messaging application. Exchange implements Microsoft's mail application programming interface (MAPI), as well as other messaging protocols such as POP, SNMP, and faxing to provide a flexible message composition and reception service. See *electronic mail, fax modem.*

FAT   See *File Allocation Table.*

fax modem   A special modem that includes hardware to allow the transmission and reception of facsimiles. See *Exchange, modem.*

File Allocation Table (FAT)   The file system used by MS-DOS and available to other operating systems such as Windows (all variations), OS/2, and Macintosh. FAT has become something of a mass-storage compatibility standard because of its simplicity and wide availability. FAT has few fault tolerance features and can become corrupted through normal use over time. See *file system.*

file system   A structure used to store data in named capsules, called *files,* on a storage device. File systems impose an ordered database of files on the mass storage device (called volumes) that uses hierarchies of directories to organize files. See *directories, file.*

File Transfer Protocol (FTP)   A simple Internet protocol that transfers complete files from an FTP server to a user running the FTP client. FTP provides a simple method of transferring files between computers but cannot perform browsing functions. You must know the URL of the FTP server to which you wish to attach. See *Internet, Uniform Resource Locator.*

file   A set of data stored on a mass storage device and identified by a directory entry containing a name, file attributes, and the physical location of the file in the volume. *See directories.*

filter   In Index Server, a filter is a program (DLL) that can parse documents of a specific format to return a list of index terms for that document. In ISAPI, a filter is a program (DLL) used to extend the capabilities of IIS. See *Internet Information Server*.

firewall   A security control device that connects two networks and determines which traffic should be allowed to pass between them. A firewall is usually implemented as a dual-homed computer attached to both the Internet and an Intranet and that protects the computers on the Intranet from intrusion by blocking connections with untrusted sources and on specific protocols. Firewalls are the strongest form of Internet security yet implemented. Firewalls incorporate the functions of packet filtering, IP masquerading, and application proxy to perform their function.

FrontPage   Microsoft's application for Web site organization and Web page content creation.

FTP   See *File Transfer Protocol*.

gateway   A computer that serves as a router, a format translator, and/or a security filter for an entire network. Gateways are also general-purpose computers that are used as routers and perform no other function.

Gopher   An Internet service that provides text and links to other Gopher sites. Gopher predates HTTP by about a year, but has been made obsolete by the richer format provided by HTTP. See *Hypertext Transport Protocol*.

hands-free setup   See *silent installation*.

hash   An algorithm that converts a string of text (such as a password) to a number. If the number can be converted back to the original text, it is referred to as a two-way hash. In a one-way hash, such as that used by Windows NT's password authentication process, the number cannot be converted back to text.

history   A list of the Web URLs visited by the user and maintained in the History folder. The user can view the URLs and revisit them from the History button in the IE 4 toolbar.

home directory   The root directory of a Web server or virtual server that contains the default document or home page. See *World Wide Web*.

home page   The default page returned by an HTTP server when a URL containing no specific document is requested. See *Hypertext Transport Protocol, Uniform Resource Locator.*

host   A host is any computer attached to the Internet with at least one unique IP address. A host is also an Internet server. Hosts are constantly connected to the Internet. See *Internet.*

HotJava   A Web browser written entirely in the Java programming language and designed to show the capability of the language. HotJava was the first browser to support Java applications.

HTML   See *Hypertext Markup Language.*

HTT   The file type used by the hypertext template files that are used by the Active Desktop to present Web View directories to the user. See *Web View.*

HTTP   See *Hypertext Transport Protocol.*

hyperlink   A link embedded in text or graphics files that have a Web address embedded within them. By clicking on the link, you jump to another Web address. You can identify a hyperlink because it is a different color from the rest of the Web page. See *World Wide Web.*

Hypertext Markup Language (HTML)   A textual data format that identifies sections of a document as headers, lists, hypertext links, etc. HTML is the data format used on the World Wide Web for the publication of Web pages. See *Hypertext Transport Protocol, World Wide Web.*

Hypertext Transport Protocol (HTTP)   Hypertext Transport Protocol is an Internet protocol that transfers HTML documents over the Internet and responds to context changes that happen when a user clicks on a hypertext link. See *Hypertext Markup Language, World Wide Web.*

Icon   A graphical representation of a resource in a graphical user interface that usually takes the form of a small (32 x 32) bitmap.

ICP mode   See *Internet Content Provider mode.*

IEAK Profile Editor   A tool distributed with the Internet Explorer Administration Kit that allows the administrator to establish and edit System Policies as well as modify autoconfiguration settings for deployed IE 4 browsers.

IEAK Wizard   A tool distributed with the Internet Explorer Administration Kit that guides the user through the steps required to build a custom IE 4 package.

IEAK   See *Internet Explorer Administration Kit*.

IExpress Wizard   A Wizard distributed with the Internet Explorer Administration Kit that automates the process of creating a custom package (CAB or EXE) to be distributed with a custom IE 4 package.

IIS   See *Internet Information Server*.

ILS   See *Internet Locator Service*.

Inbox Assistant   An Outlook Express tool that helps the user manage electronic mail by processing the mail according to rules and actions defined by the user.

INS files   IE 4 installation and autoconfiguration files that use the INS extension. The autoconfiguration mechanism of IE 4 (when enabled) will regularly check a file of this type for changes to IE 4 settings and (if settings have changed) apply those changed settings.

installation option   A collection of IE 4 components that will be installed together. The IEAK Wizard allows you to prepare up to 10 installation options for a custom IEAK package that a user installing the package may choose from.

Integrated Services Digital Network (ISDN)   A direct, digital dial-up PSTN data link layer connection that operates at 64KB per channel over regular twisted pair cable between a subscriber site and a PSTN central office. ISDN provides twice the data rate of the fastest modems per channel. Up to 24 channels can be multiplexed over two twisted pairs. See *modem, Public Switched Telephone Network*.

Intel architecture   A family of microprocessors descended directly from the Intel 8086, itself descended from the first microprocessor, the Intel 4004. The Intel architecture is the dominant microprocessor family. It was used in the original IBM PC microcomputer adopted by the business market and later adapted for home use.

intermediate system   A host that forwards datagrams between networks but is not interested in the content of those datagrams.

Internet   A voluntarily interconnected global network of computers based upon the TCP/IP protocol suite. TCP/IP was originally developed by the U.S. Department of Defense's Advanced Research Projects Agency to facilitate the interconnection of military networks and was provided free to universities. The obvious utility of worldwide digital network connectivity and the availability of free complex networking software developed at universities doing military research attracted other universities, research institutions, private organizations, businesses, and, finally, the individual home user. The Internet is now available to all current commercial computing platforms. See *FTP, Transmission Control Protocol/Internet Protocol, Telnet, World Wide Web.*

Internet Connection Wizard   The Wizard that runs when IE 4 is first installed and helps you establish a connection to the Internet.

Internet content provider (ICP) mode   The mode of using the IEAK if you are preparing a custom IE 4 package for customers of your product or service for the Internet.

Internet Explorer Administration Kit (IEAK)   A collection of tools and Wizards for creating and distributing a custom IE 4 package.

Internet Explorer   A World Wide Web browser produced by Microsoft and included free with Windows 95, Windows 98, and Windows NT 4. See *Internet, World Wide Web.*

Internet Information Server (IIS)   Serves Internet higher-level protocols, like HTTP and FTP, to clients using Web browsers. See *File Transfer Protocol, Hypertext Transport Protocol, World Wide Web.*

Internet Locator Service   A directory service that allows users to look up other Internet users, send e-mail, and establish videoconferencing connections with other users. See *Lightweight Directory Access Protocol.*

Internet Protocol (IP)   The network layer protocol upon which the Internet is based. IP provides a simple connectionless packet exchange. Other protocols such as UDP or TCP use IP to perform their connection-oriented or guaranteed delivery services. See *Internet, Transmission Control Protocol/ Internet Protocol.*

Internet Relay Chat (IRC)   An informal Internet protocol for multi-user simultaneous conversation via relayed text strings between an IRC server and multiple IRC clients.

Internet server   A server computer connected to the Internet or an Intranet. It serves Internet protocols like HTTP, FTP, and Gopher based on the TCP/IP protocol suite. See *File Transfer Protocol, Gopher, Internet, Hypertext Transport Protocol, Transmission Control Protocol/Internet Protocol.*

Internet service provider (ISP)   A company that provides dial-up connections to the Internet. See *Internet.*

Internetwork   A network of networks, usually based on a packet-switching scheme.

Internetwork Packet eXchange (IPX)   The network and transport layer protocol developed by Novell for its NetWare product. IPX is a routable, connection-oriented protocol similar to TCP/IP but much easier to manage and with lower communication overhead. See *Transmission Control Protocol/Internet Protocol.*

InterNIC   The agency that is responsible for assigning IP addresses. See *Internet Protocol, IP Address.*

Interpreter   A program that executes the commands read from a script. See *script, scripting language.*

Interrupt Request (IRQ)   A hardware signal from a peripheral device to the microcomputer indicating that it has I/O traffic to send. If the microprocessor is not running a more important service, it will interrupt its current activity and handle the interrupt request. IBM PCs have 16 levels of interrupt request lines. Under Windows NT, each device must have a unique interrupt request line. See *driver, microprocessor, peripheral.*

Intranet   A privately owned network based on the TCP/IP protocol suite. See *Transmission Control Protocol/Internet Protocol.*

intruder   Anyone who has accessed a secure resource without authorization.

IP address A four-byte number that uniquely identifies a computer on an IP internetwork. InterNIC assigns the first bytes of Internet IP addresses and administers them in hierarchies. Huge organizations (like the government or top-level ISPs) have Class A addresses, large organizations and most ISPs have Class B addresses, and small companies have Class C addresses. In a Class A address, InterNIC assigns the first byte, and the owning organization assigns the remaining three bytes. In a Class B address, InterNIC or the higher-level ISP assigns the first two bytes, and the organization assigns the remaining two bytes. In a Class C address, InterNIC or the higher-level ISP assigns the first three bytes, and the organization assigns the remaining byte. Organizations not attached to the Internet are free to assign IP addresses as they please. See *Internet, InterNIC, Internet Protocol*.

IP See *Internet Protocol*.

IRQ See *Interrupt Request*.

ISDN See *Integrated Services Digital Network*.

ISP See *Internet service provider*.

Java Virtual Machine (JVM) A fictitious machine language to which all Java applications are compiled. Java runtime environments can either interpret or compile JVM code to execute it on any computer or inside an application like a Web browser.

Java A compiled object-oriented cross-platform language based on the syntax of C++ and uses the interpreted Java virtual machine as its machine language. Since Java applications and applets can run on any platform, it is a natural candidate for Web-based programs.

JavaScript A scripting language based on the syntax of Java. JavaScript can be embedded in HTML documents to provide simple client-side active content. See *script, scripting language*.

kernel The core process of a preemptive operating system, consisting of a multitasking scheduler and the basic services that provide security. Depending on the operating system, other services such as virtual memory drivers may be built into the kernel. The kernel is responsible for managing the scheduling of threads and processes. See *driver, operating system*.

key(s)   A value or values (usually a number or a string of characters) that is used with a cipher to encrypt a message. Symmetric encryption uses one key, public key encryption uses two keys. The key (or one of the keys in public key encryption) must be kept secret in order for the message to remain private. Often keys are paired codes used to encrypt data in communication streams, one key for the sender and another for the recipient. One part of the key is kept private on the server, while the other (public) part of the key is transmitted to Web browsers. Web browsers can then encrypt data using the public portion, which can only be decrypted using the private portion of the key. The process is called public key encryption and is used in a Secure Socket Layer mechanism, as well as most other common public forms of encryption. See *encryption, Secure Socket Layer.*

keyspace   The range of all possible keys for a cipher. A cipher with a large keyspace is harder to crack than one with a smaller keyspace because there are more keys (numbers or combinations of letters) to try.

LAN   See *local area network.*

LDAP   See *Lightweight Directory Access Protocol.*

Lightweight Directory Access Protocol (LDAP)   An open standard for storing user and group information independent of the operating system that hosts the WWW service.

Linux   A free 32-bit version of the Unix operating system developed on the Internet and frequently used by hackers to attack Internet systems.

local area network (LAN)   A network of computers operating on the same high-speed, shared media network data link layer. The size of a local area network is defined by the limitations of high-speed shared media networks to generally less than one kilometer in overall span. Some LAN backbone data link protocols, such as FDDI, can create larger LANs called *metropolitan* or *medium area networks (MANs)*. See *wide area network.*

log   A database of time-based security and service-related information stored in text format.

logging   The process of recording information about activities and errors in the operating system.

Macintosh A brand of computer manufactured by Apple. Macintosh is the only successful line of computers that is based neither on the original IBM PC nor on running the UNIX operating system.

MacOS The operating system that runs on an Apple Macintosh computer. See *Macintosh*.

memory Any device capable of storing information. This term is usually used to indicate volatile semiconductor random access memory (RAM) capable of high-speed access to any portion of the memory space, but incapable of storing information without power. See *random access memory*.

message Information sent from the sender to the receiver, usually encrypted by the sender and decrypted by the receiver.

microprocessor An integrated semiconductor circuit designed to automatically perform lists of logical and arithmetic operations. Modern microprocessors independently manage memory pools and support multiple instruction lists called threads. Microprocessors are also capable of responding to interrupt requests from peripherals and include onboard support for complex floating point arithmetic. Microprocessors must have instructions when they are first powered on. These instructions are contained in nonvolatile firmware called a BIOS. See *BIOS, operating system*.

Microsoft Chat This tool lets you interact with other Internet users in real time, providing virtual spaces, or *rooms*, in which people can meet and converse. Microsoft chat supports the exchange of typed text as well as a cartoon-based visual interaction environment.

Microsoft Disk Operating System (MS-DOS) A 16-bit operating system designed for the 8086 chip that was used in the original IBM PC. MS-DOS is a simple program loader and file system that turns over complete control of the computer to the running program and provides very little service beyond file system support and what is provided by the BIOS.

Microsoft FrontPage Express A program that automates Web page editing and management and assists transferring Web pages from a workstation, where they are being developed, to a Web server where they may be accessed. FrontPage Express lets you graphically manipulate Web pages and their links.

Microsoft NetMeeting   Provides for collaboration over the Internet in real time. NetMeeting supports the Internet and telecommunications videoconferencing standards and supporting video and audio links over Internet protocols. NetMeeting also supports whiteboard collaboration, text-based chat, file sharing, and application sharing.

Microsoft NetShow Player   Accepts and plays continuous streams of video and audio broadcast over the Internet.

Microsoft Wallet   A repository for Web payment information including contact information and credit card numbers. It stores the information in encrypted form and supports Internet commerce standards such as Secure Electronic Transactions and Secure Socket Layer communications.

Microsoft Web Publishing Wizard   Automates the process of connecting to an Internet service provider (or other Web server) and transferring Web site data to that server.

MIME   See *Multimedia Internet Mail Extensions*.

modem   A modulator/demodulator. A data link layer device used to create an analog signal suitable for transmission over telephone lines from a digital data stream. Modern modems also include a command set for negotiating connections and data rates with remote modems and for setting their default behavior. The fastest modems run at about 33Kbps.

MS-DOS   See *Microsoft Disk Operating System*.

multihomed host   A computer, such as a file server, or a Web browser that resides on more than one IP network segment.

Multimedia Internet Mail Extensions (MIME)   A specification for the content types of files transmitted over the Internet. Web servers identify the type of file being sent to Web browsers using MIME types.

multitasking   The process whereby an operating system executes more than one program at the same time on the same microprocessor. The operating system does this by giving a small amount of execution time (typically 100 milliseconds) to each program in turn. To the user it appears that the programs are executing simultaneously.

NetBEUI   See *NetBIOS Extended User Interface*.

NetBIOS Extended User Interface (NetBEUI)   A simple network layer transport developed to support NetBIOS installations. NetBEUI is the fastest transport protocol available for Windows NT. NetBEUI is not routable, and so it is not appropriate for larger networks.

NetBIOS   See *Network Basic Input/Output System.*

network   A group of computers connected via some digital medium for the purpose of exchanging information. Networks can be based on many types of media, such as twisted-pair, telephone-style cable, optical fiber, coaxial cable, radio, or infrared light. Certain computers are usually configured as service providers called *servers*. Computers that perform user tasks directly and that use the services of servers are called *clients*. See *client/server, network operating system, server.*

Network Basic Input/Output System (NetBIOS)   A client/server interprocess communication service developed by IBM in the early 1980s. NetBIOS presents a relatively primitive mechanism for communication in client/server applications, but its widespread acceptance and availability across most operating systems make it a logical choice for simple network applications. Many of the network IPC mechanisms in Windows NT are implemented over NetBIOS. See *client/server.*

Network Driver Interface Specification (NDIS)   A Microsoft specification to which network adapter drivers must conform in order to work with Microsoft network operating systems. NDIS provides a many-to-many binding between network adapter drivers and transport protocols. See *transport protocol.*

Network Interface Card (NIC)   A physical layer adapter device that allows a computer to connect to and communicate over a local area network. See *Ethernet.*

network layer   The layer of the OSI model that creates a communication path between two computers via routed packets. Transport protocols implement both the network layer and the transport layer of the OSI stack. IP is a network layer service. See *Internet Protocol, Transport Protocol.*

Network Monitor   A utility used to capture and display network traffic.

Network News Transfer Protocol (NNTP)   A protocol for the transmission of a database of topical message threads between news servers and newsreader clients.

network operating system   A computer operating system specifically designed to optimize a computer's ability to respond to service requests. Servers run network operating systems. Windows NT Server and NetWare are both network operating systems. See *server, Windows NT*.

network security   Security that governs a network. Network security can be set through share permissions. See *security*.

newsgroups   Internet-wide threads of topical discussion implemented using the NNTP protocol. See *Network News Transfer Protocol, Usenet News*.

NNTP   See *Network News Transfer Protocol*.

NWLink   See *Internetwork Packet eXchange*.

object   A software service provider that encapsulates both the algorithm and the data structures necessary to provide a service. Usually, objects can inherit data and functionality from their parent objects, thus allowing complex services to be constructed from simpler objects. The term *object oriented* implies a tight relationship between algorithms and data structures. An object is also a Windows NT resource that may be shared and which has a list of services that user accounts may be permitted or denied access to.

object counters   The containers built into each service object in Windows NT. Object counters store a count of the number of times an object performs its service. You can use performance monitors to access object counters and measure how the different objects in Windows NT are operating. See *object*.

operating system   A collection of services that form a foundation upon which applications run. Operating systems can be simple I/O service providers with a command shell, such as MS-DOS, or they can be sophisticated, preemptive, multitasking, multiprocessing applications platforms like Windows NT. See *kernel, network operating system*.

optimization   An effort to reduce the workload on a hardware component by eliminating, obviating, or reducing the amount of work required of the hardware component through any means. For instance, file caching is an optimization that reduces the workload of a hard disk drive.

Outlook Express   A Microsoft program that sends and receives electronic mail from Internet SMTP and POP mail servers as well as IMAP servers such as Microsoft Exchange. Outlook Express supports file attachments, encrypted mail exchange, and HTML formatted mail, as well as Internet News reading and posting and automated news and mail filtering.

packet filter   A device used to discard undesired network traffic based on its source address, destination address, or the type of data specified by the TCP port number.

packet   A datagram.

password   A secret code used to validate the identity of a user of a secure system. Passwords are used in tandem with account names to log on to most computer systems.

PC   See *personal computer*.

Peer Web Services   Web server software for Windows NT Workstation computers.

peer   A networked computer that both shares resources with other computers and accesses the shared resources of other computers. A non-dedicated server. See *client, server*.

peer-to-peer network   A network that does not have a dedicated server. Individual workstations can share files, printers, and other services. Windows NT setups using the workgroup model are peer-to-peer networks.

Performance Monitor   A utility provided with Windows NT that provides graphical statistics that can be used to measure performance on your computer.

peripheral   An input/output device attached to a computer. Peripherals can be printers, hard disk drives, monitors, etc.

Perl   A scripting language commonly used in CGI scripts to parse user input from Web pages and dynamically create HTML documents. See *scripting languages*.

personal computer (PC)   A microcomputer used by one person at a time (that is, not a multiuser computer). PCs are generally clients or peers in a networked environment. High-speed PCs are called *workstations*. Networks of

PCs are called *LANs*. The term PC is often used to refer to computers compatible with the IBM PC.

Personal Web Server   Web server software for Windows 95 and 98 computers.

PING   A protocol used to check the connected route between two systems on an IP network. Also the name of the utility used to generate PING traffic. See *Internet Protocol*.

plaintext   The message or data in an encryption system to be sent from the sender to the receiver. This is what must be protected from being intercepted and understood. See *cleartext*.

plug-ins   The compiled components that extend the functionality of Web browsers, usually by interpreting specific types of data such as sound or video. See *Web browser*.

Point-to-Point Protocol (PPP)   A network-layer transport that performs over point-to-point network connections such as serial or modem lines. PPP can negotiate any transport protocol used by both systems involved in the link and can automatically assign IP, DNS, and gateway addresses when used with TCP/IP. See *Domain Name Service, gateway, Internet Protocol*.

Point-to-Point Tunneling Protocol (PPTP)   A protocol used to connect to corporate networks through the Internet or an ISP. See *Internet, Internet service provider*.

policies   The general controls that enhance the security of an operating environment.

policy   A specification for your network's approach to security. In Windows NT, policies affect restrictions on password use and rights assignment and determine which events will be recorded in the security log; these can be managed with the User Manager utility, and they specify general security options that apply to all users.

POP   See *Post Office Protocol*.

port   A TCP connection number used to determine which service a specific datagram should be sent to on a host.

Post Office Protocol   A protocol used for offline mail readers to manage the contents of their inbox on a mail server.

PPP   See *Point-to-Point Protocol*.

PPTP   See *Point-to-Point Tunneling Protocol*.

preferences   Characteristics of user accounts, such as the password, profile location, home directory, and logon script.

private key   The key in public key encryption that is kept private.

processor   A circuit designed to automatically perform lists of logical and arithmetic operations. Unlike microprocessors, processors may be designed from discrete components rather than be a monolithic integrated circuit. See *microprocessor*.

program   A list of processor instructions designed to perform a certain function. A running program is called a process. A package of one or more programs and attendant data designed to meet a certain application is called software. See *applications, microprocessor, software*.

protocol   An established communication method that the parties involved understand. Protocols provide a context in which to interpret communicated information. Computer protocols are rules used by communicating devices and software services to format data in a way that all participants understand. See *transport protocol*.

proxy   A service running either on a server or a firewall which receives service requests from clients and then reissues them as if the request originated from the proxy server. This hides the identity of the client and provides the ability to cache often-requested data on the proxy to reduce bandwidth on lower-speed connections to the Internet.

proxy server   A server dedicated to the function of receiving Internet Web requests from clients, retrieving the requested pages, and forwarding them to clients. Proxy servers cache retrieved Web pages to improve performance and reduce bandwidth, and also serve the security function of protecting the identity of internal clients.

PSTN   See *Public Switched Telephone Network*.

public key algorithm   An algorithm in which a different key is used for encryption than for decryption. For this reason, the encryption key can be made public without compromising security because it cannot be used to decrypt the ciphertext.

Public Switched Telephone Network (PSTN)   A global network of interconnected digital and analog communication links originally designed to support voice communication between any two points in the world, but quickly adapted to handle digital data traffic when the computer revolution occurred. In addition to its traditional voice support role, the PSTN now functions as the physical layer of the Internet by providing dial-up and leased lines for the interconnections. POTS (Plain Old Telephone Service) is another common acronym for the PSTN. See *Internet, modem.*

RAM   See *random access memory.*

random access memory (RAM)   Integrated circuits that store digital bits in massive arrays of logical gates or capacitors. RAM is the primary memory store for modern computers, storing all running software processes and contextual data. See *microprocessor.*

Random numbers   A series of numbers that cannot be predicted, even from identical starting conditions. Truly random numbers also satisfy other criteria, such as incompressibility and having an even distribution.

RAS   See *Remote Access Service.*

Receiver   The receptor and decryptor of a message.

Recreational Software Advisory Council   The organization promoting the RASCi content ratings system. RASCi provides for the rating of Web pages according to their content in four areas: language, nudity, sex, and violence.

Registry   A database of settings required and maintained by Windows NT and its components. The Registry contains all of the configuration information used by the applications and services running on the computer. It is stored as a hierarchical structure and is made up of keys, hives, and value entries. You can use the Registry Editor (REGEDT32 command) to change these settings.

Remote Access Service (RAS)   A service that allows network connections to be established over PSTN lines with modems. The computer initiating the connection is called the RAS client; the answering computer is called the RAS host. See *modem, Public Switched Telephone Network*.

remote access   A suite of related technologies that allow the extension of private networks over dial-up circuits.

resource   Any useful service, such as a shared network directory or a printer. See *share*.

roaming user profile   A user profile that is stored on and downloaded from a server. Roaming user profiles allow a user to access their profile from any location on the network. See *user profile*.

route   The list of intermediate systems between two specified end systems.

router   A network layer device that moves packets between networks, usually implemented by specially designed computers optimized for routing packets. Routers provide internetwork connectivity. See *network layer*.

routing   The process of forwarding datagrams among end systems to reach a specified end system.

RSACi   See *Recreational Software Advisory Council*.

script   A list of commands to be executed by an interpreter. Web browsers can be interpreters for scripts embedded in HTML documents. See *Interpreter, scripting language, Web browser*.

scripting language   A specific syntax and structure for commands in scripts. See *Interpreter, script*.

search engine   Web sites dedicated to responding to requests for specific information, searching massive locally stored databases of Web pages, and responding with the URLs of pages that fit the search phrase. See *Universal Resource Locator, World Wide Web*.

Secure Socket Layer (SSL)   An encrypted transmission protocol that uses TCP/IP to implement a secure public key encrypted data channel between a client and a server. See *encryption, Transmission Control Protocol/Internet Protocol*.

security   Measures taken to secure a system against accidental or intentional loss, usually in the form of accountability procedures and use restrictions.

security zones   IE 4 divides network-reachable computers into zones (separate areas that can have different levels of security established for them). The zones set up in IE 4 are: Local Machine, Trusted Sites, Local Intranet, Internet, and Restricted Sites.

sender   The originator and encryptor of a message.

Serial Line Internet Protocol (SLIP)   An implementation of the IP protocol over serial lines. SLIP has been obviated by PPP. See *Internet Protocol, Point-to-Point Protocol.*

serial   A method of communication that transfers data across a medium one bit at a time, usually adding stop, start, and check bits to ensure quality transfer. See *modem.*

server   A computer dedicated to servicing requests for resources from other computers on a network. Servers typically run network operating systems such as Windows NT Server or NetWare. See *client/server, Windows NT.*

service packs   These files contain bug fixes and operating system enhancements for Microsoft operating systems. IE 4 requires Service Pack 3 for Windows NT.

service   A process dedicated to implementing a specific function for other processes. Most Windows NT components are services used by user-level applications.

servlet   A server-side application written in Java.

session layer   The layer of the OSI model dedicated to maintaining a bidirectional communication connection between two computers. The session layer uses the services of the transport layer to provide this service. See *transport layer.*

share   A resource (such as a directory, printer, etc.) shared by a server or a peer on a network. See *peer, resource, server.*

shell   The user interface of an operating system; the shell launches applications and manages file systems.

signing code   Using a digital certificate to digitally sign a CAB or EXE file so that those who download the files can be assured that they have not been tampered with and that the signer is a reputable entity.

silent installation   A silent installation requires the minimum of user input during the installation process. Most or all input is done before the installation using the IEAK or using command-line options. A silent installation places some restrictions on how the custom IE 4 package must be built.

Simple Mail Transfer Protocol (SMTP)   An Internet protocol for transferring mail between Internet hosts. SMTP is often used to upload mail directly from the client to an intermediate host, but can only be used to receive mail by computers constantly connected to the Internet. See *Internet.*

site   A related collection of HTML documents at the same Internet address, usually oriented toward some specific information or purpose. See *Hypertext Markup Language, Internet.*

SLIP   See *Serial Line Internet Protocol.*

SMTP   See *Simple Mail Transfer Protocol.*

snooping   Gathering information about a target network or computer by interrogating the targeted computers.

Software Distribution Channel   An Active Channel established for the automatic distribution of software to computers equipped with IE 4. See *Active Channel.*

software   A suite of programs sold as a unit and dedicated to a specific application. See *applications, program.*

SSL   See *Secure Socket Layer.*

strong password   A password that is difficult to guess. Strong passwords always include punctuation or numbers and are longer than eight characters.

subdirectory   A directory contained in another directory. See *directories.*

subnet   A single broadcast network defined by the fact that no routing need occur for any two computers in the subnet to communicate.

subnet mask   A number mathematically applied to Internet protocol addresses to determine which IP addresses are a part of the same subnetwork as the computer applying the subnet mask. See *Internet Protocol*.

subnetwork   A broadcast network wherein all clients can communicate directly on a shared medium. See *Internetwork, network, subnet*.

surf   To browse the Web randomly looking for interesting information. See *World Wide Web*.

symmetric algorithm   An algorithm in which the same key is used for encryption and decryption.

System Policies   The policies used to control the user's environment and what a user can do. System Policies can be applied to a specific user, group, computer, or all users. See *Registry, System Policy Editor*.

System Policy Editor   A utility found within the Administrative Tools group used to create System Policies. See *System Policies*.

Taskbar   The bar in Windows 95 and NT that contains the Start menu, icons for open windows, a status bar, and (with Windows Desktop Update) a toolbar for quickly launching applications.

TCP/IP   See *Transmission Control Protocol/Internet Protocol*.

TCP   See *Transmission Control Protocol*.

telnet   A terminal application that allows a user to log into a multi-user UNIX computer from any computer connected to the Internet. See *Internet*.

TFTP   See *Trivial File Transfer Protocol*.

thin client   A computer designed to remotely control a user session on a more powerful multi-user computer.

throughput   The measure of information flow through a system in a specific time frame, usually one second. For instance, 28.8Kbps is the throughput of a modem: 28.8 kilobits per second can be transmitted.

time-to-live indicator   A metric used to determine when a packet should be discarded.

Transmission Control Protocol (TCP)   A transport layer protocol that implements guaranteed packet delivery using the Internet Protocol (IP). See *Internet Protocol, Transmission Control Protocol/Internet Protocol.*

Transmission Control Protocol/Internet Protocol (TCP/IP)   A suite of Internet protocols upon which the global Internet is based. TCP/IP is a general term that can refer either to the TCP and IP protocols used together or to the complete set of Internet protocols. TCP/IP is the default protocol for Windows NT.

transport layer   The OSI model layer responsible for the guaranteed serial delivery of packets between two computers over an internetwork. TCP is the transport layer protocol for the TCP/IP transport protocol.

transport protocol   A service that delivers discreet packets of information between any two computers in a network. Higher-level connection-oriented services are built upon transport protocols. See *Internet, Internet Protocol, Transmission Control Protocol, Transmission Control Protocol/Internet Protocol, transport layer.*

Trivial File Transport Protocol (TFTP)   A simple file transport protocol often used during the booting of diskless workstations. FTP is more robust and therefore more common. See *File Transfer Protocol.*

Trojan horse   A malicious software program (or an attachment to another benign program) designed to look harmless in order to entice a user to install it. Once installed, the Trojan horse software opens a vector for further attack, such as answering the modem or listening on a TCP/IP port and vectoring inbound data to the console.

trust   A relationship between domains that allows users of one to access the other without separate authentication.

UDP   See *User Datagram Protocol.*

Uniform Resource Locator (URL)   An Internet standard naming convention for identifying resources available via various TCP/IP application protocols. For example, `http://www.microsoft.com` is the URL for Microsoft's World Wide Web server site, while `ftp://gateway.dec.com` is a popular FTP site. A URL allows easy hypertext references to a particular resource from within a document or mail message. See *Hypertext Transport Protocol, World Wide Web.*

UNIX A multitasking, kernel-based operating system developed at AT&T in the early 1970s and provided (originally) free to universities as a research operating system. Because of its availability and ability to scale down to microprocessor-based computers, Unix became the standard operating system of the Internet and its attendant network protocols and is the closest approximation to a universal operating system that exists. Most computers can run some variant of the Unix operating system. See *Internet, multitasking*.

Usenet News A distributed news database implemented on NNTP and divided into topical discussion threads called *newsgroups* that are distributed among news servers. Clients using newsreaders can subscribe to specific newsgroups and have them automatically downloaded when they open their newsreader.

User Agent string A string built into a custom IE 4 Web browser by the IEAK. The browser will provide the User Agent string to Web servers to identify the custom version of IE 4.

User Datagram Protocol (UDP) A non-guaranteed network packet protocol implemented on IP that is far faster than TCP because of its lack of flow-control overhead. UDP can be implemented as a reliable transport when some higher-level protocol (such as NetBIOS) exists to make sure that required data will eventually be retransmitted in local area environments. At the transport layer of the OSI model, UDP is a connectionless service and TCP is a connection-oriented service. See *Transmission Control Protocol*.

User Manager for Domains A Windows NT application that administers user accounts, groups, and security policies at the domain level.

username A user's account name in a logon-authenticated system. See *security*.

user profile A storage location for the user's Desktop configuration. See *roaming profile*.

VBScript A variant of Visual Basic used as a scripting language in Internet Explorer and Active Server Pages. See *scripting language*.

Virtual Machine   A fictitious machine language that can be interpreted on a number of actual machines. Programs compiled to the Virtual Machine specification can then be run on any computer that can interpret that Virtual Machine specification. See *Java*.

virtual memory   A kernel service that stores memory pages not currently in use on a mass storage device to free up the memory occupied for other uses. Virtual memory hides the memory-swapping process from applications and higher-level services. See *kernel*.

Virtual Reality Modeling Language (VRML)   A syntax that describes the position of three-dimensional objects in a space, which can be transmitted from a server to a client and rendered on the client.

virus   A malicious program that copies itself between computers and occasionally damages data. Viruses can infect disk boot sectors, executable files, and documents in applications (such as Microsoft Word) that support macro languages.

WAN   See *wide area network*.

weak password   A password that is easy to guess, such as a word or number relating to the account holder, a single letter, or words appearing in a word processor's spell-check dictionary.

Web browser   An application that makes HTTP requests and formats the resulting HTML documents for users. The preeminent Internet client, most Web browsers understand all standard Internet protocols and scripting languages. See *Hypertext Markup Language, Hypertext Transfer Protocol, Internet*.

Web page   Any HTML document on an HTTP server. See *Hypertext Markup Language, Hypertext Transfer Protocol, Internet*.

Web View   Directory windows and special windows (such as the Control Panel, My Computer, and Printers windows) that are displayed like Web pages and may include HTML formatting. See *HTT*.

well-known ports   Common port assignments for services that listen for public connections. Well-known ports are used when no prior information about how to connect to a specific host is known.

Wide Area Information Service (WAIS)   An Internet-based distributed database connection protocol that allows the simultaneous query of multiple separate databases.

wide area network (WAN)   A geographically dispersed network of networks that is connected by routers and communication links. The Internet is the largest WAN. See *Internet, local area network*.

Windows 3.11 for Workgroups   The current 16-bit version of Windows for less-powerful, Intel-based personal computers; this system includes peer networking services.

Windows 95   The current 32-bit version of Microsoft Windows for medium-range, Intel-based personal computers; this system includes peer networking services, Internet support, and strong support for older DOS applications and peripherals.

Windows Desktop Update   This feature of IE 4 extends the Windows NT and Windows 95 operating systems to support Active Desktop. See *Active Desktop*.

Windows Internet Name Service (WINS)   A network service for Microsoft networks that provides Windows computers with Internet numbers for specified NetBIOS names, facilitating browsing and intercommunication over TCP/IP networks.

Windows NT   The current 32-bit version of Microsoft Windows for powerful Intel, Alpha, PowerPC, or MIPS-based computers; the system includes peer networking services, server networking services, Internet client and server services, and a broad range of utilities.

Windows Sockets   An interprocess communications protocol that delivers connection-oriented data streams used by Internet software and software ported from UNIX environments.

workstation   A powerful personal computer that usually runs a preemptive, multitasking operating system like UNIX or Windows NT.

World Wide Web (WWW)   A collection of Internet servers providing hypertext-formatted documents for Internet clients running Web browsers. The World Wide Web provided the first easy-to-use graphical interface for the Internet and is largely responsible for the Internet's explosive growth.

WWW   See *World Wide Web*.

APPENDIX

C

System Policies

Before you begin your tour through the possible policy settings, you should understand that you don't necessarily have to use *all* of the settings available to you. Many of the settings won't make your network any more secure—some just make the administrator's job easier when there are large numbers of computers and computer users. You should just select the policies that fit the specific circumstances of your network, and leave the default settings for the rest.

Working with IE 4 System Policy Settings

The two tools most often used to set Internet Explorer 4 System Policy settings are the IEAK Profile Manger and the IEAK Wizard. When you make changes to the System Policy using these tools, the settings are stored in INS and INF files that either are included in a custom IE 4 package or can be placed in a Web location for the IE 4 autoconfiguration mechanism of the installed IE 4 browsers to access. You can also use the System Policy Editor of Windows NT to import the IE 4 policy settings (by importing the ADM files that contain the settings) and create Windows 95 or Windows NT policy files (that have the POL extension). The policy files do not use the IE 4 autoconfiguration mechanism to update operating system settings. Instead, the policy files must be placed in a location where the computers can access them when logging on to a Windows network.

The Internet Explorer 4 System Policy settings are arranged in seven areas (more if you import other ADM files):

- Microsoft Chat
- Microsoft NetMeeting

- Internet Restrictions
- Internet Settings
- Outlook Express
- Web Desktop
- Subscriptions

Microsoft Chat

Microsoft Chat isn't a very complicated program, so there isn't much you will want to lock-down for this program. For the convenience of your users or customers, you may want to set the default chat server and default chat room to point to your own chat server and room.

Change Chat Server List   This is a semicolon separated list of the Internet names of chat servers.

Change Default Chat Server   This is the chat server that Microsoft Chat will connect to by default. The value in this field should be an Internet name and port number (if other than the default port).

Change Default Chat Room   This is the name of the chat room that Microsoft Chat will go to by default (on the default chat server) when it launches.

Change Default Character   For Comic Chat, this is the character that Microsoft Chat will use.

Change Default Backdrop Bitmap   This is the default background scene that Microsoft Chat will use in Comic Chat mode.

Change User's Profile for Microsoft Chat   In this field, you can enter a default user profile that will be displayed when other chat users query for information about the user.

Turn On Option to Show Only Registered Rooms in Room List   This option restricts users of Microsoft to only those chat rooms that have been registered (i.e. authorized) in the chat server.

Microsoft NetMeeting

NetMeeting is a bit more complicated than Microsoft Chat, and the System Policies reflect the increased complexity. The policy items are divided into two sections: NetMeeting Settings (which is extensive) and NetMeeting Protocols (which is limited).

Administrators may want to establish policies for NetMeeting with one of two goals in mind: restricting bandwidth use or enhancing network security. Administrators who want to restrict network bandwidth use by NetMeeting users may disable application sharing, restrict audio conferencing, and/or restrict video conferencing. (Rather than disabling audio and video, a network administrator may simply set a limit on the bandwidth to be used by NetMeeting for audio and video conferencing.)

An administrator concerned about network security may restrict the use of application sharing, restrict clipboard sharing, disable file downloading, and prevent the user from sharing the Desktop Explorer. In addition, the administrator may disable the NetMeeting protocols by disabling TCP/IP (if null modems are used for most conferencing) or disabling the null modems (if just TCP/IP is used).

NetMeeting Settings

The settings section of NetMeeting System Policies concerns the operation of the NetMeeting program, including features restrictions and settings defaults.

Restrict the Use of File Transfer   An administrator concerned about users downloading viruses or exporting confidential documents may want to restrict file transfer. The administrator can:

- Prevent the user from sending files

- Prevent the user from receiving files

Restrict the Use of Application Sharing   Application sharing allows two users to manipulate the same program (such as Microsoft Word or Excel) that has been written to take advantage of application sharing. This can pose a security threat because it allows another user elsewhere on the Internet to command the local computer to execute programs. Similarly, when you share Desktop Explorer windows, you are permitting strangers to access and control your computer's operating system. Application sharing policies include:

- Disable all application sharing
- Prevent the user from sharing the clipboard
- Prevent the user from sharing MS-DOS windows
- Prevent the user from sharing Explorer windows
- Prevent the user from collaborating

Restrict the Use of the Options Dialog   The administrator of a public-access computing lab or a general-use computer may not want the users changing NetMeeting program settings. The following settings disable the user's ability to change settings in various NetMeeting windows:

- Disable the "General" options page
- Disable the "My Information" options page
- Disable the "Calling" options page
- Disable the "Audio" options page
- Disable the "Video" options page
- Disable the "Protocols" options page
- Prevent the user from answering calls
- Prevent the user from using audio features

Restrict the Use of Video   NetMeeting videoconferencing can soak up any available network bandwidth. The first two options disable this Net-Meeting feature. The third policy setting prohibits NetMeeting from connecting to LDAP directory servers to establish conference sessions. The following settings are available to restrict video use:

- Prevent the user from sending video
- Prevent the user from receiving video
- Prevent the user from using directory services

Set the Default Directory Server   If your organization has its own directory server you may want to enter its Internet name.

Set Exchange Server Property for NetMeeting Address   This setting enables NetMeeting call setup to interoperate with Exchange Server on your LAN.

Preset User Information Category   This is the user profile data that is shown by default for NetMeeting users until the users enter their own information.

Set the NetMeeting Home Page URL   This is the default home page for NetMeeting.

Set Limit for Audio/Video Throughput   This feature allows audio and videoconferencing but prohibits the conferencing from exceeding a preset limit for bandwidth use.

NetMeeting Protocols

These two NetMeeting policy settings are primarily of interest for computers that have both serial connections and TCP/IP Internet connections.

Disable TCP/IP   If you are using NetMeeting for videoconferencing over dedicated serial connections (using the Null Modem feature), you might want to disable TCP/IP so that network intruders don't attempt to exploit the NetMeeting ports and so that users don't try to make conference calls to unauthorized locations.

Disable Null Modem   If conferencing only happens over TCP/IP, you might want to disable the Null Modem feature.

Internet Restrictions

The Internet Restrictions portion of the system policies concern Internet Explorer 4's use of HTTP and the operation of Internet Explorer 4 on the Windows operating system. Within Internet Restrictions are nine sections: General, Security, Content, Connection, Programs, Advanced, Code Download, User Profiles, and Channels Settings.

General

If you want to restrict which features of Internet Explorer 4 the user can change (if the computer is a general-use PC or one of the computers in a public-access lab, for example), you might want to select several (or all) of the following policy restrictions:

- Disable changing home page settings
- Disable changing cache settings
- Disable changing history settings
- Disable changing color settings
- Disable changing link color settings
- Disable changing font settings
- Disable changing language settings
- Disable changing accessibility settings

Security

The following settings are appropriate when the user cannot be trusted to abide by the organization's security policy (in public-access computer labs, for example). Users may attempt to circumvent security restrictions by changing the policies for security zones or adding or removing computers from security zones. You can remove the temptation by selecting the following:

- Use ONLY machine settings for security zones
- Do not allow users to change policies for any security zone
- Do not allow users to add/delete sites from a security zone

Content

As with the Security Policies, computer users may attempt to circumvent ratings restrictions by changing the content ratings settings of the installed Internet Explorer 4 browser. Automatic tracking of credit card numbers and payment information is seldom appropriate for general use computers, so you may want to disable Microsoft Wallet for these computers. You can lock-down the settings by selecting the following:

- Disable changing ratings settings

- Disable changing certificate settings

- Disable changing Profile Assistant settings

- Disable changing Microsoft Wallet settings

Connection

For computers on a LAN, you may want to disable the Connection Wizard and keep users from changing connection settings. You can still administer these settings using Automatic Configuration (INS files). Users' changes to network settings often make centralized network management more difficult. You have the following options:

- Disable calling Connection Wizard

- Disable changing connection settings

- Disable changing proxy settings

- Disable changing Automatic Configuration settings

Programs

Within Internet Explorer 4, the Messaging, Calendar, and Contact settings configure which programs are launched for mail, calendar, and contact data. If you don't want users to change these settings, they can be locked-down. IE 4 will check to see if it is the default Web browser unless you disable that feature. You have the following options:

- Disable changing Messaging settings

- Disable changing Calendar and Contact settings

- Disable changing checking if Internet Explorer is the default browser

Advanced

The Advanced tab gives the user the ability to change many settings configured in the IEAK Wizard, the IEAK Profile Manger, or in other tabs of Internet Explorer 4. You can prevent users from changing those settings by selecting this policy option:

- Disable changing settings on Advanced tab

Code Download

The only software distribution channel built in to Internet Explorer 4 by default is for IE 4 itself. If you enable this channel, IE 4 users will be notified of updates to IE 4. IE 4 will look for updates in the following path.

Path   This is the path (Internet URL) that Internet Explorer will use to download updates to Internet Explorer 4 and components.

User Profiles

Roaming profiles can wreak havoc when the user routinely uses dissimilar computers (computers who's hardware or software configuration require different settings in a user's profile). Also, when items such as favorites and Start menu items are included in the profiles, the download time and bandwidth used to move the profiles can be considerable. You can disable the roaming profile cache with the following option:

- Disable Roaming Cache

Channels Settings

Not every network administrator appreciates the Active Channels and site subscriptions feature of Internet Explorer 4. Active Channels and site subscriptions can complicate the administration of IE 4 and can monopolize network bandwidth if they are improperly used. The Channels Settings portion of the IEAK allows you to disable this feature or restrict users from changing Active Channels and site subscriptions settings, including settings involving subscribing to channels and sites, automated dialing, scheduling, and establishing schedule groups (custom times for retrieving new content other than the default daily, weekly, and monthly schedules). You have the following options for restricting Active Channel Settings:

- Disable Channel UI
- Disable adding and subscribing to channels
- Disable editing channel properties and channel subscriptions
- Disable removing channels and subscriptions to channels
- Disable adding site subscriptions
- Disable editing site subscriptions

- Disable removing site subscriptions

- Disable channel logging

- Disable Update Now and Update All for channels and subscriptions

- Disable all scheduled channel and site subscriptions

- Disable unattended dialing by subscriptions

- Disable password caching for channel and site subscriptions

- Disable downloading of channel subscription (content-notification will still work)

- Disable downloading of channel subscription (content-change notification will still work)

- Disable editing of and creating schedule groups

Internet Settings

The Internet Settings portion of the Internet Explorer 4 System Policies governs how IE 4 displays HTML information, how it uses a modem, how it interacts with other programs, and how miscellaneous IE 4 features (such as Autocomplete and the Java JIT compiler) operate. This portion is divided into the following six sections: Colors, Fonts, Languages, Modem Settings, Programs, and Advanced Settings.

Colors

By default, different parts of a Web page have different colors. Any particular Web page can override the default settings, but when a Web page does not specify the color of the background or the color of a hyperlink, Internet Explorer 4 draws it in the default color specified here.

General Colors   You can specify the background and text colors for displaying textual information (choose colors that contrast!) or use Windows colors. You have the following options for setting default general colors:

- Background color

- Text color

- Use Windows colors

Link Colors Hyperlinks (text or graphics areas on a Web page that direct the Web browser to another area) are indicated by an underline and by different colored text than the surrounding text. You can specify the color for hyperlinks that have not been visited as well as hyperlinks that already reside in that browser's history folder. Also (if you so specify) Internet Explorer 4 will highlight whichever link the cursor is on with a different color. You have the following options for setting link colors:

- Link color
- Visited link color
- Use hover color
- Hover color

Fonts

You can specify the font that Internet Explorer 4 will use by default for HTML pages (when a different font is not specified by the HTML page).

Western Proportional Font Times New Roman is the default font.

Western Fixed Font Courier New is the default font.

Languages

Internet Explorer 4 can show Web pages in a variety of languages, but IE 4 itself must be prepared for a particular language—the language the menus, windows, etc. will be displayed in. You can determine which language will be the default language for IE 4.

Choose the Default Language Preference(s) The most common default is English (United States).

Modem Settings

The vast majority of home users of Internet Explorer 4 connect to the Internet via a modem. IE 4 will automatically dial the modem to connect to an ISP when the user opens IE 4. This section controls how IE 4 (using the Internet Connection Manager) makes the connection.

Connection Type This option can be PPP, SLIP, or a null modem connection.

Enable Autodialing   If you want the computer to automatically start dialing, enable this option. Otherwise, the user will have to tell the computer to start dialing.

Number of Times to Attempt Connection   The Internet Connection Manager can be configured to retry the connection before giving up. This feature is helpful for ISPs that often have busy phones.

Number of Seconds to Wait between Attempts   The Internet Connection Manager will wait the set amount of time before retrying the connection.

Connect without User Intervention   Enabling this option allows the computer to log on automatically. Otherwise the user is required to initiate the logon attempt.

Disconnect if Idle After Specified Number of Minutes   When the user is paying for the connection by the minute, or when long-distance rates are in effect, the user may appreciate the computer disconnecting if left alone for a period of time.

Minutes to Wait Before Disconnecting   This is the number of minutes the Internet Connection Wizard will remain idle before disconnecting.

Perform Security Check Before Dialing   This option checks Internet security before dialing.

Programs

Internet Explorer 4 is primarily used for browsing the Web. Other specialized tools do a better job of keeping track of appointments, storing phone numbers, and videoconferencing. For these tasks, IE 4 launches another program. The following three settings are the default programs that IE 4 will launch for scheduling, contact information, and conferencing.

Program to Use for Calendar   There is no default.

Program to Use for Contacts   Address Book is the default program.

Program to Use for Internet Call   Microsoft NetMeeting is the default program.

Advanced Settings

This section of Internet Explorer 4 System Policies settings contains a grab bag of configuration options for various features of IE 4.

Browsing   These options govern how Internet Explorer 4 displays pages to the user. The only network performance setting that an administrator may be concerned about is Enable Scheduled Subscription Updates; you may not want to enable this if bandwidth is at a premium in your network. The other settings (the debugger, the screen mode, smooth scrolling and page transitions) all make the browser nicer to use on a fast computer but may degrade performance on a slower computer. They do not, however, impact network performance or security. You have the following options for changing the default browsing behavior:

- Disable script debugger
- Launch channels in full screen mode
- Launch browser in full screen mode
- Use autocomplete
- Show friendly URLs
- Enable smooth scrolling
- Enable page transitions
- Browse in a new process
- Enable page hit counting
- Enable scheduled subscription updates
- Underline links (always, never, hover)

Multimedia   These settings govern how Internet Explorer 4 presents non-textual data (i.e. pictures, animation, and sound). You may want to disable pictures if the network link is extremely slow. Smart image dithering will enhance a picture that is downloaded in a resolution that the video card does not support; this takes more processing power but does not take up more networking bandwidth. The five multimedia policy options are as follows:

- Show pictures
- Play animations

- Play videos

- Play sounds

- Smart image dithering

Security   You can configure Internet Explorer 4 to be relaxed or strict about security. In a computer that is used by several people, you might like IE 4 to delete cached pages so that the next user can't search the hard drive and see what the previous person has been viewing. Warnings about redirected forms (perhaps going to a different Web server without your knowledge), changing security modes, and cookie use can enhance security. You have the following options for browser security settings:

- Enable Profile Assistant

- Delete saved pages when browser closes

- Do not save encrypted pages

- Warn if forms submit is being redirected

- Warn if changing between secure and insecure mode

- Cookies (always accept cookies, prompt before accepting cookies, disable all cookie use)

Java VM   The JIT compiler makes Java run faster but requires more memory. Java logging enhances security and enables debugging, but it slows down Java execution and requires more memory and more hard drive space. Your two options for the Java VM are as follows:

- JIT compiler enabled

- Java logging enabled

Printing   The background image (which is often just there to be pleasing to the eye) can drastically slow down Web page printing and can use up expensive colored ink in ink-jet printers. You can disable printing the background colors and images in HTML pages. You have only the following option for configuring printing:

- Print background colors and images

Searching   Internet Explorer 4 allows you to turn off the autocomplete feature and prompt about searching when the first attempt to connect to the site fails. The following options are available to configure how Internet Explorer 4 will perform searches:

- Autoscan common root domains

- Search when URL fails (always search, always ask, never search)

Toolbars   Internet Explorer 4 gives you the option of showing the toolbar using smaller fonts (which gives you more screen space for HTML pages) and showing the font button, with which you can change the font size of displayed HTML pages. You have the following two options to configure the appearance of the toolbar:

- Show font button

- Small icons

HTTP 1.1 Settings   HTTP 1.1 improves on the HTTP 1.0 standard for Web page transmission by allowing resumed downloading of interrupted files, enabling the PUT command to place Web pages on Web servers, and recognizing time validity information in Web pages. You have the following options for configuring HTTP protocol use:

- Use HTTP 1.1

- Use HTTP 1.1 through proxy connections

Outlook Express

Outlook Express is less complex than Internet Explorer or NetMeeting. All it does is allow you to read and send e-mail and Internet News messages. Therefore, the system policies for Outlook Express are less detailed than those for Internet Explorer 4 and NetMeeting and have only two sections: General Settings and View Customization.

General Settings

The General Settings for Outlook Express allow you to specify the security zones for mail and news server connections and the default form of a mail or news message.

Mail and News Security Zones   By placing the mail and news servers in the Restricted Sites zone instead of the Internet zone, you acknowledge the fact that mail and news sites are popular targets for network intruders, and therefore are an indirect risk to your computers and your network. You have only the following option for configuring Mail and News security zones:

- Put mail and news in the Restricted Sites zone instead of the Internet zone

HTML Mail and News Composition Settings You can specify for mail and for news that the default form of the message be either plain text or HTML text, which can include text formatting (fonts, colors, bold, underline, etc.) and graphics. You have the following options:

- **Mail** Make a plain text message composition the default for mail messages (instead of HTML mail)

- **News** Make an HTML message composition the default for news posts (instead of plain text)

View Customization: Folder and Message Navigational Elements

The four View Customization options for Outlook Express all deal with how the folders and navigational features of Outlook Express are presented to the user. The options are the following:

- Turn on Outlook Bar

- Turn off Folder List (tree view of folders)

- Turn on Folder Bar (horizontal line that displays the selected folder's name)

- Turn off Tip of the Day

Web Desktop

In Internet Explorer 4, the Internet browser technology has been extended into the Windows operating system in the form of the Windows Desktop Update. You can lock-down the settings for sections of the WDU in the Web Desktop portion of the System Policies. There are six sections to the Web Desktop portion: Desktop, Start menu, Shell, Printers, and System.

Many of the settings in the Web Desktop portion of the System Policy settings for Internet Explorer 4 duplicate settings you can import from the

Windows 95 or Windows NT ADM files. You can see the duplicates by selecting Tools ➤ Show Duplicates in the IEAK Wizard or the IEAK Profile Manager after importing the operating system ADM file.

Desktop

The Desktop section controls what users can change about the Active Desktop (the background image or HTML, icons on the desktop, and toolbars on the desktop).

Desktop Restrictions   The following options allow you to turn off Active Desktop, lock-down all desktop settings, and hide some or all of the items on the desktop (including Internet Explorer and Network Neighborhood):

- Disable Active Desktop

- Do not allow changes to Active Desktop

- Hide Internet Explorer icon

- Hide Network Neighborhood icon

- Hide all items on desktop

Active Desktop Items   Internet Explorer 4 allows you to place HTML-coded Web items on the Active Desktop. You may want to keep users from changing how the Active Desktop items you have installed are arranged. You have the following options:

- Disable adding ANY desktop items

- Disable deleting ANY desktop items

- Disable editing ANY desktop items

- Disable closing ANY desktop items

Desktop Wallpaper Settings   The entire background of the desktop can also be specified to use HTML, and you can disallow this feature and/or keep users from changing their wallpaper settings. You have the following options:

- Disable selecting HTML as wallpaper

- Disable changing wallpaper

Desktop Toolbars Settings   In order to maintain a consistent environment for your users, you may want to keep them from changing or resizing the toolbars on the Active Desktop. You have the following options:

- Disable adding new toolbars

- Disable resizing ALL toolbars

Start Menu

The Windows Desktop Update extends Internet Explorer into the Windows Start menu. If you prefer a more "classical" look to your Windows desktop, you can use system policies to remove some or all of these extensions to the Start menu. You can also keep users from being able to change the Start menu. You can even remove the Shutdown and Logoff options of the Start menu. You have the following options:

- Remove Favorites menu from Start menu

- Remove Find menu from Start menu

- Remove Run menu from Start menu

- Remove the Active Desktop item from the Settings menu

- Disable Drag and Drop context menus on the Start menu

- Remove the Folder Options menu item from the Settings menu

- Remove Documents menu from Start menu

- Do not keep the history of recently opened documents

- Clear the history of recently opened documents

- Disable logoff

- Disable the Shut Down command

- Disable changes to Printers and Control Panel Settings

- Disable changes to the Taskbar and Start Menu Settings

- Disable the context menu for the Taskbar

- Hide the custom Programs folders

- Remove the Windows Update item from the Settings menu (Windows 98 only)

Shell

The Shell options of Internet Explorer 4 System Policies (duplicated in the Windows operating system policies described later) are most appropriate for computers that will be used for a single purpose—for example, as a public-access Web terminal where the user is not allowed to run programs other than IE 4. On a single-purpose computer you may not want users to be able to use the File menu to access arbitrary files in the computer, copy files to floppy disks, or change network connections on the computer. You have the following options:

- Disable File menu in Shell folders
- Disable context menu in Shell folders
- Only allow approved Shell extensions
- Do not track Shell shortcuts during roaming
- Hide Floppy Drives in My Computer
- Disable net connections/disconnections

Printers

If you don't want users to change how their printers are set up, you can keep them from adding or removing printers. You have the following options:

- Disable deletion of printers
- Disable addition of printers

System

For the truly draconian network administrator, the System Policies allow you to list which programs are OK for the user to run. The user can be kept from rebooting in MS-DOS mode (where, of course, no Windows system policies will apply). You have the following options:

- Run only specified Windows applications
- Do not allow computer to restart in MS-DOS mode (Windows 95 only)

Subscriptions

The Subscriptions portion of the Internet Explorer 4 System Policies (which has just one section called, imaginatively, Subscriptions) let you control how much bandwidth Active Channels, Site Subscriptions, and Software Update Channels take up in your network. These settings are not as useful for computers that are isolated and connect to an ISP via a dial-up modem; they are most useful when a number of computers in a LAN can swamp the available bandwidth of the LAN's Internet connection with subscription updates.

Maximum KB of Site Subscription   This setting limits how much data may be downloaded from a single Web site that is *not* defined by an Active Channel (CDF) file.

Maximum KB of Channel Subscription   This setting limits how much data may be downloaded from a single Web site that *is* defined by an Active Channel (CDF) file.

Maximum Number of Site Subscriptions That Can Be Installed   This places a maximum limit on how many Web sites a user may keep track of (and, combined with the previous two settings, how much bandwidth the user may soak up).

Maximum Number of Minutes between Scheduled Subscription Updates   Frequent polling of a Web site for new data can overload a network, so you can use this option to spread out update times to allow other network traffic.

Beginning of Range in which to Exclude Scheduled Subscription Updates   This is the beginning of a subscription-free time zone measured in minutes from midnight. This and the following setting are the most effective ways to keep a network free of subscription traffic during office hours.

End of Range in Which to Exclude Scheduled Subscription Updates
This is the end of the subscription-free time zone measured in minutes from midnight.

Maximum Site Subscription Crawl Depth   This option restricts how many links Internet Explorer 4 will follow when retrieving Web site pages from a URL.

Working with Windows NT Computer System Policy Settings

If you import Windows NT ADM files into the IEAK Wizard or IEAK Profile Manager, you have many more settings to work with. On the other hand, you may have imported the Internet Explorer 4 ADM files into the System Policy Editor of NT. In either case, you need to know that Windows operating systems break the policies into two sections: computer policy settings and user policy settings. The following sections walk you through each of the options that you can specify using a Windows NT computer policy.

Network: System Policies Update and Remote Update

The Remote Update key governs where the Windows NT operating system will look for the Config.nt file. This is the setting you must change if you store the policy files in a nonstandard location. The settings for this key are as follows.

- **Update mode:** Automatically instructs the operating system to look in the default location for the policy files (the Netlogon share of the PDC). Manual instructs the operating system to look in the location indicated by the path field, below.

- **Path for manual update:** This is the manual location for the policy file. You enter a UNC path here (in the form \\server\share\file.pol).

- **Display error messages:** Instructs the operating system to report if there are errors accessing the policy file.

- **Load balancing:** Allows the operating system to load the policy from a domain controller other than the primary domain controller when the PDC is heavily loaded.

System

This section of the computer policy contains two keys: SNMP, which governs how the network error and status portion of Windows NT interoperates with Internet management tools, and Run, which lists those programs that will run when the computer starts up. The SNMP settings govern who may access the SNMP component for administration, and the Run settings activate security software that must start when the system starts.

SNMP

SNMP stands for Simple Network Management Protocol, and it is how devices based on Internet technology (including file servers and clients that use TCP/IP) report error conditions and their operational status. The SNMP service must be installed for you to use this option in your computer.

Communities   SNMP devices can be organized into communities, which may be administered as a group. The Communities button allows you to add entries for the SNMP communities that this computer will join.

Permitted Managers   You can restrict who can manage the SNMP service. The Permitted Managers button presents you with a list that you may add managers to.

Traps for Public Community   You may elect not to configure the SNMP service as part of a community. The Public Community list identifies recipients of trap messages in this case. Click the Trap Configuration button to edit the list of destinations for trap messages when communities are not in effect for this computer.

Run

This key lists the programs that the computer will run when it starts up. The programs you add to the list can perform almost any security or administrative function, from scanning for viruses to resetting the contents of the hard drive to a preset state. Click the Items to Run at Startup button to edit the list of programs that will start automatically when the operating system starts.

Windows NT Network: Sharing

The following two keys control hidden shares in Windows NT. The hidden drive shares make it easier for administrators to connect to and manipulate the hard drive partitions of Windows NT computers—but hackers target hidden shares.

Create Hidden Drive Shares (Workstation)   Selecting this option instructs Windows NT Workstation computers to create the C\$, D\$, and other volume hidden shares, as well as the admin\$ hidden share. Clearing this option inhibits the creation of these shares.

Create Hidden Drive Shares (Server)   Selecting this option instructs Windows NT Server computers to create the C\$, D\$, and other volume hidden shares, as well as the admin\$ hidden share. Clearing this option inhibits the creation of these shares.

Windows NT Printers

The Security Policy Editor has three options for printers, only one of which has an impact on network security (the Disable Browse Thread option).

Disable Browse Thread on This Computer   Checking this option instructs the computer not to inform network browsers of the existence of printers that are connected to this computer. In order for other computers to print to a printer on this computer you must type the UNC path to the printer directly rather than selecting it from a browse list. The security risk of a browsable printer is minimal—you should only enable this option if you are concerned about misuse of the printers connected to the computer.

Scheduler Priority   This option affects the performance of the print service, not the security of your computer or your network. You can set the print scheduler priority to above normal (enhancing printing speed at the cost of application performance) or below normal (enhancing application performance at the expense of printing speed).

Beep for Error Enabled   By checking this option you instruct the computer to beep every 10 seconds while there is an error on a print server.

Windows NT Remote Access

The first option in this section of the computer policy tree directly affects the security of your network; the other two are optimization settings. You will want to evaluate these options for each of the computers that have the Remote Access Service installed.

Maximum Number of Unsuccessful Authentication Retries This is the number of times a caller can attempt to type a user name and password. It is important to have a low number of retries, because a common network attack is to guess passwords. When the attacker must dial your RAS server repeatedly, the attack will take longer and you are more likely to discover that your RAS server is under attack.

The number of retries defaults to two, which allows three total attempts to log on per connection.

Maximum Time Limit for Authentication This setting tells the operating system how long to wait for the user to type in a user name and password. The user is given two minutes by default. You may want to reduce this setting if your modems are in frequent use. The Length in Seconds defaults to 120.

Wait Interval for Callback This is how long the RAS server will wait before calling back an RAS client that has callback enabled (callback enhances security by requiring that the client computer be at a specified phone number). You might extend the interval if your modem line takes a while to reset; you might reduce it if your system will support it. Length in Seconds defaults to two.

Auto Disconnect This feature keeps users from monopolizing the RAS connections—after a set number of minutes you can have RAS automatically drop the connection. This feature does not enhance the security of your network. Disconnect After (Minutes) has no default setting.

Windows NT Shell: Custom Shared Folders

With the System Policy Editor you can customize the locations of Desktop components in your Windows NT computers. Changing these settings will not significantly increase the security of your network.

Custom Shared Programs Folder Path to the location of shared Programs items—the default is `%SystemRoot\Profiles\All Users\Start Menu\Programs`.

Custom Shared Desktop Icons Path to the location of shared Desktop icons. The default is `%SystemRoot\Profiles\All Users\Desktop`.

Custom Shared Start Menu   Path to the location of shared Start menu items. The default is `%SystemRoot\Profiles\All Users\Start Menu`.

Custom Shared Startup Folder   Path to the location of shared Startup items. The default is `%SystemRoot\Profiles\All Users\Start Menu\ Programs\Startup`.

Windows NT System

The Windows NT System section allows you to modify some aspects of logging on to Windows NT and some details of file system behavior. Of these configuration settings, displaying the logged-on user name is the most pertinent to computer security. The other settings are more appropriate for optimizing the performance of your Windows NT computer at the expense of compatibility with older programs.

Logon

Logon characteristics you can modify include the banner, the authentication dialog box, and how scripts are run, as follows.

Logon Banner   The purpose of this setting is to inform users of the proper use of computers in your network when they log on. You can include legal warnings, computer-use assignments, or organization identification in the logon banner text. You can customize the following.

- **Caption**: This field contains what will be shown in the banner title.

- **Text**: This is the body of the message that will be displayed to the user when they log on.

Enable Shutdown from Authentication Dialog Box   It may appear that a shutdown option in the logon box reduces security because anyone can select it, but think about it. Anyone can also simply turn off the computer or unplug it. A methodical shutdown, even from the logon window, is much safer for the data stored on the computer than just turning the computer off.

Do Not Display Last Logged On User Name   Enabling this option increases security in your network because one objective of network intruders is to collect valid user names. The convenience of not having to type your user name in again if you used the computer last is not worth the security risk.

Run Logon Scripts Synchronously Enabling this option increases compatibility at the expense of performance. It does not measurably enhance security.

File System

The three file system options primarily enhance the performance of your system at the expense of older programs that expect a file system to conform to the restrictions of older versions of MS-DOS. You should only enable these options if you are sure that your older programs will work properly in the new environment.

Do Not Create 8.3 File Names for Long File Names Older programs often expect file names to have no more than eight letters in the name with an extension of just three letters. Windows 95 and Windows NT both allow you to have file names up to 254 characters in length. If this option is disabled, Windows NT must maintain two file names—a longer one for new programs and a shorter one for older programs. Enabling this option causes Windows NT to respond only to the longer file names.

Allow Extended Characters in 8.3 File Names File names in MS-DOS and Windows are limited to a subset of the ASCII characters. Windows NT supports a much wider range of characters, encoded in UNICODE. Selecting this option enables the use of UNICODE characters in older 8.3 file names.

Do Not Update Last Access Time In comparison with the other two file system options, enabling this option will give you the greatest performance gain. By default, after every access, even a read access, NTFS will update the time of the last access for the file. This update takes a considerable amount of time. High security environments should leave this setting enabled.

Windows NT User Profiles

The User Profile options primarily increase the performance of Windows NT when the user is logging on to a network file server over a slow network link. You never know; perhaps some hacker will find a way to exploit cached copies of roaming profiles, so you'll want to delete them.

Delete Cached Copies of Roaming Profiles   Enabling this option will cause the Windows NT client computer to delete the user profile after the user logs off. This saves disk space, especially when there are a large number of users that use the same computer, such as in a college computer lab.

Automatically Detect Slow Network Connections   This option enables the operating system to detect whether or not the logon is occurring over a slow dial-up link or a fast network connection.

Slow Network Connection Timeout   If downloading the profile is taking too long (the timeout has been exceeded) then the download will be canceled and a stored or default profile will be used instead. The time default value is 2000 milliseconds.

Timeout for Dialog Boxes   If the Profile dialog boxes are ignored, the process will proceed without user intervention. The time default is 30 seconds.

Working with Windows 95 Computer Policy Settings

Windows 95 is a different operating system internally than Windows NT, and the Windows 95 computer policies reflect those differences. Many of the options are similar, however.

There are only two top-level sections, Network and System, and the policy options they allow you to set are as follows.

Network

The Network section of a Windows 95 computer policy contains the lion's share of policy options. You'll find settings similar to those in Windows NT in the Logon, SNMP, and Update keys. You'll also find more settings that apply to network security in the Windows 95 computer policies, because Windows 95 does not have any other method of enforcing computer security.

Access Control: User-Level Access Control

Windows 95 does not maintain its own security structures for users and groups, but it can refer to the security databases of a network server to control access to some resources (and to network shares, in particular).

- **Authenticator Name:** This is the name of the server that maintains the security database for the network.

- **Authenticator Type:** Your two options are a Windows NT domain or a NetWare 3.*x* or 4.*x* server.

Logon

Windows 95, like Windows NT, can present you with a logon banner when you first log on to the computer. A more useful feature from the security viewpoint is to require that the user log on to a network before they are allowed to use the Windows 95 computer.

Logon Banner   This banner, like the banner for Windows NT, can contain any message you want to put there. You may want to display a legal message, a company welcome message, or a message about the use that the particular computer should be dedicated to. You can customize the following.

- **Caption:** This is the title of the logon message.

- **Text:** This field contains the body of the message that will be displayed when the user logs on.

Require Validation by Network for Windows Access   When you enable this option the user will be required to log on to the network before they can use the resources of the Windows 95 computer.

Microsoft Client for NetWare Networks

Windows 95 comes with client software for connecting to NetWare networks, and that client software is installed and configured by default when you install the networking software.

Preferred Server   Windows 95 can connect to NetWare 3.12 networks, as well as those running NetWare 4.1 and later versions. How you present the server name depends on the kind of network you are connecting to. A simple server name will suffice for NetWare 3.12 networks or 4.1 networks with bindery emulation enabled. The Server Name field is a simple text field that should contain the name of the server or the NetWare server context.

Support Long File Names   Windows 95 can provide support for long file names in networks that do not natively support them. NetWare 4.1 and later versions of NetWare support long file names natively. The Support Long File Names option presents you with two choices of platforms for long file names: all NetWare servers that support long file names, or NetWare 3.12 and above.

Search Mode   You can select the search mode of Windows 95 for NetWare networks with this option. The Search Mode option is a numeric value with a default of zero.

Disable Automatic Netware Logon   Windows 95 will attempt to automatically log on to a NetWare network if there is one present and the Client for NetWare redirector is present on the client computer. This can present a security problem.

Microsoft Client for Windows Networks

If you have Windows NT Servers on your network, then you will most likely have Microsoft Client for Windows installed on your Windows 95 computers. There are three policy options for the client software for Windows.

Log On to Windows NT   This is the information that governs the domain membership of the Windows 95 computer. You have the following options.

- **Domain Name:** This should contain the name of the domain.

- **Display Domain Logon Confirmation:** This presents the logon information to the user when the user logs onto the domain.

- **Disable Caching of Domain Password:** This keeps the Windows 95 computer from keeping the password that was used to log on to the Windows NT Server computer.

Workgroup   This is the group of computers that the Windows 95 computer will consider as peers for file and print sharing. The Workgroup Name field may contain any valid workgroup name.

Alternate Workgroup   In the event that the regular workgroup is not accessible, this workgroup may be joined. The Workgroup Name field may contain any valid workgroup name.

File and Printer Sharing for NetWare Networks: Disable SAP Advertising

In larger networks, especially networks with bridges or routers that are configured to route SAP traffic, you should disable SAP advertising on all computers that are not actually hosting a network resource (such as a shared printer or network file share) in order to reduce traffic and broadcast storms.

Passwords

Password settings are always very important in network security because the password is the gateway to the network. Until thumbprints and retina scans become commonplace, the password will continue to confirm the identity of the user.

Hide Share Passwords with Asterisks   Under the default setting for Windows 95 computers, anyone is able to see what password is being required for a Windows 95 share simply by examining the shares for that computer (from that computer, of course).

Disable Password Caching   By default, Windows 95 keeps passwords in password files on the computer's hard drive so that users do not have to type the password each time they attempt to access a network resource.

Require Alphanumeric Windows Password   This setting guarantees that a password will not be found in a dictionary or other common word list.

Minimum Windows Password Length   Short passwords are easier to guess than long ones, and are more quickly discovered in a brute force attack on your network. The default value for length is three characters. Increase the minimum password length to at least seven characters in order to make it harder for hackers to discover a user's password.

Dial-Up Networking: Disable Dial-In

This option prevents users from dialing in to a Windows 95 computer if it has a modem attached.

Sharing

One of the strengths of Windows 95 is its ability to share files and printers with other computers in a workgroup. In most LAN environments the benefits of peer-sharing outweigh the security risk. In untrusted environments, such as college computer labs or public-access computers in coffee shops, file sharing can be exploited to circumvent network security.

Disable File Sharing   This option prevents Windows 95 from sharing directories from its hard drives.

Disable Print Sharing   This option prevents Windows 95 from sharing printers that are attached to it.

SNMP

The SNMP section of the policy tree for Windows 95 is very similar to the SNMP section for Windows NT.

Communities   Clicking this button takes you to a list of communities that this computer is a member of.

Permitted Managers   Clicking this button lists those who may manage the SNMP service.

Traps for Public Community   Clicking this button lists destinations for SNMP traps when communities are not specified for this computer.

Internet MIB (RFC1156)   This field accepts the contact information required for RFC1156 compliance. The following fields are available.

- **Contact Name:** The individual responsible for the SNMP service (the administrator responsible for the Windows 95 computer)

- **Location:** Where the administrator can be reached

Update: Remote Update

The Update fields for Windows 95 are exactly the same as they are for Windows NT.

- **Update Mode:** This can be automatic (the default setting) or manual.

- **Path for Manual Update:** If the update mode is manual, this is where the computer will look for the file.

- **Display Error Messages:** If there are error messages, this setting informs the operating system to display them to the user.

- **Load Balance:** This setting allows the computer to retrieve the policy file from a BDC if the PDC is busy.

System

The System section of the Windows 95 computer profile governs how Windows 95 starts up. It contains several settings that are not necessarily designed with security in mind but can certainly be used to increase security in your network.

Enable User Profiles

While they are a requirement in Windows NT, user profiles are an option in Windows 95. If this option is disabled, then all of the users of the Windows 95 computer will share the same user profile. That means that changes one user makes to the background, Start menu, sounds, and so forth will affect the other users of the computer. Enabling user profiles will give each user their own profile, just like in Windows NT.

Network Path for Windows Setup

The Network Path for Windows Setup option locates the Windows 95 setup program, which can be used to fix a damaged Windows 95 installation or reinstall Windows 95 on your computer. The path can be a UNC location on the network.

Network Path for Windows Tour

The Windows Tour gives new users an introduction to Windows 95. This entry must end in TOUR.EXE.

Run

Windows 95 maintains a list of programs to run whenever you log on. There are many programs you can use (virus scanners, especially) that can run in the background and protect your computer while you are doing other things with it. The Items to Run at Startup button presents you with a list of programs that will be executed when the system starts.

Run Once

This option probably won't help you much. Installation programs use the Run Once feature to continue the installation process once the computer reboots. The Items to Run Once at Startup button presents you with a list of programs that will run the next time the computer is started, but which will then remove themselves from the Run Once list.

Run Services

Services are parts of the operating system that perform special functions, such as hosting WWW files. Services persist through logon sessions. You should have no reason to change Run Services settings. The Services to Run at Startup button presents you with a list of services that will be executed when the system starts.

Working with Windows NT User or Group Policy Settings

If you are using the IEAK Wizard or the IEAK Policy Editor, then the policy settings changes you make that pertain to a particular user (instead of to the computer the user is working on) will take effect for that user when Internet Explorer 4 copies those settings to the Registry of the computer. If, on the other hand, you are importing the IE 4 policy settings to the System Policy Editor, more options are available to you in how policies take effect for users. You can even establish policy settings that will take effect for groups of users when the computers connect to the file server and the user logs on to the network.

A computer policy affects a single computer or (in the case of the default computer policy) all computers that do not have a specific computer policy defined for them. User policies are similar to computer policies—if there is no specific user policy for a user who logs on, then the default user policy is applied.

But wait, there's more! If the user belongs to a group for which a policy is defined, then that policy is also applied.

Since a user can belong to more than one group, there may be more than one policy that may apply to that user. In the Options menu of the System Policy Editor you can establish priority among the groups; when policy settings conflict, the group policy with the highest priority will take precedence.

As with computer policies, you can create new user and group policies from the Edit menu of the System Policy Editor. The policies that are created will be blank: No options will be selected in the policy trees. Once you have made policy changes in a policy file, however, you can copy that policy and those changes will be in effect in the new policy.

The six sections of the Windows NT user and group policies will be described in more detail in the sections that follow.

Control Panel: Display

The Control Panel policy options in Windows NT are primarily concerned with display settings. Since Windows NT adequately controls who may make changes to the display hardware without requiring the intervention of the System Policy Editor, these settings simply enforce a consistent environment and make administration easier for the administrator. The following settings are available.

- **Deny Access to Display icon:** Denies all access to the display control panel item.

- **Hide Background tab:** Keeps the user from changing the background.

- **Hide Screen Saver tab:** Keeps the user from changing the screen saver.

- **Hide Appearance tab:** Keeps the user from modifying the appearance settings.

- **Hide Settings tab:** Keeps the user from accessing the hardware configuration settings.

Desktop

The Desktop settings, like the display settings, enforce conformity on the network. The settings you can lock down are for the wallpaper and the color scheme.

Wallpaper

This option sets the bitmap that will appear as the screen background.

- **Wallpaper Name:** This option should specify a BMP file. It may refer to another computer via a UNC path.

- **Tile Wallpaper:** This option causes the image to be tiled (repeatedly) instead of centered with a border.

Color Scheme

The color scheme defines the colors and Desktop object characteristics, such as font size and selection. The scheme name may be any of the schemes defined in the Windows NT Colors control panel.

Shell: Restrictions

This section and the next, "System: Restrictions," contain the user policy settings that have the most impact on security. You should be careful when applying these options because you can quickly render a Windows NT computer unusable with them, and then not be able to change the settings back.

Remove Run Command from Start Menu   This option makes the Run Start menu item go away—making it more difficult for the user to start a program not found in the Start menu.

Remove Folders from Settings on Start Menu   This option keeps the user from modifying computer settings and adding or removing printers.

Remove Find Command from Start Menu   A clever user could use the Find command to locate a program, and then execute the program. This option removes the Find command from the Start menu.

Hide Drives in My Computer   A user can click programs in drive windows that are displayed. This menu option removes access to the drives.

Hide Network Neighborhood   The Network Neighborhood can show you remote shares containing programs that the user can execute. It can also show the user printers and other resources that the user can map to. This option removes the Network Neighborhood from the Desktop.

No Workgroup Contents in Network Neighborhood   You may wish to allow network browsing but only of network shares covered by domain security—in that case you might want to disallow browsing of workgroup contents that may have shares secured by the less stringent Windows 95 security model.

Hide All Items on Desktop   This option removes everything from the Desktop. You would enable this option if you are dedicating the user account to run just one program (such as a data entry or process control application).

Disable Shutdown Command   This option prevents the user from shutting down the computer. Since Windows NT can be shut down remotely, you might want to make that an administrative function for computers dedicated to a particular purpose.

Don't Save Settings on Exit   This option preserves the Desktop settings as they were when the user logged on—any changes are transient and are gone when the user logs off.

System: Restrictions

The following two system restrictions can go a long way toward securing a network against hacking from internal sources. Once a hacker has access to a computer on your network, he or she will need access to the Registry and to hacking tools in order to exploit the information stored on the computer.

Disable Registry Editing Tools   This setting keeps the user from running the Registry Editor, the System Policy Editor, or any other Registry editing tool.

Run Only Allowed Windows Applications   This option can be even more restrictive than disabling certain tools. You can use this option to restrict the user to only certain allowed programs—all others will not run. You can then make sure that the allowed programs (such as a word processor, spreadsheet, and Web browser) are safe to run. The List of Allowed Applications button shows you a list of the programs that Windows NT will allow this user to run.

Windows NT Shell

You can customize the appearance and function of the Windows NT shell for particular groups of users. You might, for example, want to provide members of the Engineering group one set of programs that show up on the Desktop or in the Start menu, and members of the Finance group a different set of programs that are shared by members of their group. The option to choose the location of the custom folders gives you a mechanism for giving each group a different environment in which you can specify the Desktop and Start menu programs.

Custom Folders

The Custom Folders options describe the locations of the directories that will contain the new items, icons, and menus. These directory locations should already exist.

Custom Programs Folder Path to the location of program items; the default is %USERPROFILE%\Start Menu\Programs.

Custom Desktop Icons Path to the location of Desktop icons; the default is %USERPROFILE%\Desktop.

Hide Start Menu Subfolders If you have a custom programs folder for Desktop items, select this option as well so that the original subfolders will not appear.

Custom Startup Folder The path to the location of startup items—the default is blank. This directory contains the items that will be started when the user logs on.

Custom Network Neighborhood The path to the location of Network Neighborhood items—the default is blank. This directory contains the items that will show up in the Network Neighborhood. You can configure this folder to contain only those resources you want the user to have access to.

Custom Start Menu The path to the location of Start menu items; the default is %USERPROFILE%\Start Menu.

Restrictions

The shell restrictions work in addition to the above settings, as follows.

Only Use Approved Shell Extensions This keeps users from extending the shell or replacing it in an insecure manner (it disables third-party shell extensions that may contain a Trojan horse).

Remove Common Program Groups from Start Menu This option leaves only the individual program groups in the Start menu, which may either be the default program groups or program groups as defined in the previous section, "Custom Folders."

Windows NT System

The two options in the Windows NT System section of a user policy govern what happens just after the user logs on to the account.

Parse Autoexec.bat When the user first logs on, Windows NT must establish the user environment. Windows NT, by default, will not parse and execute commands in the `autoexec.bat` file, but by enabling this option you can configure it to do so.

Run Logon Scripts Synchronously This option requires Windows NT to wait for logon scripts to complete before it starts the user's shell. That way any logon script effects (including abnormal termination) will be communicated to the user's shell.

Working with Windows 95 User or Group Policy Settings

Just as there are quite a few differences between Windows NT and Windows 95 computer policies, there are also quite a few differences between Windows NT and Windows 95 user and group policies. However, Windows 95 policies behave the same as Windows NT policies: If there is no policy that specifically applies to a user, the default User policy will take effect. Group policies are also applied to the user account and are applied in order of group priority.

Since Windows 95 has no other security mechanisms to speak of, you should be particularly careful about how you configure security in the Windows 95 security policy for users and groups. There are five Windows 95 User Policy sections, which are explained in detail in the following section.

Control Panel

In contrast to what you saw in the Windows NT Control Panel policy options, there is quite a lot for you to do in the Control Panel policy tree for Windows 95. This is where you control access to the display, to network configuration, to passwords, to printers, and even to the System Control Panel.

Display: Restrict Display Control Panel

This option is very much like the Windows NT Display Control Panel option. It offers the following options.

- **Disable Display Control Panel:** Removes the user's access to any display options.

- **Hide Background Page:** Removes the ability to change the background.

- **Hide Screen Saver Page:** Removes the ability to change the screen saver.

- **Hide Appearance Page:** Removes the ability to change the colors, font size and choice, and so on.

- **Hide Settings Page:** Removes the ability to change the display hardware settings.

Network: Restrict Network Control Panel

The Network Control Panel option governs how the Windows 95 computer connects to the domain. The following options are available.

- **Disable Network Control Panel:** Removes all access to network settings.

- **Hide Identification Page:** Keeps the user from changing which network the computer will connect to.

- **Hide Access Control Page:** Keeps the user from changing the share settings for the computer.

Passwords: Restrict Passwords Control Panel

The Passwords Control Panel option is another sensitive location in Windows 95. Most users have no reason to modify remote administration or user profile settings. The following options are available.

- **Disable Passwords Control Panel:** Keeps users from making any changes to passwords, remote access, or user profiles.

- **Hide Change Passwords Page:** Keeps users from changing passwords.

- **Hide Remote Administration Page:** Keeps users from changing remote administration settings.
- **Hide User Profiles Page:** Keeps users from deleting profiles.

Printers: Restrict Printer Settings

Printer settings are not usually a security issue, but they can become a nuisance issue if you have users that are prone to mischief. Using the following settings can make your life easier.

- **Hide General and Details Pages:** Keeps users from changing printer settings for individual printers.
- **Disable Deletion of Printers:** Keeps users from removing printers.
- **Disable Addition of Printers:** Keeps users from connecting to printers without permission.

System: Restrict System Control Panel

The System Control Panel contains settings that can compromise the security of the Windows 95 computer or cause the computer to fail to operate properly. The System option allows you to restrict access to the following parts of the System Control Panel.

- **Hide Device Manager Page:** Keeps users from adding and removing devices.
- **Hide Hardware Profiles Page:** Keeps users from changing the hardware environment that the computer boots to.
- **Hide File System Button:** Keeps users from modifying the operation of the file system (enabling 16- or 32-bit access, for example).
- **Hide Virtual Memory Button:** Keeps users from changing the location, amount, and method of operation of virtual memory.

Desktop

The Desktop settings for Windows 95 are the same as for Windows NT.

Wallpaper

This option sets the bitmap that will appear as the screen background.

- **Wallpaper Name:** This should specify a BMP file. It may refer to another computer via a UNC path.

- **Tile Wallpaper:** This option causes the image to be tiled (repeatedly) instead of centered with a border.

Color Scheme

The color scheme defines the colors and Desktop object characteristics, such as font size and selection. The scheme name may be any of the schemes defined in the Windows NT Colors Control Panel.

Network: Sharing

Windows 95 does not provide the same level of control over file and print sharing that Windows NT does. File and print sharing make many kinds of computer collaboration much easier than it might be, however. You must balance the need for security on your network with the need to facilitate the user's work.

Disable File Sharing Controls   This option removes the ability to share directories from the hard drives of the Windows 95 computer.

Disable Print Sharing Controls   This option removes the ability to share printers that are attached to the Windows 95 computer.

Shell

The shell section of a user policy allows you to configure how the Desktop appears in Windows 95 for that user or group of users. The shell restrictions for Windows 95 are more important than they are for Windows NT because the Windows NT and NTFS security structures provide much of the required security in Windows NT. The ability to change the location of the custom folders gives you a mechanism for giving each group a different environment.

Custom Folders

The Custom Folders options describe the locations of the directories that will contain the new items, icons, and menus. These directory locations should already exist. The options are the same as for Windows NT; refer to the Custom Folders section for Windows NT earlier in this chapter for a description of each option.

The shell restrictions for Windows 95 are the same as the shell restrictions for Windows NT. See "Shell: Restrictions" in the section "Working with Windows NT User or Group Policy Settings" for a description of the restrictions' options.

System: Restrictions

The first two system restrictions are the same for Windows 95 as they are for Windows NT. Windows 95 adds two more, however, that have to do with the running of MS-DOS applications.

Disable Registry Editing Tools   This setting keeps the user from running the Registry Editor, the System Policy Editor, or any other Registry editing tool.

Run Only Allowed Windows Applications   This option can be even more restrictive than disabling certain tools. You can use this option to restrict the user to only certain programs—all others will not run. You can then make sure that the allowed programs (such as a word processor, spreadsheet, and Web browser) are safe to run. The List of Allowed Applications button shows you a list of the programs that Windows 95 will allow this user to run.

Disable MS-DOS Prompt   This denies the user the ability to launch programs from the DOS prompt. If you wish to limit which programs the Windows 95 user can use, you should disable the MS-DOS prompt.

Disable Single-Mode MS-DOS Applications   One way around Windows 95 security is to leave Windows 95 behind and reboot to MS-DOS only. A hacker could then run any DOS-mode tools that can be loaded from a floppy disk, and since the computer is most likely connected to your network, that could include packet sniffers or alternate operating systems. This option removes the user's ability to reboot to MS-DOS.

Index

Note to reader: Throughout this index *italic* page numbers refer to figures; **boldfaced** page numbers refer to primary discussions of the topic.

B

M

O

Z

MCSE ELECTIVE STUDY GUIDES
FROM NETWORK PRESS®

Sybex's Network Press expands the definitive study guide series for MCSE candidates.

ISBN: 0-7821-2224-8
688pp; 7¹/₂" x 9"; Hardcover
$49.99

ISBN: 0-7821-2261-2
848pp; 7¹/₂" x 9"; Hardcover
$49.99

ISBN: 0-7821-2248-5
704pp; 7¹/₂" x 9"; Hardcover
$49.99

ISBN: 0-7821-2172-1
672pp; 7¹/₂" x 9"; Hardcover
$49.99

ISBN: 0-7821-2194-2
576pp; 7¹/₂" x 9"; Hardcover
$49.99

ISBN: 0-7821-1967-0
656pp; 7¹/₂" x 9"; Hardcover
$49.99

Microsoft® Certified
Professional
Approved Study Guide

NETWORK PRESS®
SYBEX

STUDY GUIDES FOR THE MICROSOFT CERTIFIED SYSTEMS ENGINEER EXAMS

NETWORK PRESS® PRESENTS
MCSE TEST SUCCESS

THE PERFECT COMPANION BOOKS TO THE MCSE STUDY GUIDES

ISBN: 0-7821-2146-2
352pp; 7½" x 9"; Softcover
$24.99

ISBN: 0-7821-2148-9
352pp; 7½" x 9"; Softcover
$24.99

ISBN: 0-7821-2149-7
400pp; 7½" x 9"; Softcover
$24.99

ISBN: 0-7821-2147-0
442pp; 7½" x 9"; Softcover
$24.99

Here's what you need to know to pass the MCSE tests.

- **Review concise summaries of key information**

- **Boost your knowledge with 400 review questions**

- **Get ready for the test with 200 tough practice test questions**

Other MCSE Test Success titles:

- **Core Requirements Box Set**
  (4 books, 1 CD)
  [ISBN: 0-7821-2296-5] April 1998

- **Windows® 95**
  [ISBN: 0-7821-2252-3] May 1998

- **Exchange Server 5.5**
  [ISBN: 0-7821-2250-7] May 1998

- **TCP/IP for NT® 4**
  [ISBN: 0-7821-2251-5] May 1998

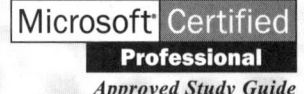

NT® IN THE REAL WORLD

THE INFORMATION YOU NEED TO BUILD, SECURE, AND OPTIMIZE NT® NETWORKS

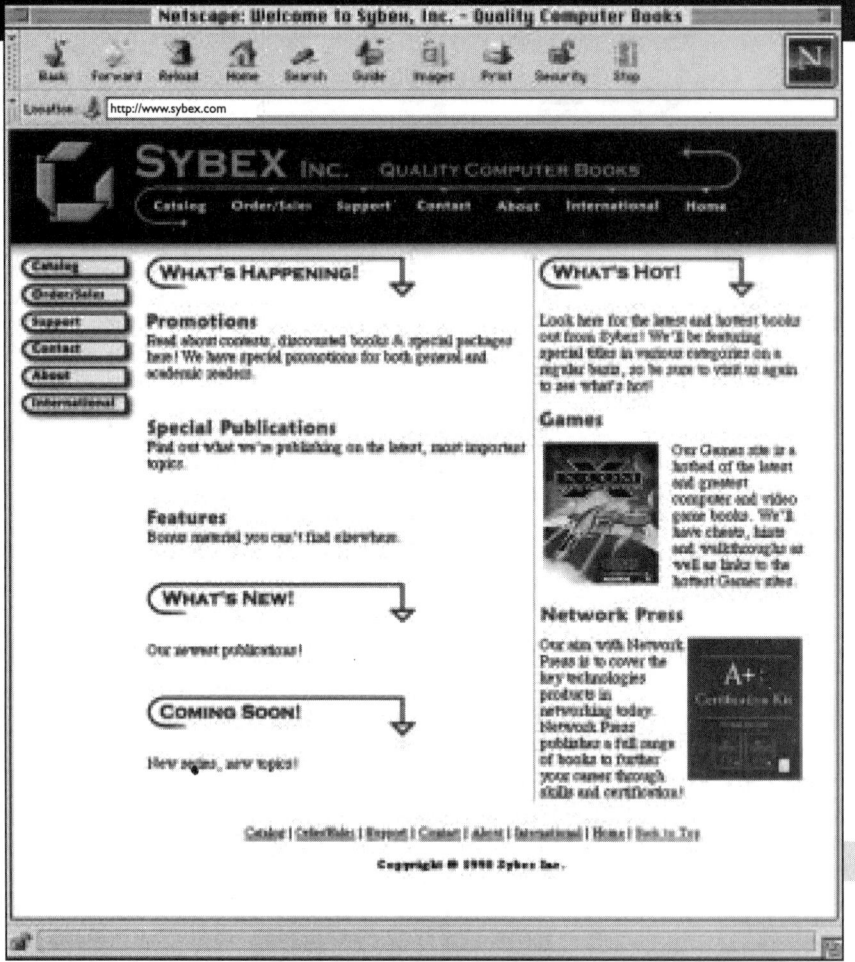

Implementing and Supporting Microsoft® Internet Explorer 4.0 by Using the Microsoft® Internet Explorer Administration Kit

Exam: 70-079: Objectives

OBJECTIVE	PAGE
PLANNING	
In corporate administrator mode or Internet service provider mode, choose the appropriate installation of Internet Explorer 4.0, with or without the Windows Desktop Update.	171
Develop custom installation strategies for Internet Explorer 4.0.	170
In corporate administrator mode, develop appropriate security strategies for using Internet Explorer 4.0 for various sites. Sites include public kiosks, end-user sites, and business sites.	171
Choose Active Desktop items and develop Active Channels.	296
Develop strategies for replacing other Internet browsers. Other browsers include Microsoft Internet Explorer 3.x and Netscape Navigator.	184
Develop strategies for replacing other Internet mail clients. Other mail clients include Internet Mail and News, Netscape Mail, and Eudora.	185
Choose the appropriate configuration strategy for Microsoft® Outlook Express.	185
Choose the appropriate configuration strategy for Microsoft® NetMeeting™. Elements include settings and restrictions.	187
Choose the appropriate configurations for the NetMeeting client. Configurations include Internet Locator Service (ILS) server connectivity, IP connectivity, peer-to-peer networking, proxy server settings, and proxy client settings.	152
In corporate administrator mode or Internet service provider mode, choose strategies for managing automatic configuration by using the IEAK Profile Manager. Methods include Microsoft® JScript™ autoproxy, .ins files, and .adm files.	182
Develop a configuration plan for Active Setup components.	170
Develop strategies for using the Internet Connection Wizard in Internet service provider mode. Elements include modem detection, stack installation, and configuration of dial-up connections.	177, 257
INSTALLATION AND CONFIGURATION	
Install and configure Internet Explorer 4.0, with or without the Windows Desktop Update, on computers that run various operating systems. Operating systems include Microsoft® Windows NT® Server 4.0, Microsoft® Windows NT® Workstation 4.0, Microsoft® Windows® 3.x, Microsoft® Windows® 95, and Macintosh.	67
Specify and customize Active Setup components.	72, 248
Customize the browser.	94, 104
Configure built-in and custom components of Internet Explorer 4.0 by using the IEAK wizard. Components include Microsoft® Outlook Express and Microsoft® NetMeeting.	261
Configure channels, software distribution channels, and site subscriptions.	100
Configure Outlook Express for custom installations of Internet Explorer 4.0.	122